THE MILITARY AND COLONIAL POLICY OF THE UNITED STATES

ADDRESSES AND REPORTS

BY

ELIHU ROOT

COLLECTED AND EDITED BY

ROBERT BACON

AND

JAMES BROWN SCOTT

AMS PRESS
NEW YORK

Reprinted from the edition of 1916, Cambridge, Mass.
First AMS EDITION published 1970
Manufactured in the United States of America

International Standard Book Number: 0-404-05399-8

Library of Congress Card Catalog Number: 70-121030

AMS PRESS, INC.
NEW YORK, N.Y. 10003

CONTENTS

INTRODUCTORY NOTE

The collected addresses and state papers of Elihu Root, of which this is one of several volumes, cover the period of his service as Secretary of War, as Secretary of State, and as Senator of the United States, during which time, to use his own expression, his only client was his country.

The many formal and occasional addresses and speeches, which will be found to be of a remarkably wide range, are followed by his state papers, such as the instructions to the American delegates to the Second Hague Peace Conference and other diplomatic notes and documents, prepared by him as Secretary of State in the performance of his duties as an executive officer of the United States. Although the official documents have been kept separate from the other papers, this plan has been slightly modified in the volume devoted to the military and colonial policy of the United States, which includes those portions of his official reports as Secretary of War throwing light upon his public addresses and his general military policy.

The addresses and speeches selected for publication are not arranged chronologically, but are classified in such a way that each volume contains addresses and speeches relating to a general subject and a common purpose. The addresses as president of the American Society of International Law show his treatment of international questions from the theoretical standpoint, and in the light of his experience as Secretary of War and as Secretary of State, unrestrained and uncontrolled by the limitations of official position, whereas his addresses on foreign affairs, delivered while Secretary of State or as United States Senator, discuss these questions under the reserve of official responsibility.

Mr. Root's addresses on government, citizenship, and legal procedure are a masterly exposition of the principles of the Constitution and of the government established by it; of the duty of the citizen to understand the Constitution and to conform his conduct to its requirements; and of the right of the people to reform or to amend the Constitution in order to make representative government more effective and responsive to their present and future needs. The addresses on law and its administration state how legal procedure should be modified and simplified in the interest of justice rather than in the supposed interest of the legal profession.

The addresses delivered during the trip to South America and Mexico in 1906, and in the United States after his return, with their message of good will, proclaim a new doctrine — the Root doctrine — of kindly consideration and of honorable obligation, and make clear the destiny common to the peoples of the Western World.

The addresses and the reports on military and colonial policy made by Mr. Root as Secretary of War explain the reorganization of the army after the Spanish-American War, the creation of the General Staff, and the establishment of the Army War College. They trace the origin of and give the reason for the policy of this country in Cuba, the Philippines, and Porto Rico, devised and inaugurated by him. It is not generally known that the so-called Platt Amendment, defining our relations to Cuba, was drafted by Mr. Root, and that the Organic Act of the Philippines was likewise the work of Mr. Root as Secretary of War.

The argument before The Hague Tribunal in the North Atlantic Fisheries Case is a rare if not the only instance of a statesman appearing as chief counsel in an international arbitration, which, as Secretary of State, he had prepared and submitted.

The political, educational, historical, and commemorative speeches and addresses should make known to future generations the literary, artistic, and emotional side of a statesman of our time, and the publication of these collected addresses and state papers will, it is believed, enable the American people better to understand the generation in which Mr. Root has been a commanding figure and better to appreciate during his lifetime the services which he has rendered to his country.

ROBERT BACON.
JAMES BROWN SCOTT.

APRIL 15, 1916.

FOREWORD

The addresses and those portions of Mr. Root's reports printed in the present volume deal with the problems which may be regarded as the consequence or aftermath of the war with Spain in 1898, except such as refer to the Chinese Relief Expedition due to the Boxer troubles of 1900. It therefore seems advisable to prefix an introductory note of a general nature, in addition to such introductory matter as precedes certain of the addresses and reports.

The insurrection in Cuba, which finally cost Spain not only Cuba but Porto Rico, broke out during the year 1895. The cause was the same as made twenty-one republics out of the European colonies in America — misgovernment by the mother-country and the desire on the part of the colonists to be free and independent states. On April 11, 1898, President McKinley sent a special message to Congress devoted to Cuba and recommending that the United States should intervene in Cuba for the following reasons:

First. In the cause of humanity and to put an end to the barbarities, bloodshed, starvation, and horrible miseries now existing there, and which the parties to the conflict are either unable or unwilling to stop or mitigate. It is no answer to say this is all in another country, belonging to another nation, and is therefore none of our business. It is specially our duty, for it is right at our door.

Second. We owe it to our citizens in Cuba to afford them that protection and indemnity for life and property which no government there can or will afford, and to that end to terminate the conditions that deprive them of legal protection.

Third. The right to intervene may be justified by the very serious injury to the commerce, trade, and business of our people and by the wanton destruction of property and devastation of the island.

Fourth, and which is of the utmost importance. The present condition of affairs in Cuba is a constant menace to our peace and entails upon this

Government an enormous expense. With such a conflict waged for years in an island so near us and with which our people have such trade and business relations; when the lives and liberty of our citizens are in constant danger and their property destroyed and themselves ruined; where our trading vessels are liable to seizure and are seized at our very door by war ships of a foreign nation; the expeditions of filibustering that we are powerless to prevent altogether, and the irritating questions and entanglements thus arising — all these and others that I need not mention, with the resulting strained relations, are a constant menace to our peace and compel us to keep on a semi-war footing with a nation with which we are at peace.

Congress replied to this message by the following joint resolution, approved by the President on April 20, 1898:

WHEREAS: The abhorrent conditions which have existed for more than three years in the island of Cuba, so near our own borders, have shocked the moral sense of the people of the United States, have been a disgrace to Christian civilization, culminating, as they have, in the destruction of a United States battle-ship [the *Maine*] with 266 of its officers and crew, while on a friendly visit in the harbor of Havana [on February 15, 1898], and cannot longer be endured, as has been set forth by the President of the United States in his message to Congress of April 11, 1898, upon which the action of Congress was invited:

Therefore,

Resolved by the Senate and House of Representatives of the United States of America in Congress assembled,

First. That the people of the island of Cuba are and of right ought to be free and independent.

Second. That it is the duty of the United States to demand, and the Government of the United States does hereby demand, that the Government of Spain at once relinquish its authority and government in the island of Cuba and withdraw its land and naval forces from Cuba and Cuban waters.

Third. That the President of the United States be, and he hereby is, directed and empowered to use the entire land and naval forces of the United States and to call into the actual service of the United States the militia of the several States to such extent as may be necessary to carry these resolutions into effect.

Fourth. That the United States hereby disclaims any disposition or intention to exercise sovereignty, jurisdiction, or control over said island except for the pacification thereof, and asserts its determination, when that is accomplished, to leave the government and control of the island to its people.

The joint resolution of Congress was communicated by the American Minister to the Spanish Government, and inasmuch as Spain responded by treating, as President McKinley informed Congress, "the reasonable demands of this Government" as measures of hostility, that body passed the following act, approved April 25, 1898:

Be it enacted by the Senate and House of Representatives of the United States of America in Congress assembled,

First. That war be, and the same is, hereby declared to exist, and that war has existed since the 21st day of April, A.D. 1898, including said day, between the United States of America and the Kingdom of Spain.

Second. That the President of the United States be, and he hereby is, directed and empowered to use the entire land and naval forces of the United States and to call into the actual service of the United States the militia of the several States to such extent as may be necessary to carry this act into effect.

It is no part of the purpose of this introduction to enter into the details of the war. Suffice it to say that, by virtue of a protocol of August 12, 1898, due to the good offices of the French Republic, a general agreement was reached upon the terms of peace and an armistice was concluded between the erstwhile belligerents; and that peace was concluded between Spain and the United States by a treaty signed at Paris on December 10, 1898, of which ratifications were exchanged on April 11, 1899. Inasmuch as the protocol and the treaty state the results of the war and the obligations assumed by the United States growing out of it, these documents are appended to the foreword.

Even a hasty reading of the treaty of Paris shows the nature, variety and extent of the problems confronting the United States by reason of the Spanish-American War, and as Portò Rico, Cuba and the Philippines were placed under the supervision of the War Department it followed that the Secretary of War was, by virtue of his office, forced to consider these problems and to find if possible an appropriate solution. Mr. Root recognized from the beginning that the United States was confronted with problems of a colonial policy, and that Porto Rico, Cuba and the Philippines should not be considered separately but as part of a larger whole.

As the result of a careful study of colonial government and misgovernment, he formulated the principles of colonial policy to be found under the caption " Insular Government " in his first annual report as Secretary of War, which was and always will be considered to be a masterly statement of the principles of colonial government and administration.

On July 20, 1899, President McKinley offered Mr. Root the position of Secretary of War in his Cabinet, to succeed General Russell A. Alger of Michigan, and he was appointed and entered upon duty on August 1, 1899, under circumstances which are best described by Mr. Root himself, in an address he made before the New York County Lawyers Association, in 1915, which is printed in another volume of the series. " Sixteen years ago ", he said, " in the month of July, having just finished the labors of the year and gone to my country home, I was called to the telephone and told by one speaking for President McKinley, ' the President directs me to say to you that he wishes you to take the position of Secretary of War.' I answered, ' Thank the President for me, but say that it is quite absurd, I know nothing about war. I know nothing about the army.' I was told to hold the wire, and in a moment there came back the reply, ' President McKinley directs me to say that he is not looking for any one who knows anything about war or for any one who knows anything about the army; he has got to have a lawyer to direct the government of these Spanish islands, and you are the lawyer he wants.' Of course I had then, on the instant, to determine what kind of a lawyer I wished to be, and there was but one answer to make, and so I went to perform a lawyer's duty upon the call of the greatest of all our clients, the Government of our country."

In the same address, Mr. Root described the fundamental principles upon which he worked out his colonial policy in Cuba, Porto Rico, and the Philippines; and his own words supply the most appropriate conclusion to this foreword:

"It was a fascinating work. It was the work of applying to some ten millions of people in Cuba and Porto Rico and the Philippines, the principles of American liberty. They were living under laws founded upon the customs of their lives, customs drawn from old Spain and developed in social and industrial activity quite unlike that of the United States; and the problem was to apply those principles which are declared in our constitutions, which embodied the formative idea of the Declaration of Independence that all men are endowed with inalienable rights, among which are life and liberty and the pursuit of happiness, to the customs and the laws of peoples which had come down from the Spain of Philip the Second and the Inquisition. Those principles were alien to their thoughts and their conceptions, to their habits of life, to their ideas of the relations between men and between men and their governments. In the first instance they had to be applied at the hand of the military officers who had their own code and methods of procedure. It was a test not to be undervalued, of the vitality, the universality, and the essential truth of the principles themselves. Through the strong and sagacious control of Governor Taft in the Philippines; through the sound administrative instincts and devotion to duty of Leonard Wood in Cuba; through the loyalty of George W. Davis, and his successors in Porto Rico, those principles of justice, principles of state morality, which we have embodied in our constitutions, constitutions which are but the expression of the conception of individual liberty that has grown through a thousand years of Anglo-Saxon freedom, proved still to be vital, and the laws of these Spanish countries received, embodied and made effective the preservation of individual liberty and the protection of the individual against the tyranny of government. The ideas that were forced upon King John when he signed the Magna Charta, — that great and conquering conception of liberty which has been the formative power moulding the social and political life of the hundred and ten million people who inhabit this continent north of the Rio Grande, — prevailed and became effective as applied to the daily life, the protection, the prosperity and the happiness of the little brown brothers in the Philippines; of the men whom we fought the war of 1898 to liberate in Cuba and of our wards in Porto Rico. Surely no lawyer was ever more fortunate than in the opportunity to help in the demonstration of the eternal verity of the principles of justice and liberty which underlie all the efforts and the struggles of our American bar." [1]

[1] *Addresses on Government and Citizenship*, by Elihu Root, pp. 504, 505. Harvard University Press, 1916.

APPENDIX TO THE FOREWORD

TEXTS OF THE PROTOCOL OF AGREEMENT AND OF THE TREATY OF PARIS

I. Protocol of Agreement. Embodying the Terms of a Basis for the Establishment of Peace Between the United States and Spain. Signed August 12, 1898.[1]

William R. Day, Secretary of State of the United States, and His Excellency Jules Cambon, Ambassador Extraordinary and Plenipotentiary of the Republic of France at Washington, respectively possessing for this purpose full authority from the Government of the United States and the Government of Spain, have concluded and signed the following articles, embodying the terms on which the two Governments have agreed in respect to the matters hereinafter set forth, having in view the establishment of peace between the two countries, that is to say:

Article I

Spain will relinquish all claims of sovereignty over and title to Cuba.

Article II

Spain will cede to the United States the island of Porto Rico and other islands now under Spanish sovereignty in the West Indies, and also an island in the Ladrones to be selected by the United States.

Article III

The United States will occupy and hold the city, bay and harbor of Manila, pending the conclusion of a treaty of peace which shall determine the control, disposition and government of the Philippines.

Article IV

Spain will immediately evacuate Cuba, Porto Rico and other islands now under Spanish sovereignty in the West Indies; and to this end each Government will, within ten days after the signing of this protocol, appoint Commissioners, and the Commissioners so appointed shall, within thirty days after the signing of this protocol, meet at Havana for the purpose of arranging and carrying out the details of the aforesaid evacuation of Cuba and the adjacent Spanish islands; and each Government will, within ten days after the signing of this protocol, also appoint other

[1] *United States Statutes at Large*, Vol. 30, pp. 1742–1743.

Commissioners, who shall, within thirty days after the signing of this protocol, meet at San Juan, in Porto Rico, for the purpose of arranging and carrying out the details of the aforesaid evacuation of Porto Rico and other islands now under Spanish sovereignty in the West Indies.

Article V

The United States and Spain will each appoint not more than five Commissioners to treat of peace, and the Commissioners so appointed shall meet at Paris not later than October 1, 1898, and proceed to the negotiation and conclusion of a treaty of peace, which treaty shall be subject to ratification according to the respective constitutional forms of the two countries.

Article VI

Upon the conclusion and signing of this protocol, hostilities between the two countries shall be suspended, and notice to that effect shall be given as soon as possible by each Government to the commanders of its military and naval forces.

Done at Washington in duplicate, in English and in French, by the undersigned, who have hereunto set their hands and seals, the 12th day of August, 1898.

[SEAL] William R. Day
[SEAL] Jules Cambon

II. Treaty of Peace. Concluded at Paris, December 10, 1898; ratification advised by the Senate February 6, 1899; ratified by the President February 6, 1899; ratifications exchanged April 11, 1899; proclaimed April 11, 1899.[1]

The United States of America and Her Majesty the Queen Regent of Spain, in the name of her august son Don Alfonso XIII, desiring to end the state of war now existing between the two countries, have for that purpose appointed as plenipotentiaries:

The President of the United States,

William R. Day, Cushman K. Davis, William P. Frye, George Gray, and Whitelaw Reid, citizens of the United States;

And Her Majesty the Queen Regent of Spain,

Don Eugenio Montero Ríos, president of the senate, Don Buenaventura de Abarzuza, senator of the Kingdom and ex-minister of the Crown; Don José de Garnica, deputy to the Cortes and associate justice of the

[1] *United States Statutes at Large*, Vol. 30, pp. 1754–1758.

supreme court; Don Wenceslao Ramirez de Villa-Urrutia, envoy extraordinary and minister plenipotentiary at Brussels, and Don Rafael Cerero, general of division;

Who, having assembled in Paris, and having exchanged their full powers, which were found to be in due and proper form, have, after discussion of the matters before them, agreed upon the following articles:

ARTICLE I

Spain relinquishes all claim of sovereignty over and title to Cuba.

And as the island is, upon its evacuation by Spain, to be occupied by the United States, the United States will, so long as such occupation shall last, assume and discharge the obligations that may under international law result from the fact of its occupation, for the protection of life and property.

ARTICLE II

Spain cedes to the United States the island of Porto Rico and other islands now under Spanish sovereignty in the West Indies, and the island of Guam in the Marianas or Ladrones.

ARTICLE III

Spain cedes to the United States the archipelago known as the Philippine Islands, and comprehending the islands lying within the following lines:

A line running from west to east along or near the twentieth parallel of north latitude, and through the middle of the navigable channel of Bachi, from the one hundred and eighteenth (118th) to the one hundred and twenty-seventh (127th) degree meridian of longitude east of Greenwich, thence along the one hundred and twenty-seventh (127th) degree meridian of longitude east of Greenwich to the parallel of four degrees and forty-five minutes (4° 45′) north latitude, thence along the parallel of four degrees and forty-five minutes (4° 45′) north latitude to its intersection with the meridian of longitude one hundred and nineteen degrees and thirty-five minutes (119° 35′) east of Greenwich, thence along the meridian of longitude one hundred and nineteen degrees and thirty-five minutes (119° 35′) east of Greenwich to the parallel of latitude seven degrees and forty minutes (7° 40′) north, thence along the parallel of latitude of seven degrees and forty minutes (7° 40′) north to its intersection with the one hundred and sixteenth (116th) degree meridian of longitude east of Greenwich, thence by a direct line to the intersection of the tenth (10th) degree parallel of north latitude with the one hundred and eighteenth (118th) degree meridian of longitude east of Greenwich, and thence along the one hundred and eighteenth (118th) degree meridian of longitude east of Greenwich to the point of beginning.

The United States will pay to Spain the sum of twenty million dollars ($20,000,000) within three months after the exchange of the ratifications of the present treaty.

Article IV

The United States will, for the term of ten years from the date of the exchange of the ratifications of the present treaty, admit Spanish ships and merchandise to the ports of the Philippine Islands on the same terms as ships and merchandise of the United States.

Article V

The United States will, upon the signature of the present treaty, send back to Spain, at its own cost, the Spanish soldiers taken as prisoners of war on the capture of Manila by the American forces. The arms of the soldiers in question shall be restored to them.

Spain will, upon the exchange of the ratifications of the present treaty, proceed to evacuate the Philippines, as well as the island of Guam, on terms similar to those agreed upon by the Commissioners appointed to arrange for the evacuation of Porto Rico and other islands in the West Indies, under the Protocol of August 12, 1898, which is to continue in force till its provisions are completely executed.

The time within which the evacuation of the Philippine Islands and Guam shall be completed shall be fixed by the two Governments. Stands of colors, uncaptured war vessels, small arms, guns of all calibres, with their carriages and accessories, powder, ammunition, livestock, and materials and supplies of all kinds, belonging to the land and naval forces of Spain in the Philippines and Guam, remain the property of Spain. Pieces of heavy ordnance, exclusive of field artillery, in the fortifications and coast defences, shall remain in their emplacements for the term of six months, to be reckoned from the exchange of ratifications of the treaty; and the United States may, in the meantime, purchase such material from Spain, if a satisfactory agreement between the two Governments on the subject shall be reached.

Article VI

Spain will, upon the signature of the present treaty, release all prisoners of war, and all persons detained or imprisoned for political offences, in connection with the insurrections in Cuba and the Philippines and the war with the United States.

Reciprocally, the United States will release all persons made prisoners of war by the American forces, and will undertake to obtain the release of all Spanish prisoners in the hands of the insurgents in Cuba and the Philippines.

The Government of the United States will at its own cost return to Spain and the Government of Spain will at its own cost return to the United States, Cuba, Porto Rico, and the Philippines, according to the situation of their respective homes, prisoners released or caused to be released by them, respectively, under this article.

Article VII

The United States and Spain mutually relinquish all claims for indemnity, national and individual, of every kind, of either Government, or of its citizens or subjects, against the other Government, that may have arisen since the beginning of the late insurrection in Cuba and prior to the exchange of ratifications of the present treaty, including all claims for indemnity for the cost of the war.

The United States will adjudicate and settle the claims of its citizens against Spain relinquished in this article.

Article VIII

In conformity with the provisions of Articles I, II, and III of this treaty, Spain relinquishes in Cuba, and cedes in Porto Rico and other islands in the West Indies, in the island of Guam, and in the Philippine Archipelago, all the buildings, wharves, barracks, forts, structures, public highways and other immovable property which, in conformity with law, belong to the public domain, and as such belong to the Crown of Spain.

And it is hereby declared that the relinquishment or cession, as the case may be, to which the preceding paragraph refers, cannot in any respect impair the property or rights which by law belong to the peaceful possession of property of all kinds, of provinces, municipalities, public or private establishments, ecclesiastical or civic bodies, or any other associations having legal capacity to acquire and possess property in the aforesaid territories renounced or ceded, or of private individuals, of whatsoever nationality such individuals may be.

The aforesaid relinquishment or cession, as the case may be, includes all documents exclusively referring to the sovereignty relinquished or ceded that may exist in the archives of the Peninsula. Where any document in such archives only in part relates to said sovereignty, a copy of such part will be furnished whenever it shall be requested. Like rules shall be reciprocally observed in favor of Spain in respect of documents in the archives of the islands above referred to.

In the aforesaid relinquishment or cession, as the case may be, are also included such rights as the Crown of Spain and its authorities possess in respect of the official archives and records, executive as well as judicial, in the islands above referred to, which relate to said islands or the rights and property of their inhabitants. Such archives and records shall be carefully preserved, and private persons shall without distinction have the right to require, in accordance with law, authenticated copies of the contracts, wills and other instruments forming part of notarial protocols or files, or which may be contained in the executive or judicial archives, be the latter in Spain or in the islands aforesaid.

Article IX

Spanish subjects, natives of the Peninsula, residing in the territory over which Spain by the present treaty relinquishes or cedes her sovereignty, may remain in such territory or may remove therefrom, retaining in either event all their rights of property, including the right to sell or dispose of such property or of its proceeds; and they shall also have the right to carry on their industry, commerce and professions, being subject in respect thereof to such laws as are applicable to other foreigners. In case they remain in the territory they may preserve their allegiance to the Crown of Spain by making, before a court of record, within a year from the date of the exchange of ratifications of this treaty, a declaration of their decision to preserve such allegiance; in default of which declaration they shall be held to have renounced it and to have adopted the nationality of the territory in which they may reside.

The civil rights and political status of the native inhabitants of the territories hereby ceded to the United States shall be determined by the Congress.

Article X

The inhabitants of the territories over which Spain relinquishes or cedes her sovereignty shall be secured in the free exercise of their religion.

Article XI

The Spaniards residing in the territories over which Spain by this treaty cedes or relinquishes her sovereignty shall be subject in matters civil as well as criminal to the jurisdiction of the courts of the country wherein they reside, pursuant to the ordinary laws governing the same; and they shall have the right to appear before such courts, and to pursue the same course as citizens of the country to which the courts belong.

Article XII

Judicial proceedings pending at the time of the exchange of ratifications of this treaty in the territories over which Spain relinquishes or cedes her sovereignty shall be determined according to the following rules:

1. Judgments rendered either in civil suits between private individuals, or in criminal matters, before the date mentioned, and with respect to

which there is no recourse or right of review under the Spanish law, shall be deemed to be final, and shall be executed in due form by competent authority in the territory within which such judgments should be carried out.

2. Civil suits between private individuals which may on the date mentioned be undetermined shall be prosecuted to judgment before the court in which they may then be pending or in the court that may be substituted therefor.

3. Criminal actions pending on the date mentioned before the Supreme Court of Spain against citizens of the territory which by this treaty ceases to be Spanish shall continue under its jurisdiction until final judgment; but, such judgment having been rendered, the execution thereof shall be committed to the competent authority of the place in which the case arose.

Article XIII

The rights of property secured by copyrights and patents acquired by Spaniards in the Island of Cuba and in Porto Rico, the Philippines and other ceded territories, at the time of the exchange of the ratifications of this treaty, shall continue to be respected. Spanish scientific, literary and artistic works, not subversive of public order in the territories in question, shall continue to be admitted free of duty into such territories, for the period of ten years, to be reckoned from the date of the exchange of the ratifications of this treaty.

Article XIV

Spain shall have the power to establish consular officers in the ports and places of the territories, the sovereignty over which has been either relinquished or ceded by the present treaty.

Article XV

The Government of each country will, for the term of ten years, accord to the merchant vessels of the other country the same treatment in respect of all port charges, including entrance and clearance dues, light dues, and tonnage duties, as it accords to its own merchant vessels, not engaged in the coastwise trade.

This article may at any time be terminated on six months' notice given by either Government to the other.

Article XVI

It is understood that any obligations assumed in this treaty by the United States with respect to Cuba are limited to the time of its occupancy thereof; but it will upon the termination of such occupancy, advise any Government established in the island to assume the same obligations.

Article XVII

The present treaty shall be ratified by the President of the United States, by and with the advice and consent of the Senate thereof, and by Her Majesty the Queen Regent of Spain; and the ratifications shall be exchanged at Washington within six months from the date hereof, or earlier if possible.

In faith whereof, we, the respective Plenipotentiaries, have signed this treaty and have hereunto affixed our seals.

Done in duplicate at Paris, the tenth day of December in the year of Our Lord one thousand eight hundred and ninety eight.

[seal] William R. Day
[seal] Cushman K. Davis
[seal] William P. Frye
[seal] George Gray
[seal] Whitelaw Reid

[seal] Eugenio Montero Rios
[seal] B. de Abarzuza
[seal] J. de Garnica
[seal] W. R. de Villa-Urrutia
[seal] Rafael Cerero

THE MILITARY AND COLONIAL POLICY OF THE UNITED STATES

PART I

THE AMERICAN SOLDIER

ADDRESS BY THE SECRETARY OF WAR AT THE MARQUETTE CLUB IN CHICAGO, OCTOBER 7, 1899, IN RESPONSE TO THE TOAST, "THE AMERICAN SOLDIER"

I AM not unmindful of the fact that the easiest way to be interesting is to be indiscreet, and that the most attractive aids to oratory are extravagant expressions which, while conforming to the heat of the evening, do not commend themselves to the sober judgment of the morning.

Happily, the subject to which I am assigned tonight finds its own interest in every American heart, and no eloquence is needed to strike the chords of sympathy or of sentiment in loyal souls, where the American soldier is the theme.

You do not wish me to speak of the soldier of the past. We are a peaceful, not a military people, but we are made of fighting fiber, and whenever fighting is by hard necessity the business of the hour we always do it as becomes the children of great, warlike races; and on every field from the day when along the stone walls that line the Cambridge road, the men of Concord and of Acton made each his own disappearing gun carriage, to the day when the flag floated over the citadel of Manila, the American soldier has answered loyally to every call of duty.

It is the soldier of today of whom you wish me to speak and of whom I wish to speak. The American soldier today is a part of a great machine which we call military organization; a machine in which, as by electrical converters, the policy of government is transformed into the strategy of the general, into the tactics of the field and into the action of the man behind the gun. Through that machine he is fed, clothed, transported and armed, equipped and housed.

The machine today is defective; it needs improvement; it ought to be improved. Thirty-three years of profound peace have evolved in it some men upon whom the stress of harsh requirement has proved that they are unfit for the positions to which they have attained. Some square pegs have got into round holes and some round pegs have got into square holes. Some men who, in the ordinary days of peace, have seemed to be equal to all requirements, in the stern necessities of war have failed to answer to the demands; and whereever that has occurred the machinery has stopped and failed to accomplish its purpose. This was inevitable. It could be avoided only by the true Anglo-Saxon method of improvement by experiment.

The machine was the machine by which was fought, through which were clothed and armed, equipped, transported and ordered, the armies which fought, the greatest civil war of modern times. It was the machinery that we received through that great generation of men whom we all honor as we look back over a third of a century, and it has required the experience of another war to teach the American people where it needs improvement and change.

It rests with you, through the senators and representatives in Congress whom you shall elect, to determine whether the lesson of this later war shall be learned, and the army organization of America shall be put in the front of American progress; but in the meantime let me say to you that within the limits of that great army machinery there are today in the city of Washington and in every military department, scores, hundreds of men doing faithful, devoted, and able service in the cause of their country and of their country's army, of whom any people upon the face of this earth might well be proud.

When the history of these troublous years comes to be written with cold and unimpassioned pen, the names of many men whose hair has been streaked with gray through the strenuous labors of these days in the staff of the army, will be written high in the list of those entitled to their country's gratitude.

This army of ours is concentrated or concentrating largely in the wonderful islands of the East, toward which all American eyes are turned today. May I say a word to you of what it has been doing there and how the American soldier has been performing his duty? Will you go back with me to that May morning when all American hearts were made bright and joyous by the news of the Nelsonic victory of Dewey?

Upon that day the title of Spain to the Philippine Islands stood unchallenged and unquestioned. But a few months before, the Philippine insurrection had ceased, ceased by an agreement under which Spain had promised to give to the Philippine Islands certain reforms, moderate in their character, reasonable in their nature, and to pay a sum of money to the leaders of the Philippine forces. Aguinaldo and his companions, as one of the terms of the treaty, had been exiled from Luzon; and, although disorganized riot and bloodshed had followed Spain's failure to keep her promise of reform, when, as a result of the destruction of the Spanish fleet, Dewey held Manila at his mercy, he was the potential master of an empire, to which the title of the Spanish foe was as unquestioned and indisputable as the title of the Queen of England to the island over which she reigns.

Admiral Dewey brought Aguinaldo in an American ship from exile. He set him upon the soil of Luzon and put in his hands the arms and ammunition by which he might gather the forces of the Philippines to aid the American army; and then for three long months, from May until the twelfth of August, he waited for reënforcements to come from America to make him strong enough to capture Manila — not to capture Manila, but to hold Manila when it was captured—

and during that time the Filipino leaders were gathering their forces, practically without opposition, with the guns of Dewey's fleet protecting them, and with the paralyzed Spaniards within the walls of Manila.

On the twelfth of August the protocol between Spain and the United States was signed, and by that we assumed the solemn obligation of holding the bay and harbor of Manila until the final treaty of peace was executed and ratified. We took possession of the city, and for six long weary months, while the slow processes of negotiation wore on, while the slower processes of discussion and ratification dragged their weary way, we stood on the ramparts of Manila waiting; and the American soldier, in those six months of inaction under the tropical sun, not knowing why he waited, not knowing that he was waiting under peremptory orders from Washington based upon the necessity of maintaining national faith, waited still — waited while the army of the Filipinos which had been gathered about the walls and promised the loot of Manila, exasperated by being kept from their plunder, grew more and more defiant, grew at last contemptuous, showered upon him abuse and ridicule and defiance and insult.

And the stern resolve, the self-control, the power in obedience to orders and to duty to restrain themselves from even the resentment of insult, entitled the soldiers of America to the admiration of civilized and law-obeying men, while it won for them only the contempt of their half-civilized opponents.

It was this contempt and the certainty it bred that the Americans would not fight and were cowards, and could be swept into the sea, that led to the attack of February fifth, when the hordes of the Filipinos precipitated themselves upon our ranks. They speedily learned their mistake. What was it that the American soldier had before him then? You all understand that the Congress of the United States, not expecting that these Filipinos, to whom we were ready to give a hundred times what they accepted from Spain a few months before, would reject the offer, had passed a law disbanding the army in effect, so that twenty-five days after the attack upon the American soldiers in Manila General Otis had left but 4,498 soldiers, officers, and men whom he was entitled to command, and the remaining 17,000 of his 22,000 soldiers were entitled to be discharged and returned to the United States.

The problem before him, then, was to hold back the uncounted hordes who surrounded Manila, to keep in subjection the two hundred thousand Filipinos in the city who had received orders to rise and massacre every European and American within its limits; to wait, with the rainy season coming upon him, until a new army could be raised and sent a third of the way around the world to take the place of the old army which must be sent back to their homes.

And then, again, the American soldier, the volunteer soldier and the thousands of regulars who were entitled to their discharge, showed what stuff they were made of. Homesick, longing for a sight of their old homes in temperate climes, enfeebled and sick from their long stay under a tropical sun and in tropical rains, nevertheless in this desperate strait of their country they abandoned the bright visions of home and stayed, without obligation, except that of patriotism, until a new army could be raised and sent to stand behind the flag.

Impatience is exhibited here and there. In many places we hear it; in many newspapers we see it. Impatience, like the old "On to Richmond" cry of 1861, like the "On to Havana" cry of 1898. But let me tell you that the events of 1899 on the island of Luzon were events that followed a fixed, settled, and wise purpose.

In face of the fact that the country was about to become a morass impossible for military operations; that the rains were coming on, which gave, in fact, during the first twenty days of July in this year forty-two inches of rainfall — three feet and a half in twenty days — which have given more than half a foot of rain in a single day; in the face of the approach of that climatic condition, with an army that must be succored from a third of the way round the world, the problem was to establish the American position against foes within and foes without, so that it could be held and maintain the flag until the men came to fight and there was land for them to fight on.

The temporary forays to punish too impertinent guerrillas have been magnified into great military movements, and when the party of foray has returned as a part of the plan of their operations, the return has been magnified into a retreat; but in fact, the steady, consistent, and unswerving purpose has run through every movement of every month and of every day in Luzon.

Well, the army, 17,000 of them, have been brought back from the other side of the world. Twenty-seven thousand — another army — have been sent, and are there today. Seventeen thousand more are on the road, and 17,000 more are in camp today, ready. By the fifteenth of next month, 49,000 American troops will answer to the commands of Otis and Lawton and MacArthur. By the end of the following month 65,000 will be there.

They are the best youth of America. Let me tell you that in the month of July we enlisted 2,900 men for the regular army, and they were enlisted out of 14,000 applications, of which 11,000 were rejected on examination. They are well officered by the best intelligence of America. Let me speak of what I know — that of the 700 officers of the fifteen regiments which have been officered since the first of August, not one has been appointed who has not seen actual service in the regular army, or in war, and not one has been appointed who was not appointed on his efficiency record as a soldier.

Well, against whom are we fighting? Are we fighting the Philippine nation? No. There is none. There are hundreds of islands, inhabited by more than sixty tribes, speaking more than sixty different languages, and all but one are ready to accept American sovereignty — and many of them have already accepted it and welcomed the Stars and Stripes to float over them. Many of them are already engaged in learning the rudiments of government under the tuition of the American soldier. We are opposed by only the single tribe of the Tagalos, who inhabit less than one-half of the single island of Luzon.

Are we fighting a people who are capable of self-government? No. The practically unanimous declaration of the men who have been there and studied the subject and studied the people, is that they are not now capable of self-government. Senator Beveridge, of Indiana, who has been there qualifying himself in noble fashion for the performance of his duties in the Senate, says that they are not fit for it. General Merritt says they are not fit for it; General Greene says they are not fit for it; President Schurman says they are not fit for it; Admiral Dewey says they are not fit for it.

Are we fighting a people who themselves consider that they are capable of their own protection? No. For never has the most advanced and violent of them gone further than to say that they want to be allowed to govern themselves under the protection of the United States. Their proposition is that they should be at liberty to make the wars and that we should fight them.

Are we fighting the whole of the single tribe with which alone we are engaged? No; for the vast majority of that tribe want peace, law, order, and are ready and anxious for the protective government of the United States. The men who own the property, the men who do the business, the men of intelligence among them are anxious that the Government of the United States shall protect them in their interests and their industries.

Are we fighting in breach of faith with an ally or for any right which we have promised to forego? No. Immediately upon Aguinaldo's appearance on the scene, Admiral Dewey was instructed to enter into no alliance with the insurgents and make no promises to them. He replied that he had made no alliance and no promises. Will any one question his statement?

We are fighting against the selfish ambition of a military dictator who was brought from exile by an American ship, furnished with arms by American soldiers and sailors; who was permitted to gather all the forces of disorder, all the men who prefer a life of brigandage to a life of industry, around the paralyzed Spaniards during the ten months when America was prevented by her international obligations and the faith of her protocol from interfering; who has attained supreme power by the assassination of his rival, and who maintains it by the arrest and punishment of every one who favors the United States, and the murder of every one whom he can reach who aids her.

The closest analogy to Aguinaldo to be found in our experience is the perpetual military revolutionist of Central America.

Gentlemen, the title of America to the island of Luzon is better than the title we had to Louisiana. It rests upon a more just foundation than the title we had to Texas. It rests upon the sure foundation of international law, and the surer foundation of high duty in the family of nations and to the cause of humanity. No president has the power or the right, no executive officer has the will or the wish to take away from American sovereignty one rod of the soil that belongs to it; and so long as the American people stand behind the American soldier he will maintain the honor of the flag and the integrity of that sovereignty on the island of Luzon, come who may against him.

But the finest thing about the American soldier is that he is an American citizen. He carries with him not the traditions of a military empire, but the traditions of a self-governing people. He comes from a land where public discussion has educated every citizen in the art of self-government; from a land where such debates as that between Lincoln and Douglas, where such great schools of public government as we see in the discussion before every presidential election, where the affairs of city and county and town and village, have made the art of government the alphabet of life for every citizen, where every citizen has learned that obedience to law, and respect for the results of popular elections, is a part of the order of nature.

And so the American soldier is different from all other soldiers of all other countries since the world began, and today I am prouder of him for what he is doing in poor, bleeding Cuba and devastated Porto Rico, and what he is doing in that tumultuous city of Manila, than I ever was for the greatest victory he ever won.

Poor Cuba, torn by years of war and dissension, with her people gathered starving in her towns, with no knowledge of the art of government, almost forgetful of the arts of peace, has had her wounds bound up, her people returned to their homes, the tillage of her soil recommenced, the industry of her factories, the activity of her commerce, all the arts of peace revived, under the kindly tuition of the American soldier. He goes with the sword, with the bayonet, with the cannon; but the moment that the enemy ceases to fire he is ready with open hand, with the spirit of John Howard and

Florence Nightingale, to heal the sick, to succor the poor, to teach the ignorant, to set up the arts of peace and to turn the scene of warfare into the smiling land of plenty.

The soldiers of the United States in Porto Rico, when that island was swept by the frightful hurricane of the eighth of August, turned into a hospital corps every one, from general down to private. I am prouder of Wood in Santiago and Wilson in Mantanzas and Ludlow in Havana, cleaning the streets and disinfecting the pest holes and teaching the Cubans how to live cleanly and orderly lives, teaching them the simple elements of civil government; teaching them how to go back to work, to earn their living; teaching them how to become self-governing citizens of a free state, than I ever could be of a hero on the ramparts amid the hail of shot.

I will leave to others the task of lauding those qualities in the American soldier which he has in common with the legions of Cæsar and the battalions of Napoleon, and I claim for him the higher honor that while he is as stern a foe as ever man saw on the battlefield, he brings the schoolbook, the plow, and the Bible. While he leads the forlorn hope of war, he is the advance guard of liberty and justice, of law and order, and peace and happiness.

I stood last month on the battlefield of Gettysburg. Two gray-haired veterans of the Civil War — one an officer of the Union and the other an officer of the Confederate army — who had fought upon that field, accompanied me. They vied with each other in recounting the story of those eventful days, themselves a happy type of our reunited land. They showed the spot where Reynolds fell. They marked the places where Hancock and Barlow shed their blood. They traced the line of Pickett's charge, and the field across which Pettigrew swept with his North Carolinians; and I thought, as I listened to their story, how dear to their hearts and to the heart of every true American is the name and the fame of every hero who fought upon that field.

My friends, today our brothers are lying in the trenches in Luzon, and today over the length and breadth of this land lying and envious tongues, for political effect, are spreading vile slanders concerning the American soldiers in Luzon. The day will come when the fair fame of these, our brothers of today, is as dear to the American people as that of the heroes of Gettysburg.

I protest in the name of the American soldier against all those who, believing because they wish to believe, without opportunity for explanation or contradiction, circulate and print the idle stories which fly through the air from malicious tongues, impugning the honor of the true and noble Americans who are protecting the honor of our flag.

I ask your condemnation upon all those who speak and print imputations upon them while they are enduring the hardships of that distant land, dying, it may be, for the honor of your flag and theirs. They will be faithful to you and to the Republic. Oh, Americans, be faithful and fair to them.

THE CHARACTER AND OFFICE OF THE AMERICAN ARMY

AN ADDRESS AT A BANQUET AT CANTON, OHIO, JANUARY 27, 1903, IN HONOR OF THE BIRTHDAY OF THE LATE PRESIDENT McKINLEY

I THANK you for your greeting in memory of your friend and mine. Never can I forget the sweet and tender associations that have gathered about your city since I walked and drove through your streets with that tenderest and sweetest of natures.

It is noteworthy that the greatest American presidents who have passed into history have been the most patient, most peaceable, and most just of all the men whose names are found upon the pages of our national life; and yet, that each one of them, Washington, Lincoln, and McKinley, led his country through the dark and bloody paths of war. Washington, the embodiment of considerate justice, could not obtain justice for the colonies except after the sacrifice and the struggle. Lincoln, agonizing for peace and union, nevertheless was devoted by fate to those years of weary effort when the blood of his countrymen flowed like water for the freedom of mankind. And McKinley, with a soul of the tenderest sympathy, straining to the utmost the efforts of diplomacy to secure justice for bleeding Cuba, was forced to become the leader in dreadful war in the islands of the East and the islands of the West.

Do not forget or be deaf to the lesson. No sense of justice, no desire for peace, no kindliness of heart can turn aside the inexorable decrees of the overwhelming powers that bring war and will bring war in the future, as they have brought it in the past. It lies not in the will of rulers, it lies not in the generous impulses of the human heart, but it lies in the working out of the destiny of mankind that no people can avoid. Controversies will arise as they have arisen, when each side believes itself to be right and the weak and feeble will go to the wall. Great and overbearing injustice walks the earth still, and the people who are unable or unwilling to strive for their rights will find small respect.

In the slow progress of the ages — progress ever but progress slow, as "the mills of God grind slowly" — it is still the part of manhood and self-respect to be able to defend one's self against injustice, to hold the arm of strength out for the protection of the weak, and, if need be, to sacrifice life that the reign of justice and righteousness may still approach upon earth.

Poor China today stands helpless, seeing, piece by piece, parts of her territory peopled by her citizens, cut out from her living body and subjected to the domination of foreign power — China, which has carried the arts of civilization to a high, if not the highest, point — China, whose people are industrious, and frugal and enterprising, among the best workmen, the most honest merchants, the most successful business men of the earth — China, whose people cultivate the domestic virtues, the affections, a high type of morality, and fear not death at all — is helpless today because centuries ago she forgot that the part of manhood required that men shall be able to defend their rights.

The nation least able to defend itself most invites aggression. It is to repel and prevent aggression and to defend and assert the right, that the army of the United States exists. Not because we love war or seek war; not because we would infringe upon the rights of any other power or of any other people, but because we have that manhood in us, and we have that respect and love for the right to make us willing to defend it with life itself, we have the army of the United States. It is an insurance against aggression. Among the eighty million people of the United States the cost of this insurance is less than a dollar apiece. For the hundred billions of property of the people of the United States the cost of this insurance is less than one-tenth of one per cent.

The character of the army of the United States conforms to the high and pacific purpose for which it exists. It is ar army of citizens of the United States — volunteers all o: them. It is a volunteer army. It is an army of citizens, each one of whom is educated, for there is an educational test upon admission. It is an army in which the door of opportunity, the open door of opportunity to youth which is the crowning and chief glory of our American institutions, is never closed, for up from the ranks each common soldier of the United States may pass by promotion to the highest rank. Aye, they do pass, and no star upon the breast, no marshal's baton held by any prince of Europe, can compare for credit with the stars on the shoulders of that Ohio boy who through gallantry in the Civil War of '61 to '65, gallantry in command in Cuba, gallantry in the march to Peking, wise administration as commander in the Philippines, has reached the high rank of major-general in the army of the United States — Adna R. Chaffee.

The officers of the army conform in their character and conduct to the purpose for which the army is maintained, and the character of the people from whom they come. I wish to say to you, not in the language of rhetoric, but as a sober statement of what I have found by careful observation, that they are free to a degree which I never dreamed of, until I commenced to know of them, from the vices which have prevailed in most armies of the world during all history. They are a temperate set of men. They are freer from the vice of drinking to excess than almost any other class I know of in this country. They are free from the vice of gambling. No such thing as duelling, which disgraces and deforms many military services, obtains in our army. The man who is dissipated is out of favor, and the public sentiment of the officers of the army is opposed to dissipation and excess. The man who does not pay his debts falls into disfavor, and it is an offense which is punished in our army by court-martial if a man does not pay his honest debts.

No one ever knew of the American army seeking to make itself a political agent. No one ever knew of the American army seeking to make itself a Pretorian guard to set up a president or an emperor. No one ever knew of the American army seeking to throw off that civil control of the military arm which our fathers inherited from England and which is ingrained in the desires, the prejudices and the instincts of the Anglo-Saxon race. It does its duty under presidents, Republican or Democratic. Whatever the political policy of the American people may be, when the army is called upon it does its duty, asking no questions, doubting not, begrudging no sacrifice, fearing no danger, and hesitating not at death itself.

Whenever the enlarged army of the United States finds the duty of the hour accomplished it melts back into the mass of the people unnoticed. When the Civil War was over, the million of men under Grant's command took their way to their homes. The greatest military power which to that day had ever existed never dreamed for a moment of threatening the institutions of our free government. And when the war with Spain was over, the 250,000 men who had been raised for that war disappeared as quietly to their homes, never thinking for a moment of exercising the slightest influence upon the political life of the country. That this is so unnoticed, and causes so little surprise among our people, is the highest testimony to the abiding confidence of the people in the soldiers of the American army. They have their faults, but their faults are small and their virtues are great; and they are justly the pride of the American people from whom they come, and to whom, when their duty is done, they return. They embody and act upon the traditions of the farewell address, the traditions of Grant's dying message to his countrymen, "Let us have peace." They are an engine not of war for war's sake, but of peace, and war for the sake of peace. They are not the scourge of God. They are the advance agents always of peace and justice. They are missionaries of ordered liberty, and wherever they go ordered liberty follows. "By their fruits ye shall know them."

Under the administration of President McKinley and his true and loyal successor, the American army undertook three great tasks after the capture of Santiago. It undertook to march to the relief of the beleaguered legations in the city of Peking; and when the work of rescue there had been accomplished, to set up a government in that city, to do justice and protect the weak until the Chinese government could resume its sway. Let me read to you not what I say or what the army says, but what the people of Peking say about the way in which these American citizens wearing the uniform of the United States performed the duty of civilization in those times of dire distress and disorder. I will read the translation of a petition addressed by a mass meeting of the Chinese in Peking on the twenty-eighth of March, 1901, to Captain John C. F. Tillson, Fourteenth United States Infantry, Provost-Marshal, American District, Chinese City, Peking; for after the city was taken it was divided into districts, and over each district the troops of one country held sway. Two thousand Chinese signed this paper:

SIR: We, the people, and proprietors of two thousand (2,000) business houses in the American section have the honor to beg you to intercede in our behalf to secure a postponement of the withdrawal of the United States troops from this section, as we have been perfectly protected by you from the beginning till now.

After the relief expedition the city was divided into different sections, and we were under your jurisdiction.

We are profoundly grateful because we have been so well treated. You have, under the wise government established by you, justly punished criminals; given us letters of protection that have saved us from molestation from bad soldiers, and enabled us to lead peaceful lives.

You have opened charity eating houses and saved the poor from starvation.

You have employed policemen to prevent crime; gambling houses and opium dens have been closed and thieves driven from the district.

We have been made very happy and we are grateful to you because you have protected us so kindly.

We learned recently that your Government will withdraw her troops before the other nations withdraw theirs.

We were very sorry to learn this, because we fear that criminals will prey upon us upon your departure.

With the best protection you could give us there was still some crime.

Should the United States troops leave here it is certain that criminals will again pillage the people.

Though we may come under the protection of some other power, we fear that that other power will not be so efficient as the United States has been and the officer not so kind and just as you.

From the beginning we have been perfectly protected by you, but after you leave we may be robbed and harmed by bad men and badly treated by the new officer.

That would be a case of a good beginning with a bad ending which we would keenly regret.

After mature consideration we have concluded to beg you to ask your Government for us to kindly permit you to remain here until the negotiation is concluded.

This will prevent our being harmed, robbed, and badly treated, and we can continue our business with content.

If this, our petition, be granted, we shall be more grateful than words can express.

For these reasons we have the honor to submit our petition with our names written on another sheet.

A petition addressed to Major Robertson, Ninth Infantry, Provost-Marshal, Tartar City, reads as follows:

We, the people of the American section, consider ourselves fortunate to be protected under the glorious flag of the United States, a flag which has indeed secured us better protection than we have ever had before. In addition to the commercial prosperity and individual privileges we have enjoyed since the arrival of the allied forces at Peking, we have been favored with many beneficial institutions, such as police station, charity house, board of health, vaccination, etc.

The Court of Provost-Marshal which seldom, if ever, leaves innocence without recognition and the guilty unpunished is the center of justice. The watchfulness with which the American policemen perform their duties has protected many a merchant from being robbed by foreign soldiers and native rascals. Everything moves on as smoothly as could be desired.

Thousands of homeless people, who otherwise would starve to death, are being fed by the American Charity House. The excellence of the present sanitary arrangements, which was once so foreign to us, cannot but win our admiration. We believe that Peking has never enjoyed such good health in her history as she is enjoying at present. In short, as a conquered people, we are more privileged than we are entitled to. We earnestly and sincerely request you, the American authorities, not to leave us until the time when all the nations withdraw their forces.

This petition was signed by five thousand six hundred leading merchants and citizens.

The second great task which the American army undertook was to lead Cuba in the unaccustomed paths of self-government, and to establish a stable government in that island. Let me read the views of the people of Cuba regarding the way in which the army fulfilled that task:

HAVANA, May 20, 1902.

HONORABLE GENERAL LEONARD WOOD.

I take this solemn occasion, which marks the fulfillment of the honored promise of the Government and people of the United States in regard to the island of Cuba, and in which our country is made a ruling nation, to express to you, the worthy representative of that grand people, the immense gratitude which the people of Cuba feel toward the American nation, toward its illustrious President, Theodore Roosevelt, and toward you, for the efforts you have put forth for the successful accomplishment of such a precious ideal.

T. ESTRADA PALMA.

HAVANA, May 20, 1902.

THEODORE ROOSEVELT,
President, Washington, D. C.

The government of the island having been transferred, I, as Chief Magistrate of the Republic, faithfully interpreting the sentiments of the whole people of Cuba, have the honor to send you and the American people testimony of our profound gratitude and the assurance of an enduring friendship, with wishes and prayers to the Almighty for the welfare and prosperity of the United States.

T. Estrada Palma.

The third great task which the army of the United States undertook, was to assert the sovereignty and just authority of the United States in the Philippine Islands, put down the insurrection against our authority there, and establish a civil government which should bring to those people the blessings of law and order and civil liberty. The army accomplished that task, established a government which, upon the first day of last July, received the sanction of Congressional enactment, and I beg to read to you some recent expressions sent by cable half-way around the world from the Philippine people indicating the character of that government so established; the government which followed the swift, resistless march of General Young and General Lawton through the island of Luzon:

Manila, January 7, 1903.

President Roosevelt, Washington, D. C.

The Philippine people have absolute confidence in Taft. Taft! once representing the intelligence and virtue of Ohio in the Capital of the nation; now representing the virtue and intelligence and living power of American institutions before all the people of the world. At the present moment departure of Taft would have deplorable effects in the country. The confidence won by Taft could not be improvised today. We believe it our duty to state to the President that the presence of Taft in the Philippines is indispensable for the ceremonial peace and the maintenance of faith which, by reason of him, the people of the Philippine Islands have in the intentions of the American people. We solemnly affirm that feelings Philippine people would be deeply hurt by the departure of Taft. We fulfill sacred duty requesting the continuance of Taft.

Tavera, Legarda, Luzuriaga,
Government Commissioners.
Arellano, Torres, Mapa,
Supreme Court Justices.
Aranata, *Solicitor-General.*
Herrera, *President of the Municipal Board of Manila.*
Albert, *President of the Federal Party.*

The greatest names, the most distinguished men of the Philippine Islands.

MANILA, January 10, 1903.

ROOSEVELT, Washington.

Native press thinks Taft's untimely departure ruinous public order. Prays he should be retained for preservation peace success American policy here.

GUITO RINACIMIENTO PATRIA,
Fraternidad Democracia.

MANILA, January 10, 1903.

ROOSEVELT, Washington.

Federals, Liberals, Nationalists request continuance Taft to complete work of America in Philippines.

MANILA, January 11, 1903.

ROOSEVELT, Washington.

International Club reports Philippine people deplore Taft's departure, which causes serious perturbation.

ROSARIO.

MANILA, January 11, 1903.

ROOSEVELT, Washington.

The Philippine lawyers having met together consider the withdrawal of Taft as fraught with disaster to the Philippine people, and ask that he may remain.

MANILA, January 12, 1903.

ROOSEVELT, Washington.

People Manila in grand demonstration Malacanang yesterday ask for continuance Taft as governor Philippines.

HERRERA, *Mayor.*

MANILA, January 12, 1903.

PRESIDENT ROOSEVELT, Washington.

Real estate owners' association considers necessary Governor Taft's stay.

MANILA, January 12, 1903.

ROOSEVELT, Washington.

Filipinos not belonging existing political parties consider Taft unchangeable maintenance moral material peace.

GUERRERO LUNA,
GENERALS MALIVAR, LUYBAN.

My friends, the establishment by the American army of those governments in far distant China and the islands of the East and West, making for peace and justice and ordered liberty, are greater achievements than the winning of any stricken field, are just cause for pride to every American citizen, and are a just title to confidence, respect and gratitude for every officer and soldier of the army of the United States. For the army of the United States breathes the spirit of William McKinley. It makes war only that peace and justice may follow. Behind the gun is the school book. After the footsteps of American soldiers the harvests spring into fruition and the sickle reaps in peace and safety. The harsh lesson of force administered by American soldiers is followed by the blessed lessons of religion and learning.

But the army of the United States is not merely the little body of men whom we call the regular establishment. The army of the United States always has been and always will be in time of war that greater army, when the whole people of the United States, putting forth their strength by militia and volunteer, second the efforts of the regular army. And in that greater army of the country the regular army performs the function of a teacher and an organizer. We have a duty to perform to that greater army. We have a duty to maintain and preserve for them an organizing power in the regular army of the United States which shall make victory possible. There is no trouble, and there never will be trouble, in this country about plenty of brave men to fight. All Americans are brave, all Americans are ready to fight for their country. The difficulties of war are met with us not in the raising of soldiers; they are met in the equipping, the supplying, the transporting and the organizing of soldiers. And, in order that this may be done, the organization of the regular army must be made adequate to the accomplishment of the task. It is our duty to see, and Congress by wise legislation during the present session is seeing, that when another war comes upon us — and it is sure to come however much we may long for peace — the young men of America shall not for the want of adequate organization die of disease in camp, perish upon the march for lack of food and clothes, fall under hostile shot and shell because misled by incompetent officers; but that the great volunteer army of the United States in the future shall have an adequate organization for its medical attendance, its supply of clothing and food and arms, its transportation, its organization, its command.

Already the Congress at the present session has passed a bill for the organization of the militia which substantially every administration of this country has endeavored to secure since 1794, when George Washington sent his first message to Congress asking for militia legislation. Already Congress has advanced to the last stage, where it now awaits action, a bill for the establishment of a general staff which makes possible adequate organization for the volunteer armies of the future. Superior intelligence shows itself by prevision and provision for the future. The people of the country owe it to the American army that that prevision and provision shall be given to the organization which will enable it to accomplish the tasks of the future as it has accomplished the tasks of the past. And I pledge you the faith of that army that never in all the years of the future will it depart from the highest standards of American citizenship. Never will it depart from the lofty ideals and the beneficent purposes for the blessings of mankind which inspired its great commander in the recent wars, the beloved friend whose memory we honor tonight.

THE UNITED STATES AND THE PHILIPPINES IN 1900

ADDRESS OF THE SECRETARY OF WAR, AT CANTON, OHIO
OCTOBER 24, 1900

A HEAVY burden of proof rests upon those who ask the American people to reject the further services of the Republican administration. Under that administration the legitimate objects of government have been attained to a degree which challenges comparison with the happiest periods in the life of any nation in any age. Never in human history anywhere on earth have security for life and property, unfettered opportunity for intelligence and energy, individual freedom, and the self-respect of manhood, attained a higher level than now marks the condition of this fortunate Republic.

The material results of wise and successful government are visible on every hand. We never before have had so many million people owning their own homes unencumbered, so many million people with accumulated earnings in savings banks, such universal employment of labor at such good wages, such abundant production from farm and factory and workshop of all material things which meet the necessities and contribute to the comfort and pleasure of life. The markets for our products are extending over the whole earth. Abundant home capital is obtainable at lower rates of interest than were ever known before for the productive enterprise which employs labor and creates wealth. We are rapidly paying our debts to Europe for the money borrowed to build our railroads and develop our country, so that the constant drain upon our earnings for the payment of interest abroad is ceasing; and we are lending money to Europe, so that the current of annual payments is setting in our direction. There never was in this world a greater body of people so well fed, well clothed and well housed.

Above and beyond all these material things are universal opportunities for education and the general exercise and training of intelligence. The newspaper, the magazine and the book find their way into the humblest home. The doors of our free schools are open to every child, and it is rare indeed that poverty withholds access. The patriotism of the rich is devoting millions to the building up of colleges, technical schools and great universities, in which the poorest boy can rise to the loftiest heights of learning and intellectual power. Freedom of thought, freedom of speech and the constant consideration and discussion of political problems are training and exercising the whole people to a degree of competency for self-government never before equaled. The aristocracy of America is the aristocracy of achievement. It is with intellectual and moral qualities that our people achieve fame and fortune. The pathway to the highest distinction is open to every boy who thumbs his primer in the common school. Inherited wealth is a hindrance rather than an aid in the race of life. Call the roll of those whom the nation has honored — the president and his cabinet, the great judges, the great senators, the great congressmen, the great governors — call the roll of the men whose great fortunes are the cause of envy and disparagement, and among them all you will find that the man who cannot look back upon a youth of privation and struggle, with no capital but his own energy and ambition, is the exception. The softening and ennobling influences of charity and religion find sway in every community. Hospitals and asylums and libraries and schools and churches grow apace with homes and manufactories, and the swift response to every appeal of humanity for the relief of misfortune answers to the quickened activity of industrial enterprise.

Of course this happy condition has not been created by government, but without good government it could not have been created. Without sound governmental policy and wise and efficient governmental administration, the blessings we have enumerated would have been impossible. Government does not make crops grow, or weave cloth, or mould iron; but wise government opens the markets for crops and for cloth and for iron; and for the want of them you and I have seen corn burned for fuel in the valley of the Mississippi, cloth unsalable gathering dust in the warehouses of New England, ores unquarried and furnaces unfired among the hills of Pennsylvania and Alabama, and the productive power of millions of American workingmen idle and helpless. Government does not make enterprise; but wise government evokes enterprise by the certainty of reward for its activity. Government does not invest capital; but wise government gives to capital that confidence in security for its investment which draws it from the hiding places of distrust and transmutes it into the plant and material out of which labor creates prosperity. Government does not give employment to labor, but wise government creates the conditions under which industrial activity employs labor. Prosperity does not come by chance. History is full of examples of earth's fairest regions nourishing only poverty, misery and degradation, because of the folly and incompetency or corruption of government. We are not without illustrations in our own land, of the ruin which can be wrought by unwise government and the attempts of men in power to apply crude and impracticable theories to the complicated and delicate machinery of industrial life. Under bad government no fertility of soil, no thrift or industry of population, can bring prosperity to a people. Security, opportunity, confidence, activity of trade and labor, are the fruits of good government alone. All these the American people secured for themselves when in the election of 1896 they committed the powers of government to the hands of President McKinley and a Republican Congress.

There is another field in which the decision of 1896 has justified itself. I am sure no really patriotic American who loves his country more than he desires office can have failed to be gratified by a certain competency and effectiveness in President McKinley's dealings with other powers. No administration during this generation at least has been confronted with such a succession of difficult undertakings outside of our own country. There may be just criticism in details, and there certainly has been much that was unjust; but what are the results ?

In April, 1898, Spain had an army of 400,000 veteran troops, and a navy which in numbers and armament appeared and was generally believed to be at least equal to ours. The whole continent of Europe anticipated that Spain would hold the land and sweep the seas, blockade our ports, and frustrate our arms until European intervention should paralyze our superior ultimate resources. But whose ships were ready and staunch and sound ? Whose ammunition was honest and effective ? Whose soldiers and sailors were trained ? Who swept the seas ? Whose flag floats over Santiago and San Juan and Havana and Manila ? Find if you can anywhere in history so great results secured against so considerable a foe by force of arms on land and sea in so brief a time, and with so small a loss of life.

The attack of the Tagalog insurgents upon our troops at Manila, in February, 1899, required the President, under the authority of Congress, to raise and equip and train an army, and transport it a third of the way round the world for the defense of American sovereignty against the force of arms.

When that army arrived in the fall of last year, a Tagalog sympathizer declared exultingly that we held no more territory in the Philippines than a bicycle rider could circle in a single day. Within three months the insurgent army and the insurgent government ceased to exist, and we hold all the islands which were subject to Spanish rule without opposition, save from fugitive bands, half guerrilla and half bandit, who are shooting our men from ambush, and blackmailing, and pillaging, and murdering their own countrymen until that happy day when their prayers may be answered by the election of an American president who will yield American sovereignty to savage force and deliver over the peaceful and unresisting people of the Philippines and the wealth and commerce of Manila to their cruel and bloody domination.

When the Democratic convention met at Kansas City in July last, all Europe believed that dreadful massacre had swept into oblivion all the ministers and legations of the civilized world in Peking. The admirals of the European powers at Taku had agreed upon 60,000 troops as the number necessary to march to Peking, and they were awaiting the slow collection of that force from the four quarters of the globe. London had arranged a memorial service in honor of her dead. A frightful war of retribution, the destruction of the dynasty, the removal of all restraint of law over 400,000,000 of people, the partition of China, the destruction of our markets and our trade seemed inevitable; but American diplomacy opened the sealed gates of the Tartar City and revealed to the world the representatives of civilization living, defending themselves against almost overwhelming hordes, under constant fire of shot and shell, with ammunition and food nearly gone, hoping, but almost despairing, for the relief which never would have come but for American faith and American persistency. Then American soldiers and American sailors pressed for rescue, for immediate movement, and 18,000 men made the march and did the work of the 60,000, and Peking fell and the legations were saved and the world rejoiced. And now, the legations saved, we continually press for peace and reasonableness and justice. I think we may safely say that during all this trying time in China not one act of wrong, or injustice, and not one moment's faltering in the assertion of American rights mars our record.

All this and many other less conspicuous and striking things done for the benefit and honor of our country have not happened by chance. High credit, honest expenditure, sound material, ships in readiness, guns and ammunition effective, sailors and soldiers well armed, equipped, trained, and disciplined, consistent and effective diplomacy, prompt and decisive action, prosperity and order at home, respect and honor abroad, are the infallible proofs of a strong, wise, safe, and honest administration. It is easy to carp and criticise. It is easy to point to failures of government to reach the ideal standard of perfection; but as compared with all the governments there are or ever have been in this imperfect and erring world, the administration now drawing to a close should awaken the satisfaction and pride of the American people to whom it renders its account.

And has not our President so borne himself in his great office that his virtues plead trumpet-tongued? Who shall estimate the value to American character of having in this place of highest honor and power this man of blameless life, of simple and unostentatious piety, whose character is fairly resplendent with the beauty of pure and unselfish domestic virtues? How ripe is the wisdom gained from his long experience in faithful and distinguished public service as Congressman, as leader of the House, as Governor and as President. What a perpetual testimony before all the world of the living truth of popular government is his ever-anxious devotion to the people's will — a devotion in which he stands by

Lincoln's side, subject, as was Lincoln, to the sneers of the thoughtless, but certain, as was Lincoln, to win the ultimate meed of praise that always waits on loyalty to great ideals.

The logic of events has proved that the American people were right when they rejected Mr. Bryan and the theories of his false democracy in 1896. The people are confirmed in their judgment, and great numbers who honestly believed that Bryan was right then have come to a clearer vision in the light of experience and follow him no longer.

Bryan and his associate leaders, who would make up his administration if he were elected, are not convinced. They do not accept the verdict of 1896. They intend now, as they intended then, to put this country on a silver basis by the free and unlimited coinage of silver at the ratio of sixteen to one; to sacrifice our national honor and credit, and substitute in the wages of labor, and the payment of honest debts, the fifty-cent dollar in place of the dollar worth one hundred cents the world over, under which all our prosperity has been attained. They intend now, as they intended then, to destroy the protective tariff, which they declare to be unconstitutional, and subject our manufacturing industries again to the fate which befell them under the Wilson tariff. They intend now, as they intended then, to deprive of power that great bulwark of constitutional liberty, the federal judiciary. They seek now, as they sought then, to excite animosities and foment discord among the people; to deceive by false promises of the demagogue, and to profit themselves by creating a warfare of class against class. The issues of 1896 remain open, avowed, insisted upon. They have learned nothing, and they have abandoned nothing, but they have despaired of securing from the American people a judgment upon those issues reversing the decision of 1896, and they have invented a new issue which they call "imperialism" and upon this issue they ask the people to give them the power to do all that the people refused in 1896 to let them do. "This," says the Kansas City platform, "we regard as the paramount issue of the campaign." To this Mr. Bryan practically confined himself in his speech of acceptance.

What is the meaning of paramount issue? What becomes of other issues when one is paramount? We should naturally suppose that to treat one particular issue as paramount involved leaving all other questions in abeyance and undetermined, to be taken up and decided at some future time when the one all-important and burning question has been disposed of. Is that what Mr. Bryan means? Does he mean to leave the other issues of his party in abeyance, awaiting future decision? Does he declare, nay, does he leave the possibility of inference that his party, if put into power at the coming election, will not act on the silver question, will not act on the tariff question, will not act on the judiciary question? No! He proposes to act, and he will act, if elected, and a Democratic Congress will act, if elected, to reverse the judgment of 1896 upon every issue then before the people. Imperialism is not paramount enough for *him* to abandon anything. It is not paramount for him. It is paramount only for those who were opposed to him in 1896, and the effect of its being paramount is merely that the sound money men, the protective tariff men, the law and order men of 1896 are to abandon their principles and their convictions, and surrender upon every issue of the Democratic platform of 1896.

What is this issue which is so important to all Mr. Bryan's late opponents, and so unimportant to him?

Imperialism! The word has a familiar sound. The cry is one of the cheapest and most threadbare of the demagogue's stock, always certain to produce a sensation among a people alert for the protection of their liberties. Jefferson was denounced as an imperialist; Lincoln was denounced as an imperialist; Grant was denounced as an imperialist; and to all three of these great and liberty-loving men the party of opposition made the country resound with loud campaign outcries that they were about to strangle the liberties of the country by military force, just as they are now clamoring againt President McKinley. Is there any more in the cry now than there was in the days of Jefferson, of Lincoln, and of Grant ? Is the character of our institutions really about to be changed, or are our liberties really in danger ? Is the issue substantial, or is it but the demagogue's cry ?

The charge is that President McKinley has been guilty of something called imperialism, in his treatment of the people of the Philippine Islands. Something so foreign to the character of our institutions and so dangerous to our liberties that it requires the American people to ignore the wisdom and efficiency of his administration at home and abroad in other respects — to reject now and hereafter the services which have been so beneficial to them in the past and to put into power Mr. Bryan and his associates, with full warrant to accomplish all the purposes they profess, which the majority of the people believe will be so fatal to the honor, the credit, and the prosperity of our country.

What has President McKinley done in the Philippines ?

On the sixth of February, 1899, the Senate of the United States approved the treaty of peace with Spain. By the third article of that treaty, Spain ceded to the United States the archipelago known as the Philippine Islands; the United States agreed to pay Spain twenty million dollars; and in the ninth article the treaty provided that the civil rights and political status of the native inhabitants of the territory ceded to the United States should be determined by the Congress.

The examination of Mr. Bryan's charge of imperialism may commence with this treaty, because it was confirmed by the Senate in a large measure by Democratic votes, with the earnest and active support and advocacy of Mr. Bryan.

Upon the advisability, the wisdom and validity of that treaty both the candidates for the presidency, therefore, are agreed; and in considering the charge made by Mr. Bryan against President McKinley, we start with the proposition that the treaty which vested in the United States the sovereignty over the Philippine Islands and committed the rights and political status of its inhabitants to the determination of the Congress of the United States was right.

On the fourth of February, two days before the Senate approved the treaty, an army of Tagalogs, a tribe inhabiting the central part of Luzon, under the leadership of Aguinaldo, a Chinese half-breed, attacked, in vastly superior numbers, our little army in the possession of Manila, and after a desperate and bloody fight, was repulsed in every direction. The treaty was confirmed by the Senate with the full knowledge of that attack. On the second of March, both Houses of Congress, by an almost unanimous vote, appropriated twenty millions of dollars, which the treaty provided to be paid to Spain on the cession of the Philippines; and on the same day, in view of this hostile attack, Congress, by a vote which had the assent and concurrence of the leaders of the Democratic party in both Houses, authorized the President to increase the regular army from 27,500 men to 65,000, and to raise and equip 35,000 volunteers.

What President McKinley has done in the Philippines has been to defend and assert the sovereignty of the United States thus acquired with the assent of both parties and of both candidates for the presidency, with the means thus placed in his hands by Congress. What is charged against him is that he did not yield or procure Congress to authorize him to yield the sovereignty of the United States acquired by the cession of Spain with the assent of both parties, to the force of armed Tagalogs whose hands were red with the blood of American soldiers; place in their hands the government of the Philippine Islands, lower the American flag upon the walls of Manila and hurry away with our wounded and our dead from the bay made glorious by Dewey's victory.

The first specification under the charge is that it was unjust to the Filipinos not to do this. Of course it was impossible to do it. Self-respect forbade it, national honor forbade it; the whole world would have contemned and despised us if we had done it; the whole country would have risen in indignant protest against any President who dared to do it. But I will pass all that and treat the question as if it had been possible. What made it requisite as an act of justice that the government of the Philippines should be placed in the hands of Aguinaldo and his associates? Was there any promise or agreement or alliance that required it? No. This Government not only never authorized it, but the President expressly forbade anything of the kind. Admiral Dewey, who commanded our naval forces, says there was nothing of the kind. General Anderson and General Merritt, who commanded the land forces, say there was nothing of the kind. True, our Democratic friends will not believe them. No length of honorable career, no splendid record of American citizenship, in their minds, entitles the American officer to be believed who testifies in favor of the Administration against Aguinaldo. Perhaps they will believe a Tagalog witness.

We have in our possession an original document, signed by Mabini, the president of Aguinaldo's cabinet, his chief adviser, and the brains of the insurrection. It is a paper of instructions to a commissioner sent upon a secret mission by the insurgent government, dated January 4, 1899, and it reads in part as follows:

> The chief of the Philippine people has not made any agreement with the Government of the United States, but inspired by the same idea of destroying the sovereignty of Spain in these Islands, they have mutually assisted each other.

Though they believe not Moses and the Prophets, perhaps they will believe that.

Is there anything in the circumstances of the assistance which we have received from these men which entitles them to the reward of the sovereignty of the Philippines? Certainly not. When Dewey destroyed the Spanish fleet and the city of Manila lay helpless under his guns, waiting only for our troops to come in and take possession, the rule of Spain in the Philippines received its death blow. There was no insurrection then in the Philippine Islands. The sovereignty and title of Spain stood unquestioned by the people of the Philippine Islands or by any one else on earth. There had been an insurrection led by Aguinaldo, but that had been terminated in the previous December by an agreement called the Treaty of Biac-na-Bato, under which Aguinaldo and his associates were bought off by the payment of $400,000, and the promise of $400,000 more on the performance of certain specified conditions which included their leaving the country. That insurrection had not been a struggle for independence, and the people of the Philippine Islands had never in their history demanded or sought independence from Spain, or the surrender of Spanish sovereignty. When Aguinaldo and his associates were brought from China to the Philippines by Admiral Dewey some weeks after the destruction of the Spanish fleet, they were but a band of adventurers, whose assistance was availed of as is that of the disaffected inhabitants of any invaded country, upon no terms, conditions or implied obligations, other than those of reasonable reward for such services as they might render.

To make the situation perfectly clear, let me read to you from the treaty of Biac-na-Bato, which terminated the insurrection in December, 1897:

1. Don Emilio Aguinaldo in his quality as Supreme Leader of those in the Island of Luzon now waging open hostilities against their legitimate

government and Don Baldomero Aguinaldo and Don Mariano Llanera, who also exercise important commands in the forces mentioned, are to cease their hostile attitude, surrender their arms that they are using against their fatherland, and are to surrender to the legitimate authorities *claiming their rights as Spanish Filipino citizens which they desire to preserve.* As a consequence of this surrender they obligate themselves to cause the surrender of such individuals as actually follow them and those who recognize them as leaders and obey their orders.

Let me read from the program formally prepared and signed for the carrying out of this treaty:

25th December. Departure of Don Emilio Aguinaldo and his companions with Don Pedro A. Paterno and Don Miguel Primo de Rivera for Lingayan, where the Spanish government will have a merchant steamer to take them to Hong-Kong, the gentlemen going aboard may take their revolvers and the two rifles asked for by Don Emilio Aguinaldo. On the departure of these gentlemen from Biac-na-Bato the Spanish Government will give, by Don Pedro A. Paterno to Baldemero Aguinaldo, a letter payable to the order of the Spanish-Filipino bank upon some bank in Hong-Kong for the sum of $400,000, the cost of exchange being charged to the Spanish government. . . .

Nothing can be more preposterous than the proposition that these men were entitled to receive from us sovereignty over the entire country which we were invading. As well the friendly Indians, who have helped us in our Indian wars, might have claimed the sovereignty of the West. They knew that we were incurring no such obligation, and they expected no such reward. Their plan was to obtain from us arms and ammunition and protection while they collected an army; to use us to capture Manila, and then to take it from us by force of arms. In their vainglorious and half-savage estimate of their powers they believed they could do this. They believed they could drive us into the sea when the time came; and their attack upon our troops at Manila on the fourth of February, 1899, was in pursuance of a deliberate purpose and long preparation. Their plan was fully formed before they left China, and it was with truly Oriental treachery in their hearts that they accepted the hospitality and the assistance of our navy.

In Hong-Kong on the fourth of May, 1898, four days after the battle of Manila Bay, a meeting of the band was held to determine upon going to Manila with Dewey, and Agoncillo stated the proposition in these words:

> There will be no better occasion than the present for the expeditionary forces to land on those islands and to arm themselves at the expense of the Americans and assure the attainment of our legitimate aspirations against those very people.
>
> The Filipino people, unprovided with arms, will be the victims of the demands and exactions of the United States, but provided with arms will be able to oppose themselves to them and struggle for their independence, in which consists the true happiness of the Filipinos.

Agoncillo's proposition was unanimously approved, and the minutes of the meeting are in our possession, signed by the conspirators, with Aguinaldo's name at the head. Transported by us to Luzon, furnished with arms and ammunition by us, they collected and organized an army about the walls of Manila, of Tagalogs and discharged Spanish soldiers and all the bandits and pirates of those coasts, until they felt strong enough to execute their purpose.

On the ninth of January, twenty-seven days before the treaty was confirmed, Aguinaldo issued his order to prepare for the attack:

> MALALOS, 9th of January, 1899.
>
> Instructions to the Brave Soldiers of Sandatahan of Manila. . . .
>
> Article 2. All of the chiefs and Filipino brothers should be ready and courageous for the combat and should take advantage of the opportunity to study well the situation of the American outposts and headquarters. Observing especially secret places where they can approach and surprise the enemy.
>
> Article 3. The chief of those who go to attack the barracks should send in first four men with a good present for the American commander. Immediately after will follow four others who will make a pretense of looking for the same officer for some reason, and a larger group shall be concealed

in the corners or houses in order to aid the other groups at the first signal. This, wherever it is possible, at the moment of attack.

Article 4. They should not prior to the attack look at the Americans in a threatening manner. To the contrary, the attack on the barracks by the Sandatahan should be a complete surprise and made with decision and courage. One should go alone in advance in order to kill the sentinel. . . .

Article 7. All Filipinos, real defenders of their country, should live on the alert to assist simultaneously the inside attack at the very moment that they note the first movement in whatever barrio or suburb, having assurance that all the troops that surround Manila will proceed without delay to force the enemy's line and unite themselves with their brothers in the city. . . .

EMILIO AGUINALDO.

Of course our forces were ignorant then of the order and of the purpose, but they observed all over Manila Filipinos packing their goods and gathering their families and quietly slipping away from the city. They left by the thousands, and they left because they had notice of the proposed attack. One notification, signed by Aguinaldo, has fallen into our hands. It is a letter to a friend in Manila, dated January 7, 1899, four weeks before the attack, and in it he says:

MY DEAR DON BENITO:

. . . I beg you to leave Manila with your family and to come here to Malolos, but not because I wish to frighten you — I merely wish to warn you for your satisfaction, although it is not yet the day or the week.

The day was not then, but it came on the fourth of February, when a body of Filipino troops marched under cover of the night, swiftly and silently, through our lines, regardless of the sentry's challenge, and, when he fired, volleys of musketry and roar of cannon upon every side commenced the proposed destruction of our army.

The bodies of our men who fell during that dreadful night and the days of conflict which followed, have been brought back reverently across the Pacific and laid in honored graves among their countrymen. But, not yet — not yet has the soil stained by their blood been surrendered to their slayers. Not yet has the treacherous and wicked attack, which they died to defeat, been turned into victory by the act of an American president.

But we are told that, irrespective of agreements, irrespective of anything said or done by the Filipino leaders, or by ourselves, we ought to transfer to them sovereignty over the Philippine Islands, because government derives its just powers from the consent of the governed, and our maintenance of sovereignty is a violation of that great principle of the Declaration of Independence.

Nothing can be more misleading than a principle misapplied. Countless crimes have been committed by men quoting texts of Scripture or maxims of political philosophy wrested from their true context and meaning. The doctrine that government derives its just powers from the consent of the governed was applicable to the conditions for which Jefferson wrote it, and to the people to whom he applied it. It is true wherever a people exist capable and willing to maintain just government, and to make free, intelligent and efficacious decision as to who shall govern. But Jefferson did not apply it to Louisiana. He wrote to Gallatin that the people of Louisiana were as incapable of self-government as children, and he governed them without their consent. Lincoln did not apply it to the South, and the great struggle of the Civil War was a solemn assertion by the American people that there are other principles of law and liberty which limit the application of the doctrine of consent. Government does not depend upon consent. The immutable laws of justice and humanity require that people shall have government, that the weak shall be protected, that cruelty and lust shall be restrained, whether there be consent or not.

When I consider the myriads of human beings who have lived in subjection to the rule of force, ignorant of any other lot, knowing life only as the beast of the field knows it, without the seeds of progress, without initiative or capacity to rise, submissive to injustice and cruelty and perpetual ignorance and brutishness, I cannot believe that, for the external forces of civilization to replace brutal and oppressive government, with which such a people in ignorance are content, by ordered liberty and individual freedom and a rule that shall start and lead them along the path of political and social progress, is a violation of the principle of Jefferson, or false to the highest dictates of liberty and humanity.

The true question in the Philippines was, whether the withdrawal of the Spanish power which we had destroyed left a people capable of establishing and maintaining a free constitutional government; whether the humble and peaceable inhabitants, who constituted the great mass of the population, were competent to protect themselves; whether the wealth and commerce of Manila, the merchants from all the nations of Europe who were gathered there, the producers of hemp and tobacco and rice, would be protected by a rule of law and order and justice, or whether, on the other hand, the people, incapable of governing themselves, would become the subjects of a dictatorship, or the prey of bloody discord. Let me read you what high authority declares as the universal lesson of history regarding the people of countries situated as are these islands, when left to themselves. In a speech on the annexation of San Domingo, in the Senate of the United States on the eleventh of January, 1871, my friend Mr. Schurz, who now charges that it was cruel injustice not to leave the Filipinos to govern themselves without control or guidance, said:

> Read that history, read that of all other tropical countries, and then show me a single instance of the successful establishment and peaceable maintenance, for a respectable period, of republican institutions, based upon popular self-government, under a tropical sun. To show me one,

do not confine your search to the West Indies; look for it anywhere else on the face of the globe in tropical latitudes. I challenge Senators to point their fingers to a single one. There is none, sir! . . .

The tropical sun inflames the imagination to inordinate activity and develops the government of the passions. The consequences are natural, and there is a tendency to govern by force instead of by argument; revolutions are of chronic occurrence, like volcanic outbreaks, and you will find political life continually oscillating between two extremes — liberty, which there means anarchy, and order, which there means despotism.

The testimony is absolutely overwhelming that the people inhabiting the Philippine Archipelago are incapable of self-government, and that the fate here described would have befallen these islands of the tropics had American sovereignty been withdrawn. There is no Philippine people. The hundreds of islands which compose the Archipelago are inhabited by more than eighty different tribes, speaking more than sixty different languages. They have no common medium of communication, and they never had a government except the arbitrary rule of Spain. Most of them have not the first conception of what self-government means, or the first qualification for its exercise. Many of them have the capacity to learn, but they have never learned.

The first Philippine Commission said of them:

Should our power by any fatality be withdrawn, the commission believe that the government of the Philippines would speedily lapse into anarchy, which would excuse, if it did not necessitate, the intervention of other powers and the eventual division of the islands among them. Only through American occupation, therefore, is the idea of a free, self-governing and united Philippine commonwealth at all conceivable. And the indispensable need, from the Filipino point of view, of maintaining American sovereignty over the archipelago is recognized by all intelligent Filipinos, and even by those insurgents who desire an American protectorate. The latter, it is true, would take the revenues and leave us the responsibilities. Nevertheless they recognize the indubitable fact that the Filipinos cannot stand alone. Thus the welfare of the Filipinos coincides with the dictates of national honor in forbidding our abandonment of the archipelago. We cannot, from any point of view, escape the responsibilities of government which our sovereignty entails; and the commission are strongly persuaded that the performance of our national duty will prove the greatest blessing to the peoples of the Philippine Islands.

This was the testimony of President Schurman, of Cornell; of Professor Worcester, of Michigan; of that old-time Democrat, Charles Denby, our former Minister to China, and of Admiral George Dewey.

The present Philippine Commission say:

A change of policy by turning the islands over to the coterie of Tagalog politicians will blight their fair prospects of enormous improvement, drive out capital, make life and property — secular and religious — most insecure, banish by fear of cruel proscription a considerable body of conservative Filipino people, who had aided Americans in well-founded belief that their people are not now fit for self-government, and reintroduce the same oppression and corruption which existed in all provinces under the Malolos insurgent government during the eight months of its control. The result will be factional strife between jealous leaders, chaos and anarchy, and will require and justify active intervention of our government or some other.

This is the testimony of William H. Taft, of Ohio; Luke E. Wright, of Tennessee; Henry C. Ide, of Vermont; Professor Bernard Moses, of the University of California, and Professor Worcester, of Michigan. All of these commissioners were sent to the Philippine Islands to learn the truth, and to inform the President and Congress of the United States for the performance of their duty.

The President was not in the Philippine Islands. The Congress was not in the Philippine Islands. They were obliged to proceed upon evidence. And find if you can, anywhere in this land, a body of men whose conclusions are more entitled to credit and constitute a safer basis of official action than these. The year of Tagalog domination in Luzon was marked by the worst evils of semi-civilized misgovernment. The first Philippine Commission said of it:

Throughout the Archipelago at large there was trouble only at those points to which armed Tagalogs had been sent in considerable numbers.

In general, such machinery of "government" as existed served only for plundering the people under the pretext of levying "war contributions", while many of the insurgent officials were rapidly accumulating wealth. The administration of justice was paralyzed and crime of all sorts was rampant. Might was the only law. Never in the worst days of Spanish misrule had the people been so overtaxed or so badly governed. In many provinces there was absolute anarchy, and from all sides came petitions for protection and help, which we were unable to give.

Pio del Pilar, Aguinaldo's most active general, was the most notorious bandit in the Philippines. The orders for a combined attack and rising within the city of Manila on the fifteenth of February, ten days after the Senate confirmed the treaty, contained these directions:

First. You will so dispose that at eight o'clock at night the individuals of the territorial militia, at your order, will be found united in all the streets of San Pedro, armed with their bolos and revolvers and guns and ammunition if convenient.

Second. Philippine families only will be respected; they should not be molested, but all other individuals, of whatever race they may be, will be exterminated without any compassion, after the extermination of the army of occupation.

Aguinaldo and Luna were rival chieftains. Aguinaldo rose to supreme power over the body of Luna, stabbed to death with swords upon Aguinaldo's threshold. The people of the Philippine Islands never consented to that government. It was a pure and simple military domination of Tagalogs. The Visayans distrusted and feared them. The people of the great island of Negros raised the American flag, repelled the Tagalog invasion and are living today in contentment under our government. The tribes of northern Luzon received us with open arms. The ablest and the best of the Tagalogs, under the leadership of Arelliano and Torres, repudiated the government of Aguinaldo, and came into our lines with their adherence and support. The very congress that Aguinaldo had gathered at Malolos voted to accept the terms offered by the first Philippine Commission, but he refused to act upon their decision. A noble tribute to the Declaration of Independence it would have been indeed to deliver the people of Negros and the commerce of Manila and the patient and unconsenting millions of all other tribes but the Tagalogs into the hands of the assassin Aguinaldo, of the bandit del Pilar, and the authors of the massacre order of February 15, 1899!

The second specification under the charge of imperialism is, in substance, that the exercise of government must be over the people of the Philippine Islands as subjects, if not as citizens, and that this exercise of power over others will be destructive to our national character and institutions. A republic cannot have subjects and live, it is said. We have survived the government of Louisiana and the Northwest Territory and New Mexico and Alaska, and many other territories in which the people of the United States as a whole have governed the people of the territory with as much authority and power as need be exercised in the Philippine Islands. The true proposition is the precise reverse of the charge which is made. The government of the Philippine Islands will not affect the character of our institutions, but the character of our institutions will determine and mould the government of the Philippine Islands. To govern as a despot would be fatal to the character of a republic, but to govern as Congress always has and always will govern in territory outside of the limits of the States, in accordance with the spirit of our institutions, subject to all the great rules of liberty and right, and responsible for every act to a great liberty-loving people can but extend and strengthen our institutions.

"You are doing what England did when we rebelled against taxation without representation," says Mr. Bryan. Strange perversion! It was taxation for the benefit of England against which we rebelled. Where has there been a dollar taken by taxation for the benefit or use of the United

States from any island ceded by Spain? There has been no taxation in the Philippines or in Porto Rico except the ordinary taxes which the people have paid for the support of their own government, and the expenses of maintaining law and order and education among themselves.

Let me show you what kind of government exists today in the Philippine Islands. I read from the instructions of the President to the present Commission, which entered upon legislative power in those islands on the first of September, last:

> In all the forms of government and administrative provisions which they are authorized to prescribe, the Commission should bear in mind that the government which they are establishing is designed not for our satisfaction, or for the expression of our theoretical views, but for the happiness, peace and prosperity of the people of the Philippine Islands, and the measures adopted should be made to conform to their customs, their habits, and even their prejudices, to the fullest extent consistent with the accomplishment of the indispensable requisites of just and effective government.
>
> The many different degrees of civilization and varieties of custom and capacity among the people of the different islands preclude very definite instruction as to the part which the people shall take in the selection of their own officers; but these general rules are to be observed: That in all cases the municipal officers, who administer the local affairs of the people, are to be selected by the people, and that wherever officers of more extended jurisdiction are to be selected in any way, natives of the islands are to be preferred, and if they can be found competent and willing to perform the duties, they are to receive the offices in preference to any others.
>
> In the constitution of departmental or provincial governments, the Commission will give especial attention to the existing government of the island of Negros, constituted, with the approval of the people of that island, under the order of the military governor of July 22, 1899, and after verifying, so far as may be practicable, the reports of the successful working of that government, they will be guided by the experience thus acquired, so far as it may be applicable to the condition existing in other portions of the Philippines.
>
> The Central Government of the islands, following the example of the distribution of the powers between the States and the National Government of the United States, shall have no direct administration except of

matters of purely general concern, and shall have only such supervision and control over local governments as may be necessary to secure and enforce faithful and efficient administration by local officers.

Upon every division and branch of the government of the Philippines, must be imposed these inviolable rules:

That no person shall be deprived of life, liberty, or property without due process of law; that private property shall not be taken for public use without just compensation; that in all criminal prosecutions the accused shall enjoy the right to a speedy and public trial, to be informed of the nature and cause of the accusation, to be confronted with the witnesses against him, to have compulsory process for obtaining witnesses in his favor, and to have the assistance of counsel for his defense; that excessive bail shall not be required, nor excessive fines imposed, nor cruel and unusual punishment inflicted; that no person shall be put twice in jeopardy for the same offense, or be compelled in any criminal case to be a witness against himself; that the right to be secure against unreasonable searches and seizures shall not be violated; that neither slavery nor involuntary servitude shall exist except as a punishment for crime; that no bill of attainder, or *ex post facto* law shall be passed; that no law shall be passed abridging the freedom of speech or of the press, or the rights of the people peaceably to assemble and petition the Government for a redress of grievances; that no law shall be made respecting an establishment of religion, or prohibiting the free exercise thereof, and that the free exercise and enjoyment of religious profession and worship without discrimination or preference shall forever be allowed.

The articles of capitulation of the city of Manila on the 13th day of August, 1898, concluded with these words:

"This city, its inhabitants, its churches and religious worship, its educational establishments, and its private property of all descriptions, are placed under the special safeguard of the faith and honor of the American army."

I believe that this pledge has been faithfully kept. As high and sacred an obligation rests upon the Government of the United States to give protection for property and life, civil and religious freedom, and wise, firm and unselfish guidance in the paths of peace and prosperity to all the people of the Philippine Islands. I charge this Commission to labor for the full performance of this obligation, which concerns the honor and conscience of their country, in the firm hope that through their labors all the inhabitants of the Philippine Islands may come to look back with gratitude to the day when God gave victory to American arms at Manila and set their land under the sovereignty and the protection of the people of the United States.

Is that imperialism? Will giving that kind of government to these poor people who have suffered so long under Spanish tyranny degrade the character of this Republic? No. The party which governs the city of New York, the party which governs Mississippi and North Carolina, with their class of hereditary voters, may distrust its capacity to maintain its virtue while it governs others, but American love of liberty and justice will be as living a force in those islands of the sea as it has been through all the years on the Atlantic and the lakes and the plains of our own land. The doing of justice to these wards of our nation, and the leading of their steps along the pathway of liberty and progress will bring not injury but the strength and benefit which always come from unselfish effort for the good of others.

Our opponents will not believe any of the American officers civil or military, in the Philippine Islands, or all of them put together, when they tell us that the great mass of the people in those islands are favorable to American rather than to Tagalog rule.

Let me give you another bit of testimony from a Tagalog pen. It is a letter from a Tagalog officer to Sandico, Colonel and Chief of Staff, Aguinaldo's Secretary of Interior and chief lieutenant:

My Respected Chief and dear brother:

I have received your respected order, regarding the organization of the "Comite" in the towns of Zaragosa, Aliaga and Licab; from the movements and actions of these towns, I don't believe it possible to organize immediately. Before we can, it will be necessary that four or five lives be taken in each town. I believe that what ought to be done to those towns is to make a new conquest of them, especially the town of San Juan de Guimba; it is difficult there to set straight the Tagalos and Ilocanos of importance, as they are badly inclined and they care to do nothing but pervert our soldiers. This is what I am able to inform you in fulfillment of the respected order of the Chief.

God guard you many years,

C. Gonzales.

Four or five lives in each town means that the support of these people to the Tagalog cause shall be procured through the terror produced by that number of assassinations. With that accomplished, Tagalog rule in the provinces of Ilocanos would forthwith assume those just powers which are derived from the consent of the governed.

You have been told that the present activity of guerrillas in the Philippine Islands, who, from their hiding places in the mountains, ambush and murder our troops and the friendly natives, is the result, under express and explicit orders from Aguinaldo, of a desire to maintain a show of resistance, in the hope of Mr. Bryan's election, and for the purpose of producing an effect upon the people of the United States which will promote that election. General MacArthur has reported this. Judge Taft has reported it. General Wright, sturdy Democrat of Tennessee, has reported it. The whole Philippine Commission have reported it. But, of course, the opposition will not believe them. They are Americans. Let me give you testimony that even they will not dispute!

General Order to the Philippine Army, No. 202

As I have in previous letters directed that all Commanders of Guerrillas are free to attack any detachment or post of the enemy, and continually molest the same: I reiterate the order the more strongly, because its fulfillment just now is very necessary for the advantage of the cause of independence of the Philippines in the approaching Presidential election in the United States of America, which takes place in the early part of the coming month of September of the present year; on account of which, it is imperative that before that day comes, that is to say, during the months of June, July, and August, we give such hard knocks to the Americans that they will resound in our favor in all parts, and set in motion the fall of the Imperialist party, which is trying to enslave us.

Date, 27th of June, 1900.

Signed by the Captain-General,

E. Aguinaldo.

Under that order, and others like it, the guerrillas of the Philippines killed on the fourth of September, Private David

Allen, bricklayer, of Tyrone, Pennsylvania; on the thirteenth of September, Private William Andrews, painter, of Atlanta, Georgia; on the twenty-first of July, Corporal Warren Billman, farmer, of New Marion, Indiana; on the nineteenth of July, Sergeant Albert Cockayne, steam-fitter, of Milwaukee, Wisconsin; on the twenty-fourth of August, Private William Christman, machinist, of Hartford, Connecticut; and down to the fifteenth of October eighty-four others — eighty-nine officers and men, and they grievously wounded many more — all without purpose or reason or expectation of benefit, except the hopes held out to them by the Kansas City platform and the belief that it was important to Mr. Bryan's cause that America should seem unsuccessful in the Philippines.

How truly these murdered countrymen of ours could have echoed Lawton's words:

> I would to God that the truth of this whole Philippine situation could be known to every one in America as I know it.
>
> If the real history, inspirations and conditions of this insurrection, and the influences, local and external, that now encourage the enemy, as well as the actual possibilities of these islands and peoples and their relations to this great East, could be understood at home, we would hear no more talk of unjust "shooting of government" into the Filipinos, or of hauling down our flag in the Philippines.
>
> If the so-called anti-imperialists would honestly ascertain the truth on the ground and not in distant America, they, whom I believe to be honest men and misinformed, would be convinced of the error of their statements and conclusions and of the unfortunate effect of their publications here.
>
> If I am shot by a Filipino bullet, it might as well come from one of my own men, because I know from observations confirmed by captured prisoners that the continuance of fighting is chiefly due to reports that are sent out from America.

I will not say that the men here who are encouraging the Filipino soldiers are traitors to their country. I do not think they know what it is they do. But I will say, and I think with justice, that the men who are reviling and belittling America here, and the men who are shooting from ambush there, are allies in the same cause, and both are enemies to the interests and credit of our country.

In the place of the old motto "My country, right or wrong," we are told that we should adopt that other motto, "My country when right, and when wrong to be put right." But who is to be judge as between you and your country? Is it the full measure of patriotic citizenship to be for your country when it agrees with you, and against it when it does not? I cannot so estimate the impulses of loyalty. In the great tribunal of public opinion I shall strive always to bring my countrymen to the adoption of my views, but if their judgment, differing from mine, becomes the basis of national action and the cause of national conflict, I can find no satisfaction in the triumph of my country's foe; neither logic nor pride of opinion will soften the pain with which I greet the death of its defenders; with all my heart and soul and hopes and prayers I am always for my country and its victory; and in no other spirit do I see aught but discord, the dissolution of allegiance and the death of loyalty.

It is said that we have not acted fairly towards the people of Porto Rico. The charge has no foundation, unless in ignorance or malice. We have given to the people of Porto Rico the most munificent gift ever conferred upon one people by another — the free markets of the United States. The President recommended that the customs duties between the United States and Porto Rico should be removed, and Congress passed a law providing for their removal. It provided for the immediate removal of eighty-five per cent of the duties under the Dingley Tariff, and for the removal of the remaining fifteen per cent whenever the people of Porto Rico should be able by any other form of taxation to pay for the support of their own government, with the proviso that at the end of two years this remnant of duties should cease absolutely, whether the Porto Ricans supported their own government or not. We receive none of the duties. The duties collected at both ends of the line are paid into the treasury of the island. I know of no reason why the Porto Ricans should not pay for their own courts and schools and police. It is much better for them than to be treated as paupers. They do not complain of it! They would have no right to complain of it! The reason why this temporary provision for the payment of their expenses is made is that they have no reasonable and fair tax laws, and it is necessary to devise new and fair laws in the place of the oppressive and unreasonable old Spanish laws which were in existence. It takes time to change a system of taxation! It affects every industry and every interest in the country! Time had to be taken for the people of Porto Rico to be heard upon the kind and the amounts of taxation to be levied upon the different classes of property and of industry in their island. We have got the best men we could find in the country there, helping them to devise a good tax law; and when it has been devised and adopted by their legislature, which will be elected next month, then it will take more time to impose the taxes and realize money upon them. In the meantime this temporary fifteen per cent of the Dingley duties supplies them the means of supporting their government.

Mr. Bryan says that trusts have grown to an unprecedented degree during the present administration. Yes, the great industrial enterprises which are opening the whole world to American markets, which are sending nearly five hundred million dollars' worth of American manufactures abroad during this year, to pay the wages and swell the savings bank accounts of American laborers, have grown beyond precedent. Some of them are monopolies and ought to be suppressed. Most of them have no element of monopoly whatever except that which comes from selling cheaper than other competitors, and that is not monopoly but competition. Most of them are conducting the business which is free to any one on earth who has the intelligence and the skill to conduct a manufactory. Would he destroy them all? Would he close all the furnaces and all the factories and all the mines because he sees no difference between those enterprises which are, and those which are not monopolies, or would he consent that some one should sit down and scrutinize the different enterprises and ascertain which are good and which are bad and attack only the bad? He has been trying to turn what he calls "the starch trust" out of Nebraska. There can no more be a monopoly in the manufacture of starch than there can be a monopoly in the consumption of corn. Nobody can make starch who does not know how, and any one can make starch who knows how and can get corn to make it with. The trouble with Mr. Bryan's treatment of trusts is that he treats them not as a matter of business, but as a matter of politics; and he thinks that a general and indiscriminate denunciation of these great industrial enterprises which are employing the labor and increasing the wealth of America is a good campaign cry.

He has proposed two remedies for trusts; one is an amendment to the Constitution of the United States placing the control of them in the Federal Government; the other is a law forbidding any business concern manufacturing in one state from selling or transacting any business connected therewith in another state without a license from authorities in Washington. Shade of Jefferson! What doctrines are these to be preached in thy name? This is "imperialism" indeed. This would concentrate in the government at Washington entire and absolute control over every business interest in the country, for no business above the dignity of the retail store is confined within the limits of any state. The summary judgment of the officer who must issue or withhold the license would constitute a power for favoritism and oppression appalling to contemplate. Such destruction of state rights, such centering of power in the Federal Government, has never before been suggested. Coming from the Democratic party it is grotesque and absurd. No party will ever seriously consider it. It is but the crude and inconsiderate suggestion of a campaign orator designed for oratorical uses only.

It is charged that the present administration is in favor of increasing the regular army, and this is said to be *militarism*, a crime that endangers the liberty of the Republic. It is said that the President, in his message to Congress in the fall of 1898, asked that the number be fixed at one hundred thousand men. That was a reduction, not an increase. On the first of September, 1898, we had 272,000 soldiers under arms — 56,000 regulars and 216,000 volunteers. When the President's message was sent to Congress the protocol had been signed, but the treaty had not been signed, peace had not been made, Spain had not evacuated Cuba, a hostile army surrounded our troops in Manila. It would have been folly to disband our army as the preliminary to negotiations, and the President could have retained that entire army until after the ratification of the treaty of peace in April, 1899. But the volunteers were anxious to return to their homes, and insistent upon being permitted to do so, and what the President asked of Congress was to authorize the enlistment of 44,000 in the regular army to take the place of 216,000 volunteers discharged; that his request was not unreasonable is shown by the fact that Congress at that very session, by the votes of both parties, authorized an army of the precise number for which the President called, making it 65,000 regulars and 35,000 new volunteers.

What is the regular army of the United States? It is a body of American citizens provided for by the Constitution, and organized in the year 1789 under the first presidency of

George Washington. Its duty is to man the sea-coast fortifications, which protect our harbors and great cities against hostile attack, and to garrison the military posts along our frontiers, and at such strategic points in the country as Congress determines to be suitable; to be ready always to fight for our country in any sudden emergency which may come upon us before there is time to raise a volunteer force, and during the time while such a force is being raised; constantly to study, experiment upon, and exercise with all the improvements in military science, — in arms, ammunition, equipment, supplies, sanitation, transportation, drill, and tactics; to furnish a nucleus of officers thoroughly familiar with the business, for the strengthening and more ready instruction of a volunteer army whenever that shall become necessary. The kind of emergency which the regular army has to meet is well illustrated by recent events in China. Far from us as China is, our troops were sent there and did their business, and are coming away again, in less time than it would have taken to raise and equip and prepare a single regiment of volunteers. This was because the troops and the transports and material were ready to move on the instant.

The authorized number of the regular army today is 65,000, but on the thirtieth of June next it will, unless there be further legislation in the meantime, be reduced to 27,500, substantially the number at which it has stood for the past twenty-seven years; but as the country has grown in its population and its multitude of interests; as our sea-coast fortifications have been increased, under the leadership of Samuel J. Tilden, and upon plans prepared by the first administration of Cleveland; as the art of war has become more scientific and complicated, more men are necessary to perform the same duties than were needed to perform them years ago. The army of 27,500 is only about one-third as large in proportion to our population as our army was thirty years ago. The question how large the army should be is a simple business question as to how many men are necessary to perform certain specific duties. The last Congress fixed upon 100,000 in view of the conditions then existing. The next session of Congress will probably determine how many are requisite under the conditions then existing. Specially belligerent people will probably ask for too many; specially economical Congressmen will probably insist upon too few. I think we can assume that about the right conclusion will be reached.

Now does any sane American honestly believe that this threatens the liberties or the institutions of our country? Why, President McKinley had 272;000 men in arms at the close of the Spanish War. Grant had an army of 1,052,000 on the thirtieth of April, 1865, and they melted away into the peaceable body of the people like snowflakes in May. But these are volunteers, it will be said. Well, all the soldiers of the regular army are volunteers. Never in the history of the army has there been a man drafted or forced into it against his will. Their term of enlistment is but three years, and at the end of that time they go back to the occupations of civil life. They are all Americans. They are intelligent Americans. None are admitted who cannot read and write. They are sound, wholesome Americans, of good habits and regular lives, for none are admitted who are not in perfect health. Nineteen thousand five hundred and forty-nine men were enlisted in the year ending the thirtieth of last June, to take the place of those whose terms had expired, and those 19,549 were selected out of 89,243 applicants — 19,549 accepted and 69,694 rejected as not up to the standard intellectually or physically. They all swear allegiance, not to a monarch or a president, but to the United States of America. They, like the volunteer, come from American homes. The flag of their country floats always over them. They are surrounded by the memories and the traditions of comrades who have died for it. They breathe the atmosphere of probity and self-respect; for I call you all to witness that wherever in all its history the American army has gone, whether in the States or the Territories, whether in Mexico or Cuba, or Porto Rico, or the Philippines or China, there the American people have relied with confidence and with reason upon an administration, both military and civil, marked by integrity and honor. Our soldiers are conspicuous in the arts of peace. Where they go, law and order and justice and charity and education and religion follow. They are not only enduring under hardship and brave in danger, but they are patient under provocation and magnanimous after victory. During these last years in the Spanish islands they have been administering the civil law with justice and moderation. They have been feeding the hungry and clothing the naked and protecting the weak and cleaning the foul cities and establishing hospitals and organizing and opening schools and building roads and encouraging commerce and teaching people how to take the first step in self-government, with cheerful industry and zeal. I challenge their detractors to say whether, in any community where they have been, in all the years of the regular army, the officers and men have not always borne themselves as simple, unassuming, unpretentious American citizens. I challenge them to point to a single act of oppression, in all these one hundred and eleven years, to a single act of disloyalty, on the part of the regular army, to the supremacy of civil law and the principles of our free constitutional government.

"I believe," says Mr. Bryan, at New York, "that one of the reasons that they want a large army is to build a fort in this city and use the army to suppress by force that discontent that ought to be cured by legislation." What warrant has he for that belief? When or by whom has such a thing been attempted? Does he not know that it is expressly forbidden by the statutes of the United States? Does he not know that there is a constant effort on the part of the War Department to prevent establishing army posts and a constant pressure by the people of our cities to secure their establishment? Let him undertake to secure the removal of Fort Crook from the city of Omaha and see what response he would receive from its people. Let him ask why Iowa, just eastward of him, obtained the passage of a bill by Congress at the last session for the establishment of a post at Des Moines. Let him inquire why Tacoma and Seattle are contending as to which city shall have the establishment of a new post now; why the people of Prescott, Arizona, are protesting against the removal of Fort Whipple; why the representatives of Texas are urging the increase of the garrison at Fort Sam Houston; why the people of Atlanta are sending delegations to secure headquarters there; and he will learn that the people of the United States, instead of fearing, desire the establishment of army posts in their neighborhoods because they know that this pretended apprehension is but the idle vaporing of a campaign orator.

"The growing practice of using the army to repress labor," says Mr. Bryan. When and where has the army been used to repress labor? Never anywhere. Twice only in the past twenty years it has been used in any domestic affair. Once in 1896 when a Democratic President, Mr. Cleveland, sent troops to Chicago to protect the mails, and again in 1899, when, upon a formal requisition by the Democratic Governor of Idaho, certifying in accordance with the Constitution and the laws, that insurrection existed which the state authorities were unable to repress, the President, in the performance of his constitutional duty, sent 653 officers and men into the Cœur d'Alene district to aid the civil officers of the state in protecting life and property.

"Soldiers are idlers," says Mr. Bryan. The records of the Department show that since the organization of the regular army it has fought 2,545 separate engagements. In the War of 1812, in the Mexican War, in the Civil War, in the Indian Wars, in the Spanish War, in the Philippine War, it has endured hardships and privations and wounds and death. It has been the safeguard and protection of the settlers as they spread out over the West. Its men have fainted under the torrid heats of summer, and frozen under the bitter cold of winter, and nowhere have they faltered or been faithless to their trust. It has given to the country Grant and Sherman and Sheridan and Thomas and Meade and Hancock. It has given to our later memories Lawton and Liscum and Riley. It did not idle in Mexico. It did not idle when the Union was threatened. It never idled on the plains when the frontier settlements were to be rescued from savage foes. There was no idleness at San Juan and El Caney. There was no idleness in Lawton's swift, resistless march that broke the power of Tagalog rule in Luzon. Did Liscum idle before the walls of Tien-tsin? Did Riley upon the walls of Peking? The women of the legations did not deem Chaffee and his battalions idle when they wept over their children in the joy of rescue. Real soldiers who have learned their business and attend to it, in peace and in war, work hard, work long, work early and work late.

Upon the indisputable proof of more than a century's faithful service, the American soldier is not a danger to liberty and law and peace, but their defender. He has earned honor and confidence and gratitude from the American people, and I challenge the just judgment of the people as between him and the men who, for their own selfish purpose, are aspersing and maligning him while in distant lands he is braving hardship and disease and wounds and death in defense of our country's flag.

Are our opponents sincere? Is Mr. Bryan, who four years ago made his campaign upon the money issue and talked of nothing but money, and so eloquently bewailed the empty dinner pail, really sincere in pronouncing the full dinner pail to be a sordid issue? Is the party which is governing and avows its intention still to govern ten millions of black citizens in the South, without their consent, whether by law or fraud or force, really disturbed about imperialism and the Declaration of Independence? Was that distinguished company which gathered in the Louis XIV room of the Hoffman House and ate their twenty-dollar dinner, with Mayor Van Wyck, of the Ice Trust, as presiding officer, and Richard Croker, of the Ice Trust, as presiding genius, and Chairman of the Democratic National Committee Jones, of the Cotton Bale Trust, as the director of the campaign — were they really solicitous about the evils of trusts and agonizing for the delivery of their countrymen from their effects?

What evidence have these men given of capacity to govern? What warrant have we but their own promises that the men who would constitute the next administration, if the change be made, are competent to perform the great and difficult duties of government? What proof has their chosen leader ever given of capacity in public affairs? He has eloquently expounded many theories. Has any theory of his which has come to the test ever proved to be right? He eloquently denounced a protective tariff. Was he right? He eloquently declared that if the mints were not immediately opened to the free and unlimited coinage of silver, ruin and desolation would be the fate of America during the four years now closing. Was he right? During all their history, the American people have selected for their presidents men of tried and proved public service, whose capacity for safe, conservative and experienced administration had been demonstrated to the knowledge of all the people. Now they are asked to put the reins of government and all the vast interests upon which our happiness depends, in the hands of a man who never did anything but talk, and never was right in anything that he said.

When, during all the years that Mr. Bryan has been a leader of opinion, has he lifted a hand to aid his country in any one of the hard tasks with which it has been grappling ? When has there been one word of praise or credit for America or American institutions, or American government, or for any of the men who represent the dignity of the people by the people's choice ? When has there been from him aught but depreciation and disparagement and discredit for everything that is, and everything that is done in our country ? When has there come from him one word of encouragement or hope, one word to cheer the path of labor, to fire the ambition of youth, to confirm or to increase the American people's confidence in their institutions and loyalty to their flag ?

Every business is best managed by its friends, every undertaking is best prosecuted by those who have faith in it. Is it not the wisest course of the American people to leave the conduct of their affairs in the hands of those who believe that this is not the worst, but the best government on earth; that ours is not the most miserable, but the most happy of lands; that we have before us not the darkest, but the most brilliant and glorious future of all the peoples who inhabit the earth ?

To whom are the American people expected to commit the momentous interests which they are asked to take away from President McKinley, but to a motley and incongruous crowd gathered from three parties, agreeing upon no single principle or policy except the free coinage of silver, and held together only for campaign purposes, by sympathy of common detraction against all the glorious achievements of American progress under both political parties during the past generation ? They are peddlers of political discontent who, with shifty eyes for the prejudices of each community, draw from their pack, anti-trust arguments for expansionists, anti-expansion arguments for sound money men, and anti-gold arguments for silver men; always everywhere seeking to stir up bitterness and hatred by Americans against Americans. They seek to substitute for the old and happily-ended conflict of section against section, a new conflict of class against class. They strike at the root of free government, with the delusive promises of the demagogue, leading the poor and the unfortunate to look to government rather than to intelligence and thrift to make them rich and strong. They strike at the life of enterprise by challenging the right of the successful to the fruits of enterprise. The strength of free institutions in America has rested for all these centuries past upon the fact that there were no classes in America; that all men were equal before the law — equal in the rights of citizenship, equal in the dignity of manhood, unfettered in the pursuit of limitless opportunity; that the poor and humble today, having the qualities of intelligence and enterprise, are the rich and powerful tomorrow; that the rich and powerful today, lacking these qualities, are the poor and humble tomorrow; that all over the land the poorest workingmen who may no longer seek to change their own condition are looking with pride and hope upon their boys starting out upon their careers with advantages their fathers never had, with open pathways to distinction and wealth. With these conditions, which have always existed, and which exist today, there is no such thing as class. No gulf divides American citizens from each other. There is but one ideal, one title of honor, of pride and of mutual respect — the ideal and the title of American citizenship. All this these men would destroy in order that they may ride into power as the governors of an unhappy and discordant people.

AMERICAN POLICIES IN THE PHILIPPINES IN 1902

ADDRESS OF THE SECRETARY OF WAR AT PEORIA, ILLINOIS SEPTEMBER 24, 1902

ONCE before, and only once, I have visited the city of Peoria. It was on that day, in the autumn of 1899, when the stately and beautiful monument to the soldiers of the Civil War, which adorns your public square, was unveiled. It was a day of festivity and rejoicing. All business and controversy and selfish care had been laid aside, and from all the town and all the country round the people had gathered to look upon the face and listen to the voice of their beloved President, William McKinley. As his sweet and vibrant tones carried his words to the very limits of the great throng, every sentence was an impulse to patriotism. Every wave of responsive sympathy lifted the people up to higher planes of citizenship and of manhood. Not merely what he said but what he was, the intimate relation of the listener to the man himself, for the moment ennobled every heart and forever left it better than it was before. His character was so pure, so unselfish, so free from uncharitableness and malice; his sympathies were so broad and genuine; his love of country and of humanity were so sincere; his sensitive regard for the feelings and desire for the happiness of others were so considerate; the native dignity and grace which fitted his high office were so charming, that the interests of political opposition and the rancor of partisan prejudice insensibly lost the wish to assail him; and even while he lived antagonism to the party leader merged into affection and honor for the man. His wisdom, his tenacity of purpose, his quiet and unostentatious strength, the sagacity and skill of his sympathetic control and leadership over men, made his nobility of character an active force for justice and peace and righteousness. Men may find, or think they find, error in his judgments. Men may differ as to the wisdom of his policies; but that his judgments were formed in sincerity as he saw the right, that his policies were the outcome of strong desire for the peace and happiness and honor of his country and of his race, and that he worked them out, so long as he lived, along the lines of justice and of humanity, no one who knew him as we knew him, will ever doubt.

His memory lives. The powerful impress of his noble character persists. The lofty purpose with which he undertook the responsibilities and the duties which the fortunes of war cast upon the American government is still the guide of action for his party and his country. The first words spoken by his successor, when taking the oath of office at Buffalo were: "It is my purpose to continue absolutely unbroken the policy of President McKinley for the peace, prosperity and honor of our beloved country." I challenge judgment upon the truth and loyalty with which Theodore Roosevelt has redeemed his promise. The murderer's bullet robbed us of a friend; it did not produce a revolution. It changed rulers; it did not change policies. The great party which was in power has continued the same, and its policies have continued. President Roosevelt has followed them not merely because he promised but because he approved. If he had not approved he could not have promised, for there is no shadow of deceitfulness in him. With loyalty and resolution, with the vigor of his intense convictions, and with the honesty, frankness and courage for which the American people love him, he has continued the work McKinley began and pressed forward the performance of the great duties which they both believed the welfare of their country and of mankind imposed upon the Government of the United States.

The American people are now called upon to consider whether they wish to withdraw their support from the policy of McKinley and of Roosevelt and elect a House of Representatives which will oppose and, by a hostile majority, frustrate and prevent all further effective action by the President.

Of course such action as that would result in an ineffective government. A government half Republican and half Democratic can never be a government of progress or of affirmative action. It cannot deal with difficulties or accomplish beneficent results. If the honor and welfare of the country demand that things be done, that constructive statesmanship accomplish results, such a divided government would fail. That may be no reason why the people should not change the majority in the House for sufficient cause, but it is a reason why it should not be done lightly, thoughtlessly, and for the mere sake of change. Grave disapproval and loss of confidence only could justify the people in thus dividing their government against itself.

What has the Republican administration of the country done, or failed to do, to call down upon it such a disapproval and loss of confidence?

The principal, indeed almost the sole attack by the representatives of the Democratic party, which occupied the greater part of the last session of Congress, was violent denunciation of the Administration's policy in the Philippines, and of the execution of that policy. A crowd of difficulties to be dealt with by the Administration had accompanied the war with Spain. A large army had been raised, the national debt had been increased by the borrowing of $200,000,000, burdensome war taxes had been imposed. In the islands yielded or ceded by Spain, millions of men of alien races, differing in language, in laws, in customs, in traditions, in prejudices, in ways of thinking, most of them ignorant, most of them suspicious, many of them unfriendly, were to be pacified and reconciled and governed and taught self-government. New experiments in government were to be tried. There were no precedents, and precedents were to be made. There was no governmental machinery, and governmental machinery was to be constructed. The principles of American liberty were to be applied to new and strange conditions among peoples who hardly knew the alphabet of freedom.

By the spring of 1902 the Republican Administration had dealt with all these difficulties, and as to all but one had reached a point where the success of a wise policy and effective administration could not be gainsaid.

The army of 270,000 men had been disbanded, and the regular force had been reduced to two-thirds of the permanent number allowed by law to safeguard the country against future attacks. The war taxes had been repealed, and the industry and property of the country had been relieved of their burden. The process of again reducing the national debt had progressed so far that, through payment and refunding, after paying all the expense of the war in Cuba and in the Philippines, the annual interest charge upon the debt was less by $6,844,431.70 than it was at the opening of the war with Spain.

Plain duty had been done by Porto Rico, and done with such judgment and discretion that a new system of taxation, suited to her conditions, was studied out in detail, put in force, and made productive, taking the place of the customs duties upon which she had relied, without a break or embarrassment in the financial affairs of her government. American currency had replaced the Spanish pesos, civil government had been established upon just and firm foundations, the laws which protect individual liberty had been planted in that unfamiliar soil, the judicial procedure which protects the innocent had been substituted for arbitrary power, the writ of habeas corpus, the great writ of personal freedom, had supplanted the *incommunicado*. The storm of detraction and abuse which raged around the Administration in the spring of 1900 had died away and disappeared upon the demonstration of the wisdom of the Republican Porto Rican policy, and before the spectacle of a prosperous and happy people, governed by the harmonious action of their own elected legislative assembly and of the officers appointed by the President of the United States.

The work of pacification and construction in Cuba had been completed. Military government there had faithfully given effect to the humane purposes of the American people. With sincere kindness our officers had helped the Cuban people to take the steps necessary to the establishment of their own constitutional government. During the time required for that process they had governed Cuba wisely and justly; had honestly collected and expended for the interest of the people the revenues, amounting to nearly sixty millions of dollars; had executed thorough sanitary measures, improving the health and lowering the death rate. By patient, scientific research, they had ascertained the causes of yellow fever, and by good administration had put an end to that most dreadful disease which had long destroyed the lives and hindered the commercial prosperity of the Cubans; they had expedited justice and secured protection for the rights of the innocent, while they had cleansed the prisons and created healthful conditions for the punishment of the guilty; they had provided adequate hospitals and asylums for the care of the unfortunate; they had established a general system of free common schools throughout the island, in which over two hundred thousand children were in actual attendance; they had constructed great and necessary public works; they had trained the Cubans themselves in all branches of administration so that the new government, upon assuming power, had begun its work with an experienced force of Cuban civil service employees competent to execute its orders; they had borne themselves with dignity and self-control, so that nearly four years of military occupation had passed unmarred by injury or insult to man or woman; they had transferred the government of Cuba to the Cuban people amid universal expressions of friendship and good will, and had left a record of justice and liberty, of rapid improvement in material and moral conditions, and of progress in the art of government, which brought honor from all the world to the people of the United States.

Of all the executive problems following in the train of the Spanish War, the problem of the Philippines alone remained. Success there had not then been demonstrated, and it was still possible that failure there might lead the American people to withdraw power from Republican hands. Accordingly the Philippine policy of the Administration was attacked. I ask the people of the United States to consider the record made by the Democratic party in that attack.

The policy was simple. Spain, which for more than three centuries before Dewey's victory had exercised undisputed sovereignty over the Philippine Islands, ceded the islands with all her title and sovereignty there to the United States, by the treaty of peace which was signed at Paris on the tenth of December, 1898, and was confirmed by the Senate of the United States on the sixth of February, 1899. The cession was one of the terms of peace, and was upon a special consideration of $20,000,000 to be paid to Spain by the United States. Upon the ratification of the treaty and the payment of that money, sovereignty over the Philippine Islands vested in the United States; the territory of the islands became the territory of the United States; the public lands belonging to Spain in the islands became the property of the United

States; all the rights and all the obligations towards the other nations of the world which pertained to sovereignty over the Philippine Islands devolved upon the United States. The Supreme Court of the United States has declared this without difference of opinion.

For a long time before the ratification of the treaty, the army of the United States had been in possession of the city of Manila, and on the fourth of February, two days before the ratification, a body of insurgents, under the Tagalog chieftain Aguinaldo, attacked our forces in that city, and were driven back with heavy loss, and with the loss of 260 of our own soldiers, killed and wounded. Then the two armies rested, facing each other in long lines surrounding the city of Manila. Under these circumstances, and with a full knowledge of these facts, the treaty under which we acquired the Philippines and paid $20,000,000 for them was ratified by two-thirds vote of the Senate. The vote was not a party vote. Some Republicans voted against the treaty. Many leading Democrats of the Senate voted in its favor. Mr. Bryan, the great Democratic leader of the day, was urgently in favor of the ratification. Subsequently the $20,000,000 to pay for the islands was appropriated without a party division by an overwhelming vote of both Houses; and on the second of March Congress, again without a party division, authorized the increase of the regular army from 27,000 to 65,000, and the raising of 35,000 volunteers for service in the Philippine Islands, where active fighting had been resumed. The policy of the Republican administration has been to maintain the sovereignty thus acquired; to put down the insurrection against that sovereignty by the use of the means thus furnished by the people of the United States without regard to party; and then to give to the people of the Islands all the blessings of civil and religious liberty, of just and equal laws, of good and honest administration, of education, of individual freedom, of social order, and of self-government just so far as they were competent to govern themselves.

President McKinley declared that policy in his message of that year in these words:

> Until Congress shall have made known the formal expression of its will I shall use the authority vested in me by the Constitution and the statutes to uphold the sovereignty of the United States in those distant islands as in all other places where our flag rightfully floats. I shall put at the disposal of the Army and Navy all the means which the liberality of Congress and the people have provided to cause this unprovoked and wasteful insurrection to cease. If any orders of mine were required to insure the merciful conduct of military and naval operations, they would not be lacking; but every step of the progress of our troops has been marked by a humanity which has surprised even the misguided insurgents. The truest kindness to them will be a swift and effective defeat of their present leader. The hour of victory will be the hour of clemency and reconstruction.
>
> No effort will be spared to build up the waste places desolated by war and by long years of misgovernment. We shall not wait for the end of strife to begin the beneficent work. We shall continue, as we have begun, to open the schools and the churches, to set the courts in operation, to foster industry and trade and agriculture, and in every way in our power to make these people whom Providence has brought within our jurisdiction feel that it is their liberty and not our power, their welfare and not our gain, we are seeking to enhance. Our flag has never waved over any community but in blessing. I believe the Filipinos will soon recognize the fact that it has not lost its gift of benediction in its world-wide journey to their shores.

The Civil Commission, of which President Schurman was the head, after studying the subject on the ground, in the Philippines, declared their conclusions in these words:

> Deplorable as war is, the one in which we are now engaged was unavoidable by us. We were attacked by a bold, adventurous, and enthusiastic army. No alternative was left to us except ignominious retreat. It is not to be conceived of that any American would have sanctioned the surrender of Manila to the insurgents. Our obligations to other nations and to the friendly Filipinos and to ourselves and our flag demanded that force should be met by force. Whatever the future of the Philippines may be, there is no course open to us now except the prosecution of the war until the insurgents are reduced to submission. The Commission is of the

opinion that there has been no time since the destruction of the Spanish squadron by Admiral Dewey when it was possible to withdraw our forces from the islands either with honor to ourselves or with safety to the inhabitants.

In those early months of 1899, when the course of our Government towards the insurrection had to be determined, there was no difference of opinion between the two parties as to the duty of the administration. The Democratic equally with the Republican press throughout the country demanded that this policy be followed.

Said the *Atlanta Constitution* of February 6, 1899:

In the light of the thrilling news from Manila, there now remains but one course for the American Government to pursue, and that is to conquer the forces of Aguinaldo. In our own way and in our own time we can deal with the question of local government in the Philippines, but as long as an armed foe stands in the way the only work ahead of us will be to vindicate the authority of the flag.

The Louisville *Courier-Journal* of the same day declared:

There can be but one result, which will be the prompt and complete assertion of our authority over Aguinaldo and his Tagalogs as it was asserted over the Spaniards. We know how to deal with the misguided and maliciously instigated insubordination of the Filipinos.

The New Orleans *Picayune* said:

It will now be necessary to crush the insurrection and firmly establish the American control before the future form of government for the islands can be for a moment considered.

The Nashville *American* said:

We must make them know that our power is supreme, otherwise we cannot give to them the blessings freedom and individual liberty have in store. The United States cannot and will not yield to Aguinaldo. Aguinaldo must and will yield to the United States.

The New York *Journal* said:

To the unprovoked attack upon our forces at Manila while we were extending every effort to reach an amicable adjustment with the Filipinos, and while our commission of inquiry was actually on the way, there can be but one answer. Order must be restored in the Philippines. The men who have taken our forbearance for weakness must be taught their mistake. American authority must be established at once beyond challenge throughout the archipelago.

The Memphis *Commercial* said:

As long as they fight American troops our policy will be to fight back and fight to conquer.

The Denver *Daily News* said:

That act has made it impossible for the United States to leave those islands until it has administered justice to those responsible for the attack. While it may be determined not to hold these islands, and may be disadvantageous to hold them, still our national dignity and honor will not permit our forces to be driven out.

Here and there an individual voice was raised counseling surrender and retreat; but the general voice of the people, without distinction of party, and without regard to selfish interest, seconded the action of Congress and the requirements of the Constitution in demanding from the Executive the suppression of insurrection and the establishment of peaceful government in the Philippine Islands under the sovereignty of the United States.

That task also has now been accomplished. The sound of angry voices declaring that it never could and never would be done had hardly died away in our national capital when, on the fourth of July last, the last hostile gun was laid down, the last insurgent surrendered, the last remnant of military government was terminated; civil government, with just and equal laws maintaining social order and protecting property and life and liberty, was established over the last province of the Philippines outside of the Moro country; the flag under which Lawton and Logan fell floated over every island and every town, the emblem of acknowledged sovereignty; and our President celebrated the anniversary of national independence by proclaiming peace and general amnesty. The task has not been an easy one. I cannot better describe the work our soldiers had to do and the way they did it than by reading the words of the general order which signalized the termination of their most arduous labors:

The President thanks the officers and enlisted men of the army in the Philippines, both regulars and volunteers, for the courage and fortitude, the indomitable spirit and loyal devotion with which they have put down and ended the great insurrection which has raged throughout the archipelago against the lawful sovereignty and just authority of the United States. The task was peculiarly difficult and trying. They were required at first to overcome organized resistance of superior numbers, well equipped with modern arms of precision, intrenched in an unknown country of mountain defiles, jungles, and swamps, apparently capable of interminable defense. When this resistance had been overcome they were required to crush out a general system of guerrilla warfare conducted among a people speaking unknown tongues, from whom it was almost impossible to obtain the information necessary for successful pursuit or to guard against surprise and ambush.

The enemies by whom they were surrounded were regardless of all obligations of good faith and of all the limitations which humanity has imposed upon civilized warfare. Bound themselves by the laws of war, our soldiers were called upon to meet every device of unscrupulous treachery and to contemplate without reprisal the infliction of barbarous cruelties upon their comrades and friendly natives. They were instructed, while punishing armed resistance, to conciliate the friendship of the peaceful, yet had to do with a population among whom it was impossible to distinguish friend from foe, and who in countless instances, used a false appearance of friendship for ambush and assassination. They were obliged to deal with problems of communication and transportation in a country without roads and frequently made impassable by torrential rains. They were weakened by tropical heat and tropical disease. Widely scattered over a great archipelago, extending a thousand miles from north to south, the gravest responsibilities, involving the life or death of their commands, frequently devolved upon young and inexperienced officers beyond the reach of specific orders or advice.

Under all these adverse circumstances the Army of the Philippines has accomplished its task rapidly and completely. In more than two thousand combats, great and small, within three years, it has exhibited unvarying courage and resolution. Utilizing the lessons of the Indian wars, it has relentlessly followed the guerrilla bands to their fastnesses in mountain and jungle and crushed them. It has put an end to the vast system of intimidation and secret assassination by which the peaceful natives were prevented from taking a genuine part in government under American authority. It has captured or forced to surrender substantially all the leaders of the insurrection. It has submitted to no discouragement and halted at no obstacle. Its officers have shown high qualities of command, and its men have shown devotion and discipline. Its splendid virile energy has been accompanied by self-control, patience and magnanimity. With surprisingly few individual exceptions its course has been characterized by humanity and kindness to the prisoner and the non-combatant. With admirable good temper, sympathy, and loyalty to American ideals, its commanding generals have joined with the civilian agents of the Government in healing the wounds of war and assuring to the people of the Philippines the blessings of peace and prosperity. Individual liberty, protection of personal rights, civil order, public instruction, and religious freedom have followed its footsteps. It has added honor to the flag which it defended, and has justified increased confidence in the future of the American people, whose soldiers do not shrink from labor or death, yet love liberty and peace.

The President feels that he expresses the sentiments of all the loyal people of the United States in doing honor to the whole army which has joined in the performance and shares in the credit of these honorable services.

The problem to be worked out in the Philippines was not a military problem alone. At the bottom of our difficulties lay the fact that the Spaniards, to secure the assistance of the people against us, and after them the ambitious men who saw the opportunity to secure empire for themselves, had filled the minds of the ignorant and credulous people with vile slanders upon American character, and the most extravagant and grotesque tales of American tyranny and barbarity. They described us as monsters in human form, who sought to fasten upon the miserable Filipinos a tyranny worse than that of Spain, and who would respect neither the rights of man nor the virtue of woman, nor the innocence of childhood, nor the sacredness of religion. To dispel this dreadful belief words were of no avail. Assurances and promises were useless, for they were not believed. Before a genuine acceptance of our sovereignty could come, except by the sullen acquiescence of the conquered, it was necessary that we should demonstrate to the great mass of the people of the islands that our sovereignty meant justice and not oppression, liberty and not slavery, protection of law and not the license of arbitrary power. And so, without waiting until the termination of the war, we established civil government to go hand in hand with our advancing armies.

A new civil commission was created with Judge Taft at its head. As armed resistance ceased, island by island, province by province, town by town, civil government was substituted for military government; the bill of rights extended its protection over the people; the writ of habeas corpus became the guaranty of their liberty; elections were held at which the people chose the officers of their own towns and provinces; a native constabulary was organized, and proved faithful and effective for the protection of life and property; the people resumed their customary vocations under the protection of law. In this way when the insurrection breathed its last in the mountains of Batangas, the great body of the people had already commenced to learn the true and beneficent meaning of American sovereignty, and a civil government built up by the careful labor of years was already in existence, fully organized and ready for the final extension of its authority. The instructions given by the President to the Philippine Commission, which constitute both the organic law of the civil government and the code of rules and principles to guide its conduct, have been adopted by Congress without change and practically without criticism, as the future guide of that government's action. The system of government created under these instructions is continued by Congress unchanged, except by the enlargement of its power. I invite comparison between the body of laws, 441 in number, enacted by the Philippine Commission and the statutes of any state and of any country. They exhibit constructive ability, legislative skill, painstaking familiarity with conditions, and fidelity to constitutional principles. The public revenues have been honestly collected and honestly administered for the benefit of the people, under a strict and thorough audit. Notwithstanding the insurrection, the business of the islands has flourished and has become nearly double what it was in the most peaceful years under Spanish rule. I quote from a circular issued by the German government last year, for the information of German producers and exporters:

> Although the pacification of the Philippine Archipelago has not as yet been fully established, the accounts of its economic department are so favorable that it cannot be too strongly urged upon German exporters to give particular attention to this group of islands. From July, 1900, to March, 1901, the exports have increased by thirty-four per cent and the imports by fifty-two per cent, as compared with those of the same period of the preceding year. The testimony cannot be withheld that the American administration of the affairs of the Philippines has, as far as the economic betterment of the country is concerned, already achieved extraordinary success.
>
> In 1894, which was the last year of peaceful condition while under Spanish rule, the Philippine imports reached $28,500,000 and the exports $33,100,000, Mexican, in value. Under American rule, in spite of the continued insurrection of the natives, the imports increased in 1899 to $40,900,000 and in 1900 to $55,500,000, Mexican, and the exports to $38,500,000 and $53,400,000, respectively. Military supplies are not included in these figures. The detailed statistics show that Spanish trade with these islands is rapidly diminishing, but commercial relations with the United States are gaining.

A million dollars has been applied to the construction of roads, two million dollars to the improvement of the harbor of Manila; a system of free public schools has been established; 180,000 children are enrolled; and a thousand teachers brought from America and nearly four thousand native teachers are instructing them. A normal school has been established in Manila. Ten thousand adults are attending night schools to learn English. In selecting the employees of the civil government a rigid and comprehensive civil service law has been faithfully observed. A majority of the prominent men of the insurrection are taking part in the new government. Of the seven commissioners who, with the governor, exercise legislative power, three are Filipinos. The chief justice of the supreme court and an associate justice, many of the judges of the first instance and many other high officials, are Filipinos. While we have reduced our American troops in the islands from about 70,000 to about 20,000, we have enlisted about 5,000 natives, who have proved to be trustworthy and efficient, and there is no longer occasion to doubt that either as a military force or as a constabulary, the natives of the islands themselves can be trusted to take the principal burden of maintaining order, and that only a small force of American troops will be required. Our position in the Philippines today is far better than the most sanguine American could reasonably have expected in those early days of 1899, when the Democratic press and Democratic leaders were joining with the Republicans in the declaration that the insurrection must be put down.

We shall have discouragements and reverses in the future as we have in the past. Grave difficulties doubtless await us, but the greatest difficulties are past. The legislation enacted at the last session of Congress secures the good which has been accomplished, and with wise conservatism opens the way to future progress. The taking of a census under its provisions has already been ordered, and after the census will follow a legislative assembly elected by the Filipinos, in which they can test and exercise their capacity for government on the broader field as they are already doing in their local affairs. We know now that steady and faithful adherence to the course which McKinley began and Roosevelt is following, will prove beyond question or cavil the truth of the declaration that our flag has never waved over any community but in blessing, and that it has not lost its gift of benediction in its world-wide journey to the Philippine shores.

Before the American people determine whether they will withdraw from the administration which has done these things, the power to continue its effective action, and hamper it by an adverse majority in the House of Representatives, I would like to have them understand and consider what part the Democratic party has played in this history.

It concerned the credit and honor of our country that we should succeed in the Philippines. If we had failed, we should have stood before all the world, and in our own consciousness as well, convicted of weakness and inefficiency and of lacking the strength and unity of purpose and the capacity for resolute and persistent action, without which no nation can be great.

And, my fellow-citizens, there come always in every great and difficult undertaking times when failure seems possible; times when discouragements and difficulties and doubts beset the pathway of endeavor. Then it is that high courage and unshaken resolve mark the quality of a nation's greatness, and then it is that faint hearts with querulous regrets and carping complaints seek always to give up the fight. Such times came during the Philippine insurrection. Where was the Democratic party then ? Was it helping the nation to succeed, or was it helping the Administration to fail ? The very men who had cried " Down with Aguinaldo ", " Hurrah for the flag ", " The insurrection must be put down ", the very men who had voted to take the cession of the Philippines, who had voted the money to pay for the Philippines, who had voted for the troops to send to the Philippines to put down the insurrection, seized the moment of discouragement to demand that in the face of armed resistance, the war should be declared a failure, the struggle should be given up, sovereignty should be relinquished, and defeated and humiliated America should surrender the cause for which the lives of so many of her soldiers had been sacrificed. There were some honorable exceptions, but most of them retired to the background and left the leadership of the party to the men who were willing to voice this policy, which for all time would have marked us as a nation rash in counsel and feeble in execution.

The new leaders filled the air with outcries over the cost of suppressing the insurrection.

They wrung the hearts of our people by parading the sad statistics which told the story of our dead and wounded.

They protested that the islands would never pay, and pointed with triumph to the custom-house figures, which showed that although our trade with the Philippines had increased, it had not in the midst of insurrection sprung up like Jonah's gourd in a single night.

They asserted that we never could and never would succeed. "Thirty thousand, forty thousand, fifty thousand men will be required for five years, for twenty-five years," they cried. Five months have not passed and there are but 20,000 American soldiers there. They tore passion to tatters in their insistence upon the construction of the Constitution which would include the archipelago within the provisions of the Dingley Tariff, and subject that distant tropical country to the duties provided to suit the conditions of life and production of the United States. With vindictive insolence they denounced the Supreme Court for deciding otherwise, and then urged that Congress should include the islands within that tariff law. Was it because they sought the welfare of the Filipino that they desired to impose upon him the provisions of this statute, which they abhor and condemn? Certainly not. It was because those duties were so unsuited to the life of the Philippine Islands, that business there could not continue and the people could not live under them, and an attempt to govern the islands under them would have been an inevitable failure.

They gave courage and hope to the insurgent leaders by constantly insisting that terms should be made, that independence should be conceded, that the insurgents should be induced to lay down their arms by promises, and they thus continually supplied incentive to further resistance by the apparent possibility of substantial success. They slandered our title; denied that we acquired sovereignty by the cession from Spain. They asserted that we had no right to succeed because we had promised Aguinaldo independence, and the assertion of sovereignty was an act of perfidy — the perfidy of George Dewey and Wesley Merritt and William McKinley! They asserted this against the official reports and the sworn testimony of Dewey, who alone could have made the promise; against the evidence of the original written document signed by Aguinaldo and his associates, which shows that he came to Manila not relying upon any promise, but with the expressed intention to obtain arms from the Americans in order to use them first against the Spaniards and then against the Americans themselves. They asserted it against the written statement of Mabini, the prime minister of the insurrection, declaring that there was no agreement whatever, and against the admission of Aguinaldo that there was none.

They charged that the outbreak of hostilities on the fourth of February was an unprovoked and wicked attack by the American soldiers upon the peaceful Filipinos who had no thought of war; and this in the face of the written evidence, over the signature of Aguinaldo himself, by proclamation, by letter, by telegram, by military order, that the Philippine forces had been for months preparing and intending to bring on that very conflict. They charged that the officers of our army were guilty of the atrocious wickedness of making that attack to affect the ratification of the treaty by the Senate, and they charged that the dispatches which Dewey and Otis sent were sent in anticipation, before the fight occurred.

They asserted that we had no right to succeed because we found a people struggling for liberty and became their ally. There is no basis for the assertion. When Dewey destroyed the Spanish fleet in Manila Bay, the people of the Philippines were not struggling at all. There was no insurrection there. There had been an insurrection, and it had been terminated four months before by the payment of money to the leaders, the chief of whom was Aguinaldo, and their expatriation to Hong-Kong. The agreement by which that insurrection was terminated said nothing either about independence or about reforms. It was a simple agreement to stop fighting, for money; and it declared that Aguinaldo and his associates desired to preserve their Spanish citizenship.

Here is a copy of Aguinaldo's proclamation when he left his country:

BIAC-NA-BATO, December 25, 1897.

I lay down my arms because further warfare will bring not happiness but trouble and disaster, which is not the end the insurrection seeks. I quit the field since my ambitions for my people are one with the lofty desires of the noble Governor-General, Señor Don Fernando Primo de Rivera, Marquis de Estrella, who, inspired by his love for our dear country, inaugurated an era of peace from the time he took up the reins of government of this Spanish territory. I lay down arms in accordance with the patriotic advice of the intermediary, the maginoo, Pedro A. Paterno, lover of the well-being of our mutual native land. I go of my own will. I go, for in spite of the personal immunity which is given me by the laws, by promises and by Spanish honor, yet the violent passion of hatred or some other political excitement might raise its suicidal hand and make anew victims, thereby creating disturbances and interfering with the progress of our development.

Viva España, Viva Filipinas.

He declares that he leaves because his ambitions for his people are one with the desires of the Spanish Governor-General. There was surely no independence in those desires. And he concludes "Viva España, Viva Filipinas!" That was the condition of affairs at the time when the outbreak of war between Spain and the United States suggested to the little band of expatriated adventurers in Hong-Kong that they might profit by our destruction of the Spanish power with which they were in such appreciative accord. When Aguinaldo first went ashore from Dewey's ship on the nineteenth of May, 1898, to start the insurrection with the arms that Dewey furnished to him, he found no insurrection and no support, and returned discouraged to the ship and asked to be sent to Japan because he could do nothing. Dewey told him to try again and sent him back. And now his friends here say there was an implied obligation to give him the country, for Dewey found the people struggling for their liberty. After reading the proclamation announcing the accord of Aguinaldo with the lofty desires of the Spanish Governor-General, this letter which he has just written to the President is most interesting:

The Honorable THEODORE ROOSEVELT,
President of the United States of America.

SIR: I have the honor to present to you an expression of my gratitude for the amnesty which opens the prison doors and lifts the ban of banishment from many Filipinos who have honorably struggled for their ideal.

I trust that such a generous and noble course on the part of the nation which you represent will be beneficial in uniting, in the future, the friendly relations between Americans and Filipinos, and I am assured that with the disinterested and just protection of the worthy descendants of the great George Washington, the aspirations of my country will be satisfied, and which, I am sure, will fully demonstrate its gratitude for the benefits which are being done for us.

Very respectfully,
EMILIO AGUINALDO Y FAMY.

MANILA, CALLE CONCORDIA, July 5, 1902.

He is a philosopher, that Aguinaldo!

The Democrats in Congress declared that we ought not to succeed because the Filipinos were competent to govern themselves. We know that in fact their pretense of constitutional government disappeared at the first symptom of dissent from Aguinaldo's will, and he became an absolute military dictator. We know this power was made secure by the assassination of his rival, Luna, who, whether by Aguinaldo's order or not, was slain upon Aguinaldo's threshold by Aguinaldo's guards.

I read the description of that government from the report of the Commission of which President Schurman was the head:

> Throughout the Archipelago at large there was trouble only at those points to which armed Tagalos had been sent in considerable numbers. In general, such machinery of " government " as existed served only for plundering the people under the pretext of levying " war contributions ", and while many of the insurgent officials were rapidly accumulating wealth. The administration of justice was paralyzed, and crime of all sorts was rampant. Might was the one law. Never in the worst days of Spanish misrule had the people been so over-taxed or so badly governed. In many provinces there was absolute anarchy, and from all cities came petitions for protection and help which we were unable to give.

Among the captured telegrams is one from Noirel and Cailles which further illustrates the character of the government to which we would have left the millions of humble and peaceful people of the Philippines. It is dated on the thirteenth of January, 1899, just twenty-two days before the outbreak of hostilities, and it throws light also upon the Democratic assertion that we were the aggressors in that conflict:

> To the President of the Republican Government, Malolos:
>
> We desire to know the result of ultimatum which you mentioned in your telegram, and we also desire to know what reward our government is preparing for the forces who will first be able to enter Manila.

And here is the answer which we have in Aguinaldo's own handwriting:

> As to the contents of your telegram, those who prove themselves heroes will have as rewards large sums of money, lands, extraordinary promotions, crosses of Biac-na-Bato, Marquis of Malate, Ermita, and Count of Manila, etc., besides the congratulations of our idolizing country on account of

their patriotism, and more if they capture the regiments with their generals, and if possible the chief of them all, who represents our future enemies in Manila.

Where were the people to be when the Marquis of Malate, the Marquis of Ermita and the Count of Manila were established over them with their large sums of money and grants of land? What was Aguinaldo's title to be? What was to become of the sham constitution under which he was then masquerading and which forbade the granting of titles of nobility? No, acceptance of sovereignty over the Philippines carried with it acceptance of the duty of protection; and we should have been false to that duty if we had left these people under the cruel and despotic rule of this dictator, with his generals and his marquises and his counts.

Our Democratic friends brush aside with contempt all American testimony. The words of Schurman and Taft, and Otis and Wright and Chaffee are as naught to them; but I will cite to them a greater than Aguinaldo. The greatest genius and most revered patriot of the Philippines was José Rizal. Shortly before he was done to death by Spain he sent a message to his countrymen. It must have been his last message; and in it he condemned the insurrection of Aguinaldo, which terminated just before our navy appeared upon the scene, and pointed out the path his people should follow to liberty and enlightenment. This is the message:

MY FELLOW-COUNTRYMEN:

On my return from Spain I learned that my name was being used as a war-cry by men in arms. This news shocked me beyond measure, but believing it was all over I remained silent as the harm was done and the deed could not be recalled. Now I hear rumors that the disturbances continue and lest any one should be taking advantage of my name in good or bad faith, I write now to correct that abuse and to undeceive those reckless men in order that they may know the truth. When I found out what they were attempting to do, I opposed it on principle and attacked it and showed the utter impossibility of its success.

I was convinced that the idea was in the greatest degree absurd and what was worse would be fatal. When, later, in spite of my advice, the movement was begun, I offered of my own accord, not only my services, but my life and even my good name to be used in any way they might believe effective in stifling the rebellion. I thought of the disaster which would follow the success of the revolution, and I deemed myself fortunate if by any sacrifice I could block the progress of such a useless calamity. This can be proven.

My countrymen, I have given proof that I was one who sought "liberties" for our country and I still seek them. But as a first step I insisted upon the development of the people in order that, by means of education and of labor, they might acquire the proper individuality and force which would make them worthy of them. In my writings I have commended to you study and civic virtue without which our redemption does not exist. I have also written, and my words have been repeated, that reforms to be effective must come from above. These which come from below will be discountenanced, will be irregular and unstable. Permeated by these ideas, I cannot do less than condemn, and I do condemn this absurd and savage insurrection planned behind my back, which dishonors us before the Filipinos and discredits us with those who otherwise would argue in our behalf. I abominate its cruelties and I disavow any kind of connection with it, regretting with all the sorrow of my soul that these reckless men have allowed themselves to be deceived. Let them return then, to their homes, and may God pardon those who have acted in bad faith.

José Rizal.

Fort Santiago, December 16, 1896.

That message is the platform of the American government in the Philippines. What was true of the people rebelling against Spain is doubly true of the same people rebelling against the United States. That judgment of the man whose birthday the Philippine people celebrate, and whom they worship as a saint, measures the duty of American sovereignty, which the American people will surely perform.

The Democrats declared that we had no right to succeed because our assertion of sovereignty was a violation of the Declaration of Independence, which declares that governments derive their just powers from the consent of the governed. That maxim, though general in its terms, was enunciated with reference to a highly civilized, self-governing people. Its unqualified application to barbarous and semi-civilized people is contrary to the whole course of civilization. Its unqualified application without regard to the rule and progress of humanity and ordered liberty among men, is contrary to the whole course of American history. Without the consent of the hundreds of thousands of Indians whom our fathers found in possession of this land, we have assumed and exercised sovereignty over them. Without the consent of the people of Louisiana, Jefferson and the signers of the Declaration and framers of the Constitution purchased their territory and exercised sovereignty over them. Without the consent of the people of the South the Government of the United States, with appalling sacrifice of life and treasure, enforced its sovereignty over them.

Whose consent were we to ask in the Philippines, and how was it to be expressed? Were we to accept the results of the misrepresentation and calumny which had painted us to the ignorant and credulous Filipinos as monsters of cruelty, and yield our sovereignty because they did not know what it meant to them?

Among the captured insurgent documents we find original telegraphic dispatches, most of them bearing memoranda or endorsements in Aguinaldo's handwriting, which show that the people of northern Luzon did not consent to Aguinaldo's government, and that it was imposed upon them by force of arms.

I read extracts from some of the dispatches: From General Pio del Pilar, San Pedro Mascati, to Aguinaldo, December 4, 1898. "Urgent. Reliable reports from Pangasinan state there is party composed of 4,000 individuals opposed to our government. Treason on the part of our troops and civilians."

From the Director of Diplomacy, Manila, to Aguinaldo, December 27, 1898, 5 A.M.: "Most urgent. The discontent in the provinces of Pangasinan, Tarlac and Yloco (Ilocos) is increasing. The town of Bangbang rose in revolt the twenty-fifth and twenty-sixth of this month, and killed all of the civil officials. It is impossible to describe the abuses committed by the military and civil authority of said province."

From the Secretary of Interior, Malolos, to Aguinaldo, December 28, 1898: "According to my information the excitement in Tarlac increases. I do not think that the people of the province would have committed such barbarities by themselves. For this reason the silence of General Macabulos is suspicious. To speak frankly, it encourages the rebels. Some 700 of them with 150 rifles entered Panique, seized the arms of the police, the town funds, and attacked the houses of the people."

From the Director of Diplomacy, Manila, to Aguinaldo, December 29, 1898: "The question of Tarlac and Pangasinan is a serious one. Malolos government calls me to restore it in said provinces. I await your opinion and order."

Where under the rule of force to which we aided Aguinaldo in northern Luzon was the consent of the governed to be ascertained?

The great Visayan island of Negros has never from the beginning wavered in its cheerful acceptance of our sovereignty and its rejection of Tagalog rule.

The difference between that and the other islands of the Visayan group is that in the others the Tagalogs arrived first and secured control by force of arms, which, with those accustomed for centuries to follow blindly the men in authority over them, made consent a necessary sequence.

When the natives began to know us and to learn what our sovereignty really meant, they did manifest their acceptance of it by the thousands, and what happened to them then? I read from reports received in response to a circular letter to our officers sent at the instance of Governor Taft, to ascertain what was done by the bands of assassins who were supporting the power of Aguinaldo, to the Filipinos who dared to give the consent of the governed to American sovereignty. The reports show in the first district of southern Luzon, natives assassinated for sympathizing with Americans, 14; natives assaulted for sympathizing with Americans, 104. In the second district of southern Luzon, natives assassinated for sympathizing with Americans, 17; natives assaulted for sympathizing with Americans, 106. In the first district of northern Luzon natives assassinated, 100; natives assaulted, 40. In the third district of northern Luzon, natives assassinated, 106; natives assaulted, 131. And so on throughout the Islands, showing before the end of 1900, 350 natives assassinated and 442 assaulted and mutilated; 67 municipal officers assassinated and 40 assaulted and mutilated for daring to give the consent of the governed to American sovereignty. Many of them were put to death with frightful barbarity. Some of them were buried alive; some hacked to pieces; some burned. While there were hundreds slain that we knew of, there were thousands slain that we did not know of. Where there were thousands put to death, how many were deterred by fear of death? The reign of terror established throughout the islands to prevent by secret and wholesale assassination, the consent of the governed to American rule makes the Mafia seem harmless and beneficent. Are we to surrender our sovereignty because the consent was withheld by these means?

Not content with denying our right to succeed, the Democrats of Congress came to the aid of the men who were preventing Philippine acceptance of American authority by misrepresentation and slander, and furnished them with fresh material and new authority for their aspersions upon the character and purposes of the American people:

Said the junior Senator from Tennessee in the Senate on May 1:

Our dealings with the American Indians have been fitly characterized as a century of dishonor; our treaties with them have been shamefully violated; we have delivered them over to the tender mercies of thieving Indian agents; we have inflamed them with injustice and mean whiskey; and when in sheer desperation they have risen in revolt we have made them " good Indians " with powder and ball. . . .

Alaska was ceded to us by despotic Russia, and came under the benign rule of this great Republic. For thirty-five years our continuous misgovernment of that country has been a shame and disgrace to the nation. . . .

When the gloss is worn off, when the syndicated boomers have appropriated the cream of the spoils, when the Government sinks into the dull routine of administration, it will be in the Philippines precisely as it has been in Alaska. We know what kind of men as a rule will be sent to serve in the Philippine Islands. Needy and desperate adventurers, broken-down politicians looking for a job, the sons, nephews, and cousins of American politicians, the Rathbones and Neelys; men who have qualified themselves for service abroad by the dirty and villainous work they have done at home. These are the men who as a rule will find service in the Philippine Islands as they did in Cuba, as my friend from Mississippi suggests. . . .

The entire Archipelago is swarming with needy and desperate adventurers seeking to reap their inhuman harvests from the calamities of the people. American Congressmen and American officials have been forming syndicates and prowling over that country seeking to make off with something that could be turned into a dollar. The whole pack of lean and famished carpet-baggers that once feasted upon the South seem to be howling upon the scent of another victim.

Said the Senator from Utah:

I infer that this is the inauguration of a scheme of loot and plunder and exploitation — another plowing of a ruined Carthage. You have garnered the harvest of death, and now propose to rake the stubblefield of a slaughtered people. . . .

Mr. President, we have accomplished nothing for the benefit of the Islands there. The condition there is so intolerable that language is inadequate to describe it, and what has taken place, if you continue the same policy, is likely to be augmented, and multiplied in its distress and disaster in the future.

Congressman Selby, of Illinois, said:

> This "new policy" business has given birth to the biggest crop of liars at Washington and Luzon known outside the realms of Hades. It has turned out that no Republican can visit Manila and return to Washington a truthful man. Even the Commission headed by Governor Taft is largely under suspicion of prevarication, if not of fraud, while Generals Otis and Chaffee have always been under suspicion. Is it possible that large salaries and the hope of great perquisites influence these gentlemen and their retainers in distorting the situation at Luzon? Who knows, for the almighty dollar is a great magnet in all colonial schemes, and its cobra head is visible in all the Philippines.

I do not wonder that with such declarations as these in the Congress of the United States, the Filipinos distrust our assurances and wait for proof that our rule will really mean liberty and prosperity. If Senators of the United States have no faith in the justice or integrity or virtue of the American people, how can we expect the people of the Philippines to have faith?

The most violent of all attacks was made upon the army, which belongs to no party and is but the instrument of a policy in which it has no part. It happened that in the long course of guerrilla warfare against savage and treacherous foes who observed none of the rules of civilized warfare, there were instances of cruel and inhuman treatment of the natives by our men. The "water-cure," so called, was administered to extort information. These acts were not justified, and they could not be justified, but spread over years of conflict, over a vast extent of territory, over thousands of engagements and skirmishes and expeditions, in which, first and last, 130,000 of our troops were engaged, they were few and far between — exceptions in a uniform course of self-restraint, humanity, and kindness. Rumor magnified them many fold. Each new witness to the same case seemed to be producing a new case; published in thousands of newspapers day after day and week after week, they seemed to be multiplied. Many of the stories told were false, many were grossly exaggerated. All were published without the background of provocation, often dreadful provocation, of exigency, often desperate exigency, which existed to palliate, though they could not justify the acts. All of these stories, false as well as true, were paraded in Congress and discussed, and the officers and men charged were denounced, the innocent as well as the guilty, without an opportunity for hearing, while they were away on the other side of the world fighting the battles of their country.

The whole army and its generals were involved in common denunciation. The gallant and fearless Funston was stigmatized by the Senator from Tennessee as a "blatherskite brigadier." "I do not know who General Wheaton is, particularly," said the Senator from Idaho, "but I imagine he was a charity boy who was appointed to West Point by some Representative or Senator and was educated by the Government."

This was of Loyd Wheaton, who enlisted from this very town as a private in the Eighth Ohio Volunteers on the twentieth of April, 1861, the day after Lincoln's first call, who won his way up through every grade in that regiment until he was honorably discharged as its lieutenant-colonel at the close of the Civil War; who was wounded at Shiloh; was brevetted for faithful and meritorious services in the Mobile campaign; was brevetted again for gallantry at the siege of Vicksburg; was brevetted again and received a medal of honor from Congress for most distinguished gallantry at Fort Blakely, Alabama; received his appointment in the regular army for those deeds and passed through every grade until after more than forty years of exceptional and conspicuous service, he was about retiring as major-general, full of years and of honor.

When the worst charge of all, subsequently shown to be utterly false, was under discussion in the Senate, the Senator from Tennessee declared:

Of course the soldier, whatever he may have said, will promptly repudiate it as every soldier in the Philippine Islands has been required and compelled to do.

Said the Senator from Utah:

Did Chaffee alone, unaided, in coldness, and in brutality and in savage and unrelenting disregard of every human sentiment or possibility of human suffering, conceive this iniquitous scheme? Whence, from what diabolical source was it derived? The American people ought to know. Is there any penalty beneath the sun adequate to be meted out to the merciless wretch who has thus brought such dishonor upon the American name and the American people? . . .

Mr. President, I do not believe that Bell himself ever conceived this iniquity; this outline of policy. Perhaps it may have been Chaffee, who received his education in savagery and in cruelty and in barbarity over in China, where we are informed the allied forces took little children and brained them upon posts, threw them into rivers, and slaughtered and persecuted without mercy and without limit helpless women. After he had received that training, he superseded the more humane officer, General MacArthur. Then it was that this diabolical programme seems to have been adopted and carried out in all its hideousness and rigor.

This was of Adna R. Chaffee. As a boy of nineteen, on the twenty-second of July, 1861, he enlisted as a private in the Sixth Cavalry. He served through all the Civil War; was brevetted for gallantry at Gettysburg; again for gallantry at Dinwiddie Court-house; twice brevetted for gallant service in engagements with the Indians; wounded in the Gettysburg campaign; wounded again at the battle of Brandy Station; highly commended for his services as general officer at El Caney and Santiago; chief of staff in Cuba; commander of the American troops in China; commanding general in the Philippines; second ranking major-general of the United States Army. It was he who, when officers of other nations hesitated to make the march to Peking, when other generals wished to wait for reënforcements that would have come too late, — it was he who declared that whatever they might do, he proposed to march at once, and he did march, and they all marched with him, and the legations were saved. Great credit came to the American army, because in that march and after Peking was captured, American soldiers under Chaffee did not loot and were not cruel, but protected the property and the lives of the Chinese.

The quarter of Peking over which the American flag floated was crowded by the poor people when other parts were deserted, because under that flag they found protection and kindness, and upon General Chaffee's departure he was accompanied by many most touching and gratifying expressions of gratitude and affection from the people who had received the benefits of his humanity. I did not think an American could be found who was not proud of that record.

Against these contemptuous and injurious aspersions upon the soldiers of the United States, I will call four witnesses.

The first is William McKinley:

> If any orders of mine were required to insure the merciful conduct of military and naval operations, they would not be lacking, but every step in the progress of our troops has been marked by a humanity which has surprised even the misguided insurgents.

The second is President Schurman, and joining with him Admiral George Dewey and the other members of the first Philippine Commission:

> To those who derive satisfaction from seizing on isolated occurrences — regrettable, indeed, but incident to every war — and making them the basis of sweeping accusations, this Commission has nothing to say. Still less do we feel called upon to answer idle tales without foundation in fact. But for the satisfaction of those who have found it difficult to understand why the transporting of American citizens across the Pacific Ocean should change their nature, we are glad to express the belief that a war was never more humanely conducted. Insurgents wounded were repeatedly succored on the field by our men at the risk of their lives. Those who had a chance

for life were taken to Manila and tenderly cared for in our hospitals. If churches were occupied, it was only as a military necessity, and frequently after their use as forts by the insurgents had made it necessary to train our artillery upon them. Prisoners were taken whenever opportunity offered, often only to be set at liberty after being disarmed and fed. Up to the time of our departure, although numerous spies had been captured, not a single Filipino had been executed. Such wrongs as were actually committed against the natives were likely to be brought to our attention, and in every case that we investigated we found a willingness on the part of those in authority to administer prompt justice.

The third is Governor William H. Taft, of Ohio, who said in his testimony under oath before the Philippine Committee of the Senate:

I desire to say that it is my deliberate judgment that there never was a war conducted, whether against inferior races or others, in which there was more compassion and more restraint and more generosity, assuming that there was war at all, than there have been in the Philippine Islands.

The fourth is Vice-Governor Luke E. Wright, of Tennessee:

General Chaffee, as a matter of course, had no patience with any acts of oppression or cruelty, and whenever his attention has been called to them has at once taken proper steps. The howl against the army has been made mainly for political purposes and the cruelties practiced have been largely exaggerated. Of course, numerous instances of this character have occurred. There never was and never will be a war of which the same may not be said; but taken as a whole, and when the character of the warfare here is considered, I think the officers and men of the American army have been forbearing and humane in their dealings with the natives, and the attempt to create a contrary impression is not only unjust to them, but it seems to me unpatriotic as well.

No one of these positions, these arguments, these efforts, these attacks, by the Democratic leaders during the critical and trying time of our Philippine undertaking stands by itself. Men may differ upon this point and upon that point, upon this question and upon that question, and different environment and disposition will produce different views; but when we consider the whole course of these Democratic leaders; when we find them attacking the administration upon the ground of doing the very thing they themselves had authorized; when we find them denying our right of sovereignty, denying the justice of our cause, assuming the truth of the insurgents' statements upon every question, rejecting the truth of American statements upon every question, elevating and lauding Filipino insurgent character and insurgent competency, and ascribing the most disgraceful motives and the most outrageous conduct to the representatives of their own government, both civil and military; holding out to the insurgents the hope of success through further resistance, and painting for them in the blackest colors the dreadful consequences of failure, denying and impugning before all the world from their high places the good faith of the American government, the integrity of the American people, and the beneficence of American rule; arraying argument and statistics, never to encourage, but always to dishearten the American people; insisting always upon the construction of powers and methods of procedure which would make success difficult or impossible; accepting and adopting with alacrity every aspersion upon American honor, and rejecting contemptuously every evidence of American efficiency and noble purpose; I think we must say that the Democratic party which has allowed these things to be done in its name has failed in one more opportunity to secure the respect and confidence of the American people. I will not say that these men wished their country to fail, but I will say that they wished the Republican administration to fail, and blinded by partisan feeling and desire for power, they forgot that the failure of the administration in the Philippines would be the failure of their country.

Throughout all this storm of detraction and abuse, the Republican majorities of the Senate and the House labored unceasingly to frame and perfect legislation under which the people of the Philippine Islands might have peace and order and individual freedom and prosperity. They studied the needs of the Islands, the character of the people, the existing laws and system of government, and they produced and passed, against Democratic opposition, a Philippine Government bill which exhibits a high degree of wise statesmanship and opens to the Philippine people the pathway to that enlightenment and capacity for self-government for which Rizal longed, and to the blessings which the noble and gentle McKinley believed would descend upon them under the benediction of our flag. I think they and not the others were the true friends of the Philippine people. I think they and not the others used well and wisely the powers vested in them as representatives of the people in the Congress of the United States; and I submit to you, my countrymen, that they and not the others are entitled to the expression of your confidence in the coming election.

EXTERNAL POLICIES IN 1904

ADDRESS AS TEMPORARY CHAIRMAN OF THE REPUBLICAN NATIONAL CONVENTION, CHICAGO, ILLINOIS, JUNE 21, 1904

Mr. Root was elected temporary chairman of the National Republican Convention which met at Chicago, Ill., on June 21, 1904, to nominate the candidates of the Republican party for the Presidential election of that year. As temporary chairman, he delivered the opening address before the Convention, reviewing at length the record of the Republican party under the administrations of President McKinley and President Roosevelt, of which he himself had been a member as Secretary of War.

Those portions of the address are omitted which may be considered as falling beyond the scope of the topics included within the present volume.

FOUR years ago we held the island of Cuba by military occupation. The opposition charged, and the people of Cuba believed, that we did not intend to keep the pledge of April 20, 1898, that when the pacification of Cuba was accomplished we should leave the government and control of the island to its people. The new policy towards Cuba which should follow the fulfillment of that pledge was unformed. During the four years it has been worked out in detail and has received effect. It was communicated by executive order to the military governor. It was embodied in the act of Congress known as the Platt Amendment. It was accepted by the Cuban Constitutional Convention on the twelfth of October, 1901. It secured to Cuba her liberty and her independence, but it required her to maintain them. It forbade her ever to use the freedom we had earned for her by so great a sacrifice of blood and treasure, to give the island to any other power; it required her to maintain a government adequate for the protection of life and property and liberty, and should she fail, it gave us the right to intervene for the maintenance of such a government. And it gave us the right to naval stations upon her coast for the protection and defense alike of Cuba and the United States.

On the twentieth of May, 1902, under a constitution which embodied these stipulations, the government and control of Cuba were surrendered to the president and congress elected by her people, and the American army sailed away. The new republic began its existence with an administration of Cubans completely organized in all its branches and trained to effective service by American officers. The administration of President Palma has been wise and efficient. Peace and order have prevailed. The people of Cuba are prosperous and happy. Her finances have been honestly administered, her credit is high. The naval stations have been located and bounded at Guantánamo and Bahía Honda, and are in the possession of our navy. The Platt Amendment is the sheet anchor of Cuban independence and of Cuban credit. No such revolutions as have afflicted Central and South America are possible there, because it is known to all men that an attempt to overturn the foundations of that government will be confronted by the overwhelming power of the United States. The treaty of reciprocity and the act of Congress of December 6, 1903, which confirmed it, completed the expression of our policy towards Cuba; which with a far view to the future, aims to bind to us by ties of benefit and protection, of mutual interest and genuine friendship, that island which guards the Caribbean and the highway to the Isthmus, and must always be, if hostile, an outpost of attack, and if friendly, an outpost of defense for the United States. Rich as we are, the American people have no more valuable possession than the sentiment expressed in the dispatch which I will now read:

HAVANA, May 20, 1902.

THEODORE ROOSEVELT,
President, Washington.

The government of the Island having been just transferred, I, as Chief Magistrate of the Republic, faithfully interpreting the sentiment of the whole people of Cuba, have the honor to send you and the American people testimony of our profound gratitude and the assurance of an enduring friendship, with wishes and prayers to the Almighty for the welfare and prosperity of the United States.

T. Estrada Palma.

When the last National Convention met, the Philippines also were under military rule. The insurrectos from the mountains spread terror among the peaceful people by midnight foray and secret assassination. Aguinaldo bided his time in a secret retreat. Over seventy thousand American soldiers from more than five hundred stations, held a still vigorous enemy in check. The Philippine Commission had not yet begun their work.

The last vestige of insurrection has been swept away. With their work accomplished, over 55,000 American troops have been brought back across the Pacific. Civil government has been established throughout the archipelago. Peace and order and justice prevail. The Philippine Commission, guided at first by executive order and then by the wise legislation of Congress in the Philippine Government Act of July 1, 1902, have established and conducted a government which has been a credit to their country and a blessing to the people of the islands. The body of laws which they have enacted upon careful and intelligent study of the needs of the country challenges comparison with the statutes of any country. The personnel of civil government has been brought together under an advanced and comprehensive civil service law, which has been rigidly enforced. A complete census has been taken, designed to be there as it was in Cuba the basis for representative government; and the people of the islands will soon proceed under provisions already made by Congress to the election of a representative assembly, in which for the first time in their history they may have a voice in the making of their own laws. In the meantime the local and provincial governments are in the hands of officers elected by the Filipinos; and in the great central offices, in the Commission, on the bench, in the executive departments, the most distinguished men of the Filipino race are taking their part in the government of their people. A free school system has been established and hundreds of thousands of children are learning lessons which will help fit them for self-government. The seeds of religious strife existing in the bitter controversy between the people and the religious orders have been deprived of potency for harm by the purchase of the friars' lands, and their practical withdrawal. By the act of Congress of March 2, 1903, a gold standard has been established to take the place of the fluctuating silver currency. The unit of value is made exactly one half the value of the American gold dollar, so that American money is practically part of their currency system. To enable the Philippine Government to issue this new currency, $6,000,000 was borrowed by them in 1903 in the city of New York; and it was borrowed at a net interest charge of 1 5–8 per cent per annum. The trade of the islands has increased notwithstanding adverse conditions. During the last five years of peace under Spanish rule, the average total trade of the islands was less than $36,000,000. During the fiscal year ending June 30, 1903, the trade of the islands was over $66,000,000. There is but one point of disturbance, and that is in the country of the Mohammedan Moros, where there is an occasional fitful savage outbreak against the enforcement of the law recently made to provide for adequate supervision and control to put an end to the practice of human slavery.

When Governor Taft sailed from Manila in December last, to fill the higher office where he will still guard the destinies of the people for whom he has done such great and noble service, he was followed to the shore by a mighty throng, not of repressed and sullen subjects, but of free and peaceful people, whose tears and prayers of affectionate farewell showed that they had already begun to learn that " our flag has not lost its gift of benediction in its world-wide journey to their shores."

None can foretell the future; but there seems no reasonable cause to doubt that under the policy already effectively inaugurated, the institutions already implanted, and the processes already begun in the Philippine Islands, if these be not repressed and interrupted, the Philippine people will follow in the footsteps of the people of Cuba; that more slowly indeed, because they are not so advanced, yet as surely, they will grow in capacity for self-government, and receiving power as they grow in capacity, will come to bear substantially such relations to the people of the United States as do now the people of Cuba, differing in details as conditions and needs differ, but the same in principle and the same in beneficent results.

In 1900 the project of an isthmian canal stood where it was left by the Clayton-Bulwer Treaty of 1850. For half a century it had halted, with Great Britain resting upon a joint right of control, and the great undertaking of De Lesseps struggling against the doom of failure imposed by extravagance and corruption. On the eighteenth of November, 1901, the Hay-Pauncefote Treaty with Great Britain relieved the enterprise of the right of British control and left that right exclusively in the United States. Then followed swiftly the negotiations and protocols with Nicaragua; the Isthmian Canal Act of June 28, 1902; the just agreement with the French Canal Company to pay them the value of the work they had done; the negotiation and ratification of the treaty with Colombia; the rejection of that treaty by Colombia in violation of our rights and the world's right to the passage of the Isthmus; the seizure by Panama of the opportunity, to renew her oft-repeated effort to throw off the hateful and oppressive yoke of Colombia and resume the independence which once had been hers, and of which she had been deprived by fraud and force; the success of the revolution; our recognition of the new republic, followed by recognition from substantially all the civilized powers of the world; the treaty with Panama recognizing and confirming our right to construct the canal; the ratification of the treaty by the Senate; confirmatory legislation by Congress; the payment of the $50,000,000 to the French Company and to Panama; the appointment of the Canal Commission in accordance with law, and its organization to begin the work.

The action of the United States at every step has been in accordance with the law of nations, and consistent with the principles of justice and honor. It has been in discharge of the trust to build the canal we long since assumed, by denying the right of every other power to build it; and it has been dictated by a high and unselfish purpose, for the common benefit of all mankind. That action was wise, considerate, prompt, vigorous and effective; and now the greatest of constructive nations stands ready and competent to begin and to accomplish the great enterprise which shall realize the dreams of past ages, bind together our Atlantic and Pacific coasts, and open a new highway for that commerce of the Orient whose course has controlled the rise and fall of civilizations. Success in that enterprise greatly concerns the credit and honor of the American people, and it is for them to say whether the building of the canal shall be in charge of the men who made its building possible, or of the weaklings whose incredulous objections would have postponed it for another generation.

Throughout the world the diplomacy of the present Administration has made for peace and justice among nations. Clear-sighted to perceive and prompt to maintain American interests, it has been sagacious and simple and direct in its methods, and considerate of the rights and of the feelings of others.

Within the month after the last National Convention met, Secretary Hay's circular note of July 3, 1900, to the Great Powers of Europe had declared the policy of the United States:

> to seek a solution which may bring about permanent safety and peace to China, preserve China's territorial and administrative entity, protect all rights guaranteed to friendly powers by treaty and international law, and safeguard for the world the principle of equal and impartial trade with all parts of the Chinese Empire.

The express adherence of the Powers of Europe to this declaration was secured. The open recognition of the rule of right conduct imposed its limitations upon the conduct of the Powers in the Orient. It was made the test of defensible action. Carefully guarded by the wise statesman who had secured its acceptance, it brought a moral force of recognized value to protect peaceful and helpless China from dismemberment and spoliation, and to preserve the "open door" in the Orient for the commerce of the world. Under the influence of this effective friendship, a new commercial treaty with China, proclaimed on the eighth of October last, has enlarged our opportunities for trade, opened new ports to our commerce, and abolished internal duties on goods in transit within the empire. There were indeed other nations which agreed with this policy of American diplomacy, but no other nation was free from suspicion of selfish aims. None other had won confidence in the sincerity of its purpose, and none other but America could render the service which we have rendered to humanity in China during the past four years. High evidence of that enviable position of our country is furnished by the fact that when all Europe was in apprehension lest the field of war between Russia and Japan should so spread as to involve China's ruin and a universal conflict, it was to the American government that the able and far-sighted German Emperor appealed, to take the lead again in bringing about an agreement for the limitation of the field of action, and the preservation of the administrative entity of China outside of Manchuria; and that was accomplished. . . .

In 1900 the first administration of McKinley had played a great part in establishing The Hague Tribunal for International Arbitration. The prevailing opinion of Europe was incredulous as to the practical utility of the provision, and anticipated a paper tribunal unsought by litigants. It was the example of the United States which set at naught this opinion. The first international case taken to The Hague Tribunal was under our protocol with Mexico of May 22, 1902, submitting our contention for the rights of the Roman Catholic Church in California to a share of the Church moneys held by the Mexican government before the cession, and known as the Pious Fund; and the first decision of the Tribunal was an award in our favor upon that question.

When in 1903 the failure of Venezuela to pay her just debts led England, Germany and Italy to war-like measures for the collection of their claims, an appeal by Venezuela to our Government resulted in agreements upon arbitration in place of the war, and in a request that our President should act as arbitrator. Again he promoted the authority and prestige of The Hague Tribunal, and was able to lead all the powers to submit the crucial questions in controversy to the determination of that court. It is due greatly to support by the American Government that this agency for peace has disappointed the expectations of its detractors, and by demonstrations of practical usefulness has begun a career fraught with possibilities of incalculable benefit to mankind.

On the eleventh of April, 1903, was proclaimed another convention between all the Great Powers, agreeing upon more humane rules for the conduct of war; and these in substance incorporated and gave the sanction of the civilized world to the rules drafted by Francis Lieber and approved by Abraham Lincoln for the conduct of the armies of the United States in the field.

All Americans who desire safe and conservative administration which shall avoid cause of quarrel, all who abhor war, all who long for the perfect sway of the principles of that religion which we all profess, should rejoice that under this Republican administration their country has attained a potent leadership among the nations in the cause of peace and international justice.

The respect and moral power thus gained have been exercised in the interests of humanity, where the rules of diplomatic intercourse have made formal intervention impossible. When the Rumanian outrages and when the appalling massacre at Kishineff, shocked civilization and filled thousands of our own people with mourning, the protest of America was heard through the voice of its Government, with full observance of diplomatic rules, but with moral power and effect.

We have advanced the authority of the Monroe Doctrine. Our adherence to the convention which established The Hague Tribunal was accepted by the other Powers, with a formal declaration that nothing therein contained should be construed to imply the relinquishment by the United States of its traditional attitude toward purely American questions. The armed demonstration by the European Powers against Venezuela was made the occasion for disclaimers to the United States of any intention to seize the territory of Venezuela, recognizing in the most unmistakable way the rights of the United States expressed in the declaration of that traditional policy.

Mindful that moral powers unsupported by physical strength do not always avail against selfishness and aggression, we have been augmenting the forces which command respect.

We have brought our navy to a high state of efficiency and have exercised both army and navy in the methods of sea-coast defense. The joint Army and Navy Board has been bringing the two services together in good understanding and the common study of the strategy, the preparation and the coöperation which will make them effective in time of need. Our ships have been exercised in fleet and squadron movements, have been improved in marksmanship and mobility, and have been constantly tested by use. Since the last National Convention met, we have completed and added to our navy, five battleships, four cruisers, four monitors, thirty-four torpedo destroyers and torpedo boats; while we have put under construction, thirteen battleships and thirteen cruisers.

Four years ago our army numbered over 100,000 men — regulars and volunteers, seventy-five per cent of them in the Philippines and China. Under the operation of statutes limiting the period of service, it was about to lapse back into its old and insufficient number of 27,000, and its old and insufficient organization under the practical control of permanent staff departments at Washington, with the same divisions of counsel and lack of coördinating and directing power at the head, that led to confusion and scandal in the war with Spain. During the past four years the lessons taught by that war have received practical effect. The teachings of Sherman and of Upton have been recalled and respected. Congress has fixed a maximum of the army at 100,000, and a minimum at 60,000; so that maintaining only the minimum in peace, as we now do, when war threatens the President may begin preparation by filling the ranks to the maximum, without waiting until after war has begun, as he had to wait in 1898. Permanent staff appointments have been changed to details from the line, with compulsory returns at fixed intervals to service with troops, so that the requirements of the field and the camp rather than the requirements of the office desk shall control the departments of administration and supply. A corps organization has been provided for our artillery, with a chief of artillery at the head, so that there may be intelligent use of our costly seacoast defenses. Under the act of February 14, 1903, a General Staff has been established, organized to suit American conditions and requirements and adequate for the performance of the long-neglected but all-important duties of directing military education and training, and applying the most advanced principles of military science to that necessary preparation for war which is the surest safeguard of peace. The command of the army now rests where it is placed by the Constitution — in the President. His power is exercised through a military chief of staff pledged by the conditions and tenure of his office to confidence and loyalty to his commander. Thus civilian control of the military arm, upon which we must always insist, is reconciled with that military efficiency which can be obtained only under the direction of the trained military expert.

Four years ago we were living under an obsolete militia law more than a century old, which Washington and Jefferson and Madison, and almost every President since their time, had declared to be worthless. We presented the curious spectacle of a people depending upon a citizen soldiery for protection against aggression, and making practically no provision whatever for training those citizens in the use of warlike weapons or in the elementary duties of the soldier. The mandate of the Constitution which required Congress to provide for organizing, arming and disciplining the militia had been left unexecuted. In default of national provisions, bodies of state troops, created for local purposes and supported at local expense, had grown up throughout the Union. Their feelings towards the regular army were rather of distrust and dislike than of comradeship. Their arms, equipment, discipline, organization, and methods of obtaining and accounting for supplies were varied and inconsistent. They were unsuited to become a part of any homogeneous force, and their relations to the army of the United States were undefined and conjectural. By the Militia Act of January 20, 1903, Congress performed its duty under the Constitution. Leaving these bodies still to perform their duties to the States, it made them the organized militia of the United States. It provided for their conformity in armament, organization and discipline to the army of the United States; it provided the ways in which, either strictly as militia or as volunteers, they should become an active part of the army when called upon; it provided for their training, instruction and exercise conjointly with the regular army; it imposed upon the regular army the duty of promoting their efficiency in many ways. In recognition of the service to the nation which these citizen soldiers would be competent to render, the nation assumed its share of the burden of their armament, their supplies and their training. The workings of this system have already demonstrated, not only that we can have citizens outside of the regular army trained for duty in war, but that we can have a body of volunteer officers ready for service, between whom and the officers of the regular army have been created by intimate association and mutual helpfulness, those relations of confidence and esteem without which no army can be effective.

The first administration of McKinley fought and won the war with Spain, put down the insurrection in the Philippines, annexed Hawaii, rescued the legations in Peking, brought Porto Rico into our commercial system, enacted a protective tariff, and established our national currency on the firm foundations of the gold standard by the financial legislation of the Fifty-sixth Congress.

The present administration has reduced taxation, reduced the public debt, reduced the annual interest charge, made effective progress in the regulation of trusts, fostered business, promoted agriculture, built up the navy, reorganized the army, resurrected the militia system, inaugurated a new policy for the preservation and reclamation of public lands, given civil government to the Philippines, established the republic of Cuba, bound it to us by ties of gratitude, of commercial interest and of common defense, swung open the closed gateway of the Isthmus, strengthened the Monroe Doctrine, ended the Alaskan Boundary dispute, protected the integrity of China, opened wider its doors of trade, advanced the principle of arbitration, and promoted peace among the nations.

We challenge judgment upon this record of effective performance in legislation, in execution and in administration.

The work is not fully done; policies are not completely wrought out; domestic questions still press continually for solution; other trusts must be regulated; the tariff may presently receive revision, and if so, should receive it at the hands of the friends and not the enemies of the protective system; the new Philippine government has only begun to develop its plans for the benefit of that long-neglected country; our flag floats on the Isthmus, but the canal is yet to be built; peace does not yet reign on earth, and considerate firmness backed by strength is still needful in diplomacy.

The American people have now to say whether policies shall be reversed, or committed to unfriendly guardians; whether performance, which now proves itself for the benefit and honor of our country, shall be transferred to unknown and perchance to feeble hands.

No dividing line can be drawn athwart the course of this successful administration. The fatal fourteenth of September, 1901, marked no change of policy, no lower level of achievement. The bullet of the assassin robbed us of the friend we loved; it took away from the people the President of their choice; it deprived civilization of a potent force making always for righteousness and for humanity. But the fabric of free institutions remained unshaken. The government of the people went on. The great party that William McKinley led, wrought still in the spirit of his example. His true and loyal successor has been equal to the burden cast upon him. Widely different in temperament and methods, he has proved himself of the same elemental virtues — the same fundamental beliefs. With faithful and revering memory, he has executed the purposes and continued unbroken the policy of President McKinley for the peace, prosperity and honor of our beloved country. And he has met all new occasions with strength and resolution and far-sighted wisdom.

As we gather in this convention, our hearts go back to the friend — the never to be forgotten friend, whom when last we met we acclaimed with one accord as our universal choice to bear a second time the highest honor in the nation's gift; and back still, memory goes through many a year of leadership and loyalty.

How wise and how skillful he was! how modest and self-effacing! how deep his insight into the human heart! how swift the intuitions of his sympathy! how compelling the charm of his gracious presence! He was so unselfish, so thoughtful of the happiness of others, so genuine a lover of his country and his kind. And he was the kindest and tenderest friend who ever grasped another's hand. Alas, that his virtues did plead in vain against cruel fate!

Yet we may rejoice, that while he lived he was crowned with honor; that the rancor of party strife had ceased; that success in his great tasks, the restoration of peace, the approval of his countrymen, the affection of his friends, — gave the last quiet months in his home at Canton repose and contentment. . . .

But we turn as he would have us turn, to the duties of the hour, the hopes of the future; we turn as he would have us turn, to prepare ourselves for struggle under the same standard borne in other hands by right of true inheritance. Honor, truth, courage, purity of life, domestic virtue, love of country, loyalty to high ideals — all these combined with active intelligence, with learning, with experience in affairs, with the conclusive proof of competency afforded by wise and conservative administration, by great things already done and great results already achieved, — all these we bring to the people with another candidate. Shall not these have honor in our land? Truth, sincerity, courage! these underlie the fabric of our institutions. Upon hypocrisy and sham, upon cunning and false pretense, upon weakness and cowardice, upon the arts of the demagogue and the devices of the mere politician, — no government can stand. No system of popular government can endure in which the people do not believe and trust. Our President has taken the whole people into his confidence. Incapable of deception, he has put aside concealment. Frankly and without reserve, he has told them what their government was doing, and the reasons. It is no campaign of appearances upon which we enter, for the people know the good and the bad, the success and failure, to be credited and charged to our account. It is no campaign of sounding words and specious pretenses, for our President has told the people with frankness what he believed and what he intended. He has meant every word he said, and the people have believed every word he said, and with him this convention agrees because every word has been sound Republican doctrine. No people can maintain free government who do not in their hearts value the qualities which have made the present President of the United States conspicuous among the men of his time as a type of noble manhood. Come what may here — come what may in November, God grant that those qualities of brave, true manhood shall have honor throughout America, shall be held for an example in every home, and that the youth of generations to come may grow up to feel that it is better than wealth, or office, or power, to have the honesty, the purity, and the courage of Theodore Roosevelt.

WEST POINT

ADDRESS AT THE CENTENNIAL CELEBRATION OF THE ESTABLISHMENT OF THE UNITED STATES MILITARY ACADEMY, JUNE 11, 1902

From the outbreak of the war of the Revolution, the necessity for trained engineers and artillerists was evident. The want was supplied, as far as possible, by inviting foreigners to assist in the military operations. General Henry Knox, Chief of Artillery, was the first to propose the establishment of a military academy, where cadets would be educated, chiefly in the theory of war, leaving the practice to be gained in actual service. In a report to a committee of Congress dated September 27, 1776, he advocated an academy " nearly on the same plan as that of Woolwich." General Knox's views were supported by Alexander Hamilton and approved by General Washington, but the plan was not carried out until 1802, when the United States Military Academy was established at West Point.

In the first century of its existence, West Point graduated 4,121 cadets, and these officers have formed the backbone and the directing force of the regular and volunteer armies of the United States; and they furnished both the North and the South with their leading officers in the war between the states. Dr. Edward S. Holden, Librarian of the Academy, states that " every great battle of the Civil War except two was fought under the command of a graduate " of West Point.

Mr. Root delivered an address at the Centennial Celebration of the founding of West Point. He made the following reference to the anniversary in his report as Secretary of War for 1902:

> The Military Academy at West Point on June 11, 1902, celebrated with appropriate ceremonies the completion of a hundred years of honorable and useful service. The advance of the world in military science, the increasing complexity of the machinery and material used in warfare, and the difficulty of the problems involved in transporting, supplying, and handling the great armies of modern times, make such an institution even more necessary to the country now than when it was founded by the fathers of the Republic a hundred years ago. The efficiency of the institution and the high standard of honor and devotion to duty which have characterized its graduates justify the continuance of public confidence. The wise liberality of Congress has enabled the institution to begin its second century with the well-founded hope of larger and long-continued usefulness.

EVERY soldier here would more readily charge a battery than I undertake to follow the eloquence, humor and pathos of Horace Porter.[1] Fortunately, but few and brief should be the words which close this cheerful and interesting occasion. The centennial year of the Military Academy fittingly coincides with the beginning of an era of great opportunity and greater obligation. One hundred years ago the people of the United States, few as they were, were scattered in rural communities, the Indian and the game were near every door, and by every door hung the rifle, the powder-horn and the bullet mould. The men of Lexington and Concord had little training, but every man knew how to shoot. Life was closer to the simplicities of living, and every man knew how to take care of himself out of doors, to feed himself, to clothe himself under the simple and the hard conditions of warfare. Armies were small; the opportunities for supply were proportionately great. But now, with the increase of our population, the collection of a large proportion of our people in the great cities, with the disappearance of game, with the increasing luxuries and refinements of life, the volunteer armies upon which the Republic must in the main depend to fight its wars, will be made up for the most part of men who have never fired a gun. Armies are large and the problems of supply, of transportation, have become complicated and difficult, requiring the best art of the best-trained minds. The increase in the scientific qualities of attack and

[1] General Porter, to whom Mr. Root refers, is the Honorable Horace Porter, graduate of West Point of the class of 1860. During the Civil War, General Porter served in the Federal army, and during the latter part of the war he was on General Grant's staff and for his services was brevetted Brigadier-General, United States Army. After the war he served as private secretary to President Grant. From 1897 to 1905 he was American Ambassador to France and in 1907 a delegate on the part of the United States to the Second Hague Peace Conference.

General Porter, while Ambassador, discovered the burial place of John Paul Jones in Paris, and through his exertions the body of John Paul Jones was transported to the United States, where it lies appropriately buried in Annapolis.

defense, and the changes in the weapons of destruction, have made it impossible that the man should come from the counter and the plow and the workshop, and be familiar with the tools which he has to use as a soldier.

And now, at the very time that this great institution of military instruction is rounding out its first century of existence, the attention of our people has been sharply concentrated upon this increased necessity for military training and military science by the events of the past few years; and the conclusion which has been reached finds expression in the action of the national legislature, which, through long discussion, but with absolute certainty, reaches just conclusions in the end upon all great subjects of public importance. The conclusion that the country needs the Military Academy more at the beginning of the second century of its existence than it did at the beginning of the first, is expressed by the laws of Congress which have enlarged the number of your corps, and which are just now devoting to the enlargement of the accommodations of the Academy the munificent sum of two million dollars, to be immediately expended, with an authorized ultimate expenditure of five millions and a half. How well you will be able to meet the obligation and to justify this confidence, let the record of the American army of today answer. For our army of America, small as it was, and far across the sea, within a few weeks of active military operation captured the fortified city of Santiago, took prisoners an army greater in number than itself, and ended in a single short campaign the conflict with the power which once controlled almost the whole of the western world. Having accomplished that feat, the army gave to the island of Cuba what it had won; it released the imprisoned; it healed the sick; it cleaned the jails; it opened hospitals and asylums; it dotted the country from end to end with schools; it gathered the children from the fields and forests and towns, and set them in rows of bright and interested faces, with schoolbooks before them; it extirpated disease and saved more lives than were lost in all the war; it established the most wonderful school of government ever known, and for three years has been teaching Cuban people how to govern themselves; and last, it has come away leaving a free and happy and grateful people.

Its clear-sighted courage made straight the way from the sea to Peking, and after the capture of the imperial city and the rescue of the beleaguered legations, in the space of a few short weeks the district of the city controlled by the American army was found crowded with the people who had returned to their customary vocations under the protection of wise and just soldiers, who fought and who carried the blessings of peace and justice, as they fought, under the Stars and Stripes.

In the Philippines, that great stretch of country extending for more than a thousand miles from north to south, the army has put down an insurrection of seven millions of people, so that today peace reigns from the northernmost point of Luzon to the southernmost island of the Sulu Archipelago. And with the sword it has carried the schoolbook, the blessings of peace and self-government and individual liberty; and now in little more than three years after the great struggle began in February, 1899, nine-tenths of all the men who took part in the insurgent government are engaged in sustaining or carrying on the government of the Philippines, under the protection of American liberty. Our soldiers have been criticised, and some of them have been accused; but however ready men at ease here may be to believe, to repeat, to rejoice in accusations against our brethren who are fighting under the American flag in support of American sovereignty, away upon the other side of the world, let me tell you that the President and the Secretary of War, and the officers, the public officers of our government at Washington, have followed these soldiers of ours in report and in private letters and in telegraphic dispatches, and by the oral word of those who have returned, during their whole course of conflict; have seen them there often bare-footed, tramping through the jungle; have seen them one by one dropping off, murdered by the treacherous foe; have seen them fading from disease; have seen them falling by shot and by sword; have seen them courageous, patient, enduring, magnanimous, faithful, loyal always to the highest standard of American citizenship, and we give you our word that these men shall not be condemned unheard by the public officers of the United States, charged to do justice to them.

Be of good cheer, American soldiers! When the record comes to be made up in the cool judgment of the American people and of mankind; after Cuba, with its brilliant page, after China, with its glorious achievement, will be written another page equally brilliant, equally glorious, on which will be recorded the achievements in war and in peace of the American army in the Philippines.

All honor to the volunteers who have been and who must always be the main support of our country in war. All honor to the genius, the courage, the self-sacrifice of the men, many of whom I see before me now, who have won immortal renown as generals of the volunteer army. They will be the first to say aye when I declare that the formative power, the high standard of conduct, the informing spirit of every American army is to be found in the regular army of the United States. All honor to the officers of the regular army, who in true republican fashion have worked their way up from the ranks, as did Chaffee, commanding in the Philippines. And all honor to the officers who, turning aside from the allurements of wealth and honor in civil life, have been appointed to the army as civilians, accepting the slender income and the hard life that is known to accompany the duties of a soldier. They will be with the first to say aye when I say that the informing spirit, the high standard of the regular army, are derived from the graduates, the teachings and the traditions of the Military Academy. Happy augury of the future that here where for a hundred years honor has ever ruled, honor made up of courage, truth, compassion, loyalty, is to be found the formative and controlling power of the American army of the future, — regular, militia, and volunteer. No army inspired by the spirit of the Military Academy can ever endanger its country's liberty, or can ever desert its country's flag.

THE ARMY WAR COLLEGE

ADDRESS AT THE LAYING OF THE CORNER STONE, WASHINGTON, D.C., FEBRUARY 21, 1903

Mr. Root as Secretary of War created the Army War College. On February 21, 1903, its corner stone was laid, and on November 9, 1908, the building itself was dedicated. Mr. Root delivered an address on each of these occasions, the first in his capacity as Secretary of War, the second as Secretary of State and in his capacity of founder of the War College.

The reader will find the aims and purposes of the War College stated and the steps by which it was created set forth in those portions of Mr. Root's reports as Secretary of War included in the present volume, pages 387–388, 390–399.

NOT to promote war, but to preserve peace by intelligent and adequate preparation to repel aggression, this institution is founded. It is a growth and not a new departure. It is a natural and necessary development of the views with which General Grant established the Artillery School at Fortress Monroe, General Sherman established the Infantry and Cavalry School at Fort Leavenworth, and General Sheridan established the School of Application for Cavalry and Light Artillery at Fort Riley. Following the same policy an Engineers' School of Application, a School of Submarine Defense, and an Army Medical School were afterwards established. All of these institutions were practically suspended during the war with Spain and in the Philippines.

When the time came for the reëstablishment it had become evident that not merely restoration, but an advance and enlargement of military education were demanded by the enlargement of our army, the advance and greater complexity of military science, the increased proportion of officers who had not the benefit of a West Point education, and the wider range of military problems which the possibilities of our national growth force upon our attention. The growth of separate institutions had reached a point where their efficiency could be increased and the results of their work could be utilized best by bringing them into relation as parts of a general system of military education under the inspection and supervision of a single coördinating and controlling body, and by supplementing their work with a post-graduate course which should carry their best men onward along the lines of research and of thought by which experience and theory combine to the making of skillful commanders of armies. Such a system the army is now putting in force as rapidly as possible.

The controlling and directing body is the War College Board, consisting of five officers of rank specially detailed, and the Chief of Engineers, the Chief of Artillery, the Superintendent of the West Point Military Academy, and the Commandant of the Leavenworth School, all under the presidency of that gallant, experienced, and able soldier, Major-General Samuel B. M. Young. Under their direction the school at Fort Leavenworth has been reëstablished and reorganized as a General Service and Staff College, with the school at Fort Riley as an accessory school of application. The special service schools have been reëstablished. A system of schools has been established at the principal posts and is being extended to all the considerable posts of the country, under which a compulsory course, following a prescribed curriculum, is required from all junior officers.

It is the design of the Board, already provided by General Orders, that the best men from the post schools shall be graded up to the Leavenworth College and the special service schools; that the best men from the Leavenworth College and the special service schools shall be graded up to the post-graduate course of the War College, there to study and confer upon the great problems of national defense, of military science, and of responsible command. The courses of instruction in all the schools at all stages are in the highest degree practical as well as theoretical, and military aptitude tested by the exercise of actual command will hold a leading place in the determination of merit.

To the men thus sifted out from the great mass of officers by the demonstration of superior intelligence and devotion to their profession the Commander-in-Chief will naturally turn for details to important service and promotion to higher rank. Membership in the War College will mean honor and opportunity. In its confidential archives will be garnered the results of the best thought of the army, and in the continuous existence of the institution, always changing in its elements as men come and go but remaining itself unchanged, will be found continuity of knowledge, of thought, and of military policy always available for practical uses under the supervision of the General Staff, of which the War College Board will form a part.

It is a common observation, and a true one, that practical qualities in a soldier are more important than a knowledge of theory, but this truth has often been made the excuse for indolence and indifference, which, except in rare and gifted individuals, destroy practical efficiency. It is also true that, other things being equal, the officer who keeps his mind alert by intellectual exercise, and who systematically studies the reasons of action, and the materials and conditions and difficulties with which he may have to deal, will be the stronger practical man and the better soldier. The same considerations which have led individual enterprise to build up the great universities and technical schools, to which the graduates of our schools and colleges resort to perfect themselves in every profession and in every branch of applied science, apply with equal force to education in the science of war. It is fitting that our government should profit by the lesson which all its citizens have learned, that for success in any business the evolution from the simple to the complex must be accompanied by a more perfect system, a more careful selection of agents, and a broader training of the men upon whom fall the responsibilities of control.

No better illustration of the necessity for such an institution as this, and for a General Staff to make its work effective, can be found than in the fate which befell the work of a soldier to whose memory I wish to pay honor today — Brevet-Major-General Emory Upton, Colonel of the 4th Artillery. Graduated from West Point in the year 1860, he became while almost a boy one of the most distinguished officers of the Civil War. He commanded successively a battery of artillery, a regiment of infantry, a brigade of infantry, a brigade of artillery, and a division of cavalry. Constantly in the field, he exhibited in camp and march and in scores of battles dauntless and brilliant courage, strict and successful discipline, and the highest qualities of command. General James H. Wilson, in his life of Professor Michie, said of Upton:

> No one can read the story of his brilliant career without concluding that he had a real genius for war, together with all the theoretical and practical knowledge which any one could acquire in regard to it. He was the equal, if not the superior, of Hoche, Desaix, or Skobeleff, in all the military accomplishments and virtues, and up to the time when he was disabled by the disease which caused his death he was, all things considered, the most accomplished soldier in our service. His life was pure and upright, his bearing chivalric and commanding, his conduct modest and unassuming, and his character absolutely without blemish. History cannot furnish a brighter example of unselfish patriotism, or of ambition unsullied by an ignoble thought or an unworthy deed.

After the close of the Civil War, he addressed himself to the task of interpreting the lessons of that war to his countrymen for the improvement of our military system. Of his own motion he devised a new system of tactics, which being capable of adoption by a simple military order was adopted and revolutionized the tactics of the army. On the recommendation of General Sherman he was sent around the world with two associate officers to study the armies of Europe and Asia, and upon his return he made a report which gave the results of all his accumulated experience and observation. He recommended the three-battalion formation in cavalry and infantry regiments. He recommended interchangeable service in staff and line as against the permanent staff departments. He recommended examination as a condition to promotion. He recommended the establishment of a general staff, and he recommended the general and systematic extension of military education. His recommendations had behind them all the prestige of his brilliant military career. They had the advocacy and support of the great soldier who then commanded the American armies, General Sherman. They embodied the practical lessons of the Civil War and the results of military science throughout the world. Yet his voice was as the voice of one crying in the wilderness. The government did not even print his report, but with those of his associates it was filed in manuscript and forgotten among the millions of documents in the archives of the War Department. General Upton subsequently printed the report himself for the benefit of the public, through a private publisher. A copy may now and then be found at a second-hand book store.

More than a quarter of a century later, and long after death had ended the restless striving of that far-seeing intelligence, other men, working out the same problems with which he dealt, found the sanity and wisdom of his conclusions and gave them effect. Were Upton living today, still upon the active list of the army, he would see all of the great reforms for which he contended substantially secured: the three-battalion system, the interchangeability of staff and line, examinations for promotion, and now, by the wisdom of the present Congress, the establishment of a General Staff, and the completion of the system of military education under the controlling body which will find its permanent home in the building whose corner stone we lay today.

Many another officer has studied and striven and written and appealed in vain for improvements in the military service, and has passed away, and he and his work have been forgotten. The helplessness of the single individual who seeks to improve a system has settled into hopelessness. The wisdom acquired in each officer's experience has been buried with him. Only an institution perpetual but always changing in its individual elements, in which by conference and discussion a concensus of matured opinion can be reached, can perpetuate the results of individual effort, secure continuity of military policy, and command for its authorized, conclusive expression of military judgment upon military questions the respect and effectiveness to which that judgment is entitled.

I am sure that I speak truly when I say that Presidents and Congresses and Secretaries of War invariably desire such aid in the performance of their duties, and for this I look with hope and confidence to the General Staff of the army and its great adjunct, the War College, which we are now establishing.

THE ARMY WAR COLLEGE

ADDRESS AT THE DEDICATION, NOVEMBER 9, 1908

IT is not strange that on the shore of the beautiful Potomac, in a land devoted to peace, there should arise a structure devoted to increasing the efficiency of an army for wars.

The world is growing more pacific; war is condemned more widely as the years go on. Humanity and the desire to promote the happiness of men are slowly but surely gaining ground. Nevertheless, selfishness, greed, jealousy, a willingness to become great through injustice, have not disappeared, and only by slow steps is man making progress. So long as greed and jealousy exist among men, so long the nation must be prepared to defend its rights. It must be possessed of virile manhood and a capacity to prevent wrongdoing. In order that this defense may be possible and this country may not become a mere hulk of wealth, this institution has been created.

At the beginning of the Spanish-American War, our little army of 25,000 men was an effective force, but it was scattered over the entire country in little bands. Few officers had seen great bodies of troops together since the Civil War. There was no one at the head of the army to do the thinking; to keep pace with the science of war. There were no means by which the study of army officers could be made use of. There was no coördination. The officers, while of the highest personal type, were unused to the handling of large bodies of men. Although they studied, they had no common ground on which they could come together. The benefit of their study died with them. It was necessary that some measure be taken as a remedy for this lack of coördination.

The order of November 27, 1901, which promulgated a general scheme of military education for the army of the United States, and as part of that scheme created a General Staff, was the product of earnest and long-continued study on the part of the ablest officers of the army. This stately building and the group of men here engaged in the study of the highest military science, are evidence that the hope of the promulgators of this scheme has met with fruition, and that the liberality of the people and of Congress has ably seconded this plan of military education.

We are warlike enough, but not military. In this we are singularly like the English, and unlike other nations. We have political ideas, but no mould of military ideas. History shows that men are naturally brave, but that they always have gone down before military science; and we must have a knowledge of military science as well as bravery and patriotism. It remains for the officers of the army now and in years to come to justify the college in which the staff, the Congress and the people are copartners. How are the officers of the War College to justify their existence? I trust I may be pardoned if I go into this subject and state some rules which I believe to be necessary.

Be careful not to let your attention be focussed too strongly on the administration of the army. The General Staff was created with the primary object of studying military science. You are brought together to do the thinking for the army, not the mere administration.

Settle your military questions within the limits of the military establishment. Never permit a controversy of any description to pass beyond the doors of the War Department. It is you who are brought together to settle military questions. The people are generous to the army and proud of it. Don't go to them with quarrels and expect them to settle them. Thrash these questions out, and then let the proper representative of the army, the Secretary of War, go to Congress with the results.

The army should consider itself an instructor. It is the mould of form and the guide of practice for that greater army of citizens which will take up arms in case of war. Remember that when war shall come, — and it is idle to disregard the possibility of its coming — it will be fought not by our little standing army, but by the militia and the volunteers. Instruction is needed to save that volunteer and militia army from paying the frightful price our armies have repeatedly paid for not learning the fundamental lessons of organization. The regular army is to officer the citizen army.

Never forget your duty of coördination with the other branches of the service — the naval, marine, and militia. This is the time to learn to serve together without friction.

Remember always that the highest duty of a soldier is self-abnegation. Campaigns have been lost for no other cause than the lack of that essential quality. Keep dissension and jealousy out of the United States army. Officers, you have no rights to rank and position incompatible with the best interests of the service.

Do not cease to be citizens of the United States. The conditions of army life are such as to narrow your views. Strive to broaden your sympathies by mingling with those outside of the service and learning from them the things they can teach you. As you are good soldiers, be good citizens. Let our army be never one of aggression, but devoted to the interests of justice and peace.

THE ARMY MEDICAL SCHOOL

ADDRESS AT THE GRADUATION EXERCISES, WASHINGTON, D.C., APRIL 14, 1903

The Army Medical School was created by a General Order of the Adjutant General's Office, dated Washington, June 24, 1893. It is located in the city of Washington, and was opened October 1, 1893.

In his report for 1902, Mr. Root referred to the school in the following words:

> The excellent work done by the Medical Department in the Army Medical School in this city should not pass unnoticed. The school takes the young surgeon, who has already graduated fom some regular medical college, and has passed his examination and received a commission in the Medical Corps, and instructs him to adapt his knowledge to the special requirements of military service in surgery, medicine, and hygiene.

THE formula to be applied to these occasions requires the officer delivering the diplomas to say something. It also requires that what he says shall be brief.

I am glad of the opportunity to say to you that I hope the address which has just been delivered, when it is printed, as it will be, will be preserved by each one of you, and that on the fourteenth of April every year during your connection with the army you will read that address through from beginning to end and revive in your minds the wisdom enforced by charming humor and sentiment with which Dr. Billings[1] has favored you.

I will add to what he has said my congratulations to you on coming into a corps which can produce such men as he; which has already a standard that you have got to live up to, and by which you can measure your own growth or decadence in intellectual and moral stature.

About the only recognition that the Congress of the United States has given to the American army for all the labors and struggles of the past five years, is to be found in the signal

[1] Dr. John S. Billings, formerly surgeon-general of the army.

honor conferred upon a member of the Medical Corps of the army by the statute making Dr. Gorgas a colonel in recognition of his distinguished service. That same honor would have been conferred upon Dr. Walter Reed had it not been for his untimely and lamented death.[1]

It is due to the untiring effort and the trained intelligence of the Medical Corps that the army of the United States has the extraordinary distinction of having in Cuba saved more lives than it destroyed; so that the saving department of this great agent of destruction has overbalanced, preponderated over, the destructive element, and made a life-saving rather than a life-destroying army.

I congratulate you upon your opportunities, — the opportunities of science secured to you by your position in the army. I hope the opportunities are more to you than the rank and pay and allowances, — the opportunity to pursue your science, to develop yourselves, to accomplish something for mankind, for your country, for your profession, free from the restraints and difficulties that the necessity of bread and butter throws before almost every scientific man.

The opportunities of the Medical Corps of the army are constantly widening. The policy which is now being pursued of taking care of the larger army in larger posts, instead of scattering it in small posts, will greatly increase your opportunities for practice, for research and for individual growth. The large posts where there will be the attrition among many men, association with your seniors, and the opportunities that come from a great collection of men, will take the place for you of those little one and two company posts in which the isolation and the lack of occupation and of opportunity

[1] An act of Congress, approved March 3, 1905, provided for the purchase of a site and the construction of an army general hospital in Washington, which was named the Walter Reed General Hospital in honor of that distinguished officer who died on November 24, 1902, of a disease contracted during his service in Cuba.

caused so many a promising young man to dwindle and dry up before he reached maturity.

Congress is continually broadening in its treatment of every scientific branch of the army. It takes time and campaigns of education to secure the adoption of measures and the grants of money necessary for great steps in advance; but that kind of campaign is going on all the time, and I look with great confidence to see at an early date complete success following the efforts of your chief, the Surgeon-General, to secure ample endowments for a greater Army Medical School, and more complete hospital facilities for the members of your corps in the city of Washington.

So you are entering a corps which is ennobled by its past achievements and which has before it constantly broadening opportunities for good, opportunities to do great things for mankind, and to make a mark in the history of your profession and the history of the army. I congratulate you upon it. I hope that you will never allow the desire to be military men purely, — the desire to be soldiers, as distinct from doctors, to overcome you. I would rather hear a surgeon called a surgeon in charge of a hospital than the commanding officer of a hospital. I believe I have sometimes observed a tendency to sink the "Doctor" in the "Captain" or the "Colonel." I think that this is doing injustice to a noble profession, and that you will not become officers rather than remain doctors. You cannot climb any higher in rank or in title than you are when you stand on the pedestal of the profession to which you gave your first loyalty, your first adherence. But as members of two noble professions, both of which have high standards of ethics and of ambition, you ought to have every capacity that you possess developed to the highest point, and to have through life the happiness which comes, not from making fortunes, not from holding great offices or wielding power, but which comes from well-employed, well-rounded, and useful lives, — the happiness that comes from accomplishing things, from achievement, from results and from individual growth and individual worth attained by individual effort.

In the belief that you will so do honor to this institution and to the army of the United States, it is with greatest pleasure that I now hand you these diplomas.

THE CITIZENS' ARMY

ADDRESS OF THE SECRETARY OF WAR AT JUNCTION CITY, KANSAS, MAY 2, 1903

THE only reason why I obey the order of the Commander-in-Chief to speak while you are wishing to hear him, and to stand before you while you wish to see him, is that now I am before a community composed of the friends of the army whose welfare I have so deeply at heart. The post of Fort Riley, the great cavalry post of the United States, I know has friends among you. It was founded as a heritage to his country from the great cavalry general of the Civil War. It is a monument to Philip Henry Sheridan. I believe it is and always will be worthy of that great name. I am glad to have the soldiers of the United States come out upon the great rolling plains of Kansas and breathe the same air that makes the volunteer soldiers of Kansas. I wish nothing better for the regular army than that it shall have the spirit of the 20th Kansas when it goes into battle.

I beg you all to remember that you also are a part of the army of the United States. These men in uniform are but the committee of the citizens of America appointed to organize the army which will fight the battles when war comes, as war always does come sooner or later. You will be the army. You women will be looking out eagerly for news from camp and field where your brothers and husbands and fathers are fighting the battles of our country; and their health, their lives, their successes, their victories, their glory, will depend upon the way in which this organizing committee of war and they stand together in the relation of brotherhood and good fellowship. All citizens are members of the same great army of the future, and so when I pass by the post of Fort Riley and come to Junction City, I see but two branches of the military post — the organizing committee and the body of the army itself. I bespeak from you kindliness and good fellowship with the men of the regular army, and I enjoin upon them the cultivation of the duty of citizenship, of kindly relations with their fellow-citizens, in order that when times of trial come all Americans — regular and volunteer and militia — shall stand together in unity, strength and efficiency, to fight the battles of our beloved country.

I thank you for your patience in listening to me. I go away with pleasant recollections of your strong typical American faces, gladder than ever that the soldiers whose welfare I am charged to promote are among so sound and wholesome and true American people as are the people of central Kansas.

THE MILITIA ACT OF 1903

ADDRESSES AT THE FIFTH ANNUAL CONVENTION OF THE INTERSTATE NATIONAL GUARD ASSOCIATION OF THE UNITED STATES, COLUMBUS, OHIO, MAY 4, 1903

The Act to promote the efficiency of the Militia was approved January 21, 1903. On May 4 and 5 following, the Fifth Annual Convention of the Interstate National Guard Association of the United States was held in Columbus, Ohio, and the Secretary of War was invited to address the convention. The president of the convention was Major-General Charles Dick, of the Ohio National Guard, then a member of the House of Representatives (subsequently United States Senator) and chairman of the Committee on the Militia. General Dick reported the Act to Promote the Efficiency of the Militia, which is printed in this volume, page 470. General Dick introduced Mr. Root to the convention in the following address:

> The National Guard never had a better friend than Secretary Root. He has done great things for the army, but he has done as much for the National Guard. His whole purpose in the administration of his office has been patriotic and above criticism.
>
> Realizing and appreciating what the sentiment of the country would sustain, and in what the people seemed to believe, he sought by such recommendations as he was able to make and such influence as he might exert, to bring about their accomplishment. That he has succeeded all men who know will attest.
>
> In the legislation that has been accomplished for us, — I refer now to the National Guard and speak largely for it, — we have had no more efficient helper, no stronger or better influence, no more helpful and guiding judgment than that of the Secretary of War; and if as a result of it we have received more of recognition; if we have been elevated a little higher in the plane of merit and respectability; if more is to come to us in the future, it is largely due to what the Secretary of War has done for us and what he will do for us in the time to come.
>
> The legislation that Congress has passed would be useless indeed if it were not well administered. It lies now largely in its administration to accomplish the results proposed; but while he is Secretary of War we have every reason to believe that its greatest success will be accomplished.

It is a matter of great pleasure, and I esteem the privilege a great honor, one to which this Association will gladly respond, to present to you the Honorable Elihu Root, Secretary of War.

Mr. Root then spoke as follows:

I AM very glad of the opportunity offered by your kind and courteous invitation, to say a few things to the officers of the National Guard collected from all parts of the country in this convention, — nothing particularly new or original, but things which I have from time to time said to individuals.

I am not going to undertake to teach you your business, for I do not know much about it. I am going to speak to you, however, in full recognition of the fact that we are engaged in the same undertaking; that what my duty imposes upon me as Secretary of War, is the very thing which you are making sacrifices of time and effort and money to accomplish, and that is to place our country in a position where it is able " to enforce the laws, suppress insurrection, and repel invasion."

Some of my friends, both in the National Guard and in the Regular Army, have given evidence of expectation that immediately upon the passage of the Militia Act, to which your president has referred, there would be published a code of rules and regulations, and a series of decisions upon the numerous questions which arise under that law, as questions always must arise under every law. I think nothing could have been more unfortunate than an attempt to formulate a system of rules and make a series of decisions under that law, in advance of patient and careful inquiry and conference.

It is a very broad and general statute; designedly framed in very general terms, because it is to be applied to a great variety of conditions, conditions in large cities and conditions in rural communities; conditions in many different states, in widely separated parts of the country, and applied to the National Guard in different stages of development, and in communities some of them very rich and able to do a great deal, and some of them comparatively poor, and able to do but little. In determining the questions that arise, — as they arise—this law must be adjusted to these varying conditions with just as much liberality and as sincere an effort to get at the rights of things and to get at what is reasonable and fair and will promote the purposes of the law, as is possible.

In endeavoring to apply such a law, the important thing is to get at its controlling purpose, and to make every decision and reach every determination under it in such a way as to conform to that purpose and promote it, instead of frustrating it.

In determining what is the leading idea, the controlling purpose of this law, it is necessary to go into the condition which the law met — into the history of the militia of the United States. It is familiar to us all that the original idea of the founders of the Republic was, that the entire body — the male population of the country — should constitute the militia; that we should rely very little upon a standing army, but that the able-bodied male citizens of the United States between the ages of eighteen and forty-five, — each one of them — should be a member of the militia; each one of them should keep in his own home the gun and the powder horn and the bullets and the various accouterments necessary to enable him to go out and defend his country when he was called.

We all know, too, that the expectation failed to be realized in practice. We know that almost immediately after the passage of the original militia bill, in 1792, the Presidents of the United States, down, seriatim, commenced to ask Congress for further legislation regarding the militia; that Washington asked for it; Jefferson asked for it; Madison asked for it; and almost every administration since has sought to strengthen it.

The original militia system, based upon that idea, never worked, and as time passed on and the conditions of life became more complicated, it became less and less possible that it should be operative, until it was absolutely a dead letter, absolutely obsolete; so that we presented the extraordinary spectacle of a great country, a great people, whose principles were opposed to the maintenance of any considerable standing army, relying upon a citizen soldiery for its defense, and yet which had no law under which any preparation for defense whatever was made.

That was the situation which existed, so far as the national preparation for defense went, down to the last session of the last Congress.

In the meantime there had grown up in the states themselves bodies of state troops, troops for the immediate and constant uses of the state; and those troops, although called the "National Guard", were practically the army of Pennsylvania, of New York, of Ohio, of Georgia, of the different states by which they were maintained, and under the command of whose governors they acted; a separate and independent system, linked to the National Government only by the fact that quite late in their history, — but a short time ago — an appropriation was made by Congress to be distributed among the different states *in accordance with their representation in Congress,* without any reference to whether they had a large or small National Guard.

These bodies of troops were not organized as a rule with reference to the service of the United States; they were organized as a rule with reference to continuing as state troops, and not to becoming national troops under any circumstances.

Under those conditions this bill was passed. It was passed after many, a great many efforts, to secure some militia legislation. And its fundamental idea is not to attempt to revive the old militia idea and ignore the results of individual enterprise and state enterprise in the creation of our disciplined, organized, and armed bodies of soldiers, but to recognize the existing fact that there are but two ways of raising a body of soldiers; one is by selection and the other is by volunteer effort, by voluntary service; and the fact that in the National Guards of the state you will find the men who are willing to give the volunteer service. To recognize the fact that these bodies of troops in the states afford the true basis for the militia system of the country; to recognize the fact that whenever we come to fight a war, it will be fought not by the old militia of 1792, but it will be fought by a volunteer army, as the Civil War was fought, as the war with Spain was fought, — the little handful of soldiers of the regular army and the great body of volunteers; to recognize the fact that these National Guard organizations are the great school of the volunteer to which the country must look, in order that its young men, when they go out to fight the battles of their country, shall find officers competent to lead them, to organize them, to transport them, to equip them, to feed them, to keep them in health, and lead them against the enemy.

That is the fundamental idea of this law: to adopt as the basis of the popular militia system the National Guard organizations; to recognize the fact that those organizations are the great school of the volunteer soldier, and to take upon the shoulders of the United States the fair share of the burden of maintaining these organizations, which are proportionate to the advantages the nation will get from them. Not to substitute payment from the national treasury for payment from the state treasury, but to add to what the states are doing in order to secure the services of the National Guard for state purposes; to add to that what the Government of the United States can well afford to do, in return for the advantages that the United States will get from the

National Guard as the school of the volunteer soldier; to add to it so that it may not take the place of state action, but may add to the efficiency, the strength, the dignity, the importance of the National Guard.

There you find the key to the construction of this act, and you will find also the guide to the way in which you and I, in which National Guardsmen, and soldiers of the regular army, and citizens alike, ought to act under this law. The law is to be construed for the purpose of aiding, of strengthening, of promoting the National Guard, and not for the purpose of hampering, or injuring, or interfering with it; the law is to be construed with reference to its controlling purpose — the intent of the legislation.

Take the question which has frequently been asked and which has got to be settled by a regulation, when all the information about it has been acquired. That is, the question as to the minimum number in such organizations. That must be settled in such a way that it will secure the greatest possible efficiency in National Guard organizations, consistent with maintaining those organizations. The minimum number should not be fixed so that it will kill the organizations in the rural community where you cannot get a large number together, but it should be fixed so as to bring up that rural community just as far as it can be brought, to the standard of the greatest efficiency in discipline and strength. I am trying to find out where that standard is. It would be a great misfortune to decide it without getting all the information, all the light upon it possible.

Take another illustration. The question as to the requirement for five days' training during the year, preceding the distribution under section 1661, as amended.[1] Query:

[1] Sec. 1661 (Rev. Stats., U. S., p. 290) was amended June 6, 1900, increasing the annual appropriation for the militia from $400,000 to $1,000,000. Sup. to Rev. Stats., U. S., vol. 2, chap. 805, p. 1446.

Sec. 18 of the Act to Promote the Efficiency of the Militia, approved January 21,

What kind of training, exercise, is required? How far is the excuse of the governor to be allowed to go in relieving the National Guard associations from that five days' training, which is a prerequisite to the distribution of Federal money?

That question has got to be treated in accordance with the purpose of the act. It may well be that a different rule will be applied in this first year from the rule that will be applied hereafter; that is, we are not to treat the National Guard of a state the same during the year which preceded the passage of the act as we do the next year, when the state has had fair notice of the act. The purpose of that provision is perfectly distinct. It is that the millions of dollars which the National Government is going to expend shall not be made the substitute for state appropriations; that the National Government shall not step in and take all the burden of the National Guard off of the state and carry it all itself, but that the state shall do its share: it shall have a National Guard, it shall have a National Guard which meets for the purpose of training and discipline. It shall be a real genuine institution, and not a paper institution, and that is to be the condition of receiving this aid from the general Government, that the general Government is not doing everything for nothing. It is for the first time in its history giving an equivalent for what it expects to get from you; but it gives the equivalent only when the conditions are such that it can

1903, provides "that each State or Territory furnished with material of war under the provisions of this or former Acts of Congress shall, during the year next preceding each annual allotment of funds, in accordance with section sixteen hundred and sixty-one of the Revised Statutes as amended, have required every company, troop, and battery in its organized militia not excused by the governor of such State or Territory to participate in practice marches or go into camp of instruction at least five consecutive days, and to assemble for drill and instruction at company, battalion, or regimental armories or rendezvous or for target practice not less than twenty-four times, and shall also have required during such year an inspection of each such company, troop, and battery to be made by an officer of such militia or an officer of the Regular Army." U. S. Stat. at L., vol. 32, part 1, p. 778.

fairly expect to get something from you, and so a reasonable construction must be given to it.

I want to say a word or two about the action which ought to follow under this bill. The manner in which the bill undertakes to help the National Guard is:

First. By furnishing the arms, the equipments, the accouterments, the supplies, which you have been in the habit of drawing against your quota in the annual million dollar appropriation, furnishing them without charging them up against that appropriation.

Second. By authorizing the Secretary of War to pay over in cash the allotment under that appropriation, for the purposes of state encampments and field exercises.

Third. By authorizing the Secretary of War to make arrangements with the governor of any state, under which the National Guard, or any part of it, may participate in field exercise maneuvers, practice marches with the troops of the regular army, and in that case to pay the expenses just as if the National Guard troops taking part were troops of the regular army — that is, to pay the transportation out of the appropriation of Congress for the transportation of the army; to pay subsistence out of the appropriation of Congress for the subsistence of the army; to pay for the tentage, for the quarters; and to pay the men regular army rates out of the appropriation for the pay of the army — quite a distinct thing, you will observe, from the former provision which gives you your quota in cash for the purpose of state encampment.

Then, in the fourth place, by much enlarging the provisions under which the officers of the regular army, both in the active and the retired lists, may be utilized for purposes of instruction and inspection in the National Guard of the different states.

There is a consistent purpose running through the act, and through those methods of assistance. I do not think I can state it better than by saying that its fundamental idea is the idea of unity.

Whenever we come to a war — and come to it we know we shall, — when, we do not know; but that we shall come to it we do know, — whenever we come to war there will be but one army of the United States; there will not be a regular army, and a militia army, and a volunteer army; there will be but one army of the United States, carrying but one flag, answering but one command, the command of the constitutional Commander-in-Chief of the Army and Navy of the United States, with but one purpose to subserve. The victories it wins will shed glory upon regular and militia and volunteer alike, and the disasters that come from its failure will involve the homes, the fortunes and the honor of all alike.

The fundamental idea of this law is to recognize the activity of the National Guard; to utilize that as the constitutional militia of the country; to utilize it as the great school of the volunteer soldier; to make it a part of the military establishment of the United States; to lay down the lines of activity so that the regular army and the National Guard shall work together, and grow ever closer and closer together, knit in bonds of sympathy and brotherhood, preparing for a great struggle in a common cause.

No more fatal weakness exists in military affairs than jealousy and dissension among the officers and soldiers of an army. It has too often happened that there have been jealousy and misunderstanding between officers and men of the regular army and the National Guard. There has been right and wrong on both sides. Now and then we find officers of the National Guard who are suspicious and jealous; now and then we find officers of the regular army who are snobbish and supercilious. My impression is that if you trace the two causes back, they will come together back in the past, and one is the cause of the other. But they are the exception; the rule is otherwise; and there is but one way I know of to dispose of those exceptions, and that is the method of honest, sincere work, side by side in the same cause.

I venture to say — and I say it upon knowledge derived from conversations with many officers, both of the regular army and of the National Guard, who were together at Fort Riley last fall, that not one officer, either of the regular army or the National Guard, came away from the maneuvers at that post last September without increased respect and liking each for the other.

The idea of the provisions of this bill is to carry out the kind of joint education which will do continually what was done at Fort Riley.

There are certain qualities and attainments which a man gets who devotes his entire life to a particular study, that no one else can get; there are certain qualities and attainments which a man gets who is out in the free, rough-and-tumble life of the world, that no man who has devoted himself to one particular occupation can get. There are elements of strength and usefulness brought to this combination by officers of the regular army which you gentlemen need, and there are elements of strength and usefulness brought to it by you which the officers of the regular army need; together they will make a combination with which we can meet the world.

With our eighty millions of people there never will be the slightest difficulty in raising an army of any size which it is possible to put into the field. Our trouble never will be in raising soldiers; our trouble will always be the limit of possibility in transporting, clothing, arming, feeding and caring for our soldiers, and that requires organization. Every one realizes that where we strike the limit of effective action, is that line upon which you can go infinitely farther with organization than you can by the light of nature. Careful pre-arrangement and careful coördination of action of numerous different agencies will carry on the capacity for transporting, for arming, supplying, feeding and caring for soldiers far beyond the point of first impression.

Looking forward to the possibilities of the future, looking forward to the war that is coming with somebody sometime, I regard the regular army as but an organizing committee, a committee of organization for the accomplishment of certain things which cannot be done except by the action of certain people devoting their entire time to it; and I look upon the National Guard as a committee for the accomplishment of certain other things that cannot be done for that army except by organization. You have got to have your quartermaster work, your commissary work, your financial work, done by the National Government, and you have got to have it done by national organization — to one source you must go for your arms, your clothing, your food, your control of transportation, and you have got to have national organization for that. But when you come to the creation of the military spirit among the youth of the country, to the education and training of that military spirit, there you step in; that is your function of preparation, for that cannot be done at the center — that must be done all over this country.

The men who are leaders of opinion in their localities, who are in charge of the troops, gathered in the several states, enlisting the pride of their states, the two working together, I have the utmost confidence will enable America to put into the field whenever the time and the exigency come, an army against which the whole round earth cannot contend.

We are beginning a new departure. The highest duty rests upon every one who loves his country and is concerned in its military efficiency—in the regular army and in the National

Guard — to address himself to the application of this new law in a spirit of kindliness and sympathy, of kindly concession and consideration, so that these results it is designed, and I believe is destined to accomplish, may be accomplished. With the right spirit they can; without that, it is impossible; and I am confident that the whole question rests with the officers and men of the two great organizations, the regular army and the National Guard; and I am sure that if we hold fast to the provisions of the Constitution, keeping them clearly in mind — the provisions of the Constitution now first accepted by Congress in this law — we cannot go far astray.

You will remember that the eighth section of the first article provides that Congress shall have power "to raise and support armies"; "to provide for calling forth the militia to execute the laws of the Union, suppress insurrections, and repel invasions; to provide for organizing, arming and disciplining the militia, and for governing such part of them as may be employed in the service of the United States, reserving to the states respectively the appointment of the officers, and the authority of training the militia according to the discipline prescribed by Congress."

That is what this law provides. It may be that the general provisions which Congress has made for the execution of this constitutional power for organizing, arming, and disciplining the militia will to some of you be irksome. They may interfere here and there with some of the arrangements you have made in your own states, and which you prefer. But so many are the sacrifices which you have made and are making to secure an adequate military force, that surely you can make a little further sacrifice of your own preferences, of your own wishes, of your own convenience, in order that we may have one system, in order that when the time of trial comes, every officer and every soldier may be moving along the same lines, according to the same discipline, the same system, with the same arms, and accomplishing by united and never-discordant effort, the result sought.

In conclusion, I wish to call your attention to the provision of the Constitution, in the tenth section of the first article, that "no state shall, without the consent of Congress, . . . keep troops or ships of war in time of peace," and I congratulate the National Guard upon being now, probably for the first time, unquestionably a constitutional force.

Military Preparation the Guaranty of Peace

The evening of the same day, the Secretary of War was again called upon to address the Convention, and, after introductory remarks, continued as follows:

I have been this afternoon in this convention of officers of the National Guard; later at the parade and review of the students at the State University — the military battalion of that institution — later at a review of the soldiers at the Columbus Barracks. It all has a deep and serious meaning. Sooner or later the time will come when your husband, brothers, lover, — God grant that it may be so far distant that it may be your sons, — but sooner or later the time will come when what these men are doing here will mean life or death.

One of the saving things about doing work in the public service is that it is work for all time. You and I come and go; what we do for ourselves dies with us; but the great country, the institution, lives; the power of civilization, the great bulwarks of liberty, of justice, of human happiness, remain, generation after generation, century after century; and what these men, my friends, citizens of Columbus, what these men are doing is laying stones in the structure of national strength that will endure century by century.

Within the memory of men now living but a few thousand of people were gathered in the Atlantic States, with a few pioneers pushing their way out into the wilderness. Now eighty millions of people stretch from the Atlantic to the Pacific. Within the experience of those now within the sound of my voice, the eighty millions will have grown to two hundred millions; we shall have grown so large that the whole world outside of America will be jostling against us, and unless America is strong to defend its rights; unless America has not merely the men and the money, but the trained intelligence and the skill to defend its rights — by force if need be — America will break into an hundred parts and the government which we love and under which we enjoy the blessings of freedom and of justice, will cease from the face of the earth.

It is that America shall be strong to defend the right; that she shall have not merely the latent power, but the ever-ready school of knowledge to defend the right, that these men, my friends, are devoting their time, their means, their efforts to the service of their country, in the National Guard and the Regular Army of our country.

Nor does it mean war; it means peace, because undefended wealth but invites aggression. The house which has in its doorway the strong man armed is passed by the predatory hordes which still exist upon the face of the earth. The millennium is still far distant. Revenge and wrong still claim their own. Injustice still tyrannizes over the weak, and unless we are ready to defend our rights, our property, our homes, our honor, we go to the wall. But if we are ready, if the results of the work of this convention are wrought out to their true and natural end with the resources, the power, the sturdy people, and the immeasurable wealth of America, peace will reign, the peace that stays with the just man armed; and all this pomp and heraldry, all the trappings and the music, all the form and the ceremony, which to the thoughtless may seem to be but idle play or preparation for sanguinary conflict, are really but engines of peace and justice, and the reign of law and righteousness.

I thank you for the kind welcome, not only for the kind welcome which you have given to me, but for the kind welcome which you have given to these gentlemen who are working for the same cause and in the same field.

THE EXPORT OF ARMS AND MUNITIONS OF WAR TO AMERICAN COUNTRIES

ADDRESS IN THE SENATE OF THE UNITED STATES MARCH 13, 1912

On March 13, 1912, Mr. Root asked unanimous consent for the consideration of a joint resolution which he introduced. There being no objection, the Senate proceeded to consider the joint resolution (S. J. Res. 89) to amend the joint resolution to prohibit the export of coal and other material used in war from any seaport of the United States, approved April 22, 1898.

The joint resolution introduced by Mr. Root was slightly amended and passed the Senate, March 13. On March 14, it was again slightly amended and passed the House, the Senate concurring in the House amendment. As approved by the President, March 14, the joint resolution reads:

> That whenever the President shall find that in any American country conditions of domestic violence exist which are promoted by the use of arms or munitions of war procured from the United States, and shall make proclamation thereof, it shall be unlawful to export except under such limitations and exceptions as the President shall prescribe any arms or munitions of war from any place in the United States to such country until otherwise ordered by the President or by Congress.
>
> Sec. 2. That any shipment of material hereby declared unlawful after such a proclamation shall be punishable by fine not exceeding ten thousand dollars, or imprisonment not exceeding two years, or both.

In explaining the joint resolution, Mr. Root said:

I WILL explain that the joint resolution is the outcome of a conference called by the President this morning with such members of the Texas delegation in the Senate and House of Representatives and such members of the Committee on Foreign Relations of the Senate and the Committee on Foreign Affairs of the House of Representatives as he could conveniently reach, for the purpose of securing the extension of his power to prevent the wholesale passing of arms and munitions of war across the Texas frontier into Mexico. At that conference, at which quite a large number of gentlemen participated, there was a general expression of opinion that we ought to take up and amend our very antiquated neutrality laws; but the suggestion was made and met with general approval, although without any formal action, that that was a very large subject which would require long-continued consideration and discussion, affecting, as it must, all countries in the world, and all possible contingencies. It was thought, however, that the immediate situation, which is now very pressing, could be dealt with by a slight extension of the power already conferred upon the President by an existing joint resolution passed on April 22, 1898. That joint resolution is as follows:

> *Resolved, etc.,* That the President is hereby authorized, in his discretion, and with such limitations and exceptions as shall seem to him expedient, to prohibit the export of coal or other material used in war from any seaport of the United States until otherwise ordered by the President or by Congress.

The idea was to extend that joint resolution so that it would apply not only to seaports, but to exports from inland places across the border line.

The joint resolution was taken up by the Committee on Foreign Relations, was carefully considered, and, with many suggestions from different members of the committee, was perfected in such form that the Committee on Foreign Relations by unanimous vote authorized me to introduce the joint resolution in the Senate and to ask for its present consideration, with the statement that it has the approval of that committee.

The situation in Texas is such that it does not admit of delay for the purpose of the general reform of our neutrality laws, and the people of Texas are deeply interested in having this extension of power to the President made immediately.

With the extension of the application of the joint resolution from seaports to all places in the United States, the committee thought it was advisable to put some limitation upon the power which is included in the existing law, and so the power of the President to forbid the exportation of arms and munitions has been limited to countries in which he finds that domestic violence is being promoted by the procurement of arms and munitions of war from the United States. At the same time a penalty is affixed for the violation of the prohibition.

The conditions are such that thousands of Americans in Mexico are now fleeing from their homes there and abandoning their occupations, their mines, their manufactories, and their business, because it is necessary to do so to prevent their lives from being destroyed by arms and munitions which are being sold and transported across the border from the United States. I hope that the joint resolution may be promptly passed.

THE POWER OF THE PRESIDENT TO SEND UNITED STATES TROOPS OUT OF THE COUNTRY

ADDRESS IN THE SENATE OF THE UNITED STATES AUGUST 14, 1912

On August 14, 1912, the Senate having under consideration the Army Appropriation bill, Senator Bacon, of Georgia, proposed an amendment to the effect that no part of the money therein appropriated should be used for the pay or supplies of any part of the army of the United States employed, stationed, or on duty in any country beyond the jurisdiction of the laws of the United States; provided, that the prohibition should not apply to cases of emergency, within the discretion of the President, arising when Congress was not in session. In support of his amendment, Mr. Bacon said that the country had come to a stage where the Executive orders the army into foreign countries, without the authority of Congress, not only when Congress is not in session, but when Congress is in session, and without communicating the fact to Congress. He referred especially to the sending of troops into China during the Boxer War, and said that there was no communication sent to Congress at that time. He referred to the fact that Mr. Root, the then Senator from New York, was at that time the Secretary of War.

Senator Bacon's proposed amendment was rejected by *viva voce* vote, prior to which Mr. Root made the following remarks:

BEFORE this matter is disposed of I wish, not to argue the question which has been suggested by the Senator from Georgia [Mr. Bacon], but to express my dissent from the position he takes.

In my judgment there is no law which forbids the President to send troops of the United States out of this country into any country where he considers it to be his duty as Commander-in-Chief of the Army to send them, unless it be for the purpose of making war, which, of course, he cannot do.

Doubtless Congress could by law forbid the troops' being sent out of the country; doubtless Congress has not done it; and I apprehend that any Congress which undertook to do it would find a general protest from the people of the United States against depriving the Commander-in-Chief of the Army of the power to protect our citizens under those circumstances which exist widely throughout the world, in countries whose governments have not the power to maintain order within their jurisdiction. From time immemorial it has been the practice of civilized nations to send troops into those countries whose governments were too feeble or too ill-organized, too deficient in power to enforce their laws and protect foreigners. From time immemorial it has been the practice of civilized nations to render protection to their own citizens, to their own consuls, to their own ministers, ambassadors, and legations. That was the situation in China in the summer of 1900, when the minister of the United States, the members of his legation, and the American citizens who gathered there for safety, were surrounded by an armed force which the Government of China professed itself unable to control. Our troops went just far enough and not one step farther than was necessary to preserve them from murder.

And now, if I am not mistaken, Congress has appropriated money for the specific purpose of building quarters in Peking, to be used for the housing of troops who shall be stationed there to prevent a recurrence of that most deplorable condition.

It is the unanimous judgment of the men who saved the legations in Peking in 1900, of the officers who had command of the troops who rendered that great service to civilization, that the way to prevent a recurrence of that condition is to keep open the communication between the embassies and legations in Peking and the seacoast. And I say there is no law, and I do not believe there ever was a law, and I do not believe there ever will be a law, to prevent the Commander-in-Chief of the Army and Navy of the United States from rendering that service which, through all civilization, has been rendered by every nation that is entitled to the loyalty of its citizens, in giving them the protection required by self-respect.

PART II

FROM THE REPORTS OF THE SECRETARY OF WAR, 1899–1903

THE PRINCIPLES OF COLONIAL POLICY

PORTO RICO, CUBA AND THE PHILIPPINES

Extract from the Report of the Secretary of War for 1899[1]

THE Treaty of Paris provides:

> The civil rights and political status of the native inhabitants of the territories hereby ceded to the United States shall be determined by the Congress.

I assume, for I do not think that it can be successfully disputed, that all acquisition of territory under this treaty was the exercise of a power which belonged to the United States, because it was a nation, and for that reason was endowed with the powers essential to national life, and that the United States has all the powers in respect of the territory which it has thus acquired, and the inhabitants of that territory, which any nation in the world has in respect of territory which it has acquired; that as between the people of the ceded islands and the United States the former are subject to the complete sovereignty of the latter, controlled by no legal limitations except those which may be found in the treaty of cession; that the people of the islands have no right to have them treated as states, or to have them treated as the territories previously held by the United States have been treated; or to assert a legal right under the provisions of the Constitution which was established for the people of the United States themselves and to meet the conditions existing upon this continent; or to assert against the United States any legal right whatever not found in the treaty.

I assume, also, that the obligations correlative to this great power are of the highest character, and that it is our unques-

[1] Page 24.

tioned duty to make the interests of the people over whom we assert sovereignty the first and controlling consideration in all legislation and administration which concerns them, and to give them, to the greatest possible extent, individual freedom, self-government in accordance with their capacity, just and equal laws, and opportunity for education, for profitable industry, and for development in civilization.

The people of the ceded islands have acquired a moral right to be treated by the United States in accordance with the underlying principles of justice and freedom which we have declared in our Constitution, and which are the essential safeguards of every individual against the powers of government, not because those provisions were enacted for them, but because they are essential limitations inherent in the very existence of the American Government. To illustrate: The people of Porto Rico have not the right to demand that duties should be uniform as between Porto Rico and the United States, because the provision of the Constitution prescribing uniformity of duties throughout the United States was not made for them, but was a provision of expediency solely adapted to the conditions existing in the United States upon the continent of North America; but the people of Porto Rico are entitled to demand that they shall not be deprived of life, liberty, or property without due process of law, that private property shall not be taken for public use without compensation, that no law shall be passed impairing the obligation of contracts, etc., because our nation has declared these to be rights belonging to all men. Observance of them is a part of the nature of our Government. It is impossible that there should be any delegation of power by the people of the United States to any legislative, executive, or judicial officer which should carry the right to violate these rules toward any one anywhere; and there is an implied contract on the part of the people of the United States with every man who voluntarily submits himself or is submitted to our dominion that these rules shall be observed as between our Government and him, and that in the exercise of the power conferred by the Constitution upon Congress, "to dispose of and make all needful rules and regulations respecting the territory or other property belonging to the United States," Congress will hold itself bound by those limitations which arise from the law of its own existence.

The problem of civil government in the islands yielded or ceded by Spain presents itself in the simplest form in the case of Porto Rico. That island is fully and without question under the sovereignty of the United States. It came to us not only by legal right, but with the cheerful and unanimous desire of its people, who are peaceful and loyal and eager for the benefits to be derived from the application of American ideas of government. There is no obstacle in the way of our providing for Porto Rico the best government which we are capable of devising for people situated as are the inhabitants of that island.

The questions presented by the consideration of the measures which ought to be taken for the government of Porto Rico are threefold: (1) What form of government shall be established, and what participation in that government shall the people of the island have? (2) What shall be the treatment of the municipal law of the island, and how far shall the laws which now regulate the rights and conduct of the people be changed to conform to the ideas prevalent among the people of the United States? (3) What economic relations shall be established between the island and the United States?

(1) In determining the question as to the form of government, and the participation of the people of the island therein, the most important fact to be considered is that the people have not yet been educated in the art of self-government, or any really honest government. In all their experi-

ence and in all their traditions, law and freedom have been ideas which were not associated with each other, but opposed to each other; and it is impossible that a people with this history — only ten per cent of whom can read or write — should ever have acquired any real understanding of the way to conduct a popular government. I do not doubt their capacity to learn to govern themselves; but they have not yet learned. There are among them many highly educated and able men, public-spirited and patriotic, and these show what their people are capable of becoming; but there are not enough of them to make a working government which would be anything but an oligarchy, and many of them have merely a theoretical rather than a practical acquaintance with the processes of government.

The difficulty does not consist merely of a lack of familiarity with the methods and processes of government; it lies deeper than that in the fact that the Porto Ricans, as a people, have never learned the fundamental and essential lesson of obedience to the decision of the majority. They have had no opportunity to learn and they never have learned. There can be no free government without a loyal, voluntary personal subjection to the peaceful decisions reached by lawful processes.

In the experiments which have already been tried in municipal elections, and toward government by municipal boards, the minority which is voted down almost invariably refuses to participate further in the business of government.

The attitude of the defeated party is precisely that which causes the continual revolutions in the government of other West Indian islands and the Central American states in the same latitude. This habit marks a rudimentary stage of political development, and before the people of Porto Rico can be fully intrusted with self-government they must first learn the lesson of self-control and respect for the principles of constitutional government, which require acceptance of its peaceful decisions. This lesson will necessarily be slowly learned, because it is a matter not of intellectual apprehension, but of character and of acquired habits of thought and feeling. It would be of no use to present to the people of Porto Rico now a written constitution or frame of laws, however perfect, and tell them to live under it. They would inevitably fail without a course of tuition under a strong and guiding hand. With that tuition for a time their natural capacity will, it is hoped, make them a self-governing people. A form of government should be provided for Porto Rico which will assure the kind of administration to which we are accustomed, with just as much participation on the part of Porto Ricans as is possible without enabling their inexperience to make it ineffective, and with opportunity for them to demonstrate their increasing capacity to govern themselves with less and less assistance.

I think that some such provisions should be made for future government as the following:

That we should first declare definitely, by statute, what general laws of the United States are to be extended to the Porto Ricans, such as, for instance, the postal laws, the banking laws, the customs, navigation and internal-revenue laws with such modifications as may be deemed advisable, the laws against counterfeiting, the anti-trust laws, etc.; and provide for Federal officers to execute these laws just as they are executed in the various states and territories of the Union; that there should be a provision for a Federal judiciary in the island, with the same kind of jurisdiction which is exercised by the Circuit and District Courts of the United States, and that jurisdiction to review their determinations should be vested in the Supreme Court of the United States, or in a designated Circuit Court of Appeals and the Supreme Court of the United States.

That there should be a form of local insular government provided which shall have complete control over the rights, property, and obligations of the people of the island, substantially covering the field covered by the government of our respective states, and subject to limitations prescribed by Congress, of the same character as the constitutional limitations generally imposed upon our state legislatures.

That the framework of this government should be substantially as follows: A governor, to be appointed by the President of the United States with the advice and consent of the Senate; the chief officers of state customary under our system, such as secretary of state, attorney-general, treasurer, auditor or comptroller, superintendent of public works, and superintendent of education, to be appointed in like manner; and a legislative council, to be composed of the chief officers of state, and a minority selected from the people of the island by the President; that all acts of the council should be subject to the veto power of the governor or to be passed over the veto by a two-thirds vote, and no law should take effect until it has remained without disapproval for thirty days after presentation to Congress or to the President of the United States, if passed when Congress is not in session; that there should be a supreme court of the island, composed of judges appointed by the President with the advice and consent of the Senate and having appellate jurisdiction only; trial courts in separate districts, having general original jurisdiction, with judges and officers to be appointed by the governor, and a petty court in each municipality; that the several municipalities now existing in the island, with such consolidations and alterations of boundaries as the council shall prescribe, shall be governed by mayors and municipal councils, to be elected by the people of the municipalities, each municipality to be free from control in the exercise of the powers of local government, except as it shall be controlled by statute, and except as its officers shall be liable to removal by the governor in case of failure faithfully to perform their duties, and with power in the governor in case of such failure to order a new election and to fill vacancies in the meantime.

Such a system as this is not without precedent in our own experience, for the provision of a governor and council was frequently adopted in our early territorial legislation. It would give to the people of the island participation in the government, and would afford them an opportunity both to acquire and to demonstrate capacity for the conduct of government.

The question whether there might not now be provision made for a legislature elected by the people of the island is not free from doubt, but in view of their present inexperience I think that it would be better to postpone such a provision until the people can have had an opportunity for exercise in municipal government and until the first formative period of adapting the laws and procedure of the island to the new conditions shall have passed under the direction of a council composed of Porto Ricans selected for their known capacity and wisdom, and Americans from the States competent and experienced in dealing with legislative and administrative problems. The constitution of such a legislature should be contemplated as a step to be taken in the near future.

I think the basis of suffrage should be that all who can read and write, or who hold property up to a specified small amount, may vote, and no others. With a sufficient system of free primary education, the entire people should acquire the suffrage on this basis fully as soon as they are capable of using it understandingly.

For the successful working of such a scheme, or of any scheme of government for the island, it will be necessary that some cardinal rule shall be adopted and rigidly followed regarding appointment to office. Wherever a Porto Rican can be found capable and willing to perform official duties he should be selected, and the aim should be to include in the civil service of the island no greater number of Americans from the United States than are necessary for the introduction of the methods of administration in which Americans have been trained and Porto Ricans have not.

Wherever it is necessary to employ Americans, except in the chief offices, a system of civil-service examination should be provided, under which requests from the governor of Porto Rico for suitable persons to be appointed may be filled.

A necessary element to the success of this, or any scheme of government in Porto Rico, is the complete establishment of a system of education which will afford the opportunity for every child of school age in the island to acquire elementary instruction. The cost of this should be defrayed from the insular treasury if its revenues are sufficient, and if not it should be regarded as a duty of the highest obligation resting upon the United States, and the expense should be borne by the United States. . . .

(2) The answer to the second question, " What shall be the treatment of the municipal law of the island, and how far shall the laws which now regulate the rights and conduct of the people be changed to conform to ideas which prevail among the people of the United States? " presents little real difficulty. The civil code established by Spain for Cuba, Porto Rico, and the Philippines, and in force at the time of the cession, is an excellent body of laws, adequate in the main, and adapted to the customs and conditions of the people. It should be continued in force, with such gradual modification as experience from time to time suggests to those who are actually engaged in enforcing it.

The trouble has not been that the law was defective or vicious, but that it has never been fairly and honestly administered. The course of such an administration will naturally lead to amendments and improvements, regarding which the people themselves who are to be affected by them should have a voice. The customs and conditions of the people who are to be governed must furnish the true basis for the law under which they are to live, and any attempt to substitute in these southern islands a system of laws based on the experience and characteristics of a New England community would be both oppressive and futile.

In order to secure a good administration of the laws, extensive changes in procedure will be necessary, and there should be material changes in the criminal law. The conditions of life are comparatively simple, and both the criminal laws and the methods of procedure may, in the first instance at least, be made simple also.

One of the ablest groups of men who ever addressed themselves to such a question in this or any other country undertook a similar task in adapting the laws of Louisiana, long living under Spanish law, to the new conditions which followed the cession of that territory to the United States. The course above outlined closely resembles the one they worked out and followed with such signal success.

A similar course was followed after the acquisition of Lower Canada by the English in 1763. The French province had been governed by the laws and ordinances of France and the custom of Paris, a mingled system of Roman and Frankish law. By the statute of 14, George III, the English law was introduced in criminal matters, and the private law in civil matters was left undisturbed. The result appears to have been entirely satisfactory both to the French population of Quebec and to the remainder of the Dominion which has been settled and governed under English law.

(3) The question of the economic treatment of the island underlies all the others. If the people are prosperous and

have an abundance of the necessities of life, they will with justice be easily governed, and will with patience be easily educated. If they are left in hunger and hopeless poverty, they will be discontented, intractable, and mutinous. The principal difficulty now in the island of Porto Rico is that the transfer of the island from Spain to the United States has not resulted in an increase of prosperity, but in the reverse. The industry of the island is almost entirely agricultural. The people live upon the products of their own soil and upon the articles for which they exchange their surplus products abroad. Their production is in the main coffee, sugar, and tobacco. The prosperity of the island depends upon their success in selling these products.

So long as the island was a part of the Spanish possessions there was substantially free trade with Spain and with Cuba. The total exports from Porto Rico for the four years preceding 1897 averaged about $16,609,000, of which an average of less than one-sixth part ($2,630,000) was sold to the United States and an average of one-half ($8,025,000) was sold to Spain and Cuba. Immediately upon the transfer of the island from Spain to the United States, Spain erected a tariff barrier against the introduction of Porto Rican products. The interests of Cuban agriculture led to the erection of a similar barrier in the tariff adopted for Cuba, so that Porto Rico was debarred from the principal markets which she had previously enjoyed, and at the same time this country has maintained its tariff against Porto Rican products just as it existed while the island was Spanish territory. The result is that there has been a wall built around the industry of Porto Rico.

Even before the hurricane of August 8, 1899, two crops of tobacco lay in the warehouses of Porto Rico, which the owners were unable to sell at prices equal to the cost of production. Their sugar shared the prevailing depression in that commodity, arising from the competition of bounty-fed beet sugar. Their coffee was practically unknown in the United States and had no market here. It is plain that it is essential to the prosperity of the island that she should receive substantially the same treatment at our hands that she received from Spain while a Spanish colony, and that the markets of the United States should be opened to her as were the markets of Spain and Cuba before the transfer of allegiance. Congress has the legal right to regulate the customs duties between the United States and Porto Rico as it pleases; but the highest considerations of justice and good faith demand that we should not disappoint the confident expectation of sharing in our prosperity with which the people of Porto Rico so gladly transferred their allegiance to the United States, and that we should treat the interests of this people as our own; and I wish most strongly to urge that the customs duties between Porto Rico and the United States be removed.

Our temporary occupation of the island of Cuba involves a very simple plan of operation, with some difficulties in its application which are apt to be overlooked by those who are impatient for immediate results. The control which we are exercising in trust for the people of Cuba should not be, and of course will not be, continued any longer than is necessary to enable that people to establish a suitable government to which the control shall be transferred, which shall really represent the people of Cuba and be able to maintain order and discharge international obligations. When that government is established it will be its duty and right to solve for Cuba the problems above discussed in regard to Porto Rico. Our present duty is limited to giving every assistance in our power to the establishment of such a government, and to maintaining order and promoting the welfare of the people of Cuba during the period necessarily required for that process.

The conduct of the Cuban people has been admirable. There have, of course, been some agitators who have loudly voiced their discontent over not being allowed personally to conduct the government, but the substantial body of educated Cubans have shown themselves to be patriotic, appreciative, and helpful, while the great body of uneducated Cubans have been patient and law-abiding. The fact, however, that probably two-thirds of the people of the island are unable to read and write; that the people in general have had no experience in any real self-government, but have been for centuries under the dominion of arbitrary power; that the bloody conflicts which raged so long have necessarily left behind bitter factional feeling, make it necessary to proceed somewhat more slowly in the formation of a government which is to command universal respect and allegiance than would be necessary in a country accustomed to the discussion of public questions, familiar with the problems presented, and trained to the acceptance of the decisions reached by the ballot.

The year allowed by the treaty for the Spanish population of the island to elect whether they will be Cuban or Spanish citizens will expire on the eleventh of April next. It will then, for the first time, be possible to determine who are the citizens of Cuba entitled to take a part in her government. By that time it is believed that, the results of the census having been computed and tabulated, we shall be ready to provide for municipal elections, which will place all the local governments of the island in the hands of representatives elected by the people, and that when these local governments, thus elected, are established they will be ready to proceed to the formation of a representative convention to frame a constitution and provide for a general government of the island, to which the United States will surrender the reins of government. When that government is established the relations which exist between it and the United States will be matter for free and uncontrolled discussion between the two parties.

The uncertainty which retards the industrial development of Cuba and prevents the influx of capital is not only as to the character of the future government and the safety of investments, but an uncertainty as to the future market for the sugar product of the island, upon which the prosperity of the island chiefly rests. The competition of the bounty-fed beet-sugar product of Europe has already reduced the price which can be realized for cane sugar to a point so near the cost of production that the cane producer cannot pay expenses by the old method of production. Only the new and improved methods, on a large scale and in the most economical manner, and requiring large capital, make a successful competition on his part possible. The sugar producer of Cuba now finds himself confronted by two additional dangers — one, the prospect that the sugar of Porto Rico, like that of Hawaii and possibly that of the Philippines, may be admitted into the great market of the United States free of duty, while Cuban sugar is required to pay duty; and the other, the prospect of ratification by the Senate of the reciprocity treaties already negotiated, under which the sugar of the British West Indies would be admitted to the United States at a twenty per cent reduction of duties, while Cuban sugar would continue to pay the full duty.

The following table shows the comparative returns to the producers of sugar in the principal countries from which the United States derives its supply, after allowing for the duties imposed under the conditions above stated, and assuming the basis of the New York price July 1, 1899, of four and one-half cents per pound for standard, ninety-six test, centrifugal sugar:

Charges	Germany	Cuba	Java	English Colonies	Porto Rico	Hawaii
Duties:	Cents	Cents	Cents	Cents	Cents	Cents
Tariff	1.685	1.685	1.685	1.348	None	None
Countervailing	.259	None	None	None	None	None
Estimated freights	.080	.100	.300	.100	.180	.270
Insurance on f. o. b. value	.020	.025	.050	.028	.032	.090
	2.044					
Less bounty	.259					
	1.785					
F. o. b. value	2.715	2.690	2.465	3.024	4.288	4.140
	4.50	4.50	4.50	4.50	4.50	4.50
Foreign value above	2.71	2.69	2.46	3.02	4.28	4.14

It appears from this comparison that if these conditions are to exist, the Cuban producer would realize but 2.69 cents per pound for his product, as against 2.71 cents for the German, 3.02 cents for the British West Indian, 4.14 cents for the Hawaiian, and 4.28 cents for the Porto Rican producer.

Under these conditions, as the United States is the great market for Cuban sugar, and the prosperity of Cuba depends upon that market, it is highly probable that, however competent and efficient may be the government of Cuba into whose hands we surrender the control of the island, the first measure of self-preservation which that government will be compelled to consider will be to undertake to secure from the United States some tariff arrangement under which Cuba can sell her sugar at a profit. . . .

It does not seem that, so long as we retain the control of Cuba and preclude her people from making trade agreements or treaties on their own account, we ought to treat her sugar producers less favorably than we do their competitors in those of the West Indies which are subject to other powers, and I recommend that during the period of our occupation of the island the duties imposed upon the importation into the United States from Cuba of the products of that island be reduced to the same rates which will be imposed upon the goods imported from Jamaica in case the Senate shall ratify the pending reciprocity treaties. . . .

PORTO RICO

THE MILITARY AND CIVIL GOVERNMENT OF THE ISLAND

As Secretary of War, Mr. Root made two extended references to the situation in the island of Porto Rico, and the policy of the Administration as to the government of that island in passing from Spanish to American control. These were in the annual reports for 1899 and 1900. On May 1, 1900, the government of Porto Rico was transferred to the civil authorities constituted under the Act of Congress approved April 12 of that year, in accordance with Mr. Root's recommendations. Thereafter the island is not mentioned in Mr. Root's reports except that in his reports for 1902 and 1903, he dwelt upon the necessity of the construction of defensive works and of the proper fortification of the harbor of San Juan, in company with various other harbors acquired as a result of the Spanish-American War.

Conditions in Porto Rico

Extract from the Report of the Secretary of War for 1899[1]

THE year has been devoted to administering and improving the civil government of the island and instructing the people in the rudiments of self-government, and this has been done at every step in conference with the leading citizens of the island, and upon lines agreed upon between them and the military governor. The work has been retarded by the unfortunate industrial condition of the island, caused by the fact that the people were unable to find remunerative markets for their products.

The prevailing distress was heightened by the terrific hurricane which swept over the entire length of the island on August 8, 1899, followed by a deluge of rain and a tidal wave on the south coast. The result of this disaster was the loss of about three thousand lives, the destruction of sugar mills, dwellings, roads, bridges, and growing crops. The principal crop of the island is coffee, and fully two-thirds of the coffee crop of the year was destroyed. Over one hundred

[1] Page 17.

thousand people were reduced to absolute destitution, without homes or food or means to obtain food, and at the same time the avenues of communication were destroyed, so that many of the destitute were reached with the greatest difficulty.

An immediate appeal to the people of the United States through the War Department met with a prompt and vigorous response. . . . Whenever the quantities of food furnished by private charity were insufficient to maintain the regular supply, the deficiency was made up by this Department, at an aggregate cost of $392,342.63, not including cost of transportation.

For the distribution of these supplies and the succor of the unfortunate victims of the hurricane, the entire army in Porto Rico became a relief corps, and the work was prosecuted with a zeal, effectiveness, and humane spirit curiously at variance with traditional ideas of the object of a military organization. . . .

During the current year 786,290 persons (practically the entire population of the island) have been vaccinated at a cost of three cents and six mills for each person. A general system of education has been established, under a board of education consisting of two Americans and three Porto Ricans; a large number of American teachers have been secured in this country, and nearly every transport that sails from New York is carrying additions to the number. Under the former government the schools afforded opportunity for education of any description for only eight per cent of the children of school age in the island. Only from ten to twelve and a half per cent of the inhabitants of the island can read and write. At the time of American occupation the jails were found crowded with prisoners who had been confined for long periods without trial, and in many cases without being informed of the charges against them. These unfortunates have either been tried or set free. The courts have been to a great extent reorganized, and their proceedings simplified and expedited. The writ of habeas corpus has been introduced.

Arrangements have been made for the taking of the census in Porto Rico by the same methods applied to the island of Cuba.

At the time of change of sovereignty the island was in a condition of great disorder, and for a considerable period bandits collected in the mountains and committed depredations and maintained themselves by robbing the peaceful inhabitants. These have been dispersed and punished, and order has been thoroughly restored. A number of attempts have been made to secure a general participation by the people in municipal elections and the reform of municipal governments. The results in this respect have not been very satisfactory thus far. Further experiments in the way of municipal elections are now in progress.

Organization of the Civil Government

Extract from the Report of the Secretary of War for 1900[1]

On May 1, 1900, the government of Porto Rico was transferred to the civil authorities constituted under the act of Congress approved April twelfth of that year. The interval of five months since the date of the last report had been employed by the military authorities of the island in improving the civil administration, accustoming the people of Porto Rico to the exercise of the powers of government, and continuing the work of relief made necessary by the deplorable condition in which the island had been left by the great hurricane of August 8, 1899.

The further distribution of commissary supplies brought the total amount distributed from the time of the hurricane

[1] Page 37.

to the fifteenth of July, when the distribution was discontinued with the concurrence of the military governor, to a total of over 30,000,000 pounds of food, costing $831,480.16. This distribution was made by a board of charities, of which the chief surgeon of the military department was president, and in which the entire organization of the army in the department was utilized. To as great an extent as practicable the owners of the coffee plantations were utilized in the distribution of rations, and the able-bodied men receiving them were required, in return for rations, to engage in the work of recovering the plantations from the destruction wrought by the hurricane, in order that as soon as possible the production of coffee in the island might be revived.

In addition to the supplies contributed by the public, the central Porto Rican relief committee received contributions of money amounting to $81,090.58. Of this sum they applied $46,072.09 to the purchase of food and (by the special request of the board of charities of the island) of medical and hospital supplies and clothing. The expenses of the committee amounted to $2,053.16. To ascertain how the balance of $32,965.33 might most usefully be applied, the secretary of the committee made a personal visit to the island in May last, and after consulting with the board of charities and citizens of Porto Riço, he reported that it should be applied in aid of the establishment and maintenance of an asylum for the care of orphan children whose parents had lost their lives in, or in consequence of, the hurricane. That report has been approved, and that disposition will be made of the money.

For the purpose of furnishing further relief by giving employment instead of alms, and at the same time securing much-needed means of communication, the Department authorized, October 25, 1899, the expenditure of $200,000, and February 27 and May 14, 1900, the further expenditure of $750,000 for the construction of military roads. This construction has been in progress throughout the year under the direction of the engineer force of the Department, the work being continued by that body after the transfer of government by the request of the civil governor. Until the transfer of government the engineer officer of the department was also president of the board of public works, and in that capacity supervised the expenditure upon roads, public buildings, light-houses, and engineering and harbor works, for which $581,000 of civil insular funds had been allotted.

The telegraphic system of the island has been reconstructed by the Signal Corps, and the system is still operated by that corps at an approximate cost of $60,000 per year, which is paid out of the appropriations for the support of the army. . . .

The census of the island, which had been ordered at the time of the last annual report, has been completed by the same methods and covering the same subjects as in the case of the Cuban census. . . . Municipal elections were held throughout the island, under orders of the military commander prescribing qualifications of electors and the method of election. The qualifications prescribed were either the ability to read and write in some language, or the payment of at least one dollar in taxes within the preceding eighteen months.

The registration and election at each polling place were under the supervision of an officer or noncommissioned officer of the army, but no armed soldier was present at or near any voting place. There was no disturbance and no reason to question the fairness and honesty of the election. Under that election the mayors, town councils, municipal judges, and boards of education of all the towns of Porto Rico, who perform the functions of government most important for the people, were elected by the people themselves.

The system of taxation in the island was found to be exceedingly defective and burdensome. It tended to repress and penalize industry and activity, and the necessities of the people had required the remission of taxes to such an extent that there remained practically no system of internal taxation of any consequence. For the purpose of securing a new system which should be effective and which should apply sound principles to the social and business conditions of the island, the military governor asked for the assistance of a competent expert, and Professor J. H. Hollander of Johns Hopkins University was sent to the island as a special commissioner to aid the military governor in the framing of an adequate system of taxation.

Upon the organization of the civil government under the act of Congress of April 12, 1900, Professor Hollander was appointed treasurer of the island, and thus enabled to continue the work for which he originally went to the island and in which he had already made satisfactory progress. The adoption of a new system of taxation must necessarily await the action of the Porto Rican legislature, now just elected. . . . Accordingly, when legislation for the island was under consideration, the military governor requested that a portion of the existing customs duties which Congress was proposing to remove, sufficient to pay the ordinary running expenses of the insular government, should be retained until the new internal taxation should become effective. This request was complied with by the provisions of the act of April 12, 1900, which, while removing the customs duties between Porto Rico and the United States, suspended the operation of the removal as to fifteen per cent of those duties until the island should be able to pay its expenses by other taxation, limiting the period of suspension, however, to two years.

After all the disorder, lawlessness, and distress consequent upon a state of war, the withdrawal of accustomed control, the transfer of sovereignty to a people unfamiliar with the language, the customs, and the prejudices of the island, the long delay in the legislation establishing civil and political rights and business relations, the poverty, ruin, and suffering caused by the great hurricane, the military governor was able to say, at the close of his administration:

On April 30 the machinery of civil government was in the charge of experienced public officers, and the organization, with departments, bureaus, and other branches, both insular and municipal, was such that the new government ordered by Congress to be instituted could the following day be launched and carried forward in an efficient and economical manner.

The courts of the island were all in the discharge of their proper functions. The dockets were not crowded as they were a year before. The prisons and jails were well kept and were not overflowing. The public highways were in fine condition and were being rapidly extended. The amount that could be spared from the treasury for education was being applied in such a manner as to give instruction according to modern methods to over 30,000 children. The laws of taxation had been so changed that very heavy and onerous burdens had been removed from the poor.

In office in every municipality were officers who in every instance were the choice of the electors, thus granting to municipalities almost complete autonomy.

Life and property were everywhere secure, and this without the use of troops for protection. Notwithstanding the most grievous losses suffered by the people from raids of banditti, from arson, from disturbance of trade relations, from losses of Spanish markets without corresponding gains elsewhere, from unsettled conditions resulting from the use of a currency which suffered a heavy discount when referred to a gold basis, and, finally, from the almost overwhelming disaster of August of last year, when seven-tenths of all the maturing crops were blotted out of existence — notwithstanding all these obstacles and burdens, the military governor was able to turn over to the civil governor the comfortable balance in the insular treasury of over $300,000.

As commander of the Military Department of Porto Rico and the last military governor, I think I may not inappropriately say that the trust confided to the army by the President and the people has not been abused, but has been wisely and justly exercised in the interest and for the benefit of the inhabitants of this beautiful island. . . .

I concur in these statements, and I wish to add to them an expression of grateful appreciation of the devotion, judgment, good temper, and ability exhibited by General Davis in the performance of his difficult duties, and of the faithful service of the officers of his command.

CUBA

THE DEVELOPMENT AND ESTABLISHMENT OF THE REPUBLIC

President McKinley's message to Congress of April 11, 1898, recommending that the United States intervene in Cuba, disclaimed any purpose of acquiring territory by conquest, and the joint resolution of Congress of April 20, 1898, demanding that Spain withdraw from the island committed the United States to the independence of Cuba.

In Article 1 of the treaty of peace between Spain and the United States, signed at Paris, December 10, 1898, Spain relinquished "all claim of sovereignty over and title to Cuba." The island was not ceded to although it was occupied by the United States, which felt itself bound by the terms of the resolution declaring war against Spain to turn the island over to its people. This declaration of intention was not a contract, but it was properly regarded as creating an equitable estoppel against the United States in favor of the Cubans who had aided it in driving the Spanish forces from the island. The United States occupied Cuba, and during its occupation prepared it for self-government, to be turned over to its people when that time should have come. On May 20, 1902, the world saw the unwonted spectacle of a country living up to its solemn promise and turning over a coveted possession to the inhabitants thereof in pursuance of a solemnly declared purpose, the hauling down of the American flag, the symbol of sovereignty during the occupation, and the unenforced, voluntary evacuation of Cuba Libre by the American troops.

Mr. Root's task as Secretary of War, from the time of the relinquishment of Cuba under the treaty and its release to its people, was to prepare Cuba for self-government and to determine the relations between Cuba and the United States.

The solution of the problem recommended by Mr. Root and adopted and put into effect by the Government of the United States is described in Mr. Root's reports as Secretary of War. The solution was:

1. Not to sail away and leave the island to disorder and probable anarchy and bloodshed, but to remain long enough to create a complete civil government composed of Cubans trained to the performance of their duties, and to turn the island over to the Cuban people with that government in operation as a going concern.

2. To require from the Cubans guarantees for the conduct of their government and to prevent the island from falling into the hands of any other nation so that the United States would not be placed in a worse position than before by reason of turning Spain out of the island. This was accomplished by including in the Cuban constitution and in the legislation of the United States and in a treaty between the United States and Cuba the provisions known as the Platt Amendment.

These provisions were presented to the Cuban Constitutional Convention pursuant to Mr. Root's instructions to the military governor of Cuba dated February

9, 1901. They had previously been approved by President McKinley and his Cabinet.

The clause relating to sanitation, which was not included in the original instructions, was incorporated upon the suggestion of Major-General Leonard Wood, then Military Governor of Cuba.

It appearing desirable to incorporate the above provisions in the statutes of the United States, Mr. Root's instructions to the military governor of Cuba were later introduced in the Senate by Senator Orville H. Platt at the request of President McKinley and Mr. Root, and were adopted as an amendment to the Army Appropriation bill of March 2, 1901, thus becoming known as the Platt Amendment. The Platt Amendment was subsequently incorporated in identical terms in the Cuban constitution and in the treaty of July 1, 1904, between Cuba and the United States.

With unimportant changes of phraseology, Articles 1, 2, 3, and 4 of Mr. Root's instructions became Articles 1, 2, 3, and 4 of the Platt Amendment.

The provision relating to sanitation, suggested by Major-General Wood in his letter of February 19, 1901, became Article 5 of the Platt Amendment.

Article 5 of Mr. Root's instructions became Article 7 of the Amendment, and Article 6 of the Amendment, concerning the Isle of Pines, and Article 8 of the Amendment, requiring further assurance by treaty, were inserted by the Senate Committee on Cuban Relations, of which Senator Platt was chairman.

General Wood's letter, referred to in the previous paragraph, has not hitherto been printed. As it is an historical document of the first importance in connection with the transfer of Cuba to its people, it follows in full:

HEADQUARTERS MILITARY GOVERNOR,
ISLAND OF CUBA,

HAVANA, February 19, 1901.

THE HONORABLE
THE SECRETARY OF WAR,
WASHINGTON, D. C.

SIR: I have the honor to acknowledge receipt of your communication of February 9th, which was transmitted to me first by cable and later under the personal care of Colonel H. L. Scott.

On receipt of the instructions by cable I immediately assembled the Committee on Relations to Exist between Cuba and the United States and made known to them the five articles or provisions which, in the opinion of the Executive branch of the Government, represent the wishes of the United States in all that pertains to the proposed relations between the Government of the United States and the people of Cuba.

I was particularly careful to impress upon them that Congress might in its wisdom insist upon different conditions or relations, but that the proposition submitted embodied those which in the opinion of the Executive branch of the Government should exist and that they were the only ones which they could at present consider.

There seemed to be no serious objection to any of the conditions excepting the Fifth; that in reference to Naval Stations. There was also some apparent objection to the terms of the Third Article in reference to the intervention and maintenance of a stable government to protect life and property, etc., as provided for by the Treaty of Paris. I informed them that this condition was one which, in my opinion, could not be modified as it embodied the obligations which the United States had assumed under the above-mentioned treaty. I do not think the opposition on this point will be serious. The matter is now under discussion and I believe the committee is canvassing the Convention as to the acceptability of the different provisions.

In my opinion the demands are liberal, equitable and just and should be insisted on throughout. It is very probable that we shall have to exercise directly the intervention provided for under the Third Article and it is certain that we should, were it not known in Cuba that in case of lack of stability and failure to observe the provisions imposed by the Treaty of Paris the United States would promptly intervene. Such knowledge will probably act as a check on the government to come.

In reference to the Naval Stations: the objection to this seems to be a matter principally of sentiment combined with a certain amount of selfishness. Among the elements now dominating in the politics of the island there is little or no gratitude for what has been done by the United States. Among the bulk of the people there is a feeling of appreciation and gratitude.

There is another phase of this Cuban situation which seems to be of vital importance; that is the sanitary conditions which will probably exist in Havana and in other large cities under a Cuban government. As I understand it the purpose of the war was not only to assist the Cubans, but, in a general sense, to abate a nuisance. It is probable that if we leave the island of Cuba without a definite agreement with the government to come in reference to the maintenance of good sanitary conditions, that we shall soon find Havana and all other large cities in practically the same condition of sanitation as during the Spanish War and a menace to our Southern seaports and the consequent interference with commerce will continue. As a rule, the people of the island are immune to yellow fever and, consequently, take little interest in the elaborate sanitary precautions which have been instituted under the American rule and which have resulted in reducing the death rate in Havana alone, from 45 per 1000 as an average death rate in times of peace to 24 and a fraction. If possible, I think that there should also be some provision in reference to the exercise of proper control and supervision over the construction of the new system of sewers and pavements for the City of Havana. It is highly probable that after the withdrawal of the Americans this work will be carried out in anything but a complete and perfect manner.

This question of control of sanitation of Cuban ports is, in my opinion, of vital importance to the United States.

Very respectfully,

(Signed) LEONARD WOOD,

Major-General, Military Governor.

In that portion of the instructions to the Military Governor of Cuba which became Article 3 of the Platt Amendment, Mr. Root said that:

> Upon the transfer of the control of Cuba to the government established under the new constitution Cuba consents that the United States reserve and retain the right of intervention for the preservation of Cuban independence and maintenance of a stable government, adequately protecting life, property, and individual liberty, and discharging the obligations with respect to Cuba imposed by the Treaty of Paris on the United States and now assumed and undertaken by the Government of Cuba.

As the reservation of the right of intervention seemed to cause some uneasiness in the Cuban constitutional convention, it was thought advisable to interpret the sense in which the United States understood the right to intervene and the circumstances which would justify and require it. It was necessary that the right and the circumstances should be understood in the same sense by Cuba; therefore, Mr. Root put the interpretation of the Government of the United States upon this article in his telegram to the Military Governor dated April 3, 1902, directing him at the same time to lay the telegram before the Cuban constitutional convention, which was then in session, in order that the article should be adopted with the interpretation which the United States had placed upon it. The telegram which the Military Governor laid before the convention, pursuant to instructions, was thus worded:

> You are authorized to state officially that in the view of the President the intervention described in the third clause of the Platt Amendment is not synonymous with intermeddling or interference with the affairs of the Cuban Government, but the formal action of the Government of the United States, based upon just and substantial grounds, for the preservation of Cuban independence, and the maintenance of a government adequate for the protection of life, property, and individual liberty, and adequate for discharging the obligations with respect to Cuba imposed by the Treaty of Paris on the United States.

The Cuban Government, as previously stated, was turned over to the people of the island on May 20, 1902. Trouble broke out in the island in 1906, and, exercising the right of intervention contained in the statutes of the United States, the Cuban constitution and the treaty between Cuba and the United States, President Roosevelt intervened. A provisional governor was appointed for Cuba and various officials were selected to aid in the work of reorganization. American troops were sent to the island and the necessary measures taken to restore and maintain order. Upon the accomplishment of the purposes of the occupation, the United States, on March 31, 1909, again withdrew from the island (Cir. No. 92, War Dept., Dec. 31, 1909), leaving Cuba for the second time to its newly elected and duly constituted authorities. (See Foreign Relations of the United States, 1906, Part I, pp. 480, et seq.)

This chapter of Cuban history is, it is believed, a unique chapter in the world's history, and it reflects great credit upon the Republic which adopted the policy and upon the wisdom and constructive ability of the statesman who devised it. It should be said, in this connection, that Mr. Root's policy in regard to Cuba was intended by him not merely to apply to the island of Cuba but to form the basis of a future Caribbean policy for the United States. The policy was conceived in the conviction that the construction and operation of the Panama Canal under the exclusive authority of the United States impose greater burdens upon this country in that part of the world.

CONDITIONS IN CUBA

Extract from the Report of the Secretary of War for 1899[1]

ON December 13, 1898, the Division of Cuba was created, consisting of the geographical departments and provinces of the island of Cuba, with headquarters in the city of Havana. The division was placed under the command of Major-General John R. Brooke, who, in addition to the command of the troops of the division, was directed to exercise authority as military governor of the island. On January 1, 1899, pursuant to the provisions of the protocol and the arrangements made by the evacuation commission, Spanish sovereignty was formally relinquished and the government of the island was transferred to the military governor as the representative of the President of the United States. On February 6, 1899, the evacuation of Cuba was completed by the sailing of the last of the Spanish army from the port of Cienfuegos.

The United States forces stationed in Cuba at the time of the transfer of the control consisted of 1,004 officers and 22,827 enlisted men.

The retiring army left a large Spanish population, and the long war for independence had engendered an excited and bitter feeling between them and the Cubans. The country had long been with little governmental control, except that exercised in the immediate neighborhood of the troops who were about departing. The ordinary social restraints had been destroyed, the cities were crowded with thousands of refugees and *reconcentrados*, who were exasperated by suffering and the death of their families and friends, and it was deemed necessary to take especial precautions for the prevention of riot and bloodshed at the time when Spanish con-

[1] Page 12.

trol was removed. It is gratifying to note that the transfer was accomplished with entire harmony and without disorder, the troops of the United States replacing those of Spain step by step, as the latter retired, until a complete substitution was effected.

On the twenty-fourth of January the Division of Cuba was portioned into seven geographical divisions, as follows: Pinar del Rio, Province of Havana, Havana, Matanzas, Santa Clara, Santiago, and Puerto Principe.

On April 19 and July 1, 1899, these departments were consolidated into four, leaving the Division of Cuba divided into the Department of the Province of Havana and Pinar del Rio, Department of Havana, Department of Matanzas and Santa Clara, and Department of Santiago and Puerto Principe.

Since the Spanish evacuation there have been no strictly military operations, and the officers of the army in Cuba have been largely occupied in conducting, under the direction of the military governor and the department commanders, a general civil administration for which no other governmental machinery existed, and in aiding the existing municipal governments in the performance of their duties. . . .

In all these respects satisfactory progress has been made. The use of troops to maintain order was necessary for but a short period. Forces of civil police organized from the people of the island have been substituted, and are performing their duties efficiently. The part played by our troops in the maintenance of order is now substantially but the restraining influence of their presence. . . .

The sanitary conditions of the cities and towns throughout the island were found to be as bad as it is possible to conceive. Thorough and systematic inspections were made, sanitary corps were organized, streets were cleaned, sewers were opened, cesspools and sinks were emptied, public and private buildings were disinfected, methods of disposing of refuse were adopted, water supplies were improved, and rules were established and enforced to prevent a recurrence of similar conditions. In the larger cities a thoroughly good sanitary condition will require the establishment of grades, the construction of adequate sewer systems, and increase of water supplies. . . .

The city of Havana is now undergoing a house-to-house renovation and disinfection. Some two thousand houses have already been treated, and the work continues at the rate of one hundred and twenty to one hundred and twenty-five houses per day. The reports show that in no case has the process of disinfection failed to eradicate the infection, and no case of fever has occurred except from a fresh infection. The total deaths from yellow fever in Havana for the first ten months of each year since 1889 have been as follows:

Year	Deaths	Year	Deaths
1890	314	1895	512
1891	318	1896	950
1892	272	1897	991
1893	469	1898	134
1894	369	1899	63

The deaths from all causes in Havana during the first few months after our occupation were numerous, owing to the great number of sick and dying who were there at the time of the Spanish evacuation. The rate has been steadily decreased until in September it was brought down to the annual rate of 27 per thousand and in October to 26.6 per thousand.

Similar conditions existing at Santiago were treated in a similar manner and with great thoroughness and effectiveness, and an outbreak of yellow fever at that point was speedily controlled and overcome.

During the six months ending June 30, 1899, we expended from the insular revenues $1,712,014.20 for sanitation,

$293,881.27 for charities and hospitals, and $88,944.03 for aid to the destitute.

The revival of industry has been necessarily slow, but has made gratifying progress. Many of the people who had been driven into the towns during the reconcentration period have returned to the country and recommenced the cultivation of the land. Tobacco has been planted very largely and sugar to a less degree. In many parts of the island there is an adequate demand for labor at the rates which were customary before the war. . . .

The rule of administration of the civil government of the island has been to employ the people of Cuba themselves to the fullest extent possible, and to furnish to the Cubans, during our occupation, an opportunity for training in the honest and efficient performance of official duties which has never been afforded to them before.

As soon as the social conditions had become sufficiently normal to make it practicable, provision was made for taking a census of the island, designed to furnish the basis for the organization of the Cuban government to which we shall transfer the control now held by us in trust for the people of Cuba. . . . The entire force through which the census is being taken is composed of Cubans, with one well-known citizen of each of the provinces as the supervisor for that province, and with enumerators nominated by him from residents of the province. The scope of the inquiry and the blanks, forms, and orders employed were determined upon by the Department after conference between the officials of the United States Census Bureau and the supervisors who came to Washington for that purpose. The taking of the census was commenced at the appointed time, and it is now substantially completed, with entire success. . . .

The Organization of the Civil Government of Cuba

Extract from the Report of the Secretary of War for 1900[1]

The conduct of affairs in Cuba during the year has been a continuance of the process of aiding the Cuban people in the development of a Cuban government in such a way that when fully organized it shall be stable and efficient. This has been done by guiding the Cubans in the first steps of systematic self-government and by introducing, mainly through the instrumentality of Cuban officers, such reforms in the various branches of administration as shall serve to put the business of government in fairly good condition when a complete Cuban administration finally assumes control of government in the island.

The census of the island was successfully completed. . . . The results, which were carefully computed and tabulated by the methods employed in the United States, show a total population of 1,572,797, of whom 533,498, or thirty-four per cent, are able to read and write, while sixty-six per cent are illiterate. Fifty-seven and eight-tenths per cent, or considerably more than half the entire population, consist of native-born whites; the foreign whites constitute but nine per cent, and the negro and mixed race thirty-two per cent.

On the whole this exhibits rather better material for government than had been anticipated, although if sixty-six per cent of the people were to continue illiterate, the permanence of free constitutional government could hardly be expected, and a definite ascertainment of the facts emphasizes the urgent necessity for popular education. . . .

The census having been completed and the period given for Spanish residents to make their election as to citizenship having expired on April 11, 1900, steps were immediately

[1] Page 28.

taken for the election of municipal governments by the people. In view of the fact that sixty-six per cent of the people could not read and write, it was not deemed advisable that absolutely unrestricted suffrage should be established, and, after very full conference with leading Cubans, including all the heads of the great departments of state, a general agreement was reached upon a basis of suffrage, which provided that every native male Cuban or Spaniard who had elected to take Cuban citizenship, of full age, might vote if he either could read and write, or owned real estate or personal property to the value of $250, or had served in and been honorably discharged from the Cuban army; thus according a voice in the government of the country to every one who had the intelligence to acquire the rudiments of learning, the thrift to accumulate property, or the patriotism to fight for his country.

On the eighteenth of April an election law, which aims to apply the best examples of our American election statutes to the existing conditions of Cuba, was promulgated for the guidance of the proposed election. On the sixteenth of June an election was held throughout the island in which the people of Cuba in all the municipalities, which include the entire island, elected all their municipal officers. The boards of registration and election were composed of Cubans selected by the Cubans themselves. No United States soldier or officer was present at or in the neighborhood of any polling place. There was no disturbance.

After the newly elected municipal officers had been installed and had commenced the performance of their duties, an order was made enlarging the powers of the municipal governments and putting into their hands as much of the government of the people as was practicable. As soon as the new municipal governments were fairly established the following call for a constitutional convention was issued:

HEADQUARTERS DIVISION OF CUBA,
HAVANA, July 25, 1900.

The Military Governor of Cuba directs the publication of the following instructions:

WHEREAS, The Congress of the United States by its joint resolution of April 20, 1898, declared

"That the people of the island of Cuba are, and of right ought to be, free and independent:

"That the United States hereby disclaims any disposition or intention to exercise sovereignty, jurisdiction, or control over said island except for the pacification thereof, and asserts its determination, when that is accomplished, to leave the government and control of the island to its people";

And whereas, the people of Cuba have established municipal governments, deriving their authority from the suffrages of the people given under just and equal laws, and are now ready, in like manner, to proceed to the establishment of a general government which shall assume and exercise sovereignty, jurisdiction, and control over the island: Therefore

It is ordered, That a general election be held in the island of Cuba on the third Saturday of September, in the year nineteen hundred, to elect delegates to a convention to meet in the city of Havana, at twelve o'clock noon on the first Monday of November, in the year nineteen hundred, to frame and adopt a constitution for the people of Cuba, and, as a part thereof, to provide for and agree with the Government of the United States upon the relations to exist between that Government and the Government of Cuba, and to provide for the election by the people of officers under such constitution and the transfer of government to the officers so elected.

The election will be held in the several voting precincts of the island under and pursuant to the provisions of the electoral law of April 18, 1900, and the amendments thereof.

The people of the several provinces will elect delegates in number proportionate to their populations as determined by the census, viz.:

The people of the province of Pinar del Rio will elect three (3) delegates.

The people of the province of Havana will elect eight (8) delegates.

The people of the province of Matanzas will elect four (4) delegates.

The people of the province of Santa Clara will elect seven (7) delegates.

The people of the province of Puerto Principe will elect two (2) delegates.

The people of the province of Santiago de Cuba will elect seven (7) delegates.

J. B. HICKEY,
Assistant Adjutant-General.

Under this call a second election was held on the fifteenth of September, under the same law, with some slight amendments, and under the same conditions as the municipal elections. The election was wholly under the charge of Cubans, and without any participation or interference whatever by officers or troops of the United States. The thirty-one members of the constitutional convention were elected, and they convened at Havana at the appointed time. The sessions of the convention were opened in the city of Havana on the fifth of November by the military governor, with the following statement:

To the Delegates of the Constitutional Convention of Cuba:

Gentlemen: As military governor of the island, representing the President of the United States, I call this convention to order.

It will be your duty, first, to frame and adopt a constitution for Cuba, and, when that has been done, to formulate what, in your opinion, ought to be the relations between Cuba and the United States.

The constitution must be adequate to secure a stable, orderly, and free government.

When you have formulated the relations which, in your opinion, ought to exist between Cuba and the United States, the Government of the United States will doubtless take such action on its part as shall lead to a final and authoritative agreement between the people of the two countries to the promotion of their common interests.

All friends of Cuba will follow your deliberations with the deepest interest, earnestly desiring that you shall reach just conclusions, and that, by the dignity, individual self-restraint, and wise conservatism which shall characterize your proceedings, the capacity of the Cuban people for representative government may be signally illustrated.

The fundamental distinction between true representative government and dictatorship is that in the former every representative of the people, in whatever office, confines himself strictly within the limits of his defined powers. Without such restraint there can be no free constitutional government.

Under the order pursuant to which you have been elected and convened you have no duty and no authority to take part in the present government of the island. Your powers are strictly limited by the terms of that order.

The convention has completed its organization and is now in session.

Especial attention has been given by the military government to the development of primary education. The enrollment of the public schools of Cuba immediately before the last war shows 36,306 scholars, but an examination of the reports containing these figures indicates that probably less than half the names enrolled represented actual attendance. There were practically no separate school buildings, but the scholars were collected in the residences of the teachers. There were few books, and practically no maps, blackboards, desks, or other school apparatus.

The instruction consisted largely in learning by rote, the catechism being the principal text-book, and the girls occupying their time chiefly in embroidery. The teachers were allowed to eke out their unpaid salaries by accepting fees from the pupils, and since less than one-tenth of the children of school age could be accommodated, the result of the fee system was that the children of the poor were either excluded or wholly neglected. Even these poor apologies for public schools were, to a great extent, broken up by the war, and in December, 1899, the entire public-school enrollment of the island numbered 21,435. . . . In June, 1900, it had grown to 143,120.

This great development was accomplished under the Cuban secretary of public instruction and the Cuban commissioner of public schools, with the able and experienced assistance of Mr. Alexis E. Frye as superintendent. It is governed by a school law modeled largely upon the law of Ohio. . . . The schools are subject to constant and effective inspection and the attendance is practically identical with the enrollment.

The schools are separated from the residences of the teachers, and each schoolroom has its separate teacher. The courses and methods of instruction are those most approved in this country. The text-books are translations into Spanish of American text-books. For the supply of material $150,000 were, in the first instance, appropriated from the insular treasury, and afterwards, upon a single order, 100,000 full sets of desks, text-books, scholars' supplies, etc., were purchased upon public advertisement in this country at an expense of about three-quarters of a million dollars.

All over the island the old Spanish barracks and barracks occupied by the American troops, which have been withdrawn, are being turned into schoolrooms after thorough renovation. The pressure for education is earnest and universal. The appropriations of this year from the insular treasury for that purpose will amount to about four and a half million dollars; but great as the development has been, it will be impossible, for a long time yet to come, to meet fully with the resources of the island the demand for the learning so long withheld. . . .

During the past summer, through the generosity of Harvard University and its friends, who raised a fund of $70,000 for that purpose, 1,281 Cuban teachers were enabled to attend a summer school of instruction at Cambridge, designed to fit them for their duties. They were drawn from every municipality and almost every town in the island. They were collected from the different ports of the island by five United States transports, which carried them to Boston, and, at the expiration of their visit, took them to New York and thence to Havana and to their homes.

They were lodged and boarded in and about the University at Cambridge, and visited the libraries and museums and the educational institutions and manufacturing establishments in the neighborhood of Boston. Through the energy of Mr. Frye money was raised to enable them to visit New York and Washington. They were returned to their homes without a single accident or loss, full of new ideas and of zeal for the educational work in which they had found so much sympathy and encouragement.

The issue of rations which characterized the first year of American occupation has been discontinued and has been succeeded by an extensive reëstablishment, renovation, and reorganization of the charitable institutions of the island. These were left at the close of the war without funds or supplies, and, with comparatively few exceptions, consisting mainly of the Sisters of the religious orders, without attendance. Such of them as were not closed were dilapidated, filthy, and unsanitary. The hospitals were practically without apparatus, medicines, or physicians. The children in the asylums were receiving but little education, insufficient food, and insufficient care.

A comprehensive law governing the department of charities was adopted on the seventh of July last, and, under the able direction of Major Edwin St. J. Greble, the head of the department, has been put into effective operation. . . . All of the buildings have been cleaned and renovated and receive regular and systematic support.

There are now receiving Government aid in Cuba thirty-eight hospitals, four asylums for the aged, twelve orphan asylums, two dispensaries for the poor, one insane asylum, three leper hospitals, two reform schools, one training school for boys, one for girls, and one emergency hospital in Santiago de Cuba. In the orphan asylums a strong effort has been made to secure the placing of children in private families throughout the island, and the effort has met with great success.

As prosperity has increased, many parents who had been unable to support their children and had left them in these institutions have claimed them and taken them to their homes, and large numbers of other children have been placed in private families, under proper pledges for their care and education, secured by careful investigation beforehand, and afterwards by systematic personal inspection. For the children still remaining, a thorough system of industrial education which will fit them for self-support has been inaugurated.

The hospitals have been supplied with medicines and surgical apparatus and attendance, and trained nurses brought from the United States are engaged in the instruction of trained nurses in Cuba. At the civil hospital No. 1 in Havana there are five American trained nurses, and a training school for nurses has been started for women with accommodations for forty scholars. At the civil hospital in Matanzas there are four American nurses and a training school for nurses with accommodations for thirty scholars. At the civil hospital in Cienfuegos there is one American trained nurse and about sixteen scholars; at Remedios, one American trained nurse and eighteen scholars.

Each of the charitable institutions is limited in its expenditures, in excess of such funds as it may have, to a carefully considered appropriation of insular funds, the expenditure of which is subject to regular and systematic inspection. Unless it were in the Mercedes Hospital in Havana, there was not a place in Cuba at the time of American occupation to which a patient could go for either medical or surgical treatment with any reasonable prospect of proper facilities and care.

The condition of the insane was particularly distressing. They were confined in cells in the jails all over the island, filthy and ragged, and treated literally like wild beasts. All these unfortunates have been collected and taken to the large insane asylum in Havana, which has been put in good order, and they are cared for in accordance with the dictates of modern humanity.

The prisons in the island were filled to overflowing with wretched creatures living in indescribable filth and squalor.

An early inspection of the woman's prison in Havana disclosed the fact that the women had no other place to sleep than on the floor, and were unable to appear in a body because they were without clothes to cover their nakedness; and they came before the inspector one by one, passing the same garment from one to another.

The cruelty of these conditions is more impressive from the fact that many of the unfortunate inmates had never been tried, or convicted of any offense. As the simplest way of dealing with that evil, a board of pardons was constituted in January, which visited all the prisons and examined the inmates. They found many who had been for long periods waiting trial, and in one instance this period had extended for eleven years. So far as the offenses with which they were charged could be ascertained, a large part of these people had been punished far more severely, whether they were innocent or guilty, than they could have been upon conviction. . . .

The intolerable delays of criminal procedure which thus punished the innocent equally with the guilty, and punished both without any opportunity for trial, have been to a great extent obviated by the establishment of correctional courts throughout the island, modeled upon the court which, under the direction of Captain Pitcher, has proved so successful in Havana, and in which petty offenses are summarily dealt with and disposed of, and the innocent have an opportunity to be promptly relieved from prosecution.

As a further safeguard against the recurrence of the evils described, an order has been made providing for the writ of habeas corpus to go into effect in December. The character and use of that writ do not yet seem to be fully understood by the Cubans, who are quite unfamiliar with it, but it will doubtless in time become with them, as it is with us, an effective instrument for the protection of liberty.

One of the results of these changes of procedure is that many of the prisons in the island are now wholly without inmates. Many other amendments of the law, improvements of the courts, and procedure, and reforms of specific abuses have been accomplished. All these things have been done with the concurrence and mainly through the instrumentality of Cubans, and in such a way that the Cubans have been learning how to do them and how to maintain the improved conditions and continue the reforms when the government comes entirely into their hands.

Public Works

There has been great activity in public works. Our officers have been renovating, repairing, and reconstructing public buildings, building extensive and enduring roads and sewers and waterworks, and inspecting and cleansing private and public buildings and paving streets in most of the cities and towns of the island. . . .

A number of large light-houses have been constructed, beacons have been set, and harbors have been buoyed, and in every proper field of public enterprise there has been the greatest activity on the part of Cubans under American guidance in doing things for the public interest, which have been wholly neglected for the past hundred years.

The tariff has been completely revised, and an independent treasury for the island has been established in which the revenues of the island are deposited and kept as they are received. . . .

The revenues for the fiscal year ending June 30, 1900, amounted to $17,333,484.10, as against $7,397,148.57 for the preceding six months. The revival of industry continues; the tobacco crop is large and fine; the area planted in sugar cane is continually extended; the production of fruit at the eastern end of the island is increasing; the mines of Santiago are in full operation; labor is in demand at good wages.

Curiously enough, now that Spanish sovereignty has departed from the island a current of Spanish immigration is setting in. More than forty thousand Spaniards, chiefly hardy and industrious people from the north of Spain, have come to the island during the year, and it is estimated that before the end of December the number will have reached fifty thousand. They are useful and welcome additions to the industry of the island.

Only doubt as to the stability of the future government and uncertainty as to the continuance of a market for her products retards the influx of capital and the development of Cuba's extraordinary resources.

Further Progress in Civil Government

Extract from the Report of the Secretary of War for 1901[1]

The government of the island of Cuba during the past year has been peaceful and orderly. There has been no occasion for interference by the United States forces with the ordinary administration of law. Following the plan of steadily training the people in performing the duties of government, the organization of the rural guard has been perfected, and that body has been placed under one head, and now includes a total of 1,300 men and officers, armed with modern carbines and well mounted. The municipal police, which during the formative stage were supported from the general fund, have been placed finally upon the proper and intended footing of support by the municipalities themselves. In order that upon the withdrawal of our troops the island may not be without a force competent to take charge of her coast forti-

[1] Page 36.

fications, several companies of Cuban troops have been organized, which, while maintained at insular expense, are assigned to our coast artillery companies in the island as second platoons for the purpose of instruction and discipline, and to fit them for the duties of coast defense.

A gradual reduction is being made in the excessive number of municipalities in the western provinces for the purpose of lightening taxation and increasing efficiency. There has been a great reduction in the number of asylums and pauper institutions. Beggars are practically unknown in the island. There are supported by the state thirty-four hospitals, containing 2,844 beds. Six training schools for female nurses have been established under the tuition of American trained nurses, with Cuban girls as pupils, with regular courses, examinations, and degrees. The Government training schools for boys and girls have been enlarged. The bureau for placing indigent children, mentioned in my last report, has been thoroughly established, and has during the year returned over 1,200 children to their relatives and placed 437 in other families. There are still 2,010 orphans under the care and supervision of the state. The lepers of the island have been gathered into two institutions, and the total number under treatment is now 134.

Six private institutions assisted by the state contain 362 aged poor. Extensive improvements have been made in the insane asylums, and they now contain 835 inmates. The prisons have been repaired and improved, and each jail has been provided with a physician and the necessary medicines. School instruction has been inaugurated in the larger jails. Extensive repairs of streets and sanitary work have been done in Havana, Santiago, Cienfuegos, and Santa Clara. Sewerage and paving plans for Havana have been completed and advertised for, and the contract has been awarded. Plans have been prepared for harbor improvements at Matanzas, and a contract for $550,000 has been awarded for the deepening of the harbor at Cardenas. Important first-class lights have been established at Colorado Reefs and Bahía Honda on the north coast of Cuba, and many harbors have been buoyed and properly marked. Public schools have increased in efficiency. The school law has proved thoroughly successful. Its democratic character and the local control which it gives, combined with efficient central supervision are satisfactory.

There are 121 boards of education elected by the people, and as these boards become familiar with their duties the administration of the school law improves. The system has been kept entirely out of politics. The work of changing the old *cuartels* or barracks throughout the island into schoolhouses has progressed, and $250,000 have been expended upon this work during the year with good results. There is still, however, great need for additional schoolhouses and thoroughly instructed teachers.

There has been a general improvement in the administration of justice, but the courts are still far from what they should be. There is difficulty in obtaining the proper personnel. The number of men suitable for the judicial career is limited. One of the greatest dangers which confronts the new government is the difficulty in obtaining an absolutely sound judiciary. Trials, however, are in general shorter and more prompt than formerly, and witnesses are more willing to testify. . . .

A systematic combat with tuberculosis, which has one of the largest death rates, has been inaugurated. Systematic vaccination against smallpox is going on throughout the entire island. The death rate from malaria in the large towns has been much reduced by sanitary improvements. The eastern part of the island is entirely free from yellow fever. The western part is practically free, there being but a few cases in or about Havana. This dreaded disease has passed from one of the leading causes of death to one of the least frequent. The reduction of the death rate in Havana alone, as compared with the former death rate, shows an average of approximately 3,700 lives per year saved, and Havana has changed from one of the most unhealthy cities to one of the most healthy. . . . This practically absolute control of yellow fever, has come as the result of the investigations as to its causes, prosecuted under the direction of the military government.

Immediately preceding American occupation the Spanish government of Cuba was occupying and using for government purposes a large amount of valuable real estate which had formerly been the property of the Roman Catholic Church, and which was held by the Crown subject to the results of a long series of negotiations and agreements between the Crown of Spain and the Holy See. The government also held a large number of "censos" or mortgages upon property in different parts of the island which had been given to the church for various religious purposes, and which had been taken over by the Crown and held under the agreements referred to. The Crown of Spain on its part recognized and complied with an obligation to pay to the church a large annual sum for its maintenance and support.

With American occupation the payment of this annual sum ceased, while the intervening government entered into possession of the property and employed the greater part of the real estate for the same governmental purposes to which it had been devoted under Spanish control. The church thereupon claimed the right to be repossessed of its property. After a great deal of discussion and investigation the various questions as to property rights raised by the church were submitted to a judicial commission. . . . The commission decided in favor of the claims of the church, and the whole subject has been adjusted, to the apparent satisfaction of all parties, as to the real estate, by the military government's paying a rental of five per cent upon the appraised values of the property, amounting to about $2,000,000, with a five years' option to the government of Cuba, when organized, to buy the property at the appraised value, receiving credit against the purchase price for twenty-five per cent of the rental paid, and as to the "censos", by the military government's taking them at fifty cents on the dollar, and permitting the debtors to take them up at the same rate. . . .

In response to calls from the Senate Committee on Relations with Cuba, the War Department has prepared and rendered a complete detailed and itemized statement of all the receipts and expenditures of the government of Cuba from January 1, 1899, to April 30, 1900, showing the places where and dates within which the amounts were collected and the officers by whom and the authority under which the collections were made. . . .

Notwithstanding the intimate political relations which have existed between the United States and Cuba since 1898, American production has not succeeded to any considerable degree in superseding the productions of other countries in the Cuban market.

The total imports of merchandise from January 1, 1899, to June 30, 1901, amounted to $165,948,272, and the total exports of merchandise for the same period amounted to $138,104,515, leaving a trade balance against Cuba for that period of $27,843,757. This excess of purchases is doubtless in a great measure accounted for by the fact that the long period of war and devastation which preceded the Spanish evacuation left the island practically destitute of movable property necessary either for the comfort of life or the reproduction of wealth. The excessive purchases have necessarily been made in a great measure upon credit in anticipation of the revenues to be derived from increased production following upon the revival of industry.

The Constitutional Convention

The constitutional convention, which was in session at the time of my last report, has concluded its labors and adjourned *sine die*. That convention was elected: (1) To frame and adopt a constitution; (2) to agree with the Government of the United States upon the relations to exist between that Government and the Government of Cuba, and (3) to provide for the election, by the people, of officers under such constitution, and the transfer of government to the officers so elected.

In February of the present year, as the convention appeared to be drawing near the conclusion of the first branch of its work, the following instructions were sent to the military governor:

War Department,
Washington, February 9, 1901.

Sir: As the time approaches for the Cuban constitutional convention to consider and act upon Cuba's relations with the United States, it seems desirable that you should be informed of the views of the Executive Department of our Government upon that subject in a more official form than that in which they have been communicated to you hitherto. The limitations upon the power of the Executive by the resolution of Congress of April 20, 1898, are such that the final determination upon the whole subject may ultimately rest in Congress, and it is impracticable now to forecast what the action of Congress will be. In the meantime, until Congress shall have acted, the military branch of the Government is bound to refrain from any committal, or apparent committal, of the United States to any policy which should properly be determined upon by Congress, and, at the same time, so far as it is called upon to act or to make suggestions bearing upon the course of events, it must determine its own conduct by reference to the action already taken by Congress, the established policy of the United States, the objects of our present occupation, and the manifest interests of the two countries.

The joint resolution of Congress of April 20, 1898, which authorized the President to expel the Spanish forces from Cuba, declared that—

"the United States hereby disclaims any disposition or intention to exercise sovereignty, jurisdiction, or control over said island except for the pacification thereof, and asserts its determination, when that is accomplished, to leave the government and the control of the island to its people."

The treaty of peace concluded at Paris on the 10th of December, 1898, and ratified by the Senate on the 6th of February, 1899, provides in the first article that —

"as the island is, upon its evacuation by Spain, to be occupied by the United States, the United States will, so long as such occupation shall last, assume and discharge the obligations that may, under international law, result from the fact of its occupation, for the protection of life and property."

It contains numerous obligations on the part of the United States in respect of the treatment of the inhabitants of the territory relinquished by Spain, such as the provision of the tenth article, that the inhabitants shall be secured in the free exercise of their religion; of the eleventh article, that they shall be subject to the jurisdiction of the courts, pursuant to the ordinary laws governing the same, and of the ninth article, that they shall retain all their rights of property, including the right to sell or dispose thereof, and the right to carry on their industry, commerce, and professions. The sixteenth article of the treaty provides that the obligations assumed in the treaty by the United States with respect to Cuba are limited to the time of its occupancy thereof, but that it shall, upon the termination of such occupancy, advise any government established in the island to assume the same obligations.

Our occupation of Cuba has been under the binding force both of the resolution and of the treaty, and the pacification mentioned in the resolution has necessarily been construed as coextensive with the occupation provided for by the treaty, during which we were to discharge international obligations, protect the rights of the former subjects of Spain, and cause or permit the establishment of a government to which we could, in good faith, commit the protection of the lives and property and personal rights of those inhabitants from whom we had compelled their former sovereign to withdraw her protection. It is plain that the government to which we were thus to transfer our temporary obligations should be a government based upon the peaceful suffrages of the people of Cuba, representing the entire people and holding their power from the people, and subject to the limitations and safeguards which the experience of constitutional government has shown to be necessary to the preservation of individual rights. This is plain as a duty to the people of Cuba under the resolution of April 20, 1898, and it is plain as an obligation of good faith under the Treaty of Paris. Such a government we have been persistently and with all practicable speed building up in Cuba, and we hope to see it established and assume control under the provisions which shall be adopted by the present convention. It seems to me that no one familiar with the traditional and established policy of this country in respect to Cuba can find cause for doubt as to our remaining duty. It would be hard to find any single statement of public policy which has been so often officially declared by so great an array of distinguished Americans authorized to speak for the Government of the United States, as the proposition stated, in varying but always uncompromising and unmistakable terms, that the United States would not under any circumstances permit any foreign power other than Spain to acquire possession of the island of Cuba.

Jefferson and Monroe and John Quincy Adams and Jackson and Van Buren and Grant and Clay and Webster and Buchanan and Everett have all agreed in regarding this as essential to the interests and the protection of the United States. The United States has, and will always have, the most vital interest in the preservation of the independence which she has secured for Cuba, and in preserving the people of that island from the domination and control of any foreign power whatever. The preservation of that independence by a country so small as Cuba, so incapable, as she must always be, to contend by force against the great powers of the world, must depend upon her strict performance of international obligations, upon her giving due protection to the lives and property of the citizens of all other countries within her borders, and upon her never contracting any public debt which in the hands of the citizens of foreign powers shall constitute an obligation she is unable to meet. The United States has, therefore, not merely a moral obligation arising from her destruction of Spanish authority in Cuba and the obligations of the Treaty of Paris for the establishment of a stable and adequate government in Cuba, but it has a substantial interest in the maintenance of such a government.

We are placed in a position where, for our own protection, we have, by reason of expelling Spain from Cuba, become the guarantors of Cuban independence and the guarantors of a stable and orderly government protecting life and property in that island. Fortunately the condition which we deem essential for our own interests is the condition for which Cuba has been struggling, and which the duty we have assumed toward Cuba on Cuban grounds and for Cuban interests requires. It would be a most lame and impotent conclusion if, after all the expenditure of blood and treasure by the people of the United States for the freedom of Cuba and by the people of Cuba for the same object, we should, through the constitution of the new government, by inadvertence or otherwise, be placed in a worse condition in regard to our own vital interests than we were while Spain was in possession, and the people of Cuba should be deprived of that protection and aid from the United States which is necessary to the maintenance of their independence. It was, undoubtedly, in consideration of these special relations between the United States and Cuba that the President said in his message to Congress of the 11th of April, 1898:

"The only hope of relief and repose from a condition which can no longer be endured is the enforced pacification of Cuba. In the name of humanity, in the name of civilization, in behalf of endangered American interests which give us the right and the duty to speak and to act, the war in Cuba must stop.

"In view of these facts and of these considerations I ask the Congress to authorize and empower the President to take measures to secure a full and final termination of hostilities between the Government of Spain and the people of Cuba, and to secure in the island the establishment of a stable government, capable of maintaining order and observing its international obligations, insuring peace and tranquillity and the security of its citizens as well as our own, and to use the military and naval forces of the United States as may be necessary for these purposes."

And in his message of December 5, 1899:

"This nation has assumed before the world a grave responsibility for the future good government of Cuba. We have accepted a trust, the fulfillment of which calls for the sternest integrity of purpose and the exercise of the highest wisdom. The new Cuba yet to arise from the ashes of the past must needs be bound to us by ties of singular intimacy and strength if its enduring welfare is to be assured. Whether those ties shall be organic or conventional, the destinies of Cuba are in some rightful form and manner irrevocably linked with our own, but how and how far is for the future to determine in the ripeness of events. Whatever be the outcome, we must see to it that free Cuba be a reality, not a name, a perfect entity, not a hasty experiment bearing within itself the elements of failure. Our mission, to accomplish which we took up the wager of battle, is not to be fulfilled by turning adrift any loosely-framed commonwealth to face the vicissitudes which too often attend weaker states whose natural wealth and abundant resources are offset by the incongruities of their political organization and the recurring occasions for internal rivalries to sap their strength and dissipate their energies."

And it was with a view to the proper settlement and disposition of these necessary relations that the order for the election of delegates to the present constitutional convention provided that they should frame and adopt a constitution for the people of Cuba, and as a part thereof provide for and agree with the Government of the United States upon the relations to exist between that Government and the Government of Cuba.

The people of Cuba should desire to have incorporated in her fundamental law provisions in substance as follow:

1. That no government organized under the constitution shall be deemed to have authority to enter into any treaty or engagement with any foreign power which may tend to impair or interfere with the independence of Cuba, or to confer upon such foreign power any special right or privilege without the consent of the United States.

2. That no government organized under the constitution shall have authority to assume or contract any public debt in excess of the capacity of the ordinary revenues of the island, after defraying the current expenses of government, to pay the interest.

3. That upon the transfer of the control of Cuba to the government established under the new constitution Cuba consents that the United States reserve and retain the right of intervention for the preservation of Cuban independence and the maintenance of a stable government, adequately protecting life, property, and individual liberty, and discharging the obligations with respect to Cuba imposed by the Treaty of Paris on the United States and now assumed and undertaken by the Government of Cuba.

4. That all the acts of the military government, and all rights acquired thereunder, shall be valid and shall be maintained and protected.

5. That to facilitate the United States in the performance of such duties as may devolve upon her under the foregoing provisions and for her own defense, the United States may acquire and hold the title to land for naval stations, and maintain the same at certain specified points.

These provisions may not, it is true, prove to be in accord with the conclusions which Congress may ultimately reach when that body comes to consider the subject, but as, until Congress has acted, the Executive must necessarily within its own sphere of action be controlled by its own judgment, you should now be guided by the views above expressed.

It is not our purpose at this time to discuss the cost of our intervention and occupation, or advancement of money for disarmament, or our assumption under the Treaty of Paris of the claims of our citizens against Spain for losses which they had incurred in Cuba. These can well be the subject of later consideration.

Very respectfully,

Elihu Root,
Secretary of War.

Major-General Leonard Wood,
Military Governor of Cuba, Havana, Cuba.

The Platt Amendment

On the passage of the act of March 2, 1901, entitled "An act making appropriation for the army for the fiscal year ending June 30,1902", the following proviso, contained in the act and commonly known as the "Platt Amendment", was communicated to the military governor, viz.:

Provided further, That in fulfillment of the declaration contained in the joint resolution approved April twentieth, eighteen hundred and ninety-eight, entitled "For the recognition of the independence of the people of Cuba, demanding that the Government of Spain relinquish its authority and government in the island of Cuba, and withdraw its land and naval forces from Cuba and Cuban waters, and directing the President of the United States to use the land and naval forces of the United States to carry these resolutions into effect," the President is hereby authorized to "leave the government and control of the island of Cuba to its people" so soon as a government shall have been established in said island under a constitution which, either as a part thereof or in an ordinance appended thereto, shall define the future relations of the United States with Cuba, substantially as follows:

I. That the government of Cuba shall never enter into any treaty or other compact with any foreign power or powers which will impair or tend to impair the independence of Cuba, nor in any manner authorize or permit any foreign power or powers to obtain by colonization or for military or naval purposes or otherwise, lodgment in or control over any portion of said island.

II. That said government shall not assume or contract any public debt, to pay the interest upon which, and to make reasonable sinking fund provision for the ultimate discharge of which the ordinary revenues of the island, after defraying the current expenses of government, shall be inadequate.

III. That the government of Cuba consents that the United States may exercise the right to intervene for the preservation of Cuban independence, the maintenance of a government adequate for the protection of life, property, and individual liberty, and for discharging the obligations with respect to Cuba imposed by the Treaty of Paris on the United States, now to be assumed and undertaken by the government of Cuba.

IV. That all acts of the United States in Cuba during its military occupancy thereof are ratified and validated, and all lawful rights acquired thereunder shall be maintained and protected.

V. That the government of Cuba will execute, and, as far as necessary, extend, the plans already devised or other plans to be mutually agreed upon, for the sanitation of the cities of the island, to the end that a recurrence of epidemic and infectious diseases may be prevented, thereby assuring protection to the people and commerce of Cuba, as well as to the commerce of the southern ports of the United States and the people residing therein.

VI. That the Isle of Pines shall be omitted from the proposed constitutional boundaries of Cuba, the title thereto being left to future adjustment by treaty.

VII. That to enable the United States to maintain the independence of Cuba, and to protect the people thereof, as well as for its own defense, the government of Cuba will sell or lease to the United States lands necessary for coaling or naval stations at certain specified points, to be agreed upon with the President of the United States.

VIII. That by way of further assurance the government of Cuba will embody the foregoing provisions in a permanent treaty with the United States.

By direction of the Department the military governor formally communicated these provisions to the convention and advised that body that the President awaited its action thereon.

On the third of April the following dispatch was sent to the military governor, who communicated it to a committee of the convention:

WOOD, Havana:

You are authorized to state officially that in the view of the President the intervention described in the third clause of the Platt Amendment is not synonymous with intermeddling or interference with the affairs of the Cuban government, but the formal action of the Government of the United States, based upon just and substantial grounds, for the preservation of Cuban independence, and the maintenance of a government adequate for the protection of life, property, and individual liberty, and adequate for discharging the obligations with respect to Cuba imposed by the Treaty of Paris on the United States.

ELIHU ROOT,
Secretary of War.

On the twelfth of June the convention adopted an ordinance making provisions identical with those above quoted from the act of March 2, 1901, a part of the constitution.

On October first the convention performed its remaining duty by adopting an electoral law providing for a general election throughout the island, to be held on the thirty-first day of December next, to choose governors of provinces, provincial councilors, members of the house of representatives, and presidential and senatorial electors. The law also provides that on February 24, 1902, the several bodies of electors thus chosen shall meet and elect a president, vice-president, and senators. The elections are to be held under the direct supervision of a Central Board of Scrutiny, composed of the president of the convention and four other members selected for that purpose. . . .

I do not fully agree with the wisdom of some of the provisions of this constitution; but it provides for a republican form of government; it was adopted after long and patient consideration and discussion; it represents the views of the delegates elected by the people of Cuba; and it contains no features which would justify the assertion that a government organized under it will not be one to which the United States may properly transfer the obligations for the protection of life and property under international law, assumed in the Treaty of Paris.

By virtue of the ordinance of June 12, 1901, appended thereto, the constitution defines the future relations of the United States with Cuba by the provisions the presence of which Congress has made a condition precedent to the President's leaving the government and control of the island of Cuba to its people. The constitution thus adopted and perfected has been treated accordingly by the military government as an acceptable basis for the formation of the new government to which, when organized and installed, the control of the island is to be transferred; and such a transfer may be anticipated before the close of the approaching session of Congress. If the people of Cuba and their officers exhibit, under the government of their own choice, the same self-restraint and respect for law which have characterized their relations to the intervening government during our occupation under the Treaty of Paris, the success of the Cuban administration may be confidently expected.

The new republic will begin its independent career with the hearty friendship and sincere good wishes of all the officers and soldiers of the United States who have fought and labored for the good of Cuba, and who have learned to appreciate the many admirable and attractive qualities of her people. I think that as the period of American occupation draws toward its close there is more appreciation by the Cubans of what the people of the United States have done for them. During the recent severe illness of the military governor the manifestations of esteem and affection for him were especially gratifying; and the lamented death of President McKinley was followed by general expressions of sympathy and sorrow throughout the island.

The chief apparent obstacle to the future prosperity of the island is to be found in its commercial relations with the United States, and the necessity of securing some reciprocal arrangement under which a concession shall be made from the tariff duties now imposed by the United States upon the principal Cuban products.

The prosperity of Cuba depends upon finding a market for her principal products, sugar and tobacco, at a reasonable profit. Under existing conditions, or any conditions which are to be anticipated, she can find such a market for her sugar, and to a great degree for her tobacco, only in the United States. Under the existing provisions of the United States tariff law the prices which can be realized for Cuban sugar and a large part of Cuban tobacco in this market are not sufficient to pay the duties, cost of transportation and production, and yield a living profit to the producer. . . .

In reliance upon fair and generous treatment by the United States, the Cuban planters have made strenuous efforts to revive their great industry, and have raised their product of sugar from 308,000 tons in 1899 to 615,000 tons in 1900, while the output for the present year is estimated at something over 800,000 tons. Incited by our precept and trusting to our friendship, they have struggled to retrieve the disasters under which their country had suffered. All the capital they had or could borrow has been invested in the rebuilding of their mills and the replanting of their land. More than half of the people of the island are depending directly or indirectly upon the success of that industry. If it succeeds we may expect peace, plenty, domestic order, and the happiness of a free and contented people to reward the sacrifice of American lives and treasure through which Cuba was set free. If it fails we may expect that the fields will again become waste, the mills will again be dismantled, the great body of laborers will be thrown out of employment; and that poverty and starvation, disorder and anarchy will ensue; that the charities and the schools which we have been building up will find no money for their support and will be discontinued; that the sanitary precautions which have made Cuba no longer a dreaded source of pestilence, but one of the most healthy islands in the world, will of necessity be abandoned, and our Atlantic seaboard must again suffer from the injury to commerce and the maintenance of quarantines at an annual cost of many millions.

Cuba has acquiesced in our right to say that she shall not put herself in the hands of any other power, whatever her necessities, and in our right to insist upon the maintenance of free and orderly government throughout her limits, however impoverished and desperate may be her people. Correlative to this right is a duty of the highest obligation to treat her not as an enemy, not at arm's length as an aggressive commercial rival, but with a generosity which toward her will be but justice; to shape our laws so that they shall contribute to her welfare as well as our own. . . .

Cuban Commerce

Our present duty to Cuba can be performed by the making of such a reciprocal tariff arrangement with her as President

McKinley urged in his last words to his countrymen at Buffalo on the fifth of September. A reasonable reduction in our duties upon Cuban sugar and tobacco, in exchange for fairly compensatory reductions of Cuban duties upon American products, will answer the purpose, and I strongly urge that such an arrangement be promptly made. It would involve no sacrifice, but would be as advantageous to us as it would be to Cuba. The market for American products in a country with such a population, such wealth and purchasing power, as Cuba with prosperity would speedily acquire, made certain by the advantage of preferential duties, would contribute far more to our prosperity than the portion of our present duties which we would be required to concede.

A large part of the $37,000,000 worth of merchandise which Cuba now imports from countries other than the United States, and of the much greater amount which she would import if prosperous, should come, and with a proper reciprocal arrangement inevitably would come, from the United States. . . . Last year she bought over $6,000,000 worth of cotton goods, of which we supplied less than $500,000; nearly $700,000 worth of woolen goods, of which we supplied less than $22,000; over $2,000,000 worth of vegetables and vegetable fibres, of which we supplied but $171,000; over $2,700,000 worth of wines, of which we supplied but $329,000; over $526,000 worth of silk goods, of which we supplied but $24,000; nearly $2,598,000 worth of oils, etc., of which we supplied but $713,000; $1,053,000 worth of chemicals, drugs, etc., of which we supplied but $422,000; $8,476,000 worth of animals and animal products, of which we supplied but $1,994,000; $1,638,000 worth of manufactures of leather, of which we supplied but $405,000; $3,335,000 worth of rice, of which we supplied but $3,000. Substantially the whole of these items, of which we now furnish so small a part, should come from the fields and factories of the United States.

Aside from the moral obligation to which we committed ourselves when we drove Spain out of Cuba, and aside from the ordinary considerations of commercial advantage involved in a reciprocity treaty, there are the weightiest reasons of American public policy pointing in the same direction; for the peace of Cuba is necessary to the peace of the United States; the health of Cuba is necessary to the health of the United States; the independence of Cuba is necessary to the safety of the United States. The same considerations which led to the war with Spain now require that a commercial arrangement be made under which Cuba can live.

Inauguration of the Republic

Extract from the Report of the Secretary of War for 1902 [1]

In conformity to the Cuban constitution and electoral law, elections were held by the Cuban people on December 31, 1901, and by the electoral college on February 24, 1902, when a president, vice-president, senate and house of representatives were chosen. On March 24, 1902, the following instructions were given to the military governor:

Brigadier-General Leonard Wood,
Military Governor of Cuba, Havana, Cuba.

Sir: You are authorized to provide for the inauguration, on the twentieth of May next, of the government elected by the people of Cuba; and upon the establishment of said government to leave the government and control of the island of Cuba to its people, pursuant to the provisions of the act of Congress entitled " An act making appropriation for the army for the fiscal year ending June 30, 1902 ", approved March 2, 1901.

Upon the transfer of government and control to the president and congress so elected, you will advise them that such transfer is upon the express understanding and condition that the new government does thereupon, and by the acceptance thereof, pursuant to the provisions of the appendix to the constitution of Cuba adopted by the constitutional convention on the 12th of June, 1901, assume and undertake all and several the obligations assumed by the United States with respect to Cuba by the treaty between the United States of America and Her Majesty the Queen

[1] Page 6.

Regent of Spain, signed at Paris on the 10th day of December, 1898. It is the purpose of the United States Government, forthwith upon the inauguration of the new government of Cuba, to terminate the occupancy of the island by the United States and to withdraw from that island the military forces now in occupancy thereof; but for the preservation and care of the coast defenses of the island, and to avoid leaving the island entirely defenseless against external attack, you may leave in the coast fortifications such small number of artillerymen as may be necessary, for such reasonable time as may be required, to enable the new government to organize and substitute therefor an adequate military force of its own; by which time it is anticipated that the naval stations referred to in the statute and in the appendix to the constitution above cited, will have been agreed upon, and the said artillerymen may be transferred thereto.

You will convene the Congress elected by the people of Cuba in joint session at such reasonable time before the twentieth of May as shall be necessary therefor, for the purpose of performing the duties of counting and rectifying the electoral vote for president and vice-president under the fifty-eighth article of the Cuban constitution. At the same time you will publish and certify to the people of Cuba the instrument adopted as the constitution of Cuba by the constitutional convention on the 21st day of February, 1901, together with the appendix added thereto and forming a part thereof, adopted by the said convention on the 12th day of June, 1901. It is the understanding of the Government of the United States that the government of the island will pass to the new president and congress of Cuba as a going concern, all the laws promulgated by the government of occupation continuing in force and effect, and all the judicial and subordinate executive and administrative officers continuing in the lawful discharge of their present functions until changed by the constitutional officers of the new government. At the same moment the responsibility of the United States for the collection and expenditure of revenues, and for the proper performance of duty by the officers and employees of the insular government will end, and the responsibility of the new government of Cuba therefor will commence.

In order to avoid any embarrassment to the new president which might arise from his assuming executive responsibility with subordinates whom he does not know, or in whom he has not confidence, and to avoid any occasion for sweeping changes in the civil-service personnel immediately after the inauguration of the new government, approval is given to the course which you have already proposed of consulting the president-elect, and substituting before the twentieth of May, wherever he shall so desire, for the persons now holding official positions, such persons as he may designate. This method will make it necessary that the new president and yourself should appoint representatives to count and certify the cash and cash balances, and the securities for deposits, transferred to the new government. The consent of the owner of the securities for deposits to the transfer thereof you will of course obtain.

The vouchers and accounts in the office of the auditor and elsewhere relating to the receipt and disbursement of moneys during the government of occupation must necessarily remain within the control and available for the use of this Department. Access to these papers will, however, undoubtedly be important to the officers of the new government in the conduct of their business subsequent to the twentieth of May. You will accordingly appoint an agent to take possession of these papers, and retain them at such place in the island of Cuba as may be agreed upon with the new government until they can be removed to the United States without detriment to the current business of the new government.

I desire that you communicate the contents of this letter to Mr. Palma, the president-elect, and ascertain whether the course above described accords with his views and wishes.

Very respectfully, ELIHU ROOT,
Secretary of War.

These instructions, being communicated to the president-elect, Mr. Palma, received his approval, and they were completely executed on May 20, 1902. . . .

The whole governmental situation in Cuba was quite unprecedented, with its curious device of a suspended sovereignty given up by Spain, but not in terms vested in anybody else, and if vested remaining dormant, while a practical working government of military occupation in time of peace, deriving its authority from the sovereignty of another country, claimed temporary allegiance, made and enforced laws, and developed a political organization of the Cuban people to take and exercise the suspended or dormant sovereignty. It was important that in inaugurating the new government there should be no break in the continuity of legal obligation, of rights of property and contract, of jurisdiction, or of administrative action. It would not do to wait for the new government to pass laws or to create offices and appoint administrative officers and vest them with powers, for the instant that the new government was created the intervening government would cease, and the period of waiting would be a period of anarchy.

It was necessary, therefore, to take such steps that the new government should be created as a going concern, every officer of which should be able to go on with his part of the business of governing under the new sovereignty without waiting for any new authority. That everything necessary to this end should be done, and that it should be done according to a consistent and maintainable legal theory, caused the Department a good deal of solicitude. It is gratifying to report that it was done, and that the government which, until noon of May twentieth, was proceeding under the authority of the President of the United States, went on in the afternoon of that day and has ever since continued under the sovereignty which had been abandoned by Spain in April, 1899, without any more break or confusion than accompanies the inauguration of a new President in the United States. This could not have been done without the most perfect good understanding, mutual confidence, and sympathetic coöperation on the part of our officers, who were about to retire, and the newly-elected officers of Cuba, who were about to take the reins of government. Our troops withdrew from Cuba in the afternoon of the twentieth of May, amid universal expressions of gratitude, esteem, and affection. The public feeling was well illustrated by the following telegram from President Palma:

Havana, May 21, 1902.

Elihu Root,
Secretary of War, Washington:

I am deeply moved by your heartfelt message of congratulation on the inauguration of the Republic of Cuba, to the birth of which the people and the Government of the United States have contributed with their blood and treasure. Rest assured that the Cuban people can never forget the debt of gratitude they owe to the great republic, with which we will always cultivate the closest relations of friendship and for the prosperity of which we pray to the Almighty.

T. Estrada Palma.

I venture to express the hope that this strong and well-deserved friendship of Cuba may be permanent and may never be alienated by our treatment of the smaller and weaker power, and that the people of the United States may never lose their deep interest in the welfare of the new republic which they have called into being with so much labor and sacrifice. I know of no chapter in American history more satisfactory than that which will record the conduct of the military government of Cuba. The credit for it is due, first of all, to Brigadier-General Leonard Wood, the commander of the department of Santiago until December, 1899, and thenceforth military governor of the island. Credit is due also to Brigadier-General Tasker H. Bliss, who had charge of the collection of customs revenues; Major E. St. John Greble, and Major and Surgeon Jefferson R. Kean, successively heads of the department of charities; Lieutenant Matthew E. Hanna, superintendent of public schools; Lieutenant E. C. Brooks and Mr. J. D. Terrill, successively auditors of Cuba; and to the Cuban gentlemen who, as heads of the various state departments, constituted the cabinet of the military governor: Messrs. Diego Tamayo, secretary of state and government; Leopoldo Cancio, secretary of finance; José Varela, secretary of justice; José R. Villalon, secretary of public works; Enrique José Varona, secretary of public instruction; and Perfecto Lacoste, secretary of agriculture. Credit is also due to Major-General John R. Brooke, the first military governor, and the members of his administration; and to the department commanders, General James H. Wilson and General Fitzhugh Lee; to the lamented General William Ludlow, whose arduous labors in the government and sanitation of Havana made his untimely death not the least of his country's sacrifices for Cuba; to Brigadier-General Joseph P. Sanger, commander at Matanzas and later director of the census; and to Major-General (then Colonel) Adna R. Chaffee, chief-of-staff, and Colonel W. V. Richards and Colonel H. L. Scott, adjutant-generals of the department.

Especial credit is due also to the Medical Department of the army, and particularly to Major Walter Reed and Major William C. Gorgas for their extraordinary service in ridding the island of yellow fever, described in my last report; and to Dr. Jefferson R. Kean and Dr. James Carroll for their share in that work.

The brilliant character of this scientific achievement, its inestimable value to mankind, the saving of thousands of lives, and the deliverance of the Atlantic seacoast from constant apprehension, demand special recognition from the Government of the United States.

Dr. Reed is the ranking major in the Medical Department, and within a few months will, by operation of law, become lieutenant-colonel. I ask that the President be authorized to appoint him assistant surgeon-general with the rank of colonel, and to appoint Major Gorgas deputy surgeon-general with the rank of lieutenant-colonel, and that the respective numbers in those grades in the Medical Department be increased accordingly during the period for which they hold those offices.

The name of Dr. Jesse W. Lazear, contract surgeon, who voluntarily permitted himself to be inoculated with the yellow-fever germ, in order to furnish a necessary experimental test in the course of the investigation, and who died of the disease, should be written in the list of the martyrs who have died in the cause of humanity. As a slight memorial of his heroism a battery in the coast defense fortification at Fort Howard, Baltimore, Md., has been named " Battery Lazear ".

THE PHILIPPINES

THE SUPPRESSION OF THE INSURRECTION AND THE BUILDING UP OF CIVIL GOVERNMENT

The Philippine question has apparently been the most serious and difficult problem to solve bequeathed to us by the Spanish-American War. The battle of Manila occurred on May 1, 1898, and as a result the American authorities substituted themselves for the Spanish authorities in Manila and in other parts of the archipelago.

Upon the exchange of ratifications of the treaty of peace between Spain and the United States, signed at Paris, December 10, 1898, the United States found itself possessed of whatever legal title Spain had to the Philippines and of whatever possession Spain was in a position to transfer. From Manila as a center American troops took possession of the islands and when, as the result of the military operations set forth in the extracts from Mr. Root's reports, they had brought about a degree of order which made civil government seem feasible, a commission was appointed with the Honorable William H. Taft as chairman, to assume the government of the islands. The instructions to this commission drafted by Mr. Root, and signed by President McKinley with trifling verbal changes, properly may be called the organic act of the Philippines, and, with modifications had in mind when they were framed, are the basis of the Act of Congress providing for the government of the islands.

Military Operations in the Islands

Extract from the Report of the Secretary of War for 1899[1]

THE principal military operations of the year have been in the Philippine Islands. At the date of the last annual report the Eighth Army Corps, under the command of Major-General E. S. Otis, held possession of the city of Manila under the provisions of the protocol of August 12, 1898, which required the United States to occupy and hold that city pending the conclusion of the treaty of peace, and which imposed upon the troops in possession at once the obligation to protect life

[1] Page 5.

and property within the city and to refrain from infringing upon Spanish territory outside of the city limits. In the performance of this duty many annoyances were experienced from the army of the Tagalogs, who were in insurrection against the government of Spain, and who had been collected about the city, after its capture by the American forces had become inevitable, under the promise of their leaders that they should share in the plunder of the inhabitants.

General Otis was ordered to avoid any conflict with them, and, strictly complying with these orders, he made every effort to secure a peaceable understanding. The peaceable attitude of the American forces was unfortunately misconstrued as indicating weakness and fear of a conflict. On the night of February 4, 1899, our forces were attacked by the Tagalogs, who attempted to capture the city. They were promptly repulsed in a series of active engagements which extended through the night of the fourth, and the fifth, sixth, and tenth days of February. Our lines were extended and established at a considerable distance from the city in every direction. On the twenty-second of February a concerted rising of the Tagalogs, of whom there are about 200,000 in the city of Manila, was attempted, under instructions to massacre all the Americans and Europeans in the city. This attempt was promptly suppressed and the city was placed under strict control.

The troops composing the Eighth Army Corps under General Otis's command at that time were of regulars 171 officers and 5,201 enlisted men, and of volunteers 667 officers and 14,831 enlisted men, making an aggregate of 838 officers and 20,032 enlisted men.

All of the volunteers and 1,650 of the regulars were, or were about to become, entitled to their discharge, and their right was perfected by the exchange of ratifications of the treaty on the eleventh of April.

The total force which Major-General Otis was thus entitled to command for any considerable period consisted of only 171 officers and 3,551 enlisted men. The numbers of the Eighth Army Corps, above stated, give the entire numerical strength of all troops present in the islands, including those at Cavite and Iloilo, the sick and wounded, those serving in the civil departments and in the staff organizations, and deducting these, the effective men of the line, officers and soldiers, were about 14,000. Of these 3,000 constituted a provost guard necessary to preserve order within Manila and prevent the carrying-out of the known intention of the secret hostile organizations in that city to burn and sack the city when our troops were engaged on the lines of defense. Including, therefore, all the troops who were entitled to be discharged, there were not more than 11,000 officers and men available to engage the insurgent army, which was two or three times that number, well armed and equipped, and included many of the native troops formerly comprised in the Spanish army, and to occupy and hold positions in a comparatively unknown country, densely populated by inhabitants speaking in the main an unknown language. The months of the most intense heat, followed by the very severe rainy season of that climate, were immediately approaching, and for any effective occupation of the country it was necessary to await both the close of the rainy season and the supply of new troops to take the place of those about to be discharged. Practically all the volunteers who were then in the Philippines consented to forego the just expectation of an immediate return to their homes, and to remain in the field until their places could be supplied by new troops. They voluntarily subjected themselves to the dangers and casualties of numerous engagements, and to the very great hardships of the climate. They exhibited fortitude and courage, and are entitled to high commendation for their patriotic spirit and soldierly conduct.

The operations of the period extending from February to the thirty-first day of August, the date of the annual report of General Otis as commander of the Department of the Pacific, were marked by a steady maintenance and strengthening of the position occupied by our forces, a gradual extension of our lines, a restoration of security and confidence in the city of Manila, numerous sharp engagements in the field marked by unbroken success, and many instances of very gratifying conduct on the part of both officers and men. It is probable that at any time a column of troops could have been sent anywhere on the island of Luzon against any armed resistance which the insurgents could have offered after the demoralization in their ranks, resulting from the severe defeats inflicted upon them in February; but there were not the troops necessary to garrison the towns, or to maintain any far extended lines of communication. Accordingly no attempt was made to occupy the country, except in the vicinity of Manila, and at such points as were important for the protection of our lines. Such movements as passed beyond this territory were designed primarily to break up threatening concentrations of insurgent troops, and to prevent undue annoyance to the positions which we occupied.

On the eleventh of February the city of Iloilo, on the island of Panay, the second port of the Philippines in importance, was occupied. After the capture of Iloilo the navy took possession of the city of Cebu, on the island of Cebu, and on the twenty-sixth of February a battalion of the Twenty-third Infantry was dispatched to that port for the protection of the inhabitants and property.

On the first of March a military district comprising the islands of Panay, Negros, and Cebu, and such other Visayan islands as might be thereafter designated, to be known as the "Visayan Military District", was established and placed under the supervision of Brigadier-General Marcus P. Miller, commanding First Separate Brigade, Eighth Army Corps, with headquarters at Iloilo.

The Third Battalion of the First California Volunteer Infantry was thereupon ordered to the island of Negros, under the command of Colonel (now Brigadier-General) James F. Smith, and took possession of the city of Bacolod, on that island, without resistance.

On the fifth of May Brigadier-General James F. Smith assumed temporary command of the Visayan military district, and on the twenty-fifth of May, Brigadier-General R. P. Hughes, United States Volunteers, was assigned to the command of the district.

On the nineteenth of May the Spanish garrison at Jolo, in the Sulu Archipelago, was replaced by American troops.

By the thirty-first of August the number of troops stationed at Jolo and the Visayan Islands, including a small guard at the Cavite Arsenal, amounted to 4,145 men. . . .

All of the forces who were entitled to be discharged as above mentioned have now been returned to this country and mustered out. The new troops designed to take the place of those returning to this country, and to constitute an effective army for the occupation of the Philippines, have been transported to Manila. . . .

The troops now in the Philippines comprise 905 officers and 30,578 men of the regular force, and 594 officers and 15,388 men of the volunteer force, making an aggregate of 1,499 officers and 45,966 men, and when the troops on the way have arrived the total force constituting the Eighth Army Corps will be 2,051 officers and 63,483 men.

By the tenth of October the process of changing armies and the approach of the dry season had reached a point where an advance toward the general occupation of the country was justified.

At that time the American lines extended from the Bay of Manila to Laguna de Bay, and included considerable parts of the provinces of Cavite, Laguna, and Morong to the south and east of Manila, substantially all of the province of Manila, and the southern parts of Bulacan and Pampanga, dividing the insurgent forces into two widely separated parts. To the south and east of our lines in Cavite and Morong were numerous bands occasionally concentrating for attack on our lines, and as frequently dispersed and driven back toward the mountains. On the eighth of October, the insurgents in this region having again gathered and attacked our lines of communication, General Schwan with a column of 1,726 men commenced a movement from Bacoor, in the province of Cavite, driving the enemy through Old Cavite, Noveleta, Santa Cruz, San Francisco de Malabon, Saban, and Perez das Marinas, punishing them severely, scattering them and destroying them as organized forces, and returning on the thirteenth to Bacoor.

On the north of our lines stretched the great plain of central Luzon extending north from Manila about one hundred and twenty miles. This plain comprises parts of the provinces of Manila, Pampanga, Bulacan, Tarlac, Nueva Ecija, and Pangasinan. It is, roughly speaking, bounded on the south by the Bay of Manila; on the east and west by high mountain ranges separating it from the seacoasts, and on the north by mountains and the Gulf of Lingayen. Through the northeast and central portion flows the Rio Grande from the northern mountains southwesterly to the Bay of Manila, and near the western edge runs the only railroad on the island of Luzon, in a general southeasterly direction from Dagupan, on the Bay of Lingayen, to Manila. In this territory Aguinaldo exercised a military dictatorship, and with a so-called Cabinet imitated the forms of civil government, having his headquarters at Tarlac, which he called his capital, and which is situated near the center of the western boundary of the plain.

The operations commenced in October involved the movement of three separate forces: (1) A column proceeding up the Rio Grande and along the northeastern borders of the plain and bending around to the westward across the northern boundary toward the Gulf of Lingayen, garrisoning the towns and occupying the mountain passes which gave exit into the northeastern division of the island. (2) An expedition proceeding by transports to the Gulf of Lingayen, there to land at the northwestern corner of the plain and occupy the great coast road which from that point runs between the mountains and the sea to the northern extremity of the island, and to proceed eastward to a junction with the first column. (3) A third column proceeding directly up the railroad to the capture of Tarlac, and thence still up the road to Dagupan, driving the insurgent forces before it toward the line held by the first two columns. These movements were executed with energy, rapidity, and success, notwithstanding the exceedingly unfavorable weather and deluges of rain, which rendered the progress of troops and transportation of subsistence most difficult.

On the twelfth of October a strong column under General Lawton, with General Young commanding the advance, commenced the northerly movement up the Rio Grande from Arayat, driving the insurgents before it to the northward and westward. On the eighteenth the advance reached Cabiao. On the nineteenth San Isidro was captured, and a garrison established; on the twenty-seventh Cabanatuan was occupied, and a permanent station established there. On the first of November Aliaga and Talavera were occupied. In the meantime detachments, chiefly of Young's cavalry, were operating to the west of the general line of advance, striking insurgent parties wherever they were found and driving them toward the line of the railroad. By the thirteenth of November the advance had turned to the westward, and our troops had captured San José, Lupao, Humingan, San Quintin, Tayug, and San Nicolas. By the eighteenth of November the advance had occupied Asingan and Rosales, and was moving on Pozorrubio, a strongly intrenched post about twelve miles east of San Fabian. General Lawton's forces now held a line of posts extending up the eastern side of the plain and curving around and across the northern end to within a few miles of the Gulf of Lingayen.

On the sixth of November a force of 2,500, under command of General Wheaton, sailed from Manila for the Gulf of Lingayen, convoyed by ships of the navy, and on the seventh the expedition was successfully landed at San Fabian with effective assistance from a naval convoy against spirited opposition. On the twelfth the Thirty-third Volunteers, of Wheaton's command, under Colonel Hare, proceeded southeastward to San Jacinto, attacked and routed 1,200 intrenched insurgents, with the loss of the gallant Major John A. Logan and six enlisted men killed, and one officer and eleven men wounded. The enemy left eighty-one dead in the trenches and suffered a total loss estimated at three hundred.

In the meantime, on the fifth of November, a column under General MacArthur advanced up the railroad from Angeles to Magalang, clearing the country between Angeles and Arayat, encountering and routing bodies of the enemy at different points, and capturing Magalang. On the eleventh it took Bamban, Capas, and Concepcion, and on the twelfth of November entered Tarlac, from which the enemy fled on its approach. Meantime, parties, mainly of the Thirty-sixth Volunteers, under Colonel J. F. Bell, cleared the country to the right of the line of advance as far east as the points reached by General Lawton's flanking parties. On the seventeenth of November MacArthur's column had occupied Gerona and Panique, to the north of Tarlac. On the nineteenth Wheaton's troops, and on the twentieth MacArthur's troops, entered Dagupan.

On the twenty-fourth of November General Otis was able to telegraph to the Department as follows:

> Claim to government by insurgents can be made no longer under any fiction. Its treasurer, secretary of the interior, and president of congress in our hands; its president and remaining cabinet officers in hiding, evidently in different central Luzon provinces; its generals and troops in small bands scattered through these provinces, acting as banditti, or dispersed, playing the rôle of " Amigos ", with arms concealed.

Since that time our troops have been actively pursuing the flying and scattered bands of insurgents, further dispersing them, making many prisoners, and releasing many Spanish prisoners who had been in the insurgents' hands.

On the twenty-third General Young's column had reached Namacpacan, thirty miles north of San Fernando, in the province of Union, and passed north into the mountains; and on the twenty-fourth Vigan, the principal port of the northwest coast, was occupied by a body of marines landed from the battleship *Oregon*. In the meantime the destruction of the organized insurgent power in central Luzon found a response from the natives of the province of Nueva Viscaya, offering their services to drive out the insurgents who were in possession of Bayambong, the capital of that province, upon which the insurgent army had been prevented from retreating by the disposition of General Lawton's forces, commanding the passes of the mountains, and which Lawton's troops were rapidly approaching.

All these movements were accomplished under great difficulties owing to the almost impassable condition of the country. In the course of them, large quantities of insurgent supplies of all descriptions were captured, including stores of food, clothing, arms, munitions of war, quick-firing and Krupp guns, a powder factory and an arsenal, engineering tools, money, war department records, personal effects of officers, and numerous private dispatches.

It is gratifying to know that as our troops got away from the immediate vicinity of Manila they found the natives of the country exceedingly friendly, and both men and animals were able to live upon the country, and for considerable periods leave their supply trains behind. This was doubtless due in some measure to the fact that the Pampangos, who inhabit the provinces of Pampanga and Tarlac, and the Pangasinanes, who inhabit Pangasinan, as well as the more northerly tribes, are unfriendly to the Tagalogs, and had simply submitted to the military domination of that tribe, from which they were glad to be relieved. This is emphasized by a report from General Wheaton that he had been obliged to guard the mother and infant son of Aguinaldo to prevent the natives of Pampanga from killing them.

Wherever the permanent occupation of our troops has extended in the Philippine Islands, civil law has been immediately put in force. The courts have been organized and the most learned and competent native lawyers have been appointed to preside over them.

A system of education has been introduced and numerous schools have been established. It is believed that in the city of Manila a greater number of good schools, affording better facilities for primary instruction, exist today than at any previous time in the history of the city.

Continued Military Operations in the Philippines

Extract from the Report of the Secretary of War for 1900 [1]

At the date of the last report (November 29, 1899) the government established by the Philippine insurgents in

[1] Page 6.

central Luzon and the organized armed forces by which it was maintained had been destroyed, and the principal civil and military leaders of the insurrection, accompanied by small and scattered bands of troops, were the objects of pursuit in the western and the northern parts of the island. That pursuit was prosecuted with vigor and success, under conditions of extraordinary difficulty and hardship, and resulted in the further and practically complete disintegration of the insurrectionary bands in those regions, in the rescue of nearly all the American prisoners and the greater part of the Spanish prisoners held by the insurgents, in the capture of many of the leading insurgents, and in the capture and destruction of large quantities of arms, ammunition, and supplies.

There still remained a large force of insurgents in Cavite and the adjacent provinces south of Manila, and a considerable force to the east of the Rio Grande de Pampanga, chiefly in the province of Bulacan, while in the extreme southeastern portions of Luzon, and in the various Visayan islands, except the island of Negros, armed bodies of Tagalogs had taken possession of the principal seacoast towns, and were exercising military control over the peaceful inhabitants. Between the insurgent troops in Bulacan and the mountains to the north, and the insurgents in the south, communication was maintained by road and trail, running along and near the eastern bank of the Mariquina River, and through the towns of Mariquina, San Mateo, and Montalban and the province of Morong. This line of communication, passing through rough and easily defended country, was strongly fortified and held by numerous bodies of insurgents.

On December 18, 1899, a column, under the command of Major-General Henry W. Lawton, proceeded from Manila, and between that date and the twenty-ninth of December captured all the fortified posts of the insurgents, took possession of the line of communication, which has ever since been maintained, and destroyed, captured, or dispersed the insurgent force in that part of the island. In the course of this movement was sustained the irremediable loss of General Lawton, who was shot and instantly killed while too fearlessly exposing his person in supervising the passing of his troops over the river Mariquina at San Mateo. . . .

On January 4, 1900, General J. C. Bates, U. S. V., was assigned to the command of the First Division of the Eighth Army Corps, and an active campaign under his direction was commenced in southern Luzon. The plan adopted was to confront and hold the strong force of the enemy near Imus and to the west of Bacoor by a body of troops under General Wheaton, while a column, under General Schwan, should move rapidly down the west shore of the Laguna de Bay to Biñang, thence turn southwesterly and seize the Silang, Indang, and Naic road, capture the enemy's supplies supposed to be at the towns of Silang and Indang, and arrest the retreat of the enemy, when they should be driven from northern Cavite by our troops designated to attack them there, and thus prevent their reassembling in the mountains of southern Cavite and northern Batangas. This plan was successfully executed.

General Schwan's column moved with great rapidity over the lines indicated, marching a distance of over six hundred miles, meeting with and defeating numerous bodies of insurgents and capturing many intrenched positions, taking possession of and garrisoning towns along the line, and scattering and demoralizing all the organized forces of the enemy within that section of country. From these operations and the simultaneous attacks by our troops under General Wheaton in the north the rebel forces in the Cavite region practically disappeared, the members being killed or captured or returning to their homes as unarmed citizens, and a few scattered parties escaping through General Schwan's line to the south. By the eighth of February the organized forces of the insurgents in the region mentioned had ceased to exist. In large portions of the country the inhabitants were returning to their homes and resuming their industries, and active trade with Manila was resumed.

In the course of these operations about six hundred Spanish prisoners were released from the insurgents, leaving about six hundred more still in their hands in the extreme southeastern provinces of Camarines and Albay, nearly all of whom were afterwards liberated by our troops. In the meantime an expedition was organized under the command of Brigadier-General William A. Kobbé, U. S. V., to expel the Tagalogs who had taken possession of the principal hemp ports of the islands situated in Albay, the extreme southeastern province of Luzon, and in the islands of Leyte, Samar, and Catanduanes.

This expedition sailed from Manila on the eighteenth of January and accomplished its object. All of the principal hemp ports were relieved from control of the insurgents, garrisoned by American troops, and opened to commerce by order of the military governor of the islands on the thirtieth of January and the tenth and fourteenth of February. The expedition met with strong resistance at Legaspi from an intrenched force under the Chinese general, Paua. He was speedily overcome and escaped into the interior. After a few days he reassembled his forces and threatened the garrisons which had been left in Albay and Legaspi, whereupon he was attacked and defeated; he then surrendered. Thirty pieces of artillery, a large quantity of ammunition, a good many rifles, and a considerable amount of money were captured by this expedition.

On the fifteenth of February an expedition, under the supervision of Major-General Bates and under the immediate command of Brigadier-General James M. Bell, U. S. V., sailed from Manila to take possession of the north and south Camarines provinces and western Albay, in which the insurgent forces had been swelled by the individuals and scattered bands escaping from our operations in various sections of the north. The insurgent force was defeated after a sharp engagement near the mouth of the Bicol River, pursued, and scattered. Large amounts of artillery and war material were captured. The normal conditions of industry and trade relations with Manila were resumed by the inhabitants.

On the twentieth of March the region covered by the last-described operations was created a district of southeastern Luzon, under the command of General James M. Bell, who was instructed to proceed to the establishment of the necessary customs and internal-revenue service in the district. In the meantime similar expeditions were successfully made through the mountains of the various islands of the Visayan group, striking and scattering and severely punishing the bands of outlaws and insurgents who infested those islands. In the latter part of March General Bates proceeded with the Fortieth Infantry to establish garrisons in Mindanao. The only resistance was of a trifling character at Cagayan, the insurgent general in northeastern Mindanao surrendering and turning over the ordnance in his possession.

With the successful accomplishment of these operations all formal and open resistance to American authority in the Philippines terminated, leaving only an exceedingly vexatious and annoying guerrilla warfare of a character closely approaching brigandage, which will require time, patience, and good judgment to suppress. As rapidly as we have occupied territory, the policy of inviting inhabitants to return to their peaceful vocations, and aiding them in the reëstablishment of their local governments, has been followed, and the protection of the United States has been promised to them. The giving of this protection has led to the distribution of troops in the Philippine Islands at over four hundred different posts, with the consequent labor of administration and supply.

The maintenance of these posts involves the continued employment of a large force, but as the Tagalogs who are in rebellion have deliberately adopted the policy of murdering, so far as they are able, all of their countrymen who are friendly to the United States, the maintenance of garrisons is at present necessary to the protection of the peaceful and unarmed Filipinos who have submitted to our authority; and if we are to discharge our obligations in that regard the reduction of those garrisons must necessarily be gradual.

The most efficient measures for lessening the number of posts and consequently the number of troops necessary in the Philippines, will be the construction of roads, making possible rapid communication, so that each post may effectually protect the people of a larger section of country; the establishment of personal relations between our officers and the people of the country with whom they are brought in contact, so that we can tell who are trustworthy sources of information and who are not; the gradually growing appreciation of the benefits of our control and the sincerity of our professions of good intention, which will naturally follow the benefits of good civil government; and the organization of native troops under American officers.

The Beginnings of the Civil Government

Extract from the Report of the Secretary of War for 1900[1]

Spanish authority had for centuries furnished the only controlling force for the maintenance of order in the Philippine Islands, and upon the destruction of the Spanish power

[1] Page 22.

the existing administration completely ceased to perform its functions and disappeared, leaving a great body of inhabitants, without training or capacity to organize for self-control, absolutely without government. No substitute for the accustomed control was furnished under the Tagalog rule, which was built up, in the first instance, by our assistance, and afterwards under our sufferance, between the battle of Manila Bay, May 1, 1898, and the assertion of our authority by the army which arrived in the islands in the autumn of 1899. General Otis says of the interim:

> Under Tagalog domination, which was really the irresponsible dictatorship of Aguinaldo, cruelly enforced by his military officers, there was no rule by which the right or wrong of personal action could be determined, nor indeed did individual liberty of any kind exist. The so-called insurgent government, whatever it might have been at its inception, degenerated into a military despotism of low order, in which neither property nor life had the least security.

From these statements should be excepted Manila, southern Mindanao, and the islands of the Sulu Archipelago, inhabited by Moros, who continued under the direct control of their tribal chieftains, under the arrangement made by General Bates on August 20, 1899, and the island of Negros, whose people repelled the Tagalog rule and immediately substituted a government under American supervision for that of Spain. In the remainder of the archipelago, particularly in the regions inhabited or dominated by the Tagalogs, as American occupation extended it became necessary to deal with civil society thoroughly disorganized, in which all the turbulent and predatory elements of tribes ranging from barbarism to a semi-civilization had been set free from the habit of obedience to law.

In the first instance the military control of the United States superseded the military control of the Tagalogs. The military authorities, however, promptly commenced the organization of civil administration, in which, as rapidly as practicable, all the ordinary functions of government were to be vested. The substantive body of Spanish law of the Philippines was excellent and adequate if it could be applied. The first step in its application was the organization of courts. In this we were fortunate in securing the services of one of the most able and profound lawyers of the islands, Don Cayetano Arellano, who was made chief justice of the supreme court of the island, composed of six Filipino lawyers of Luzon, Panay, and Cebu, and three officers of the army, who were members of the bar of our own country. This court has been supplemented by subordinate courts, created first for the city of Manila and afterwards for other regions from time to time as our occupation has extended. In all of these courts the judges and the prosecuting attorneys have, in the main, been natives of the islands.

The Spanish criminal procedure in the islands had been exceedingly oppressive and regardless of personal rights, and native representatives in the new courts were very desirous to introduce as speedily as possible the privileges accorded by the laws of the United States to its citizens. The native and American justices of the supreme court, assisted by the attorney-general, Don Florentino Torres, also a distinguished lawyer of Manila, accordingly proceeded to the preparation of a code of criminal procedure, which was promulgated by an order dated April 23, 1900, and which for the first time affords real protection to the personal rights of persons charged with crime in the Philippine Islands.

The next step in order of importance was the establishment of municipal governments through which the people of the islands might control their own local affairs by officers of their own selection. For the accomplishment of this end the chief justice, Arellano, and Attorney-General Torres, assisted by three American judicial officers, were constituted a board on January 29, 1900. After two months of assiduous work the board reported a general statute for the organization of municipalities, which was promulgated by an order on March 29, 1900. Of this statute the board says in its report, over the signature of the distinguished Philippine members:

> For the first time the Philippine people are to exercise the right of suffrage in the election of municipal officers, a right only slightly restricted by conditions which have been imposed for the purpose of rewarding as well as encouraging the people in their just and natural aspirations to become educated and worthy to enjoy all the benefits of civilization.
>
> With the new municipalities a really autonomous and decentralized municipal government will be established in the towns. . . .
>
> A reading of the provisions of the law clearly demonstrates the purposes, tendencies, and beneficent intentions of the United States Government.

The statute thus adopted places in the hands of the municipal authorities practically the entire administration of the ordinary affairs of government, reserving to the central authority only such power of supervision and intervention as might be necessary to require the powers vested in the municipal officers to be exercised with loyalty and good faith.

The law relating to marriages was modified, upon the general demand of the people, so as to permit civil marriage, and give to persons thus married all the legal rights of those married by religious ceremony.

The patent and trade-mark laws of the United States were in substance adopted in the islands. The coasting trade was regulated; burdensome taxes imposed by Spanish law were abolished; the schools, which were established immediately upon our occupation of Manila, were extended and improved; a quarantine law was enacted and put in force; the customs and insular revenues were greatly increased, and a rigid high license and early closing law was enforced upon the saloons in the city of Manila. . . .

On consultation with the commission, and with the President's approval, a notice of amnesty was issued by the military governor, dated June 21, 1900, and supplemented by a public statement by the military governor, under date of July 2, 1900, based, in the main, upon the instructions to the commission. Something over five thousand persons, of all grades of the civil and military service of the insurrection, among them many of the most prominent officials of the former Tagalog government, presented themselves and took the following oath:

> I hereby renounce all allegiance to any and all so-called revolutionary governments in the Philippine Islands and recognize and accept the supreme authority of the United States of America therein; and I do solemnly swear that I will bear true faith and allegiance to that Government; that I will at all times conduct myself as a faithful and law-abiding citizen of said islands, and will not, either directly or indirectly, hold correspondence with or give intelligence to an enemy of the United States, neither will I aid, abet, harbor, or protect such enemy. That I impose upon myself this voluntary obligation without any mental reservation or purpose of evasion, so help me God. . . .

The commission in their legislative action are following the ordinary course of legislative procedure. Their sessions are open, and their discussions and the proposed measures upon which they are deliberating are public, while they take testimony and receive suggestions from citizens as if they were a legislative committee. Their first legislative act was the appropriation, on the twelfth of September, of $2,000,000 (Mexican), to be used in the construction and repair of highways and bridges in the Philippine Islands. The second act, on the same day, was an appropriation of $5,000 (Mexican) for a survey of a railroad to the mountains of Benguet, in the island of Luzon.

The proposed railroad, about forty-five miles in length, extending from the Manila and Dagupan road, near the Gulf of Lingayen, to the interior, will open, at a distance of about one hundred and seventy miles from Manila, a high tableland exceedingly healthy, well wooded with pine and oak, comparatively dry and cool, and where the mercury is said to range at night in the hottest season of the year between fifty and sixty degrees Fahrenheit. The value of such a place for the recuperation of troops and foreign residents will be very great.

The third act of the commission was an appropriation for the payment of a superintendent of public instruction. They have secured for that position the services of Frederick W. Atkinson, recently principal of the high school of Springfield, Mass., who was selected by the commission for that purpose before their arrival in Manila.

Before the first of September a board of officers had been engaged upon the revision of the tariff for the islands in the light of such criticisms and suggestions as had been made regarding the old tariff. The commission have considered the report of this board, and after full public hearings of business interests in the island have formulated a tariff law which has been transmitted to the Department. This has been given to the press and published in the trade journals in this country, and suggestions thereon from the business interests of the United States have been publicly invited by the Department.

A measure has been adopted for the improvement of the harbor of Manila, where now cargoes of all large vessels have to be lightered for several miles, and where the typhoons of that region frequently prevent all shipment and discharge of cargoes for weeks at a time. Plans for the construction of a system of roads, under the appropriation already mentioned, were made by the engineer force in the islands during the recent rainy season, and an additional force of engineers has been sent from this country to aid in the construction work during the dry season now opening.

The revenues of the islands are increasing, although up to this time they are derived chiefly from customs. The customs receipts deposited with the Treasurer during the year ending June 30, 1900, amounted to $5,482,448.45. The receipts for the six months ending June 30, 1900, as compared with the corresponding six months of the preceding year, show an increase of $1,785,496.26. The revenues will not, however, be sufficient for the construction of the roads, the harbor improvements, the railroad, and the establishment of necessary schools as rapidly as those undertakings ought to progress.

I recommend that provision be made by Congress either for a loan to the insular treasury, to be repaid out of the revenues of the island hereafter, of a sufficient amount for the building of the proposed railroad, or that authority be granted for the issue of bonds for that purpose constituting an obligation of the insular government secured by a lien upon the road.

A civil service board has been constituted by the commission, and a civil service law has been enacted by the commission providing for the application of the merit system to appointments in the island. . . .

Much embarrassment has been caused by the condition of the currency in the islands. Under Spanish control the business of the islands was transacted almost entirely by the use of the Mexican silver dollar of 377.17+ grains. The people of the country practically know no other currency, and it is impossible to transact business generally with American currency among a people to whom its value is unknown. Our soldiers who receive their pay in American currency and wish to spend it in the islands, our quartermasters and commissaries who wish to purchase supplies, and all other persons who come into the possession of American money which they desire to use in the islands are obliged to purchase Mexican dollars. These are worth in the neighborhood of fifty cents American money, but their price continually fluctuates with the market price of silver.

The present disturbances in China have caused a scarcity in the supply, which has sent the price up to the neighborhood of fifty-two cents, while the insular government — which, of course, has been obliged to follow some established rule for the payment of its employees—has been receiving them at fifty cents. This condition, while it is profitable to the bankers of Manila, is the cause of constant loss and annoyance to all other people, and, both because of the scarcity and the fluctuation in value, is a serious injury to business.

Two remedies have been suggested: One that we should ourselves coin a dollar for use in the islands of the same weight and fineness as the Mexican dollar, which shall be permitted equally with that coin to take its chances with the fluctuation of the market, but which would relieve us from an embarrassment caused by a limited supply of coin bearing the Mexican stamp. The other suggestion is that we should coin an insular dollar which we shall undertake to redeem in gold at fifty cents, and which, being substantially the same in value and appearance as the Mexican dollar, would pass current in the islands, and would, as rapidly as it became the medium of exchange, bring the islands to a gold basis.

Final Military Operations in the Philippines

Extract from the Report of the Secretary of War for 1901 [1]

At the date of my last report (November 30, 1900), formal and open resistance to American authority in the Philippines had practically terminated, and the Filipino insurgent forces had adopted a system of guerrilla warfare, closely approaching brigandage. To contend successfully against this condition and to suppress it, to afford protection to the peaceful and unarmed inhabitants, and to reëstablish local civil governments had necessitated the distribution of our forces to

[1] Page 31.

more than four hundred stations. This process continued until a maximum of five hundred and two stations were occupied, holding every important town and strategic point in the archipelago. The scattered guerrilla insurgent bands obtained funds and supplies from the towns and the country in the vicinity of their operations. The people thus contributing to the support of these guerrillas had been rarely interfered with. Prisoners taken in battle had been disarmed and immediately released.

This policy had been adhered to in the hope that it might make friendly neighbors of the natives, but, on the contrary, they seemed suspicious of this beneficence, and looked upon it as an evidence of weakness. It was therefore decided to apply more rigidly to the residents of the archipelago the laws of war touching the government of occupied places. Notice of this intention was given by a proclamation issued by the military governor, December 20, 1900, fully explaining the law, supplemented by letters of instruction, and followed by more vigorous field operations. It was followed immediately by the deportation to the island of Guam of about fifty prominent Filipino insurgent army officers, civil officials, insurgent agents, sympathizers, and agitators. . . .

The field work of the army was continued with renewed vigor from each of the five hundred stations and was conducted simultaneously throughout the entire archipelago with such telling results that, with the exception of Lukban in Samar and Malvar in southern Luzon, all prominent insurgent leaders with their commands were captured or surrendered.

These field operations were prosecuted notwithstanding the withdrawal from the Philippines and return to the United States of the volunteer army, comprising one regiment of cavalry and twenty-five regiments of infantry, a total of nearly 1,400 officers and 29,000 enlisted men, whose transfer across 8,000 miles of sea to San Francisco, where they were mustered out of service as required by law, was accomplished without loss.

The most important single military event of the year in the Philippines was the capture of Aguinaldo, successfully accomplished by Brigadier-General Frederick Funston, U. S. A., under the supervision and guidance of his department and division commanders, Major-Generals Wheaton and MacArthur. Soon after his capture Aguinaldo voluntarily subscribed to the oath of allegiance and issued a proclamation to the Filipino people, urging the termination of hostilities, that "lasting peace might come to them under the glorious banner of the United States." His capture was soon followed by the surrender of such prominent Filipino leaders as Tinio, Aglipay, Trías, and Cailles, with their entire following.

The operations of the field forces were so vigorous and unrelenting that more than 1,000 encounters occurred between our troops and the insurgents from May, 1900, to June 30, 1901, in which the insurgent casualties were: killed, 3,854; wounded, 1,193; captured, 6,572; surrendered, 23,095; with a total of 15,693 rifles and nearly 300,000 rounds of small-arms ammunition captured and surrendered. Our casualties during the same period were: killed, 245; wounded, 490; captured, 118; missing, 20.

I cannot speak too highly of the work of the army in the Philippines. The officers and men have been equal to the best requirements, not only of military service, but of the civil administration with which they were charged in all its details from the date of our occupancy in August, 1898, until the inauguration of a civil governor on July 4, 1901.

The recent disturbances in Samar and southern Luzon are of minor consequence, and are being stamped out by the vigorous operations of the troops. Small disturbances of this character are, unfortunately, to be expected, but will be controlled and guarded against by every means possible. The difficulties of this description are not more but less than were anticipated when my report of last year was written. . . .

The army in the Philippines has been reduced since my last report from 2,367 officers and 71,727 enlisted men to 1,111 officers and 42,128 enlisted men. When the organizations now remaining in the Philippines shall by the force of ordinary casualties and expiration of enlistments be reduced to the numbers established by the order of May 8, 1901, . . . the total enlisted strength of those organizations, exclusive of hospital corps, will be 32,079 men.

The policy indicated in my report of last year, of creating a native Philippine force which shall in time release a large part of the American army from the necessity of remaining in the Philippines, has not been neglected. The authority then asked was granted by section thirty-six of the act of February 2, 1901, Congress in that provision wisely empowering the President to proceed in his discretion by successive steps, beginning with a simple organization of scouts, and continuing, when the proper time should arrive, with the more complicated and fully officered organization of the regular army. Pursuing this policy, the small bodies of scouts mentioned in my last report have during the year been enlarged and multiplied until there are now 4,973 in the service. As command in these bodies requires special qualifications for dealing with the native soldiers, all the appointments of officers (ninety-eight in number) have been made upon the recommendations of the commanding officer in the Philippines. . . .

Reduction of Expenses. The War Department has realized the importance and the duty of following the improved conditions by a reduction of expenditures and the enforcement of economy. War always and inevitably tends toward extravagance. The conditions of active military operations frequently require that things shall be done without regard to cost. The uncertainties of the future make very liberal and often excessive estimates and requisitions the part of prudence. The difficulties of rapid transportation and extemporized storage of supplies make it impossible to enforce the ordinary standards of official accountability. The large sums expended and the greater interests involved, discourage small economies. Habits are acquired which cannot be thrown off without a positive and vigorous effort. We are making such an effort and, I think, with success. . . .

A number of improvements in the methods of transacting the business of the supply departments suited to the conditions in the Philippines have been formulated and will be followed. The economical handling of supplies will be greatly promoted by the proposed construction of much-needed storehouses and by the progressive concentration of troops at fewer stations, while the quantity of supplies required will be reduced by the gradual substitution of native troops and civil constabulary for American soldiers to maintain order.

The Civil Government of the Philippines

Extract from the Report of the Secretary of War for 1901 [1]

On February 19, 1901, in reporting upon a resolution of the Senate asking information regarding lands held in mortmain or otherwise for ecclesiastical or religious uses in the Philippine Islands, I transmitted copies of the acts of the Philippine commission numbered fifty-six to sixty-eight, inclusive, bringing the record of enactments down to January 2, 1901, and these were communicated to Congress by the message of the President dated February 25, 1901, and are printed in Senate Document 190, Fifty-sixth Congress, second session. . . .

[1] Page 53.

The presentation of this report to Congress will put the National Legislature in possession of the entire body of legislative acts, consisting of two hundred and sixty-three statutes, under which civil government in the Philippine Islands is proceeding.

A brief account of the growth and general character of the present government of the Philippines may be of service in considering these enactments.

In March, 1900, the insurgent government and the organized forces supporting it had been dispersed. The principal cities and the greater part of the country were in possession of the American forces, subject to forcible interference only by the numerous guerrilla bands which were scattered through the mountains, and considerable portions of the territory were held in apparently peaceable possession. The government was a government of military occupation, and the civil laws were being administered under the direction of military officers. All laws were subject to amendment, repealing, or overruling by the order of the military commander, which was, as must always be the case in such governments, the supreme law. Such a government is always unsatisfactory in its character, and while the conditions in many large parts of the archipelago rendered its continuance necessary, the people of the pacified provinces were eager for the resumption of peaceable conditions under a government regulated by formal and public laws which should supersede the necessarily arbitrary orders of the military commander. The first Philippine Commission, of which Mr. Schurman was chairman, had urged the early establishment of civil government, and it was manifestly desirable that as soon as possible those parts of the Filipino people who had turned to paths of peace should be relieved so far as practicable from the prejudicial effects of purely military methods.

The sole power, however, which the President was exercising in the Philippine Islands was a military power derived from his authority under the Constitution as Commander-in-Chief of the Army and Navy. The question presented was how, in the exercise of the President's military power under the Constitution, to give the peaceful people of the Philippines the real benefits of civil government. The question was answered by an analysis of the military power, which when exercised in a territory under military occupation includes executive, judicial, and legislative authority. It not infrequently happens that in a single order of a military commander can be found the exercise of all three of these different powers — the exercise of legislative power by provisions prescribing a rule of action, of judicial power by determinations of right, and of executive power by the enforcement of the rules prescribed and the rights determined. It is indeed the combination of all these powers in a single individual which constitutes the chief objection to any unnecessary continuance of military government.

It was accordingly determined that as the fundamental step in giving the substance of civil government to the people of the Philippines there should be a separation of these powers so that the executive, the legislative, and the judicial powers should be exercised by different persons throughout the pacified territory; and as it is well settled that the military authority of the President in occupied territory may be exercised through civil agents as well as military officers, it was determined that that part of the military power which was legislative in its character should be exercised by civil agents proceeding in accordance with legislative forms, while the judicial power should be exercised by courts established and regulated by the enactments of the legislative authority. The President accordingly, on March 16, 1900, appointed the second Philippine Commission of five members, with

Judge Taft as the president, and vested in them authority to exercise such legislative authority, subject to the approval and control of the Secretary of War, leaving in the military commanders the executive authority (except certain specific powers of appointment not important to notice here), and vesting judicial authority in the courts to be established through the legislative action of the commission.

On April 7, 1900, formal written instructions were given to the commission, which defined their powers and formulated the policy which was to be followed in the gradual development and conduct of civil government in the Philippines. A copy of this instrument was set forth in full in President McKinley's message to Congress on December 3, 1900. It remains the guide and rule of action of the insular government, and all the steps taken in the government of the Philippines since that time have been in conformity to its provisions. [These instructions appear on pages 287–294 of this volume.]

Legislative Power. The scope of the authority conferred upon the commission was declared in the following words:

> Exercise of this legislative authority will include the making of rules and orders, having the effect of law, for the raising of revenue by taxes, customs, duties, and imposts; the appropriation and expenditure of public funds of the islands; the establishment of an educational system throughout the islands; the establishment of a system to secure an efficient civil service; the organization and establishment of courts; the organization and establishment of municipal and departmental governments, and all other matters of a civil nature for which the military governor is now competent to provide by rules or orders of a legislative character.

With due allowance for the time necessary to reach their destination and become familiar with the conditions, the commission were directed to commence the performance of their duties on September 1, 1900; and ever since that time, with the addition to their numbers which will be hereafter stated, that body has acted as the local legislature of the

Philippine Islands. While the President vested and could vest in it no greater legislative authority than the military commander previously had, it has exercised that authority in accordance with legislative forms. Its sessions have been stated and public. Its legislative enactments have been publicly introduced and printed in the form of bills. When of general public interest they have been made the subject of public hearings before committees, which the people of the islands have freely attended and at which their views have been freely expressed. The ordinary legislative opportunities for amendment have been afforded, and finally the amendments and the bills have been publicly debated and voted upon, and the bills passed have become in effect statutes, subject to the approval of the Secretary of War, which has not in any case been withheld.

The statutes thus enacted have become the law of the land in the Philippines, and bear the same relation to governmental action and private rights in the archipelago that the statutes enacted by the Congress and the state legislatures in the United States bear within the territory for which they are enacted. Under this system the Philippine Islands have had the practical advantages of having the legislative separated from the executive authority; of having laws matured under the influence of public discussion and deliberation; of having the laws, when adopted, certain, permanent, and known; and of having the moneys of the insular government expended only pursuant to previous appropriations made by law, so that official accountability could be enforced by a rigid system of audit, testing the accounts of all disbursing officers from the lowest to the highest by reference to a fixed standard of lawful authority. I have no question that the substitution of this method for the orders of a single military commander, however competent, has been of the greatest value. I invite the attention of Congress to the two hundred and sixty-three statutes now set before them, with the hope that the work of the commission will receive the approval which I believe it merits for its high quality of constructive ability, its wise adaptation to the ends desirable to be accomplished, and its faithful adherence to the principles controlling our own government.

It should be observed that these statutes are not mere expressions of theoretical views as to how the Philippines ought to be governed, but are the practical treatment of carefully studied conditions. Many of the most important are not the beginnings but the results of patient experiment — the outcome and improvement of successive military orders dealing with the same subjects.

The Spooner Amendment. In the act making appropriation for the support of the army for the fiscal year ending June 30, 1902, approved March 2, 1901, Congress enacted the following provision (commonly known as the Spooner Amendment):

> All military, civil, and judicial powers necessary to govern the Philippine Islands, acquired from Spain by the treaties concluded at Paris on the tenth day of December, eighteen hundred and ninety-eight, and at Washington on the seventh day of November, nineteen hundred, shall, until otherwise provided by Congress, be vested in such person and persons and shall be exercised in such manner as the President of the United States shall direct for the establishment of civil government and for maintaining and protecting the inhabitants of said islands in the free enjoyment of their liberty, property, and religion: *Provided,* That all franchises granted under the authority hereof shall contain a reservation of the right to alter, amend, or repeal the same.
>
> Until a permanent government shall have been established in said archipelago full reports shall be made to Congress on or before the first day of each regular session of all legislative acts and proceedings of the temporary government instituted under the provisions hereof; and full reports of the acts and doings of said government, and as to the condition of the archipelago and of its people, shall be made to the President, including all information which may be useful to the Congress in providing for a more permanent government: *Provided,* That no sale or lease or other disposition of the public lands or the timber thereon or the mining rights

therein shall be made: *And provided further,* That no franchise shall be granted which is not approved by the President of the United States, and is not in his judgment clearly necessary for the immediate government of the islands and indispensable for the interest of the people thereof, and which cannot, without great public mischief, be postponed until the establishment of permanent civil government; and all such franchises shall terminate one year after the establishment of such permanent civil government.

These provisions were immediately communicated to the commission by cable, with the following direction:

Until further orders government will continue under existing instructions and orders.

Conditions and Policy. The conditions at that time did not permit, nor, great as has been the improvement, do they now permit, the abandonment of military government throughout the archipelago. In the more unsettled portions of the islands the restrictive and punitive force of purely civil administration would as yet be quite inadequate to the maintenance of order, even if the creation of a civil-service personnel were already accomplished. The work of securing the great number of competent and faithful civil agents necessary for the administration of government is necessarily slow, even in thoroughly pacified territory. It requires that the appointing power should become familiar with great numbers of the natives, and should learn both who are competent and who are to be trusted — a necessarily gradual process.

The policy contemplated in the instructions of April seventh, and followed by the War Department, has been to press forward steadily, as rapidly as it could be done safely and thoroughly, the gradual substitution of government through civil agents for government through military agents, so that the administration of the military officer shall be continually narrowed, and that of the civil officer continually enlarged, until the time comes when the army can, without imperiling the peace and order of the country, be relegated to the same relation toward government which it occupies in the United States. In this way we have avoided the premature abandonment of any power necessary to enforce the authority of the United States, and at the same time have held open to the people of every community the opportunity to escape from the stringency of military rule by uniting with us in effective measures to bring about peaceful conditions in the territory which they inhabit.

Municipal Governments. The first duty charged upon the commission by the instructions of April seventh was "the establishment of municipal governments, in which the natives of the islands, both in the cities and in the rural communities, shall be afforded the opportunity to manage their own local affairs to the fullest extent of which they are capable, and subject to the least degree of supervision and control which a careful study of their capacities and observation of the workings of native control show to be consistent with the maintenance of law, order, and loyalty."

In pursuance of this instruction the commission, on January 31, 1901, passed "a general act for the organization of municipal governments in the Philippine Islands." This is act No. 82, known as the "municipal code." Under this act a town when organized becomes a municipal corporation having the customary corporate powers. The municipal authority is to be exercised by a president, vice-president, and municipal council elected for a term of two years by the qualified electors of the municipality. Provision is made for a municipal secretary and a municipal treasurer, who are to be appointed by the president with the consent of the council. The qualified electors include all persons who prior to the capture of Manila had held certain municipal offices, and all persons who own real property to the value of five hundred pesos, or pay an annual tax of thirty pesos or more, and all those who speak, read, and write either English or Spanish. (Persons guilty of crime, or of certain specific acts of disloyalty, and tax delinquents are disqualified.)

The powers of government conferred upon the municipalities are similar in character and extent to those ordinarily exercised by municipalities in the United States, and include, in general, authority to fix salaries; fill vacancies in office; provide fire, police, and health regulations; make appropriations of money for municipal purposes; manage the property of the town; regulate the construction, repair, and use of streets, wharves, and piers; establish, regulate, and maintain a police force; preserve the public peace and suppress vice; establish and maintain schools; assess property for taxation; levy taxes for municipal purposes, within the limitations prescribed by law; license the sale of intoxicating liquors; fix penalties for violation of ordinances, etc.

For the accomplishment of the purposes indicated the municipal council is empowered to make such ordinances and regulations, not repugnant to law, as may be necessary to carry into effect and discharge the powers and duties conferred by the municipal code, and such as shall seem necessary and proper to provide for the health and safety, promote the prosperity, improve the morals, peace, good order, comfort, and convenience of the municipality and the inhabitants thereof, and for the protection of property therein, and enforce obedience thereto with lawful fines or penalties.

In proceedings relative to assessment of property for taxation and the levy and collection of taxes, the municipal authorities act in conjunction with the provincial authorities of the province in which the municipality is situated; and the revenues derived from the tax levies are ratably distributed between the province and the municipalities therein.

Under this code municipal governments have been organized and are maintained in seven hundred and sixty-five towns.

Provincial Governments. A further instruction contained in the instrument of April 7, 1900, was as follows:

> The next subject in order of importance should be the organization of government in the larger administrative divisions, corresponding to counties, departments, or provinces, in which the common interests of many or several municipalities falling within the same tribal lines or the same natural geographical limits may best be subserved by a common administration.

Under this direction the commission, on February 6, 1901, passed "a general act for the organization of provincial governments in the Philippine Islands," being act No. 83, and since amended in various details by act No. 133 and act No. 223. Under this act a provincial government upon organization becomes a body corporate, with customary corporate powers. The officials of the provincial government are a provincial governor, secretary, treasurer, supervisor, and fiscal. The governing body is the provincial board, composed of the governor, treasurer, and supervisor. The governor is to be chosen by the councilors of the municipalities in the province. The other officers are to be appointed by the commission, and, with the exception of the fiscal, are to be appointed under the provisions of the civil service act.

The provincial government has jurisdiction over roads, bridges, and ferries not within the inhabited pueblos or barrios; over the administration of criminal law in the province; the protection and entertainment of the courts; the assessment and collection of taxes conjointly with the municipal officers; extensive visitorial and supervisory powers over municipal officers, and over the local constabulary or police. Under this statute the commission has from time to time organized thirty-five of the provinces in the archipelago. Three of these — Cebu, Bohol, and Batangas — proved to be prematurely organized, and have been turned back to the control of the military officers. The governments of the remaining thirty-two are in full operation. The organization of these municipalities and provinces was necessarily a long and painstaking proceeding, and to accomplish it the commissioners have journeyed through the islands, familiarizing themselves with the conditions, meeting the inhabitants, and consulting with the principal men. The first provincial governors were necessarily selected by the commission, but in every case they were selected upon consultation with the citizens, and with due regard to their informally expressed wishes.

The city of Manila has been placed under a special government quite similar to that of Washington, provided by act No. 183, entitled " An act to incorporate the city of Manila", passed July 31, 1901.

Judicial Establishment. A third duty specifically imposed upon the commission was to provide for the organization and establishment of courts. In performance of this duty the commission has established a judicial system, provided for by act No. 136, entitled " An act to provide for the organization of courts in the Philippine Islands". The judicial power of the government of the islands is vested in a supreme court, consisting of a chief justice and six associate justices, sitting in Manila, Iloilo, and Cebu, and a court of first instance in each of fourteen judicial districts, which include the entire archipelago, both of these being courts of record, and a justice's court in each municipality. The judges are to be appointed by the commission. The supreme court has appellate jurisdiction to review the decisions of courts of first instance, and original jurisdiction to issue writs of mandamus, certiorari, prohibition, habeas corpus, and quo warranto, and to issue writs of certiorari and such other auxiliary writs and process as may be necessary to the complete exercise of its original or appellate jurisdiction.

The courts of first instance have original jurisdiction in all civil actions except those upon a money demand of less than

$100; in all criminal cases in which the penalty may exceed $100 fine or six months' imprisonment; in admiralty and probate cases, and to issue writs of injunction, mandamus, certiorari, prohibition, quo warranto, and habeas corpus. They have appellate jurisdiction over all cases arising in the justices' courts. The justices' courts have jurisdiction of cases involving less than $100 and of petty offenses. Under the provisions of this law justices' courts have been organized in the seven hundred and sixty-five established municipalities, courts of first instance in the fourteen judicial districts, and a supreme court, with the Honorable Cayetano Arellano, the most distinguished lawyer of the Philippines, as chief justice, and Florentino Torres, of Manila, Joseph F. Cooper, late of Texas, James F. Smith, late of California, Charles A. Willard, late of Minnesota, Victorino Mapa, of Manila, and Fletcher Ladd, late of New Hampshire, as associate judges.

On June 12, 1901, an act (No. 140) was passed defining the judicial districts, and fixing the times and places where the courts of first instance should be held.

On August 7, 1901, the commission regulated the practice and procedure of these courts by their act No. 190, entitled "An act to provide a code of procedure in civil actions and special proceedings in the Philippine Islands".

Civil Executive Organization. In the month of June of the present year affairs in the islands were in a condition to justify a further step in the progressive narrowing of military administration by a division of the executive authority, and conferring that authority, so far as the pacified provinces were concerned, upon civil agents, leaving the executive power as to the remainder of the islands still in the hands of military officers.

The following order, by authority of the President, was made on the twenty-first of June:

War Department,
Washington, June 21, 1901.

On and after the 4th day of July, 1901, until it shall be otherwise ordered, the president of the Philippine Commission will exercise the executive authority in all civil affairs in the government of the Philippine Islands heretofore exercised in such affairs by the military governor of the Philippines, and to that end the Hon. William H. Taft, president of the said commission, is hereby appointed civil governor of the Philippine Islands. Such executive authority will be exercised under and in conformity to the instructions to the Philippine Commissioners dated April 7, 1900, and subject to the approval and control of the Secretary of War of the United States. The municipal and provincial civil governments which have been or shall hereafter be established in said islands, and all persons performing duties appertaining to the offices of civil government in said islands, will in respect of such duties report to the said civil governor.

The power to appoint civil officers, heretofore vested in the Philippine Commission or in the military governor, will be exercised by the civil governor with the advice and consent of the commission.

The military governor of the Philippines is hereby relieved from the performance, on and after the said 4th day of July, of the civil duties hereinbefore described, but his authority will continue to be exercised as heretofore in those districts in which insurrection against the authority of the United States continues to exist or in which public order is not sufficiently restored to enable provincial civil governments to be established under the instructions to the commission dated April 7, 1900.

By the President:

Elihu Root,
Secretary of War.

On the fourth of July Judge Taft was inaugurated, at Manila, as civil governor under this order, and entered upon the performance of his duties. At the same time Major-General MacArthur, after an able and successful administration of both military and civil affairs, transferred the command of the military division and the authority of military governor to Major-General Adna R. Chaffee, who had recently completed his service as American commander in the China relief expedition.

On the first of September a further step toward civil executive organization was made by the establishment of separate executive departments, to which members of the commission were assigned as follows: department of the interior, Dean C. Worcester; department of commerce and police, Luke E. Wright; department of finance and justice, Henry C. Ide; department of public instruction, Bernard Moses.

The administrative affairs of the government are apportioned among these several departments as follows:

The department of the interior has under its executive control a bureau of health, the quarantine service of the marine-hospital corps, a bureau of forestry, a bureau of mining, a bureau of agriculture, a bureau of fisheries, a weather bureau, a bureau of pagan and Mohammedan tribes, a bureau of public lands, a bureau of government laboratories, and a bureau of patents and copyrights.

The department of commerce and police has under its executive control a bureau of island and inter-island transportation, a bureau of post offices, a bureau of telegraphs, a bureau of coast and geodetic survey, a bureau of engineering and construction of public works other than public buildings, a bureau of insular constabulary, a bureau of prisons, a bureau of light-houses, a bureau of commercial and street-railroad corporations, and all corporations except banking.

The department of finance and justice embraces the bureau of the insular treasury, the bureau of the insular auditor, a bureau of customs and immigration, a bureau of internal revenue, the insular cold-storage and ice plant, a bureau of banks, banking, coinage, and currency, and the bureau of justice.

The department of public instruction embraces a bureau of public instruction, a bureau of public charities, public libraries, and museums, a bureau of statistics, a bureau of public records, a bureau of public printing, and a bureau of architecture and construction of public buildings.

At the same time, by appointment of the President, three distinguished Filipinos, Señor Trinidad H. Pardo de Tavera, of Manila, Señor Benito Legarda, of Manila, and Señor José Luzuriaga, of Negros, were added to the commission.

On the twenty-ninth of October, in order to relieve somewhat the very great pressure under which Governor Taft was laboring, the following order was made, creating the office of vice-governor and appointing Commissioner Wright to that position:

WHITE HOUSE,
WASHINGTON, October 29, 1901.

By virtue of the authority vested in me as President of the United States, the Honorable Luke E. Wright is appointed vice-governor, with authority to act as civil governor of the Philippine Islands whenever the civil governor is incapacitated by illness, or certifies that his temporary absence from the seat of government will make it necessary for the vice-governor to exercise such powers and duties.

THEODORE ROOSEVELT.

Division of Jurisdiction. Since the fourth of July the civil and military agents of the government of the islands have been conducting administration within their respective jurisdictions in substantial harmony. By mutual consent the seven provinces of La Union, Ilocos Sur, Abra, Ilocos Norte, Cagayan, Isabela, and Zambales have been found to be sufficiently advanced in pacification for the organization of provincial governments, and the provisions of the provincial government act and the authority of the civil governor have been extended over them. At the same time, the three provinces already mentioned have been by like consent restored to the executive control of the military governor. . . .

Approximately 74,152 square miles, or fifty-eight per cent of the estimated area of the islands, and 4,902,837 people, or seventy per cent of the estimated population of the islands, are now under the civil administration; and approximately 53,701 square miles, or forty-two per cent of the total area, and 2,072,236 people, or thirty per cent of the total estimated population, are under military administration.

Insular Constabulary and Municipal Police. The initial step in the organization of a native police force was taken on June 18, 1900, by General Order No. 87, of the military governor. This was followed by act No. 58 of the commission, December 12, 1900, appropriating $150,000 for expenses of organization and maintenance of a police force. The municipal code of January 31, 1901, required every municipality to establish and regularly maintain a police department. The Manila charter of July 31, 1901, required the establishment and maintenance of a regular police force. On July 18, 1901, act No. 175 of the commission provided for the establishment, under the general supervision of the civil governor, of an insular constabulary, for the purpose of better maintaining peace, law, and order in the various provinces. This organization is under the general charge of a chief of the insular constabulary, and is to consist of not less than fifteen nor more than one hundred and fifty privates, properly officered, for each province. The archipelago is divided into four divisions, for each of which there is an assistant chief.

There is also a corps of inspectors consisting of not less than one nor more than four for each province, who are charged with the command of the insular constabulary, and the duty of inspecting the municipal police of the various municipalities. The sergeants, corporals, and privates in each province are selected from the residents of the province. They are enlisted for two years unless sooner discharged. The chief and the force generally are declared to be peace officers, and are authorized and empowered to prevent and suppress brigandage, unlawful assemblages, riots, insurrections, and other breaches of the peace and violations of the law. . . . The force thus constituted is the result of a progressive development covering a year and a half of experiment. These experiments appear to justify the conclusion that a native police force, well officered, can be made faithful and effective, can be trusted with arms, and will be an element of constantly increasing value in the maintenance of order. The latest reports show a little over six thousand natives employed in the various municipal police forces and between nine hundred and one thousand already enlisted in the insular constabulary.

Civil Service. In providing the personnel of the government which is thus gradually superseding military administration, the Department has proceeded upon the assumption that the honor and credit of the United States is so critically involved in creating a good government that the importance of securing the best men available should outweigh and practically exclude all other considerations. This principle of selection has been followed without deviation. No officer, high or low, has been appointed upon any one's request, or upon any personal, social, or political consideration. The general power of appointment was vested by the instructions of April seventh in the commission, which is eight thousand miles removed from all American pressure for office, and which will stand or fall upon its success or failure in getting competent men. The order of June twenty-first appointing the civil governor transferred the power to the civil governor with the consent of the commission. The exercise of this power by the commission and by the civil governor has not been interfered with or overruled in any case. The only appointments of a civil character made by the Administration in the United States since the commission entered upon its duties have been the governor, vice-governor, and members of the commission, appointed by the President on the recommendation of the Secretary of War; the auditor, deputy-auditor, and treasurer, who are officers of an independent accounting system, appointed by the Secretary of War; the director-general of posts, appointed by the Postmaster-General.

The practice regarding all appointments to offices not covered by the very comprehensive civil service law has been to refer all applications for appointment received at the White House or the War Department, with the accompanying testimonials, immediately to the commission or the civil governor, with instructions to report when the service of the applicant was desired. In numerous cases the commission have cabled for further information, which has been sought and furnished as promptly as possible. Such inquiries regarding candidates for judicial appointments have been made by the Department of Justice through the judges and district attorneys in the judicial districts in which the candidates formerly resided. Special acknowledgment is due to the officers of that Department for their active and zealous coöperation in this respect. In like manner information as to the most competent persons to fill places which in this country come under the jurisdiction of the Treasury Department, the Department of the Interior, and the Department of Agriculture has been sought through those Departments, respectively, and they have always rendered prompt and effective assistance.

The civil service law enacted by the Philippine Commission September 19, 1900 (act No. 5), has been put into successful and satisfactory operation. The civil service rules required by the act were adopted by the board and submitted to the military governor on the twenty-eighth of December last, and were promulgated on the second of January. The rules provide that examinations of a suitable and practical character, and absolutely impartial, shall be held to test the relative capacity and fitness of applicants for the positions to which they seek to be appointed, and that in making certifications to fill all vacancies the names of the highest eligibles shall be certified from which selection shall be made by the appointing officer. The board has been diligent in adapting the principles of the act to the many varying conditions; and regular examinations have been commenced. A manual of information has been printed and can be obtained upon application to the civil service board at Manila or to the War Department at Washington. . . .

System of Account and Audit. At the time of my last report the accounting system of the islands was still conducted under the provisions of an executive order promulgated on May 8, 1899. At that time the conditions of very active warfare, the confusion incident to the constant movements and changes of the military officers charged with civil disbursements, the necessity for the exercise of independent discretion in expenditures, and our slender knowledge of conditions, made it impossible to apply any such complete and detailed methods for securing official accountability as have been found useful in the United States.

At the beginning of the present year, however, a point had been reached in the development of government which made an important advance in the accounting system possible, and a complete revision of that system was undertaken. For this purpose the experience acquired in dealing with the accounts of Porto Rico, Cuba, and the Philippines was utilized, and the accounting officers of the United States Treasury, Post Office, and War Department were brought into conference. Upon their joint recommendations a new system of accounting and audit was embodied in an executive order signed by the President on February 23, 1901, and in a series of rules and regulations, approved by the Secretary of War at the same time, and promulgated by an act of the commission (No. 90, of February 28, 1901). The new regulations went into effect on April 1, 1901. They practically put into force in the Philippine Islands the accounting and auditing system of the United States, and furnish all the checks and safeguards which Congress has thrown about the moneys of the United States. Since April first they have been in force in the Philippines, and also in Cuba, with comprehensive and satisfactory results. . . .

Education. In pursuance of the instructions of April 7, 1900, the commission, on January 21, 1901, passed their act (No. 74), establishing a department of public instruction under the direction of a general superintendent, with authority to divide the archipelago into eighteen divisions, to establish schools in every pueblo; to procure buildings, material, and teachers. The act also provided for a general supervisory board, composed of the general superintendent and four other members appointed by the commission, and for a local school board in each municipality organized under the municipal code, one-half of the members to be elected by the municipal council and the remaining half to be appointed by the division superintendent. The act gave authority to the general superintendent to obtain from the United States one thousand trained teachers, with monthly salaries of not less than seventy-five dollars or not more than one hundred and twenty-five dollars.

It further provided for the establishment and maintenance in Manila of a normal school for the education of natives of the islands in the science of teaching; for the establishment and maintenance in Manila of a trade school for the instruction of the natives in the useful trades, and for the establishment and maintenance of a school of agriculture in the island of Negros.

The close relations between church and state under Spanish rule in the Philippines had resulted in the predominance of religious over secular education in such public schools as had existed. The complete separation of church and state, which is one of the fundamental principles of the new government, of course requires a complete change of method, and tends to leave the inhabitants of the islands with but very few facilities for religious education. This subject was disposed of by the following provision of act No. 74:

SEC. 16. No teacher or other person shall teach or criticise the doctrines of any church, religious sect, or denomination, or shall attempt to influence the pupils for or against any church or religious sect in any public school established under this act. If any teacher shall intentionally violate this section, he or she shall, after due hearing, be dismissed from the public service.

Provided, however, that it shall be lawful for the priest or minister of any church established in the pueblo where a public school is situated, either in person or by a designated teacher of religion, to teach religion for one-half an hour three times a week in the school building to those public school pupils whose parents or guardians desire it and express their desire therefor in writing filed with the principal teacher of the school, to be forwarded to the division superintendent, who shall fix the hours and rooms for such teaching. But no public school teacher shall either conduct religious exercises or teach religion or act as a designated religious teacher in the school building under the foregoing authority, and no pupil shall be required by any public school teacher to attend and receive the religious instruction herein permitted. Should the opportunity thus given to teach religion be used by the priest, minister, or religious teacher for the purpose of arousing disloyalty to the United States, or of discouraging the attendance of pupils at such public schools, or creating a disturbance of public order, or of interfering with the discipline of the school, the division superintendent, subject to the approval of the general superintendent of public instruction, may, after due investigation and hearing, forbid such offending priest, minister, or religious teacher from entering the public school building thereafter.

The act further provides that the English language shall, as soon as practicable, be made the basis of all public school instruction.

Under the provisions of this act $162,000 were immediately appropriated for the purchase of text-books and school stationery and supplies, and the very difficult task of securing suitable school accommodations and competent teachers was vigorously begun. The superintendent reported on the twenty-seventh of May, subsequent to the passage of the act, that there had been appointed eight superintendents, eight principals and assistants for normal, agricultural, and manual training work, and seven hundred and eighty-one teachers from the United States, and two superintendents and eighty teachers from applicants in the Philippines, and that the basis for these appointments had been more than eight thousand personal written applications with testimonials appended, and the recommendations of normal school principals, college presidents, and state officials, and the personal certification of the qualifications of applicants by leading educational men in the United States with whom the superintendent is personally acquainted, or whose character is well known to him by repute. Of the teachers appointed from the United States, six hundred and eighty-two have been sent from this country to the Philippines by army transports. One voyage of the transport *Thomas* was devoted exclusively to the transportation of teachers, and the others went upon the regular semi-monthly sailings of the other transports. The expenses of travel were paid from the insular funds.

The Manila normal school for the instruction of native teachers was opened on the tenth of April. Accommodations had been provided for 350 scholars, and by the opening day 450 had enrolled. Additional accommodations were procured, and 600 were admitted to the classes, of whom 570 studied faithfully to the end of the term. The report of the interest and application of the students and their progress in acquiring English is gratifying. The need of teachers for the establishment of the general system of schools contemplated is just beginning to be supplied. There is a great lack of suitable buildings. In most of the pueblos such buildings are not to be found, and curiously enough in that country of great forests it is very difficult to obtain lumber for construction purposes.

Many more teachers must be obtained; many buildings must be constructed. Time and persistent energy and very large amounts of money will be necessary to put the system in working order. No regular system of reports has yet been possible, but from the reports received it is estimated that not less than 150,000 children are actually enrolled in the free primary schools; that one-half of these are being compelled to wait because there are not adequate school-rooms, and that there are 75,000 children in actual daily attendance upon the schools already established. There are between 3,000 and 4,000 native elementary teachers employed. About 2,000 of these are receiving daily instruction in English.

Over 10,000 adult natives are studying English in evening schools under American teachers, and many more are applying than can be cared for as yet. The greatest eagerness is manifested to learn English. There is a widespread desire to send boys to the United States for education. Many of the towns are arranging to send and support boys here for that purpose. The educational situation is, briefly, as follows: There is a widespread and earnest desire for education among the people of the islands. There are more people anxious for education than there are teachers to furnish it. There are more teachers than there are school buildings or rooms for them to teach in. I think no one can become familiar with the facts without deep interest and a strong desire to press forward provision for education. All the good influences of American civilization may enter through this open door.

Utilization of Forest Products. The most evident and striking element of wealth in the Philippine Islands consists of its forests. The official geographic statistics of 1876 fix the forest area at 51,537,243 acres. In 1890 Fernando Castro estimated the forest area at 48,112,920 acres. But a small part of this vast area is in private ownership, and there are probably between 40,000,000 and 50,000,000 acres of forest land which formerly belonged to the Crown of Spain, and by the Treaty of Paris became the property of the United States. Pine, cedar, mahogany, and hundreds of hard woods, valuable dye woods, and rubber and gutta-percha trees exist in immense quantities.

From time immemorial the inhabitants of the islands have been accustomed to resort to these public forests for their firewood and lumber in the exercise of rights under licenses regulated by law. The forestry laws and regulations of Spain in the Philippines, while affording this use of the public forests to the people, aimed at the establishment of a scientific system of forestry similar to that which exists in Germany and other European countries. These regulations were, however, not adequately enforced. Upon the military occupation of the country by the American forces it was determined, if possible, to enforce the system and at the same time preserve and utilize the forests. The principle followed under such a system is, instead of cutting all the trees at once and leaving waste land, to cut only the full-grown trees, leaving the smaller trees to grow and in their turn become ready for cutting in a never-ending series. The annual growth of these forests is estimated at fourteen hundred million (1,400,000,000) cubic feet, about three times the cut of lumber for 1900 in the entire United States. At present more than ninety-nine per cent of this annual growth is going to waste. With proper treatment it may be made an inexhaustible source of wealth.

The forestry bureau was accordingly organized by the military governor on April 14, 1900, and placed under the direction of Captain George P. Ahern, of the Ninth United States Infantry, an officer of experience and extensive study in forestry matters. A small force of foresters and rangers was employed, and a careful study of the forests was entered upon. On June 27, 1900, the Spanish regulations were reënacted with such amendments as were necessary to adjust them to the changed conditions, in a general order of the military governor known as General Order No. 92, which went into effect on July 1, 1900, and the issue of licenses for the cutting of marked trees of full growth and down timber for firewood and for lumber, under the regulations and supervision of the officers of the forestry bureau, was continued.

Upon the passage of the act of March 2, 1901, containing the provision that no sale or other disposition of the public lands or timber thereon or the mining rights therein shall be made, coupled with a provision for the granting of such franchises by the President as were, in his judgment, clearly necessary for the immediate government of the islands, and indispensable for the interests of the people thereof, the following dispatch was received from the Philippine Commission March 7, 1901:

ROOT, Secretary of War, Washington:

High price lumber one of people's greatest burdens. Present situation very little timber on private land; people almost entirely are obliged to depend upon purchase timber from government land to repair damage owing to the war. If recent legislation abrogates general orders, headquarters department of military governor, series of last year, No. 92, fixing reasonable rates and proper limitations under which any resident may cut public timber, it will produce greatest hardship. If so, ask authority to put imported timber on free list. Is cutting public timber for public works forbidden ? Request opinion.

TAFT.

Upon consultation with such members of the committee which drafted the provisions above referred to as could be reached after the adjournment of Congress, and upon full consideration of all the circumstances in view of which Congress acted, including full reports which had already been made regarding the system followed by the forestry bureau, it was concluded that if the legislative intent had been to prohibit the issue of the customary licenses and cut the people of the Philippine Islands off from the privileges which they had long enjoyed, far different language would have been used, and that the intent was to prevent undue American exploitation and not to interfere with the existing and established practice, and thus create a timber famine in the islands.

The following reply to Judge Taft's dispatch of March seventh was accordingly sent:

March 30, 1901.

TAFT, Manila:

With reference to your telegram of the seventh, it is considered provisions act Congress, March 2, do not interfere with established system forestry regulations provided for by Spanish law as modified by military governor-general, orders 92, June 27, 1900. Full discussion of subject forwarded by mail. Advise General MacArthur.

ROOT.

The total number of timber licenses issued from the organization of the forestry bureau on July 1, 1900, to October 22, 1901, has been —

Licenses issued prior to March 2, 1901	296
Licenses issued since March 2, 1901	181
Total	477

All of these licenses are limited to one year, and 196 expire by limitation on December 1, 1901. They were distributed among forty-one different provinces and small islands. Under them there was cut between July 1, 1900, and June 30, 1901, 2,439,431 cubic feet of timber and 2,000,000 cubic feet of firewood, yielding a revenue to the insular government of $199,373.11 (Mexican). The aggregate of these cuttings, amounting to 4,439,431 cubic feet, is less than one-third of one per cent of the estimated annual growth of the forests, so that if a perfect forestry system were applied, three hundred times as much could be cut each year without decreasing the supply. Three times as much was cut for lumber alone during the year 1900 in Alabama, three times as much in Missouri, six times as much in Mississippi, eight times as much in Louisiana, ten times as much in Arkansas, eleven times as much in Texas, twenty times as much in Oregon, and twenty-five times as much in Washington — eighty-five times as much in these eight states, although the population of the Philippine Islands is about one-tenth of the population of the entire United States.

The amount cut has proved to be inadequate to the wants of the community. The inaccessibility of the forests, the absence of railroads and the prohibition against building them, the lack of proper tools and machinery and skilled labor, have combined with the limitations imposed by the forestry regulations to make it impossible to get enough timber for the uses of the people. About fifty per cent of the timber cut has been used by the Government in the construction of barracks, storehouses, bridges, and other public works, and with 40,000,000 acres of the finest timber in the world standing in the islands, great numbers of native property owners have been unable to rebuild their homes destroyed during the war, and the Government has been obliged to import from the United States nearly 1,000,000 feet of lumber for its absolutely necessary construction.

Every effort is being made to enlarge the force of competent foresters for the enforcement of the forestry regulations. I earnestly recommend, as a matter of material importance to the people of the Philippine Islands, such legislation as shall permit the building of railroads from the towns to the forests, and the employment of capital, under proper limitations and supervision, in the cutting of timber which shall supply the wants of the people and utilize the now wasting growth of the forests. . . .

Agriculture. It is manifest that with their great extent of fertile land, and wide variations of elevation, and consequently of temperature, improvements in the agriculture of the Philippine Islands can be made to the immense advantage of the people. The methods of cultivation are primitive and ineffective. The ordinary vegetables, notwithstanding the fertility of the land, are small and poor, and the stock is evidently run out and should be renewed. Many grains which are unknown to the people can undoubtedly be raised. They live chiefly on rice, and raise less than they consume. They imported during the last fiscal year 392,932,908 pounds, valued at $5,490,958.

The kind of work toward improvement and diversity of crops and instruction in methods which is being done in this country by the Department of Agriculture would be of inestimable benefit in the Philippines. On the eighth of October the commission created a bureau of agriculture, and the Secretary of Agriculture has kindly consented to spare for a time, to serve as the chief of this bureau, Professor F. Lamson-Scribner, one of the chiefs of division and the leading agrostologist of his Department. It is very desirable that the request which the Secretary of Agriculture will make for authority to establish an agricultural experiment station in the Philippines should be granted.

Public Works. The harbors of the Philippines are generally shallow. At Manila all the freight of sea-going vessels of over sixteen feet draft has to be transferred by lighters between the ship and the shore for several miles at very great expense and risk. Storms frequently interrupt business altogether, especially in the season of typhoons, and great damage is often caused to the unprotected shipping. The burden imposed upon commerce by this method of transacting business is great. The freight rate between Manila and Hong-Kong, a distance of about seven hundred miles, is as much as, and sometimes more than, between San Francisco and Hong-Kong, a distance of about eight thousand miles.

The commerce of Manila urgently demands the creation of a thoroughly protected harbor with sufficient depth of water to accommodate the largest ships, where they can lie in safety and load and discharge their cargoes in all weathers. More than twenty years ago the Spanish government formulated an elaborate scheme for the improvement of the harbor, and had completed about thirty per cent of the work before the cession of the islands to the United States. After a careful examination of the plans and specifications of the Spanish engineers by Major Biddle, now the Engineer Commissioner of the District of Columbia, and then chief engineer of the Division of the Philippines, they were adopted with some modifications. By act No. 22, passed October 15, 1900, and an amendatory act No. 101, passed March 19, 1901, a sum of $1,000,000 in American money was appropriated for the improvement of the harbor, and contracts were authorized for an additional amount not exceeding $2,000,000. . . .

Nearly every account of the Philippines dwells upon the wretched condition of roads, or rather the absence of roads, which practically prevents internal commerce except immediately upon the navigable waters. On September 12, 1900, the commission, by act No. 1, appropriated $2,000,000 (Mexican) to be expended in the construction of highways and bridges. Both this work and the river and harbor work above referred to have been placed under the charge of the United States Corps of Engineers. The force of engineers in the Philippines was greatly increased for that purpose, and they have been working during the year on over eight hundred miles of roads. Seventy-five thousand dollars have been expended in the construction of a road from the town of Pozorrubio, in the province of Pangasinan, to the town of Baguio, in the province of Benguet, mentioned in my last report.

A cold-storage and ice plant, ample to supply the needs of both the army, and the civilians in Manila who are accustomed to the use of ice, has been completed at an expense of about $700,000. Two market houses in the city of Manila have been built, and two others are in course of erection. The Bridge of Spain has been widened, the erection of the Santa Cruz Bridge has been commenced, repairs to the Ayala Bridge have been undertaken, and all of the small bridges in Manila, of which there are a great many, have either been practically rebuilt or extensively repaired. Two crematories for the disposal of garbage have been erected in Manila, and an appropriation has been made for the erection of another in that city. A new building for the customs offices has been erected, and new warehouses, affording additional storage space for about thirteen thousand tons, have been built. About four hundred and seventy-two cubic meters of cut stone have been utilized in the extension of the Luneta sea wall.

The Mariveles quarantine station has been improved by the repairing of the old existing barracks and the construction of a hospital for contagious diseases, at a cost of $25,166.50; by the construction of a wharf, at an expenditure of $64,500; by the construction of four new buildings on the wharves and two on shore, at a cost of $38,900; the installation of an electric-light plant, at an expense of $23,175; the repairing of old buildings, the building of sewers, and modern plumbing. The station is now practically complete, and provides accommodation for eight hundred steerage and forty cabin passengers. . . .

Currency and Banking. I beg to call attention to the statements made in my last report upon the urgent need of reforming the currency of the Philippines, which is in as bad a condition as is possible. Time has confirmed the opinion in which I then concurred with the Secretary of the Treasury that the wise course is to coin and pay out for Government uses pesos of a little less than the weight and fineness of the Mexican pesos of 377.17 + grains of pure silver, at the rate of two silver pesos for one gold dollar, the ratio now maintained in the islands between Mexican dollars and American gold dollars, and to maintain that same relation between the new coins and gold by exchanging gold for them at that rate.

I am satisfied that such coins, being substantially identical in size and exchange value with the coins to which the people are accustomed, will pass into circulation, and that as rapidly as this is accomplished the business of the country will come upon a gold-standard basis representing a fixed relation between the proposed coins and American money.

There is urgent need for greater banking facilities in the Philippines. There are no American banks there, and there is no power to create any banking corporation. The effect of this is that the banking establishments which were established under Spanish rule still monopolize the field, while American capital is excluded. I recommend the extension of the national banking act to the Philippines, with such modifications as the circumstances demand. . . .

Tariff. The tariff bill mentioned in my last report as having been prepared by the commission has been completed. The publication of the bill in the trade and other newspapers of this country, accompanied by an invitation of criticism, resulted in a large volume of correspondence, all of which was carefully considered, and in some changes, which were made with the concurrence of the commission. The appraisers of the New York custom-house, and other tariff experts in this country, were consulted as to the descriptive language used, in order to avoid, so far as possible, ambiguities which might lead to litigation.

After being first approved by the Secretary of War, the bill was enacted by the Philippine Commission on the sixteenth of September as act No. 230, and went into effect on the fifteenth of November. It represents more than a year of painstaking consideration and discussion by competent men thoroughly familiar with the business conditions and government needs of the Philippines, with the benefit of three years' experience of the good and bad points of the former law, with the benefit of the best expert assistance and advice, and with full opportunity for public criticism and suggestion by the business men both of the Philippines and of the United States.

Commerce and Revenue. Notwithstanding the serious disadvantages under which it has labored, the business of the islands has increased during the past year. The total value of merchandise (exclusive of army supplies) imported during the fiscal year 1901 was $30,279,406, as against $20,601,436 for the fiscal year 1900, and the total value of merchandise exported during the fiscal year 1901 was $23,214,948, as against $19,751,068 for the fiscal year 1900 — an increase of forty-seven per cent in the value of imports and an increase of seventeen and one-half per cent in the value of exports.

The imports came from the following countries:

United States	$2,855,685	China	4,339,941
United Kingdom	6,956,145	Hong-Kong	2,340,585
Germany	2,135,252	British East Indies	2,182,892
France	1,683,929	All other countries	5,623,625
Spain	2,161,352		

The exports went to the following countries:

United States	$2,572,021	China	73,701
United Kingdom	10,704,741	Hong-Kong	2,697,276
Germany	81,526	British East Indies	759,286
France	1,934,256	All other countries	2,736,886
Spain	1,655,255		

The imports from the United States show an increase of 72.4 per cent over the imports of 1900, and the exports to the United States show a decrease of twenty-seven per cent from the exports of 1900. The imports from the United Kingdom, from Germany, from France, and from the British East Indies have increased in a greater proportion than the imports from the United States.

The revenues of the Philippine government during the fiscal year 1901 amounted to $10,817,662.31, as against $6,723,852.18 during the fiscal year 1900. The total expenditures during the fiscal year 1901 amounted to $6,763,821.68, as against $5,218,381.12 in 1900, making an increase of revenues of over $4,000,000, and an increase of expenditures of about $1,500,000, and a surplus of revenues over expenditures of $4,053,840.63, as against a surplus of $1,505,471.06 for the preceding year. Of course the great expenditures which have been undertaken for public works, education, insular constabulary, extension of the judicial system, etc., will rapidly dispose of this surplus. . . .

Power to Contract Loans. Many of the things which call urgently for attention — such, for instance, as education and public works — ought to be pressed forward without waiting for the slow process of saving from annual revenues, and authority ought to be given, under proper restrictions, to the insular government and to the cities of the archipelago to raise money by the issue of bonds in pursuance of the same policy which has been followed by our American states and cities.

Lands of Religious Orders. One of the purposes for which the borrowing of money should be authorized is the acquisition of the tracts of land held by religious orders in the islands. The policy of the Executive in its treatment of the new relations necessarily assumed by the church toward the state under American rule was expressed in the instructions of April 7, 1900. . . .

Three religious orders, the Dominicans, Augustinians, and Recolletos, who were established under Spanish rule, had at the time of American occupation a holding of about 403,000 acres of agricultural lands. These lands are occupied by a native tenantry intensely hostile to the friars, and that hostility is unquestionably shared by the vast majority of the people of the islands. The relation of these landlords to their tenants and to the entire people was one of the chief causes of irritation and rebellion under the Spanish government.

The new conditions make it manifestly for the interest of the religious orders that they should convert into money this property, which they can obviously no longer peacefully enjoy or practically make useful. At the same time the peace and order of the community, the good will of the people toward the Government of the United States, and the interest of an effective settlement and disposition of all questions arising between the church and state in the islands, make it equally desirable that these lands should be purchased by the state and that title upon proper and reasonable terms should be offered to the tenants or to the other people of the islands. For this purpose it will be necessary that money should be obtained from other sources than the ordinary revenues of the Philippine government. The receipts from sales of the lands to natives can be devoted to the payment of any bonds issued to raise money for the purchase.

Slavery. It is gratifying to report that the efforts of the American officers to bring about a cessation of the practice of slavery among the Moros are not fruitless. The character of the slavery practiced is quite unlike that formerly practiced in the United States in this, that the Moro slave, so-called, becomes a member of the owner's family, enjoying many privileges, often having voluntarily sold himself into slavery to better his condition. The so-called slaves themselves exhibit no special anxiety to change their condition. All who seek freedom receive it upon coming into the American lines.

The following proclamation has been issued by the Dato Mandi, one of the most powerful of the Moro rulers:[1]

[1] This is a literal copy of the original, which was written in Arabian characters.

To the Datos, Principals, and Old Men of the
Moro Rancherias of this District:

Being aware that some Moros in villages within my jurisdiction continue to engage in slavery, some by loan made to poor families, some buying them for trading, all doubtless forgetful of the orders issued by the old Government of Spain, which strictly prohibited slavery, and in order not to wait to be again instructed by the civil Government of the United States, I direct all my subjects, especially the datos, principals, and old men of all villages in my jurisdiction, beginning with this date, to comply and enforce the rules provided in the following sections, viz.:

First. In view of the fact that slavery has not and never will bring any progress with it, you shall prevent Moros having slaves of their own or other race.

Second. If actually some are in such condition because of debt contracted for his immediate needs, he will not be considered as such slave, but as a hired man who receives a salary for his services, and with the view of extinguishing the debt in from eight to ten months.

Third. It is strictly prohibited from this date illegal trading of Moro slaves and also slavery among themselves. Offenders of these rules will be liable to a penalty or a fine.

The Dato Rajahmuda. Mandi.
Zamboanga, April 19, 1901.

It is believed that the peaceful process, the rapid advance of which is indicated by this proclamation, will accomplish the desired result much more readily than it could be accomplished in any other way.

Progress of Government. In general the progress of good government in the Philippines during the past year has been greater than the most sanguine American familiar with the obstacles to be overcome could have anticipated. Mutual understanding and confidence are necessary elements to success in such a field. These cannot be extemporized or forced; they must come freely, naturally, and slowly. I think our legislators and administrators in the Philippines are winning the confidence of the people by deserving it. For hundreds of years the Filipino people had been accustomed to fair promises never fulfilled. We have made similar promises, and what we have already done in the way of performance has been a revelation of unexpected good faith.

The organization of the Federal party in the Philippines, which has extended throughout the provinces, loyally accepting the sovereignty and asserting the sincerity and beneficent purpose of the American people, has been of the utmost value. The character of the military officers who have commanded, of Governor Taft and the members of the commission, and of the assistants whom they have gathered around them, has commanded respect and dispelled suspicion throughout a field of influence widening steadily as they have become known. A country is very fortunate which can draft from its citizens such men into the public service.

I believe that each successive step in the practical development of American purpose in the Philippines will result in wider appreciation and approval in the islands, and that we may reasonably look forward to a time not far distant which will be characterized by general good feeling, established confidence, and active coöperation on the part of all the peoples of the archipelago in our efforts for their benefit. The course will not be without its difficulties, discouragements, and reverses, but cheerful and persistent courage, faithful to the spirit of our institutions, will prevail.

General Policy of Government. The policy followed by the American Executive in dealing with the government of the Philippines (and also in dealing with the government of the other islands ceded or yielded by Spain, which have been under the control of the War Department) has been to determine and prescribe the framework of insular government, to lay down the rules of policy to be followed upon the great questions of government as they are foreseen or arise, to obtain the best and ablest men possible for insular officers, to distribute and define their powers, and then to hold them responsible for the conduct of government in the islands with the least possible interference from Washington.

Notwithstanding a rigid adherence to this policy, and consistently with it, the demands upon the Department for action in the vast and complicated business of the island governments have been constant and imperative. Different civilizations, different systems of law and procedure, and different modes of thought have evolved a great crowd of difficult questions for determination. New facts ascertained and changed conditions have called for the interpretation and application of our own rules of policy and the establishment of further rules. Different views as to the scope of authority under the distribution of powers have required reconciliation. The application of the law of military occupation to rights and practices existing under the laws of Spain, and the process of overturning inveterate wrongs have brought about frequent appeals to the highest authority, which, being made in the name of justice, have required consideration. The work undertaken has been the building up of government from the foundation upon unfamiliar ground. We have had no precedents, save the simple and meager proceedings under the occupation of California and New Mexico, more than half a century ago, and it has been necessary to decide every question upon its own merits and to make our own precedents for the future.

For the performance of all these duties full and accurate knowledge of the conditions and proceedings of all the governments in all the islands on the part of the authorities in Washington has been required. It has been necessary to follow them step by step. The President and Congress have looked to the War Department for information as to how the trust of government in the various islands was being performed, and tens of thousands of applications by the people of the United States for every conceivable kind of information regarding the islands have poured into the Department in an uninterrupted stream.

Only thorough system could arrange, record, and keep available for use the vast and heterogeneous mass of reports and letters and documents which this business has involved, furnish answers to the questions, conduct the correspondence, and keep the Secretary of War from being overwhelmed in hopeless confusion. The War Department had no machinery for the purpose. No provision for any such administrative machine was made by law. Of necessity, by the detail of officers and the employment of the temporary clerks authorized by law, such machinery has been created in the Department with a chief, an assistant chief, a law officer, a competent force of translators, accountants, stenographers, and recording and indexing and copying clerks. It is called the Division of Insular Affairs of the War Department, and it performs with admirable and constantly increasing efficiency the great variety of duties which in other countries would be described as belonging to a colonial office, and would be performed by a much more pretentious establishment. . . .

Instructions to the Philippine Commission[1]

War Department,
Washington, April 7, 1900.

Sir: I transmit to you herewith the instructions of the President for the guidance of yourself and your associates as Commissioners to the Philippine Islands.

Very respectfully,
Elihu Root,
Secretary of War.

Honorable William H. Taft,
President Board of Commissioners to the Philippine Islands.

Executive Mansion, April 7, 1900.

Sir: In the message transmitted to the Congress on the 5th of December, 1899, I said, speaking of the Philippine Islands: "As long as the insurrection continues the military arm must necessarily be supreme. But

[1] Extract from the Report of the Secretary of War of 1900, p. 72.

there is no reason why steps should not be taken from time to time to inaugurate governments essentially popular in their form as fast as territory is held and controlled by our troops. To this end I am considering the advisability of the return of the commission, or such of the members thereof as can be secured, to aid the existing authorities and facilitate this work throughout the islands."

To give effect to the intention thus expressed I have appointed the Honorable William H. Taft, of Ohio; Professor Dean C. Worcester, of Michigan; the Honorable Luke E. Wright, of Tennessee; the Honorable Henry C. Ide, of Vermont, and Professor Bernard Moses, of California, commissioners to the Philippine Islands to continue and perfect the work of organizing and establishing civil government already commenced by the military authorities, subject in all respects to any laws which Congress may hereafter enact.

The commissioners named will meet and act as a board, and the Honorable William H. Taft is designated as president of the board. It is probable that the transfer of authority from military commanders to civil officers will be gradual and will occupy a considerable period. Its successful accomplishment and the maintenance of peace and order in the meantime will require the most perfect coöperation between the civil and military authorities in the island, and both should be directed during the transition period by the same executive department. The commission will therefore report to the Secretary of War, and all their action will be subject to your approval and control.

You will instruct the commission to proceed to the city of Manila, where they will make their principal office, and to communicate with the military governor of the Philippine Islands, whom you will at the same time direct to render to them every assistance within his power in the performance of their duties. Without hampering them by too specific instruction, they should in general be enjoined, after making themselves familiar with the conditions and needs of the country, to devote their attention in the first instance to the establishment of municipal governments, in which the natives of the islands, both in the cities and in the rural communities, shall be afforded the opportunity to manage their own local affairs to the fullest extent of which they are capable, and subject to the least degree of supervision and control which a careful study of their capacities and observation of the workings of native control show to be consistent with the maintenance of law, order, and loyalty.

The next subject in order of importance should be the organization of government in the larger administrative divisions, corresponding to counties, departments, or provinces, in which the common interests of many or several municipalities falling within the same tribal lines, or the same natural geographical limits, may best be subserved by a common administration. Whenever the commission is of the opinion that the condition of affairs in the islands is such that the central administration may safely be transferred from military to civil control, they will report that conclusion to you, with their recommendations as to the form of central government to be established for the purpose of taking over the control.

Beginning with the 1st day of September, 1900, the authority to exercise, subject to my approval, through the Secretary of War, that part of the power of government in the Philippine Islands which is of a legislative nature is to be transferred from the military governor of the islands to this commission, to be thereafter exercised by them in the place and stead of the military governor, under such rules and regulations as you shall prescribe, until the establishment of the civil central government for the islands contemplated in the last foregoing paragraph, or until Congress shall otherwise provide.

Exercise of this legislative authority will include the making of rules and orders, having the effect of law, for the raising of revenue by taxes, customs, duties, and imposts; the appropriation and expenditure of public funds of the islands; the establishment of an educational system throughout the islands; the establishment of a system to secure an efficient civil service; the organization and establishment of courts; the organization and establishment of municipal and departmental governments, and all other matters of a civil nature for which the military governor is now competent to provide by rules or orders of a legislative character.

The commission will also have power during the same period to appoint to office such officers under the judicial, educational, and civil-service systems and in the municipal and departmental governments as shall be provided for. Until the complete transfer of control the military governor will remain the chief executive head of the government of the islands, and will exercise the executive authority now possessed by him and not herein expressly assigned to the commission, subject, however, to the rules and orders enacted by the commission in the exercise of the legislative powers conferred upon them. In the meantime the municipal and departmental governments will continue to report to the military governor and be subject to his administrative supervision and control, under your direction, but that supervision and control will be confined within the narrowest limits consistent with the requirement that the powers of government in the municipalities and departments shall be honestly and effectively exercised and that law and order and individual freedom shall be maintained.

All legislative rules and orders, establishments of government, and appointments to office by the commission will take effect immediately, or at such times as they shall designate, subject to your approval and action upon the coming in of the commission's reports, which are to be made from time to time as their action is taken. Wherever civil governments are constituted under the direction of the commission, such military posts, garrisons, and forces will be continued for the suppression of insurrection and brigandage, and the maintenance of law and order, as the military commander shall deem requisite, and the military forces shall be at all times subject under his orders to the call of the civil authorities for the maintenance of law and order and the enforcement of their authority.

In the establishment of municipal governments the commission will take as the basis of their work the governments established by the military governor under his order of August 8, 1899, and under the report of the board constituted by the military governor by his order of January 29, 1900, to formulate and report a plan of municipal government, of which His Honor Cayetano Arellano, president of the audiencia, was chairman, and they will give to the conclusions of that board the weight and consideration which the high character and distinguished abilities of its members justify.

In the constitution of departmental or provincial governments, they will give especial attention to the existing government of the island of Negros, constituted, with the approval of the people of that island, under the order of the military governor of July 22, 1899, and after verifying, so far as may be practicable, the reports of the successful working of that government, they will be guided by the experience thus acquired, so far as it may be applicable to the condition existing in other portions of the Philippines. They will avail themselves, to the fullest degree practicable, of the conclusions reached by the previous commission to the Philippines.

In the distribution of powers among the governments organized by the commission the presumption is always to be in favor of the smaller subdivision, so that all the powers which can properly be exercised by the municipal government shall be vested in that government, and all the powers of a more general character which can be exercised by the departmental government shall be vested in that government, and so that in the governmental system which is the result of the process the central government of the islands, following the example of the distribution of the powers between the States and the National Government of the United States, shall have no direct administration except of matters of purely general concern, and shall have only such supervision and control over local governments as may be necessary to secure and enforce faithful and efficient administration by local officers.

The many different degrees of civilization and varieties of custom and capacity among the people of the different islands preclude very definite instruction as to the part which the people shall take in the selection of their own officers; but these general rules are to be observed: That in all cases the municipal officers, who administer the local affairs of the people, are to be selected by the people, and that wherever officers of more extended jurisdiction are to be selected in any way, natives of the islands are to be preferred, and if they can be found competent and willing to perform the duties, they are to receive the offices in preference to any others.

It will be necessary to fill some offices for the present with Americans which after a time may well be filled by natives of the islands. As soon as practicable a system for ascertaining the merit and fitness of candidates for civil office should be put in force. An indispensable qualification for all offices and positions of trust and authority in the islands must be absolute and unconditional loyalty to the United States; and absolute and unhampered authority and power to remove and punish any officer deviating from that standard must at all times be retained in the hands of the central authority of the islands.

In all the forms of government and administrative provisions which they are authorized to prescribe, the commission should bear in mind that the government which they are establishing is designed, not for our satisfaction or for the expression of our theoretical views, but for the happiness, peace, and prosperity of the people of the Philippine Islands, and the measures adopted should be made to conform to their customs, their habits, and even their prejudices, to the fullest extent consistent with the accomplishment of the indispensable requisites of just and effective government.

At the same time the commission should bear in mind, and the people of the islands should be made plainly to understand, that there are certain great principles of government which have been made the basis of our governmental system which we deem essential to the rule of law and the maintenance of individual freedom, and of which they have, unfortunately, been denied the experience possessed by us; that there are also certain practical rules of government which we have found to be essential to the preservation of these great principles of liberty and law, and that these principles and these rules of government must be established and maintained in their islands for the sake of their liberty and happiness, however much they may conflict with the customs or laws of procedure with which they are familiar.

It is evident that the most enlightened thought of the Philippine Islands fully appreciates the importance of these principles and rules, and they will inevitably within a short time command universal assent. Upon every division and branch of the government of the Philippines, therefore, must be imposed these inviolable rules:

That no person shall be deprived of life, liberty, or property without due process of law; that private property shall not be taken for public use without just compensation; that in all criminal prosecutions the accused shall enjoy the right to a speedy and public trial, to be informed of the nature and cause of the accusation, to be confronted with the witnesses against him, to have compulsory process for obtaining witnesses in his favor, and to have the assistance of counsel for his defense; that excessive bail shall not be required, nor excessive fines imposed, nor cruel and unusual punishment inflicted; that no person shall be put twice in jeopardy for the same offense, or be compelled in any criminal case to be a witness against himself; that the right to be secure against unreasonable searches and seizures shall not be violated; that neither slavery nor involuntary servitude shall exist except as a punishment for crime; that no bill of attainder or *ex post facto* law shall be passed; that no law shall be passed abridging the freedom of speech or of the press, or the rights of the people peaceably to assemble and petition the Government for a redress of grievances; that no law shall be made respecting an establishment of religion or prohibiting the free exercise thereof, and that the free exercise and enjoyment of religious profession and worship without discrimination or preference shall forever be allowed.

It will be the duty of the commission to make a thorough investigation into the titles to the large tracts of land held or claimed by individuals or by religious orders; into the justice of the claims and complaints made against such landholders by the people of the island, or any part of the people, and to seek by wise and peaceable measures a just settlement of the controversies and redress of wrongs which have caused strife and bloodshed in the past, In the performance of this duty the commission is enjoined to see that no injustice is done; to have regard for substantial rights and equity, disregarding technicalities so far as substantial right permits, and to observe the following rules:

That the provision of the Treaty of Paris pledging the United States to the protection of all rights of property in the islands, and as well the principle of our own Government which prohibits the taking of private property without due process of law, shall not be violated; that the welfare of the people of the islands, which should be a paramount consideration shall be attained consistently with this rule of property right; that if it becomes necessary for the public interest of the people of the islands to dispose of claims to property which the commission finds to be not lawfully acquired and held, disposition shall be made thereof by due legal procedure, in which there shall be full opportunity for fair and impartial hearing and judgment; that if the same public interests require the extinguishment of property rights lawfully acquired and held, due compensation shall be made out of the public treasury therefor; that no form of religion and no minister of religion shall be forced upon any community or upon any citizen of the islands; that upon the other hand no minister of religion shall be interfered with or molested in following his calling, and that the separation between state and church shall be real, entire, and absolute.

It will be the duty of the commission to promote and extend, and, as they find occasion, to improve, the system of education already inaugurated by the military authorities. In doing this they should regard as of first importance the extension of a system of primary education which shall be free to all, and which shall tend to fit the people for the duties of citizenship and for the ordinary avocations of a civilized community. This instruction should be given in the first instance in every part of the islands in the language of the people. In view of the great number of languages spoken by the different tribes, it is especially important to the prosperity of the islands that a common medium of communication may be established, and it is obviously desirable that this medium should be the English language. Especial attention should be at once given to affording full opportunity to all the people of the islands to acquire the use of the English language.

It may be well that the main changes which should be made in the system of taxation and in the body of the laws under which the people are governed, except such changes as have already been made by the military government, should be relegated to the civil government which is to be established under the auspices of the commission. It will, however, be the duty of the commission to inquire diligently as to whether there are any further changes which ought not to be delayed; and if so, they are authorized to make such changes, subject to your approval. In doing so they are to bear in mind that taxes which tend to penalize or repress industry and enterprise are to be avoided; that provisions for taxation should be simple, so that they may be understood by the people; that they should affect the fewest practicable subjects of taxation which will serve for the general distribution of the burden.

The main body of the laws which regulate the rights and obligations of the people should be maintained with as little interference as possible. Changes made should be mainly in procedure, and in the criminal laws to secure speedy and impartial trials and at the same time effective administration and respect for individual rights.

In dealing with the uncivilized tribes of the islands the commission should adopt the same course followed by Congress in permitting the tribes of our North American Indians to maintain their tribal organization and government, under which many of those tribes are now living in peace and contentment, surrounded by a civilization to which they are unable or unwilling to conform. Such tribal governments should, however, be subjected to wise and firm regulation; and, without undue or petty interference, constant and active effort should be exercised to prevent barbarous practices and introduce civilized customs.

Upon all officers and employees of the United States, both civil and military, should be impressed a sense of the duty to observe not merely the material but the personal and social rights of the people of the islands, and to treat them with the same courtesy and respect for their personal dignity which the people of the United States are accustomed to require from each other.

The articles of capitulation of the city of Manila on the 13th of August, 1898, concluded with these words:

"This city, its inhabitants, its churches and religious worship, its educational establishments, and its private property of all descriptions are placed under the special safeguard of the faith and honor of the American army."

I believe that this pledge has been faithfully kept. As high and sacred an obligation rests upon the Government of the United States to give protection for property and life, civil and religious freedom, and wise, firm, and unselfish guidance in the paths of peace and prosperity to all the people of the Philippine Islands. I charge this commission to labor for the full performance of this obligation, which concerns the honor and conscience of their country, in the firm hope that through their labors all the inhabitants of the Philippine Islands may come to look back with gratitude to the day when God gave victory to American arms at Manila and set their land under the sovereignty and the protection of the people of the United States.

WILLIAM MCKINLEY.

THE SECRETARY OF WAR, Washington.

THE WORK OF THE PHILIPPINE COMMISSION

Extract from the Report of the Secretary of War for 1902[1]

The Philippine Government Act of July 1, 1902, adopts and continues with enlarged powers the system of government built up under the President's instructions of April 7, 1900. The growth and character of that government were described in my last annual report. I transmit herewith all the statutes passed by the Philippine Commission from and including act No. 264, passed October 14, 1901, to and including act No. 424, passed July 1, 1902. These, together with the acts previously transmitted to Congress, constitute

[1] Page 59.

the entire body of legislation by the Philippine Commission prior to the passage of the Philippine Government Act by Congress.

The enacting clause of all these laws is "*By authority of the President of the United States, be it enacted by the United States Philippine Commission.*" Their authority as law rests: First, upon the power vested in the Commission by the President in the exercise of his war powers under the Constitution, in the instructions of April 7, 1900. Second, upon the sanction given to those instructions in that part of the act of March 2, 1901, commonly known as the "Spooner Amendment", which provided:

> All military, civil and judicial powers necessary to govern the Philippine Islands, acquired from Spain by the treaties concluded at Paris on the 10th day of December, 1898, and at Washington on the 7th day of November, 1900, shall, until otherwise provided by Congress, be vested in such person and persons and shall be exercised in such manner as the President of the United States shall direct for the establishment of civil government and for maintaining and protecting the inhabitants of said islands in the free enjoyment of their liberty, property, and religion.

And, third, upon the provision of the Philippine Government Act of July 1, 1902.

> That the action of the President of the United States in creating the Philippine Commission and authorizing said Commission to exercise the powers of government to the extent and in the manner and form and subject to the regulation and control set forth in the instructions of the President to the Philippine Commission, dated April 7, 1900, . . . is hereby approved, ratified, and confirmed.

The statutes passed by the Philippine Commission after July 1, 1902, will rest upon the authority conferred beforehand upon the Commission by Congress in that act, and the enacting clause will be: "*By authority of the United States, be it enacted by the Philippine Commission.*" . . .

Sections 63, 64, and 65 of the Philippine Government Act of July 1, 1902, authorize the Commission to acquire title to lands of religious orders held in such large tracts as to affect injuriously the peace and welfare of the people of the islands, to issue bonds in payment for such land, to sell the land, with a preference to actual settlers and occupants, and to apply the proceeds to paying the principal and interest of the bonds. After the bill containing these provisions had been reported favorably by the committees of both Houses, but before the passage of the bill, Governor Taft being about to return from Washington to his post at Manila via the Suez Canal, was directed to stop at Rome for the purpose stated in the following extract from his instructions:

> In view, therefore, of the critical situation of this subject in the Philippines, and of the apparent impossibility of disposing of the matter there by negotiation with the friars themselves, the President does not feel at liberty to lose the opportunity for effective action afforded by your presence in the West. He wishes you to take the subject up tentatively with the ecclesiastical superiors who must ultimately determine the friars' course of conduct, and endeavor to reach at least a basis of negotiation along lines which will be satisfactory to them and to the Philippine government, accompanied by a full understanding on both sides of the facts and of the views and purposes of the parties to the negotiation, so that when Congress shall have acted the business may proceed to a conclusion without delay.

These instructions were complied with and resulted in a very full and satisfactory understanding as to the methods to be adopted for disposing of the various questions arising out of the separation of church and state in the Philippine Islands required by the change of sovereignty. . . . The negotiations are now proceeding at Manila between Governor Taft and Monsignor Guidi, the papal delegate to the Philippines, in accordance with the understanding reached at Rome. I have no doubt that, although many of the questions involved are delicate and difficult, just conclusions will be reached, satisfactory to both sides.

The trade of the islands has been greatly hampered during the past year by the ravages of rinderpest, causing a mortality in some provinces of over ninety per cent among the *carabaos,* and a consequent shortage of food crops. Business in many sections has been seriously interrupted by an epidemic of cholera, yet the imports for the fiscal year 1902 were greater than in any previous year in the history of the archipelago, and exports were exceeded in but two previous years, 1870 and 1889. The total merchandise, exclusive of gold and silver and Government supplies, imported during the fiscal year 1902 was $32,141,842, as against $30,279,406 for the fiscal year 1901 and $20,601,436 for the fiscal year 1900, and the total value of merchandise exported during the fiscal year 1902 was $23,927,679, as against $23,214,948 for the fiscal year 1901 and $19,751,068 for the fiscal year 1900, an increase of six per cent in the value of imports for the fiscal year 1902 over the fiscal year 1901 and of fifty-six per cent over the fiscal year 1900, and an increase in the value of exports for the fiscal year 1902 over the fiscal year 1901 of three per cent and over the fiscal year 1900 of twenty-one per cent. . . .

The imports from the United States amounted to $4,035,243 in 1902 as against $2,855,685 in 1901 and $1,657,701 in 1900, or an increase for the past year over 1900 of 143 per cent. The value of merchandise exported to this country in 1902 was $7,691,743 as against $2,572,021 in 1901 and $3,522,160 in 1900, showing an increase in favor of the latest period over 1900 of 118 per cent.

The United States shows greater gains of imports for the fiscal year 1902 than any other country, except the French East Indies, which shows a great increase in the quantity of rice exported to the islands to make up for deficient crops. In exports the United States gained more than any other country.

The showing made by the United States on the basis of direct shipments to and from the islands discloses a marked increase during the past few years; yet it does not take into account purchases made in this country entered at the Philippine customs-houses free of duty for use of the United States military departments of the insular government or its subordinate branches. In these figures also this country is deprived of the proper credit for its imports into the islands by shipments passing through Hong-Kong and eventually reported as originating at that point. Although this applies also to European countries to some extent, it has been found that only a small part of their export credits is affected, for the reason that nearly all their shipments come direct via Singapore; and the transshipment at that port and at Hong-Kong and Saigon are rarely attended by the issue of new shipping documents, under which the port of transshipment can be taken as the port of origin.

As to the Philippine export trade to the United States, in which this country has trebled its figures during the last two years, the results stated represent more nearly the proper credit, but there are numerous instances of shipments of hemp in large quantities, intended for the United States, to Europe and Hong-Kong under documents in which these countries are given as the ports of final destination. This will appear from the fact that approximately $7,500,000 worth of hemp was exported from the Philippines to the United Kingdom during the year 1902, while during the same period the importations of this fiber into the United States from the United Kingdom amounted to nearly $4,250,000, presumably included in indirect shipments, credit for which should be given to this country. If credit is given for these importations the United States is placed far in advance as the leading market for Philippine products at the present time. . . .

Immigrants to the number of 30,094 arrived in the Philippine Islands during the fiscal year 1902 as against 17,108 in the fiscal year 1901. Of this number 12,751 (including

10,101 Chinese) had been in the islands before. Among the 17,343 who came for the first time there were 15,312 or 88 per cent, Americans, 368 Chinese, 451 Japanese, 222 English, 358 Spaniards, 129 East Indians, and 503 of other nationalities. There were 2,497 females and 928 children under 14 years of age. With the exception of 8,349 Chinese but 3 per cent of the immigrants were illiterates. Among the Americans there were 176 merchant dealers and grocers, 790 teachers, 122 clerks and accountants. The greater number of Americans are, however, not described by occupation. More than three-fourths of the Chinese were laborers, and more than half the remainder merchants. . . .

The total revenues have amounted to $33,589,819.05 and the total expenditures to $23,253,573.13, American money. The relative income and expenditure by fiscal years has been as follows:

	Income	Expenditure
1899	$3,508,682.83	$2,376,008.62
1900	6,763,527.73	4,758,677.75
1901	10,686,188.97	6,073,766.44
1902	12,631,419.52	10,045,120.32

The surplus of income over expenditure has in a great measure been allotted to the payment of various contracts for public improvements and public benefit, so that the real surplus of free cash in the treasury is comparatively small.

I shall defer comment and recommendation generally upon Philippine affairs until I transmit the report of the commission, now on the way to this country.

I ask the attention of Congress to two subjects upon which, I think, if the conditions and needs of the islands could be fully understood, there would be but little controversy, and upon which very simple enactments would be of immense value to the people of the islands, whose welfare the Government of the United States is bound to promote. I earnestly urge, first, that the duties levied in the United States upon products of the Philippine Archipelago imported therefrom be reduced to twenty-five per cent of the Dingley tariff rates; second, that the government of the island be permitted to establish the gold standard for its currency, and to take such measures as it finds to be practicable and prudent to keep the silver coinage which it is authorized to issue at parity with gold, without in any way committing the United States to responsibility therefor.

I shall not now undertake, nor is it the proper office of such a report as this, to argue the economic questions which may be raised by the consideration of these recommendations. The views upon which they are based have been presented in my former reports and in the reports of the Philippine Commission. The reason for presenting them now is that the ills which have recently befallen the people of the islands call urgently for active and immediate measures of relief. The people of a country just emerging from nearly six years of devastating warfare, during which productive industry was interrupted, vast amounts of property were destroyed, the bonds of social order were broken, habits of peaceful industry were lost, and at the close of which a great residuum of disorderly men were left leading a life of brigandage and robbery, had a sufficiently difficult task before them to restore order and prosperity. In addition to this, however, the people of the Philippine Islands have within the past year been visited by great misfortunes.

The rinderpest has destroyed about ninety per cent of all their *carabaos*, leaving them without draft animals to till their land and aid in the ordinary work of farm and village life. *Carabaos* have increased in price from $20 to $200 Mexican. The Eastern disease known as " surra " has killed and is killing the native and American horses, further crippling transportation. The rice crop has been reduced to twenty-five per cent of the ordinary crop. Last year in the Visayan Islands and this year in Luzon a plague of locusts has come upon the land, destroying much of the remaining twenty-five per cent of the rice crop. A drought in China and the fall in the price of silver have raised the price of rice from $4 to $7 a *picul*. The commission have been obliged to go out of the islands and use insular funds to buy over 40,000,000 pounds of rice to save the people from perishing by famine. Cholera has raged and is raging throughout the islands. The ignorance of the people and their unwillingness to submit to sanitary regulations have made it almost impossible to check the ravages of the disease, which, it is estimated, will claim not less than 100,000 victims. The decline in the price of silver has carried Mexican dollars down from a ratio of two to one in gold to a ratio of over two and one-half to one, and this has borne heavily on the commercial interests and on the wage earners.

The insular government has in ten months lost over $1,000,000 gold by the decline in silver because it was operating on a silver basis, and this has changed the surplus of revenues into a deficit at the very time when the other causes mentioned have caused an extraordinary demand for the use of the revenues for the relief of the people. Agriculture is prostrated. Commerce is hampered and discouraged. All the political parties in the Philippines urgently demand a change of the present currency standard. Some relief would be afforded by opening a profitable market in the United States to the products of the islands. Still greater relief would be afforded by delivering the business of the islands from the disastrous effects of the decline in the price of silver and the fluctuations in exchange, and putting it upon the substantial basis of the gold standard currency which exists in the United States, where we wish them to do their business, which exists on the continent of Europe and in India and Japan, and the adoption of which is now under consideration in the Straits Settlements.

Conditions in the Philippines

On January 9, 1902, Mr. Root appeared before the House Committee on Military Affairs, then considering the military appropriation bill, and made the following statement concerning the necessity for a liberal appropriation for work in the Philippines:

I think I can state quite briefly what I regard to be the situation. About two-thirds of the people of the Islands are now under civil government. The other third are largely composed of non-Christian tribes. There are now thirty-one provinces under civil government. They are all new. The communities have been in a state of unrest and disorder for a number of years, five or six years. There has been an almost entire absence of all the customary limitations of civil society.

There is active warfare going on in certain parts of the Islands, in Batangas and Tayabas and Luzon, and in Samar, and, until recently, in Cebu. The great mass of the people in the organized provinces, which are under civilized government, wish for nothing so much as to be allowed to go on in peace, rearing their children and earning their livelihood under the sovereignty of the United States; but there are still in these provinces a considerable number of men who are giving aid and comfort to the insurrectionists in the other provinces, and who are all the time trying to work up insurrection, to keep the people stirred up and to keep up their secret societies. The process of settlement — of restoring the settled conditions of a peaceable community — is necessarily a slow one, and while that is going on the moral force of the American troops is a very important element in maintaining the condition of peace.

Every year and every month and every day tends to consolidate the peaceable conditions, to reduce the number of disorderly and discontented and turbulent characters, and to restore the domination of the peaceable, law-abiding citizens; and the process has been hindered by the fact that we have been prohibited by law, up to this time, from giving to the people the ordinary advantages of good government in the way of permitting industrial enterprises. The limitations which were imposed in the so-called Spooner provision upon the granting of franchises, upon the giving of titles to public lands, upon all the active industries which give profitable employment and which develop the resources of a country, have held us in a state of suspense there, and there are a great many people who are conspirators now who would cease to be if they got something to do. You see we have gone into a country which had been under a sixteenth-century government, and we have been prevented by law from introducing a twentieth-century government there. The forests have been cut off to a great extent near the water; what remain cannot be reached except by building railroads. We have been prohibited from permitting anybody to build railroads there. Last month there were actually over a thousand prospectors sitting on mineral lands waiting for the chance to acquire rights to them and work their mines. Copper and gold and coal exist there, and those minerals have been there in the earth for three or four hundred years under Spanish rule without the people's ever scratching them. Now, if we can have laws under which mining claims can be taken up and people can go to work getting out the mineral, there will be money spread through the community and there will be employment.

And the same way about agricultural lands. A large part of the agricultural lands are unavailable because there is no communication except by water, and therefore only strips along the edge of the water are available to raise anything for the market. The people live largely upon rice. They did not raise the rice they used last year; they had to import $5,000,000 worth of rice into a country fertile beyond description. We are not able to open up the rich agricultural lands away from the water. Of course there has never been a census taken. There are no surveys. The records are all destroyed; land titles are all in air.

A year ago an estimate was made that between two hundred thousand and three hundred thousand Filipinos were living on lands without any title to their lands. Give them titles and it will be worth while to improve their lands, and you will get a contented set of people, who are interested in the peace and prosperity of the country, instead of having a lot of floaters. But we are prohibited from giving titles. We cannot permit railroads to be built, we cannot permit a manufacturing establishment to acquire rights, we cannot permit a mine to be opened, we cannot permit any of the industries which make a community prosperous and contented to go on there. If you will take those limitations off, under proper restrictions, of course, and enable the wheels of industry to move there, you will see content in the place of discontent and conspiracy.

You see it is a peculiar situation. In a country, with, by a rough estimate, 73,000,000 acres of land, only about 5,000,000 are held in private ownership. The remaining 68,000,000 acres, in round numbers, have become the property of the United States. The Philippine government has had no power to alienate an acre of it, and is expressly prohibited, by the legislation of a year ago, from leasing an acre of it. How can you expect a community to have the progress and the industrial activity that brings contentment under those conditions? They have just been holding on by main strength and tenacity.

Mr. Jett. Would you be in favor of extending the homestead-exemption laws of the United States?

Secretary Root. With modifications. Of course you have to have your laws framed to meet the communities and the conditions. Bills have been prepared with a great deal of care to remedy the evils that I have just referred to. A bill was introduced in the House by Mr. Cooper, a bill in the Senate by Mr. Lodge, and they have gone to the appropriate committees — the Philippine Committee in the Senate and the Insular Committee in the House. Those bills contain a great number of provisions designed to meet these conditions; but up to this time there has been a suspension of industrial activity over there.

Mr. Adams. Mr. Secretary, the same thing has happened in Cuba, has it not, retarding the development of industry?

Secretary Root. It has retarded Cuba, although it is not so bad in Cuba because Cuba was a more settled country and her sugar and tobacco productions formerly reached a very high point. They have been gradually working back toward that point. The trouble in Cuba is, that the decline in the price of sugar throughout the world has reached a figure where the Cuban product cannot be sold profitably under our existing tariff conditions here. But in Cuba the railroads, which were very much needed, have been prevented by the limitations of what is called the Foraker Amendment.

The Van Horne people have been building a private railroad. Under the existing laws there, any one has a right to buy land and build a railroad upon it. They bought their land or had it given to them. The people in the eastern end of the island are exceedingly anxious for a railroad, and the promoters of the railroad have been helped along in every way, and they have gone ahead and built railroads without any franchises. Where they have come to a road they have crossed under a revocable license, and that license can be taken away at any time.

The Finances of the Philippines

Extract from the Report of the Secretary of War for 1903[1]

Philippine Coinage. Under the authority of sections 76 to 83, inclusive, of the Philippine Government Act, and of the act entitled " An act to establish a standard of value and to provide for a coinage system in the Philippine Islands " approved March 2, 1903, the Philippine government has coined 14,145,000 silver pesos, 3,100,000 50-centavo pieces or half pesos, 5,350,000 20-centavo pieces, 5,100,000 10-centavo pieces, 8,850,000 5-centavo pieces, 10,600,000 1-centavo pieces, 11,950,000 half-centavo pieces, making an aggregate in face value of 17,883,250 silver pesos, each of the face value of one-half an American gold dollar, and having an aggregate face value of $8,941,625 gold money of the United States. Eleven million three hundred and fifty-five thousand of the pesos were coined at the San Francisco mint, the remaining pesos and all the subsidiary coins at the Philadelphia mint. . . .

The silver bullion purchased for this coinage amounted to 13,520,895.82 ounces. The cost of the bullion amounted to $7,372,990.11. The purchases were made through the officers of the mint. Of the amount purchased, 1,115,234.52 ounces were purchased from the Mexican Pious award fund in the hands of the Department of State. These purchases were made at the London price at the time of delivery at the San Francisco mint. The remainder was purchased from various firms and corporations upon offers tendered to the director of the mint Mondays and Thursdays of each week, in response to a public invitation by him. Of the total amount of silver bullion purchased for coinage purposes there remain 43,324.85 ounces not used in the above-mentioned coinage, and the cost of this surplus amounted to $30,401.22, leaving

[1] Page 43.

the total quantity of silver bullion actually consumed in making the coins above specified 13,478,448.07 ounces and the cost thereof $7,342,588.89. The surplus of 43,324.85 ounces of silver will be used for further subsidiary coinage.

The prices at which this silver bullion was purchased ranged from 49.10 cents per ounce to 60.47 cents per ounce. The average price paid was 55.193 cents per ounce. This makes the cost to the Philippine government of the silver in each peso coined equal to 43.05 cents. The difference between the actual cost of the bullion consumed in making the coins above mentioned, including the cost of base metal for alloy and minor coins, and the total face value of the coinage, is $1,495,644.85. The total cost of coining, transportation, insurance, packing, and miscellaneous expenses was $256,930.35, leaving a seigniorage or profit to the Philippine government consisting of the difference between the face value of the new coins and the total cost of the new coins delivered in Manila, amounting to $1,238,714.50. This sum will go into the special fund for the maintenance of parity between the new coins and the money of the United States.

Silver Certificates. Section 8 of the act of March 2, 1903, authorized the treasurer of the Philippine Islands, in his discretion, to receive deposits of the standard silver coins of one peso in sums of not less than twenty pesos, and to issue silver certificates therefor in denominations of not less than two nor more than ten pesos, retaining the deposited coin in the treasury "to be held and used for the payment of such certificates on demand, and for no other purpose"; thus supplying for public convenience government notes representing silver coin actually held by the government as against the notes.

Under this provision certificates have been engraved, printed, and delivered at Manila representing 10,000,000 silver pesos. Of these, 4,000,000 were in 10-peso notes,

4,000,000 in 5-peso notes, and 2,000,000 in 2-peso notes. This work was admirably done by the very considerate and public-spirited coöperation of the Bureau of Engraving and Printing. The 10-peso notes bear the engraved vignette of President Washington; the 5-peso notes, of President McKinley, and the 2-peso notes, of the Philippine patriot and poet Rizal. . . .

Issue of Certificates of Indebtedness. The money for the purchase of bullion and expense of coinage was furnished in part from the general funds of the Philippine government and in part by the issue of certificates of indebtedness under the authority of section 6 of the Philippine coinage act of March 2, 1903. That section provides that in order to maintain parity between said silver Philippine pesos and the gold pesos provided for by the act, the Philippine government may issue temporary certificates of indebtedness to the extent of $10,000,000 or 20,000,000 pesos, running not more than one year and bearing interest not to exceed four per cent. And it provides that the proceeds of such certificates shall be used exclusively for the maintenance of said parity, except that a sum not exceeding $3,000,000 at any one time may be used as a continuing credit for the purchase of silver bullion.

Under these provisions certificates of indebtedness payable one year after date and bearing four per cent interest have been issued and sold in the United States to the amount of $6,000,000. Three million dollars thereof, issued specifically for the purchase of bullion, were sold on April 20, 1903, at a premium of 2.513 per cent. The other $3,000,000 thereof, issued specifically for the creation of a gold reserve fund for the maintenance of parity, were sold on August 25, 1903, at a premium of 2.24 per cent, making an average premium of 2.3765 per cent, and making the interest charge to the Philippine government for the use of the money borrowed for one year 1.6235 per cent, or in round figures $1\frac{5}{8}$ per cent.

These sales were made upon public advertisement for bids, and the extraordinarily favorable result was due not merely to the credit of the Philippine government, but to the fact that the Secretary of the Treasury authorized the War Department to announce that the certificates would be received by the Treasury Department as security for the deposit of United States funds in the national banks, under certain specified conditions. . . .

Circulation. It is estimated that there are now in circulation in the archipelago between eleven and twelve million pesos of the Spanish-Filipino coinage of all denominations. It is the purpose of the Philippine government to take steps to get this coinage into the treasury and to recoin the silver thus supplied into the new Filipino coins, thus bringing the aggregate of the new coinage up to about twenty-eight million pesos. This will, in the judgment of the Commission, meet the present requirements of the islands. The purchase of silver bullion for coinage purposes has accordingly been suspended.

It is the purpose of the Philippine government to exercise the authority conferred upon it by section 7 of the Philippine coinage act of March 2, 1903, and declare the Mexican silver dollars heretofore in use in the Philippine Islands to be no longer receivable for public dues after January 1, 1904.

In anticipation of the demonetization of Mexican dollars those coins have been largely shipped out of the islands, leaving in circulation there an amount which is estimated at not exceeding 4,000,000 pesos. To supply the need for currency thus created 8,210,307 pesos of the new coinage have already passed into circulation (including 3,305,116 pesos deposited in Manila banks, about one-third of which probably remains in the hands of the banks). No serious difficulty is anticipated in the absorption of the entire amount coined after the demonetization of Mexicans, January 1, 1904.

Monetary Commission. The intimate trade relations between the Philippines and the silver-currency countries of Asia make the relations between gold and silver in those countries a matter of great practical importance to the Philippine government. That government has followed with great interest the course of the Commission recently appointed by the Government of the United States upon the request of the Governments of Mexico and China that the United States should join them in seeking to establish a more stable relation between the moneys of the gold-standard countries and of the countries now upon the silver standard.

Under the recent legislation of Congress the business of the Philippine Islands is about to be put upon the gold-standard basis. Any action which leads to the adoption of a gold monetary system in China will be of material advantage to the Philippines. The promotion of that object during the past summer by the conferences between the above-mentioned American commission, the commission from the Republic of Mexico, and the similar commissions of the chief countries of Europe is regarded with gratification by the Philippine government, which hopes that this effort may receive further encouragement and support from the Congress of the United States. . . .

I earnestly renew the recommendation which I have already made for a reduction of duties upon Philippine imports into the United States. As matters stand at present we have practically deprived the Philippines of their Spanish market, and we have so arranged the tariff laws of the two countries that American consumers are making money at the expense of the Philippine revenues. I submit that there is no just reason why the people of the Philippines should not be treated with some fair approach to the advantages which are awarded to the people of Porto Rico and the Hawaiian Islands. . . .

Navigation Laws. Section 3 of the act of Congress of March 8, 1902, relating to the Philippine tariff, provides —

> That until July 1, 1904, the provisions of law restricting to vessels of the United States the transportation of passengers and merchandise directly or indirectly from one port of the United States to another port of the United States shall not be applicable to foreign vessels engaging in trade between the Philippine Archipelago and the United States or between ports in the Philippine Archipelago.

But for this suspension, under the decision of the Supreme Court in the Porto Rican case of Huus *v.* The New York and Porto Rico Steamship Company,[1] the navigation laws of the United States may be held to prohibit any vessel not built in the United States and owned by a citizen of the United States from engaging in either one or two entirely distinct classes of trade: First, inter-island trade throughout the archipelago; and second, trade between the United States and the Philippine Islands. As to the inter-island trade it is quite certain that unless there be a further suspension of the navigation laws or other legislative relief consequences very disastrous to the islands will result.

The waterways among the islands are, of course, the great internal highways of the country. The business is largely done by a great number of small vessels, in the main owned by the people of the islands. There are now engaged in the coastwise trade of the islands 3,471 vessels, with an aggregate tonnage of about 108,000 tons. Of these, 135 are steamers, with a gross tonnage of 49,790 tons; 46 are steam launches, and the remainder sailing vessels. None of the steamers is of American origin and ownership, and but three of the sailing vessels, and their gross tonnage is 610 tons.

The present tonnage is inadequate for the demands of the growing trade of the islands, and there is undoubtedly a field

[1] Decided in 1900, and reported in 182 *United States Reports*, 392.

for the profitable use of American shipping in the inter-island trade. Some provision, however, should be made to prevent a situation in which the laws of the United States will make it illegal for the Philippine people to use their own vessels in their own internal trade and which will practically require the trade of the islands to be carried on in violation of law.

As to the trade between the United States and the Philippines, the returns show that during the fiscal year 1903, out of the $13,863,059 of exports from the Philippines into the United States, nearly ninety-seven per cent, and of the imports from the United States into the Philippines approximately ninety per cent were carried in foreign vessels. At the time of the passage of the act of March 8, 1902, the supply of American vessels on the Pacific was quite inadequate to the transaction of this business. . . .

Philippine Railroads. On January 5, 1903, the Senate adopted the following resolution:

Resolved, That the Secretary of War be, and he is hereby, directed to inform the Senate what effect, in his opinion, an adequate system of railroads in the Philippine Islands would have upon the cost of maintaining law and order and protecting life and property in those islands, and whether, in his opinion, the expense of protecting life and property and maintaining a stable government would be reduced by such a system of railroads in a sum sufficient to equal the interest on the money necessary to build and operate such roads.

To which the Secretary replied as follows:

In my opinion an adequate system of railroads in the Philippine Islands would greatly reduce the cost of maintaining law and order and protecting life and property in those islands. I think the difference between the cost of maintaining a stable government, accomplishing these ends with such a system of railroads, and maintaining a government of equal efficiency without railroads would be greater than the interest on the money necessary to build and operate the roads.

Experience has shown that the building of a railroad in an unsettled country does not merely reduce the cost of policing the country, but greatly decreases the necessity of policing it. The moral effect of rapid communication with central authority is to discourage disorder. The increase in the value of property, the improvement of business, the distribution of money, the employment of labor, the constant travel and communication among the inhabitants, dispelling ignorance and prejudice — all these combine to reduce the cost and increase the efficiency of peaceful and orderly government.

In Luzon alone there are some thirty provinces, in which eight or nine different languages and over sixty different dialects are spoken, and there is special need of means to make the people homogeneous and capable of uniting in common self-government.

We have on this continent two notable illustrations of the foregoing views — in the discontinuance of insurrection following the building of railroads in Mexico and in the effect on Indian disturbances produced by our own transcontinental roads.

My predecessor, Secretary Alger, urged the adoption of such a policy for Cuba in his report for 1898. The road which he proposed has now been built by private capital, and I do not doubt that it will prove to be a powerful agent in the maintenance of peace and order.

I think sound policy requires that we should either build or procure the building of railroads in the larger islands of the Philippine Archipelago without any avoidable delay.

In pursuance of the views thus expressed and in order to be ready with any further information which Congress might desire on the subject of the Senate's inquiry, the War Department procured for the Philippine government the services of two experienced engineers familiar with the work of locating railroads in the tropics, and these engineers have personally examined and located a line of railroad from Manila up the easterly side of the great plain of central Luzon, over the mountains near Carranglan, down the valley of the Cagayan to the north coast of Luzon at Aparri; another line from the termination of the present railroad on the Gulf of Lingayen up the west coast to Laoag, and a third line from Manila southerly through Cavite and Batangas to the south coast at the city of Batangas.

The estimated cost of constructing these roads is $11,140,-095. I am satisfied that the Philippine government could afford to pay the entire interest on the cost of construction in return for the benefit which the government will receive in greater efficiency and reduced cost of administration. The increase in the taxable value of property and the benefits to the people of the island of Luzon will of course be very great. It is probable that private capital cannot be obtained for investment at the risk of this enterprise without some state aid or a loan of credit by means of a guaranty or otherwise. I strongly recommend that should the powers of the Philippine government be deemed insufficient for this purpose, such legislation as may be necessary to confer the power be enacted by Congress.

Philippine Accounts. The general deficiency act of July 1, 1902, appropriated $30,000 to enable the Secretary of War to compile for the information of Congress a detailed statement of the receipts and expenditures by the military government of Cuba, in continuation of statements theretofore rendered to May 1, 1900, and further —

> to enable the Secretary of War to pay all necessary expenses in compiling for the information of Congress a similar statement relating to the Philippine Islands of all receipts and expenditures from the date of American occupation.

The itemized audited accounts showing the disposition of the entire revenue receipts of the military government in Cuba, including both the government of Santiago and the government of the entire island, down to the transfer of government to the Cubans, were submitted to Congress on December 13, 1902. A similar statement containing the itemized audited accounts of all receipts and expenditures of the military and civil governments of the Philippine Islands from the date of American occupation to June 30, 1902, was sent to Congress on February 13, 1902.

The material for the statement for the fiscal year ending June 30, 1903, has been completed in the Philippines and is about to be forwarded to the War Department in pursuance of law. The receipts and expenditures during the period of American occupation have been as follows:

	Fiscal Year Ended June 30 —					Total
	1899	1900	1901	1902	1903	
Revenues						
Customs	$3,097,864.15	$5,739,297.40	$9,105,754.67	$8,550,758.49	$9,686,533.29	$36,180,208.00
Postal	42,954.87	104,282.54	122,816.83	137,811.99	146,659.44	554,525.67
Internal	240,754.00	561,993.18	966,400.47	225,505.09	222,980.40	2,217,633.14
Provincial	....	....	....	1,993,270.97	2,559,601.94	4,552,872.91
City of Manila	....	....	....	1,199,590.01	1,561,473.61	2,761,063.62
Miscellaneous	127,109.81	357,954.61	491,217.00	524,482.97	1,148,877.05	2,649,641.44
Total	$3,508,682.83	$6,763,527.73	10,686,188.97	12,631,419.52	15,326,125.73	48,915,944.78
Expenditures						
Customs	28,817.90	100,194.09	267,446.88	490,126.40	587,142.89	1,473,728.16
Postal	30,410.75	89,149.51	155,347.77	175,156.57	226,730.33	676,794.93
Provincial	....	....	....	746,586.80	1,163,585.01	1,910,171.81
Loans and refunds to provinces	....	....	....	324,479.35	1,760,563.87	2,085,043.22
City of Manila	....	....	....	1,744,344.56	1,813,118.10	3,557,462.66
Other expenditures	2,316,779.97	4,569,334.15	5,659,971.79	6,564,426.64	8,711,363.27	27,812,875.82
Total	2,376,008.62	4,758,677.75	6,073,766.44	10,045,120.32	14,262,503.47	37,516,076.60

Captured Philippine Documents. There are now on file in the Bureau of Insular Affairs some 200,000 documents captured at different times from the insurgents in the Philippines. Few of them are of value as military records, but they contain the material for a history of the insurgent government both during its open existence and during the ensuing guerrilla war. They include many of the orders and regulations and much of the correspondence of the insurgent officers, and throw much light upon many important matters of which, from the American point of view alone, but a partial understanding can be obtained. These papers, since their receipt in October, 1902, have been carefully arranged, recorded, and filed, and those of special interest indexed and translated. It seems well worth while to print the more important of these documents with such explanatory notes as can be furnished by officers who are familiar with the transactions to which they relate. The Chief of the Bureau reports that the papers of permanent interest can be included in about five volumes of about five hundred pages each. It is estimated that the publication will cost at the Public Printing Office about $15,000. The first volume is practically ready to go to the printer in case Congress shall authorize the printing. I recommend an appropriation for this purpose.

The End of the Philippine Insurrection

Extract from the Report of the Secretary of War for 1902[1]

At the time of my last report Malvar, in the provinces of Batangas and Tayabas, in the island of Luzon, and Lukban, in the island of Samar, were the only insurgent leaders of importance who still maintained guerrilla warfare. We hoped that these leaders with their followers would yield to the example and advice of the great body of the Philippine people who had become friendly to the United States, and would voluntarily lay down their arms. It soon became evident, however, that this would not be the case. Malvar grew stronger, rather than weaker, under the effect of a conciliatory and peaceful policy, and the fierce natives of Samar were excited to greater hostile activity by a successful surprise at Balangiga in September, by which the people of the town, who had given every appearance of friendliness and were treated as friends, set upon a company of the Ninth Infantry while at breakfast and murdered most of them.

Active campaigns were accordingly inaugurated in both regions; and these resulted in the surrender of Malvar on the sixteenth of April, and in the capture of Lukban and the surrender of Guevara, his successor, on the twenty-seventh of April. General Frederick D. Grant reports that the surrenders in Samar included every gun known to exist in the

[1] Page 11.

island, except two; and General J. F. Bell, who conducted operations against Malvar in Batangas, reports that during the campaign we secured 3,561 guns, 625 revolvers, with many thousand bolos, rounds of ammunition, etc., and detected, captured, or forced to surrender some eight or ten thousand persons actively engaged in one capacity or another in the insurrection. These surrenders put an end to the guerrilla warfare in the Philippines, which had been waged with great ferocity ever since the destruction of Aguinaldo's government in the latter part of 1899, and had been accompanied by constant treachery, assassination, cruelty, and disregard of the laws of war.

The way was now clear to complete the establishment of civil government, and by energetic action and hearty co-operation on the part of both the civil and military authorities in the Philippines this was accomplished coincidently with the enactment by Congress of the Philippine government bill of July 1, 1902.

On July 4, 1902, the remainder of the military government was ended by the following order:

War Department,
Washington, July 4, 1902.

The insurrection against the sovereign authority of the United States in the Philippine Archipelago having ended, and provincial civil governments having been established throughout the entire territory of the archipelago not inhabited by Moro tribes, under the instructions of the President to the Philippine Commission, dated April 7, 1900, now ratified and confirmed by the act of Congress approved July 1, 1902, entitled "An act temporarily to provide for the administration of affairs of civil government in the Philippine Islands, and for other purposes", the general commanding the Division of the Philippines is hereby relieved from the further performance of the duties of military governor, and the office of military governor in said archipelago is terminated. The general commanding the Division of the Philippines, and all military officers in authority therein, will continue to observe the direction contained in the aforesaid instructions of the President, that the military forces in the Division of the Philippines shall be at all times subject, under the orders of the military commander, to the call of the civil authorities for the maintenance of law and order and the enforcement of their authority.

By the President:

ELIHU ROOT,
Secretary of War.

On the same day the President issued a proclamation of peace and amnesty. . . .

The dual process by which the military power had steadily acquired control over the various provinces of the archipelago, and at the same time had been superseded progressively by civil administration, was then finished, and a complete system of civil government, built up under the authority of the President, was in operation, ready to go on under the authority of Congress.

I described in my last report the important bearing which the continuous offer and bestowal of civil rights and local self-government as the result of pacification had upon the attitude of the people toward the insurrection. It is evident that the insurrection has been brought to an end both by making a war distressing and hopeless on the one hand, and by making peace attractive, through immediate and present demonstration of the sincerity of our purpose to give to the people just and free government, on the other. This result could not have been accomplished except by genuine and hearty coöperation of both the military and civil authorities acting together under the general direction of the War Department. The good temper and mutual consideration and helpfulness, and subordination of personal to public interests, displayed by General MacArthur and General Chaffee on the one hand, and by Governor Taft, Vice-Governor Wright, and the Civil Commission on the other, frequently under circumstances of great delicacy and difficulty, are worthy of high praise. Some of their subordinates, through incomplete knowledge and from widely differing points of view, have sometimes expressed discordant opinions, but both soldiers and civilians, with very few exceptions, have rendered loyal and devoted support to the prescribed policy.

There was at one time in the public press and on the floor of Congress much criticism of the conduct of the army in the Philippines, as being cruel and inhuman. All wars are cruel. This conflict consisted chiefly of guerrilla warfare. It lasted for some three years and a half, and extended over thousands of miles of territory. Over 120,000 men were engaged upon our side, and much greater numbers upon the other, and we were fighting against enemies who totally disregarded the laws of civilized warfare, and who were guilty of the most atrocious treachery and inhuman cruelty. It was impossible that some individuals should not be found upon our side who were unnecessarily and unjustifiably cruel. Such instances, however, after five months of searching investigation by a committee of the Senate, who took some three thousand printed pages of testimony, appear to have been comparatively few, and they were in violation of strict orders obedience to which characterized the conduct of the army as a whole.

The two observers who, as the heads of the civil government in the Philippines, had the best opportunities for information, and at the same time were naturally free from any military bias, have given what I believe to be a true statement of the character of our military operations.

Vice-Governor Luke E. Wright says, in a letter written on the twentieth of July last:

> General Chaffee, as a matter of course, had no patience with any acts of oppression or cruelty, and whenever his attention has been called to them has at once taken proper steps. The howl against the army has been made mainly for political purposes, and the cruelties practiced have been largely exaggerated. Of course, numerous instances of this character have occurred. There never was and never will be a war of which the same may not be said, but taken as a whole, and when the character of the

warfare here is considered, I think the officers and men of the American army have been forbearing and humane in their dealings with the natives, and the attempt to create a contrary impression is not only unjust to them, but it seems to me unpatriotic as well.

Governor Taft, in his testimony under oath before the Philippine Committee of the Senate on the fourth of February last, said:

After a good deal of study about the matter, and, although I have never been prejudiced in favor of the military branch, for when the civil and military branches are exercising concurrent jurisdiction there is some inevitable friction, I desire to say that it is my deliberate judgment that there never was a war conducted, whether against inferior races or not, in which there was more compassion and more restraint and more generosity, assuming that there was war at all, than there have been in the Philippine Islands.

Relations with the Moro Tribes

Extract from the Report of the Secretary of War for 1902 [1]

The establishment of civil government in the Philippines still left a function for the army to perform in the control of the Moros in the Sulu Archipelago, southern Mindanao, and the southern part of Palawan very similar to that which it has long performed in relation to the Indian tribes in the western part of the United States. It was only through an extended series of decisions by the Supreme Court of the United States, dealing with specific questions as they arose in the early years of the last century, that the precise legal relations between the Federal Government, the State and Territorial governments, and the Indian tribes of North America were determined.

The court said in the case of The Cherokee Nation *v.* The State of Georgia: [2]

The Indians are acknowledged to have unquestionable and heretofore an unquestioned right to the lands they occupy until that right shall be extinguished by a voluntary cession to the Government. It may well

[1] Page 16. [2] 5 Peters 1.

be doubted whether those tribes which reside within the acknowledged boundaries of the United States can with strict accuracy be denominated foreign nations. They may more correctly, perhaps, be denominated domestic dependent nations. They occupy territory to which we assert a title, independent of their will, which must take effect in point of possession when their right of possession ceases; meanwhile they are in a state of pupilage. Their relations to the United States resemble that of a ward to his guardian. They look to our Government for protection; rely upon its kindness and its power; appeal to it for relief to their wants, and address the President as their great father.

A similar process of judicial decision will probably be called for by the numerous questions certain to arise from our relations to the Moro tribes; but in the meantime the close general analogy to the relations of the North American Indians indicates a duty, for the present at least, of limited supervision and control operating upon the tribal governments of the Moros, rather than an attempt to substitute an American or Philippine government acting directly upon the individual Moros. In the performance of this duty we find ourselves exercising powers and following methods plainly contemplated by the Constitution, and sanctioned by the judicial decisions and established usage of the entire existence of the Government of the United States.

The instructions of the President to the Philippine Commission of April 7, 1900, contained the following direction based upon the foregoing view:

In dealing with the uncivilized tribes of the islands the Commission should adopt the same course followed by Congress in permitting the tribes of our North American Indians to maintain their tribal organization and government, and under which many of those tribes are now living in peace and contentment, surrounded by a civilization to which they are unable or unwilling to conform. Such tribal governments should, however, be subjected to wise and firm regulation, and without undue or petty interference constant and active effort should be exercised to prevent barbarous practices and to introduce civilized customs.

The same instructions provide that the military forces in the Philippines shall be at all times subject, under the orders of the military commander, to the call of the civil authorities for the maintenance of law and order and the enforcement of their authority.

These instructions were approved and adopted by Congress in the Philippine Government Act of July 1, 1902, and they will continue to guide the civil and military authorities in the Philippines in their dealings with the Moros. The questions to be worked out in that process are altogether apart from the general questions of government in the Philippines, and such measures of force as are necessary to control the various Moro tribes have no more relation to the recent Philippine insurrection than our troubles with the Sioux or the Apaches had to do with the suppression of the Southern rebellion.

The Moros of the Sulu Archipelago and Palawan, and those living upon or in immediate communication with the seacoast in Mindanao, have been as a rule, friendly and well behaved. Some of the Malanao Moros who inhabit the borders of Lake Lanao, in the interior of Mindanao, resented attempts made by Americans to examine the interior of the country, and in the spring of this year entered upon a regular system of attacking our men when found alone or in small parties, and stealing our horses and mules. Several of our men were murdered, and in April a demand was made for the return of the property and the surrender of the murderers. This demand was met by defiance, and after long continued and repeated efforts to secure redress and a discontinuance of the practice by peaceable means, an expedition was organized under Colonel (now Brigadier-General) Frank D. Baldwin, which on the second and third of May attacked and captured the stronghold of the Sultan of Bayang and the Dato of Binadayan on Lake Lañao, with a loss of seven killed and forty-four wounded. . . .

After this lesson many of the lake datos came in and established friendly relations. Some of them, however, remained recalcitrant, and continued the practice of annoyance and attack. General Chaffee reported on the sixth of September that since the second of May our troops had been attacked twelve times, with a loss of four killed and twelve wounded. On the twenty-eighth of September another well-conducted expedition under Captain John J. Pershing, of the Fifteenth Cavalry, inflicted severe punishment upon the Maciu Moros, capturing many of their fortified places, killing one of their sultans and forty or fifty of their fighting men, with a loss of two Americans wounded.

Some further punishment may yet be necessary, but the present indications since this last experience seem to be peaceful.

The numbers of the Lake Lanao Moros are estimated variously from 100,000 to 400,000. The smaller number is probably nearer the fact. No attempts appear to have been made by Spain to exercise any control over them between the middle of the seventeenth century and the year 1890. Some unsuccessful efforts were made by small forces in the years 1890 and 1891; and in 1898, before the war between Spain and the United States, extensive preparations had been made by the Spanish forces in the Philippines for the subjugation of the lake tribes.

Farther in the interior of Mindanao are numerous heathen tribes still more savage and lower in the scale of civilization than the Moros. In 1897 the Spanish governor of Mindanao estimated the numbers of sixteen of these tribes at an aggregate of 262,000. From time immemorial the Moros have been in the habit of raiding their villages and carrying away captives into slavery, and a considerable slave trade appears to have been carried on between the southwest coast of Mindanao and ports in the Sulu Archipelago. It is only by asserting and establishing our right of control over the Moro tribes that we can put a stop to this nefarious business; and if there were no other reason, that alone would make it impossible for us to follow the example of Spain and leave the Moros of the interior to themselves.

Now that the insurrection has been disposed of we shall be able to turn our attention, not merely to the slave trade, but to the already existing slavery among the Moros. We cannot immediately free the slaves by a single act, first, because it would require a war of extermination in which a large part of the slaves would probably be found fighting against us; and, second, because a large part of them would have nowhere to go and no way to live if deprived of the protection and support of their present masters. I believe, however, that we can maintain a process of gradual and steady reduction, resulting ultimately in the extinction of the practice of slavery. Some of the results of our efforts in that direction are stated in my last report. The process will be slow, and will require patience and good judgment, but I believe the result will be worth the trouble. The task of improving the Moros is by no means hopeless. General George W. Davis, who commanded in Mindanao, and now commands the Division of the Philippines, says of them:

> Whatever may be the number of Moros, whether a few, or many hundred thousands, all, and many times more than all, of these people will be needed as agricultural and mechanical laborers and helpers in the cultivation of the soil and the utilization of its productions for the benefit of themselves and mankind. They are able to produce rice, sugar cane, coffee, corn, cattle, beautiful woven fabrics, and thrusting and cutting weapons; they manufacture bronze cannon and gunpowder, and give surprising proofs of their ingenuity and industry. Their Moro boats are fashioned and rigged and sailed with the utmost skill, and are admired by all strangers. A race of men who are capable of doing all this and who possess many manly qualities, should be kept alive and not shot down in war. They should be aided and encouraged and taught how to improve their own natural and social condition, and benefit us at the same time. Mohammedans in Turkey and India and Java have proved to be industrious and useful members of the communities. Mohammedan Malays in Sarawak, a British Protectorate in Borneo, perform all the

skilled and unskilled labor of that prosperous colony, and are as plainly showing their adaptability for the higher duties and occupations as did the Japanese. The Moros have certainly equal or greater capacity for usefulness.

The report from which this quotation is taken is among those transmitted herewith, and I commend it to special attention. It exhibits the breadth of view and sound judgment which uniformly characterize that officer's work.

The End of the Moro Rebellion

Extract from the Report of the Secretary of War for 1903 [1]

The last report of the Secretary of War contained an account of the punitive expeditions which had been found necessary in the Lake Lanao region in the months of May and September, 1902. I then said:

Some further punishment may yet be necessary, but the present indications since this last experience seem to be peaceful.

In April, 1903, a body of American troops under Captain John J. Pershing, engaged in the exploration of the west shore of Lake Lanao, was attacked by the Sultan of Baccalod and the Sultan's fort was captured and destroyed. In May, while exploring the east shore of the lake, the force under Captain Pershing was opposed and fired upon by the Taraca Moros, and their forts were assaulted and captured. Both General Sumner, in command of the Department, and General Davis, in command of the Division, characterize the conduct of Captain Pershing and his officers and men in terms of high commendation. On the eleventh of May the following dispatch was sent by the Secretary of War to General Davis:

I congratulate you and Brigadier-General S. S. Sumner on the work done in Mindanao. Express to Captain John J. Pershing and the officers and men under his command the thanks of the War Department for their able and effective accomplishment of their difficult and important task.

[1] Page 33.

In the Sulu Archipelago the conduct of the Moros has been growing steadily more unsatisfactory during the entire year. The agreement made by General Bates with the Sultan of Jolo on August 10, 1899, and submitted to Congress February 1, 1900, recognized the sovereignty of the Sultan and depended upon him for the maintenance of order. Fuller experience with these people, however, has shown that the sovereignty of the Sultan is little more than nominal and that he has not the power, even if he has the will, to maintain order. The people are really governed by a number of chiefs or " dattos," who pay very little attention to the theoretical authority of the Sultan. Some of these are friendly to the Americans and some of them have become exceedingly insolent and defiant, committing or permitting their people to commit frequent thefts and assaults and contemptuously repudiating any subordination to American sovereignty. I said in my last report:

> Now that the insurrection has been disposed of we shall be able to turn our attention, not merely to the slave trade, but to the already existing slavery among the Moros. We cannot immediately free the slaves by a single act, first, because it would require a war of extermination in which a large part of the slaves would probably be found fighting against us, and, second, because a large part of them would have nowhere to go and no way to live if deprived of the protection and support of their present masters. I believe, however, that we can maintain a process of gradual and steady reduction, resulting ultimately in the extinction of the practice of slavery.

The conditions which I have described, as long as they exist, will be an insuperable barrier to carrying out the intention thus expressed, as it is found that the Sulu Moros are not only continuing the practice of slavery, but are actively engaged in the slave trade.

It has thus become plain that the Bates agreement of 1899, which served a useful purpose at that time can no longer be depended upon as an instrument of government, and that a new arrangement must be substituted in its place under which American authority operates directly upon the dattos, who are the real controlling powers in the Sulu Archipelago. General Samuel S. Sumner, commanding the Department, in his report of June 30, 1903, said of that agreement:

> Without going into a discussion of the Bates agreement, I do not believe any development can take place or any advance be made so long as the treaty stands. It was made, as I am informed, to meet and cover an emergency; its use as a temporary measure has passed, and we should now replace it by some wise and just measures that will allow us to get into personal contact and have more direct control and supervision of these people.

THE ARMY IN CUBA AND THE PHILIPPINES

A TRIBUTE TO ITS COURAGE AND EFFICIENCY

Extract from the Report of the Secretary of War for 1902 [1]

THE conduct and service of the army, both in Cuba and in the Philippines, were summed up in the following order:

War Department,
Washington, July 4, 1902.

To the Army of the United States:

The President upon this anniversary of national independence wishes to express to the officers and enlisted men of the United States army his deep appreciation of the service they have rendered to the country in the great and difficult undertakings which they have brought to a successful conclusion during the past year.

He thanks the officers and the enlisted men who have been maintaining order and carrying on the military government in Cuba, because they have faithfully given effect to the humane purposes of the American people. They have with sincere kindness helped the Cuban people to take all the successive steps necessary to the establishment of their own constitutional government. During the time required for that process they have governed Cuba wisely, regarding justice and respecting individual liberty; have honestly collected and expended for the best interests of the Cuban people the revenues, amounting to over $60,000,000; have carried out practical and thorough sanitary measures, greatly improving the health and lowering the death rate of the island. By patient, scientific research they have ascertained the causes of yellow fever, and by good administration have put an end to that most dreadful disease, which has long destroyed the lives and hindered the commercial prosperity of the Cubans. They have expedited justice and secured protection for the rights of the innocent, while they have cleansed the prisons and established sound discipline and healthful conditions for the punishment of the guilty. They have reëstablished and renovated and put upon a substantial basis adequate hospitals and asylums for the care of the unfortunate. They have established a general system of free common schools throughout the island, in which over 200,000 children are in actual attendance. They have constructed

[1] Page 14.

great and necessary public works. They have gradually trained the Cubans themselves in all branches of administration, so that the new government upon assuming power has begun its work with an experienced force of Cuban civil-service employees competent to execute its orders. They have borne themselves with dignity and self-control, so that nearly four years of military occupation have passed unmarred by injury or insult to man or woman. They have transferred the government of Cuba to the Cuban people amid universal expressions of friendship and good will, and have left a record of ordered justice and liberty, of rapid improvement in material and moral conditions, and progress in the art of government which reflects great credit upon the people of the United States.

The President thanks the officers and enlisted men of the army in the Philippines, both regulars and volunteers, for the courage and fortitude, the indomitable spirit and loyal devotion with which they have put down and ended the great insurrection which has raged throughout the archipelago against the lawful sovereignty and just authority of the United States. The task was peculiarly difficult and trying. They were required at first to overcome organized resistance of superior numbers, well equipped with modern arms of precision, intrenched in an unknown country of mountain defiles, jungles, and swamps, apparently capable of interminable defense. When this resistance had been overcome they were required to crush out a general system of guerrilla warfare conducted among a people speaking unknown tongues, from whom it was almost impossible to obtain the information necessary for successful pursuit or to guard against surprise and ambush.

The enemies by whom they were surrounded were regardless of all obligations of good faith and of all the limitations which humanity has imposed upon civilized warfare. Bound themselves by the laws of war, our soldiers were called upon to meet every device of unscrupulous treachery and to contemplate without reprisal the infliction of barbarous cruelties upon their comrades and friendly natives. They were instructed, while punishing armed resistance, to conciliate the friendship of the peaceful, yet had to do with a population among whom it was impossible to distinguish friend from foe, and who in countless instances used a false appearance of friendship for ambush and assassination. They were obliged to deal with problems of communication and transportation in a country without roads and frequently made impassable by torrential rains. They were weakened by tropical heat and tropical disease. Widely scattered over a great archipelago, extending a thousand miles from north to south, the gravest responsibilities, involving the life or death of their commands, frequently devolved upon young and inexperienced officers beyond the reach of specific orders or advice.

Under all these adverse circumstances the Army of the Philippines has accomplished its task rapidly and completely. In more than two thousand combats, great and small, within three years, it has exhibited unvarying courage and resolution. Utilizing the lessons of the Indian wars, it has relentlessly followed the guerrilla bands to their fastnesses in mountain and jungle and crushed them. It has put an end to the vast system of intimidation and secret assassination by which the peaceful natives were prevented from taking a genuine part in government under American authority. It has captured or forced to surrender substantially all the leaders of the insurrection. It has submitted to no discouragement and halted at no obstacle. Its officers have shown high qualities of command, and its men have shown devotion and discipline. Its splendid virile energy has been accompanied by self-control, patience, and magnanimity. With surprisingly few individual exceptions, its course has been characterized by humanity and kindness to the prisoner and the noncombatant. With admirable good temper, sympathy, and loyalty to American ideals its commanding generals have joined with the civilian agents of the Government in healing the wounds of war and assuring the people of the Philippines the blessings of peace and prosperity. Individual liberty, protection of personal rights, civil order, public instruction, and religious freedom have followed its footsteps. It has added honor to the flag which it defended, and has justified increased confidence in the future of the American people, whose soldiers do not shrink from labor or death, yet love liberty and peace.

The President feels that he expresses the sentiments of all the loyal people of the United States in doing honor to the whole army which has joined in the performance and shares in the credit of these honorable services.

This General Order will be read aloud at parade in every military post on the fourth day of July, 1902, or on the first day after it shall have been received.

Elihu Root,
Secretary of War.

THE CHINESE RELIEF EXPEDITION

JULY–DECEMBER, 1900

During the year 1898 a widespread movement was started in China to introduce western learning and civilization. The then emperor was an enthusiastic advocate of the movement and issued a number of edicts calculated to transform China into a modern state. It was opposed by the bureaucracy and other vested interests of China, backed by the popular superstition and conservatism of the people. The empress-dowager took advantage of this situation, made the emperor practically a prisoner, and compelled him to issue an edict restoring her regency. Drastic efforts were then made to stamp out the reform movement. This reactionary tide continued to rise until it culminated, in 1900, in the organization of the "Boxers," a secret society whose avowed object was to "exterminate the foreigners and save the dynasty." Foreign missionaries and native converts were massacred, and the chancellor of the Japanese legation, Mr. Sugiyama, and Baron von Ketteler, the German minister, were murdered. The legations, the foreign missionaries and residents and the native converts to Christianity, together with a number of bluejackets and marines of various nationalities, sent to protect the legations, were closely besieged. Peking was cut off from all communication with the rest of the world, and efforts to restore communication were at first unsuccessful. Finally, a force composed of American, British, French, Japanese, and Russian troops large enough to take the offensive was collected, and the native city of Tien-tsin was captured July 14, 1900. However, it was not until August 4 that the combined forces were ready to start for Peking; and on August 14, after a series of severe engagements and trying marches, they entered the city and raised the siege.

The American contingent was under the command of Major-General Adna R. Chaffee. The total number of American troops (not including sailors or marines) sent to and serving in China during the disturbances was 191 officers and 4,809 enlisted men. General Chaffee states in his official report that on August 14, "Two companies of the Fourteenth Infantry, under the immediate command of Colonel Daggett, had scaled the wall of the Chinese city at the northeast corner, and the flag of that regiment was the first foreign colors unfurled upon the walls surrounding Peking." The casualties among the American troops were two officers killed and seven wounded; and thirty-one enlisted men killed and 169 wounded.

By a joint note of December 22, 1900, the powers presented to China their demands for "equitable indemnities for governments, societies, companies, and private individuals, as well as for Chinese who have suffered during the late events in person or in property in consequence of their being in the service of foreigners." The final protocol between China and the intervening powers under which the troops were withdrawn, signed at Peking, September 7, 1901, fixed the amount of this indemnity at 450,000,000 Haikwan taels, equivalent in round numbers to $333,000,000 United States gold. China agreed to pay this sum, with interest at four per cent per annum, by installments running through a period of thirty-nine years. The share allotted to the United States was $24,440,778.81, for which a bond dated December 15, 1906, was given by China to the United States; but in a note of June 15, 1907, Mr. Root, then Secretary of State, informed the Chinese Minister that

> It was from the first the intention of this Government at the proper time, when all claims should have been presented and all expenses should have been ascertained as fully as possible, to revise the estimate and account against which these payments were to be made, and, as proof of sincere friendship for China, to voluntarily release that country from its legal liability for all payments in excess of the sum which should prove to be necessary for actual indemnity to the United States and its citizens.[1]

The revised estimate of American losses placed their amount at $11,655,492.69, and President Roosevelt in his annual message of December 3, 1907, asked for authority from Congress to remit and cancel the obligation of China for the payment of all that part of the indemnity in excess of that sum. By a joint resolution of Congress approved May 25, 1908 (U. S. Statutes at Large, Vol. 35, Part 1, p. 577), authority was given to reduce the amount of the indemnity to $13,655,492.69 and to remit the remainder, which amounted to $10,785,286.12. The two million dollars added by the joint resolution to the estimate of the American losses given in the President's message was withheld to abide the result of rehearings on private claims against the indemnity before the Court of Claims, with the proviso that any balance remaining after all such claims had been adjudicated should also be returned to China. The settlement of these claims was completed in 1914, and the awards of the Court of Claims amounted to $824,164.36, thus making the total amount retained for the United States and its citizens $12,479,657.05, with interest at the stipulated rate, and the amount remitted to China $11,961,121.76.

An executive order issued December 28, 1908, authorized the reduction of the amount of the bond of December 15, 1906, to $13,655,492.69, in accordance with the joint resolution of May 25, 1908, and directed that after January 1, 1909, there be retained by the United States from the monthly installments made by China on account of the original bond only such sums as would, with the amount previously paid by China, satisfy at the end of the period contemplated in the original bond the principal and interest of the reduced amount of the bond, and that the remainder of each monthly installment be returned to China. (Foreign Relations, 1908, p. 72.)

The balance of $1,175,835.64 remaining after the Court of Claims had made its awards from the two million dollars reserved for that purpose and included in the $13,655,492.69 retained by the United States, has been returned in installments from the United States to China out of the sums previously paid by China and retained by the United States as a part of the reduced indemnity.

Although the remission was made by the United States unconditionally, the Chinese Government, in appreciation of this generous and friendly act, decided to devote the remitted money to the education and support of Chinese students in the United States, a certain number of whom are to be sent to the United States throughout the period of the indemnity payments. (Foreign Relations, 1908, pp. 67–72.) This undertaking is now in operation.

[1] Foreign Relations, 1907, Part 1, p. 174.

Because of the unusual nature of the transaction and its interest to the two countries, the note of Mr. Root, written in behalf of the United States, informing China of the remission, and the note of Prince Ch'ing of July 14, 1908, on behalf of China, accepting the remission, and stating the purposes to which the money thus released would be devoted, are printed in full below:

The Secretary of State to the Chinese Minister in Washington

DEPARTMENT OF STATE,
WASHINGTON, June 15, 1907.

SIR: After the rescue of the foreign legations in Peking during the Boxer troubles of 1900, the note of the Powers to China prescribing the conditions upon which the occupation of Peking and the Province of Chili would be ended, dated December 22, 1900, required in its sixth article the payment of "equitable indemnities for governments, societies, companies, and private individuals, as well as for Chinese who have suffered during the late events in person or in property in consequence of their being in the service of foreigners."

The final protocol under which the troops were withdrawn, signed at Peking, September 7, 1901, fixed the amount of this indemnity at 450,000,000 Haikwan taels, equivalent in round numbers to $333,000,000 United States gold. China agreed to pay this sum, with interest at 4 per cent per annum, by installments running through a period of thirty-nine years.

The share of this indemnity allotted to the United States was $24,440,778.81, and on account of the principal and interest of that sum China has paid to the United States, down to and including the 1st day of June, 1907, the sum of $6,010,931.91.

It was from the first the intention of this Government at the proper time, when all claims should have been presented and all expenses should have been ascertained as fully as possible, to revise the estimate and account against which these payments were to be made, and, as proof of sincere friendship for China, to voluntarily release that country from its legal liability for all payments in excess of the sum which should prove to be necessary for actual indemnity to the United States and its citizens.

Such a revision has now been made by the different executive departments concerned, and I am authorized by the President to say that, in pursuance of that revision, at the next session of the Congress he will ask for authority to reform the agreement with China under which the indemnity is fixed by remitting and cancelling the obligation of China for the payment of all that part of the stipulated indemnity which is in excess of the sum of $11,655,492.69 and interest at the stipulated rate.

Accept, Mr. Minister, etc., (Signed) ELIHU ROOT.

The Prince of Ch'ing, President of the Chinese Foreign Office, to Minister Rockhill

FOREIGN OFFICE,
PEKING, July 14, 1908.

YOUR EXCELLENCY: I have the honor to acknowledge the receipt of your dispatch of July 11, informing me that you had been directed by the Secretary of State to notify me that a bill has passed the Congress of the United States authorizing the President to modify the indemnity bond given the United States by China under the provision of Article VI of the final protocol of September 7, 1901, from $24,440,000 United States gold currency, to $13,655,-492.29, with interest at 4 per cent per annum. Of this amount $2,000,000 are held pending the result of hearings on private claims presented to the Court of Claims of the United States within one year. Any balance remaining after such adjudication is also to be returned to the Chinese Government in such manner as the Secretary of State shall decide. The President is further authorized under the bill to remit to China the remainder of the indemnity as an act of friendship, such payments to be made at such times and in such a manner as he may deem just. As directed by the Secretary of State, your excellency requests the Imperial Government kindly to favor him with its views as to the time and manner of the remissions, and asks an early reply to communicate to your excellency's Government.

On reading this dispatch I was profoundly impressed with the justice and great friendliness of the American Government, and wish to express our sincerest thanks.

Concerning the time and manner of the return to China of the amounts to be remitted, the Imperial Government has no wishes to express in the matter. It relies implicitly on the friendly intentions of the United States Government and is convinced that it will adopt such measures as are best calculated to attain the end it has in view.

The Imperial Government, wishing to give expression to the high value it places on the friendship of the United States, finds in its present action a favorable opportunity for doing so. Mindful of the desire recently expressed by the President of the United States to promote the coming of Chinese students to the United States to take courses in the schools and higher educational institutions of the country, and convinced by the happy results of past experience of the great value to China of education in American schools, the Imperial Government has the honor to state that it is its intention to send henceforth yearly to the United States a considerable number of students there to receive their education. The board of foreign affairs will confer with the American minister in Peking concerning the elaboration of plans for the carrying out of the intention of the Imperial Government.

The China Relief Expedition

Extract from the Report of the Secretary of War for 1900[2]

A BELIEF that the protection of American interests in China would soon require a larger land force than our naval vessels on that station could supply, led, as early as June 14, 1900, to an inquiry by the Department of the commanding general in the Philippines as to the time within

[1] Stat. L. Vol. 35, Pt. I, pp. 577, 578. [2] Page 11.

which he could send troops to Taku, and on the sixteenth of June to an order for the dispatch of a regiment of infantry from Manila with suitable transportation, medical officers, and rapid-fire guns, and with instructions that the commanding officer should confer with the admiral commanding the American fleet at Taku, and report to the American minister at Peking for the protection of the lives and property of American citizens in China.

On the seventeenth of June occurred the battle in which the Taku forts were captured by the European squadrons at that point, and on the twentieth Admiral Kempff telegraphed to the Secretary of the Navy that he considered one brigade necessary to represent our Government properly. On the twenty-seventh the Ninth Infantry, under Colonel Emerson H. Liscum, after some delay caused by a typhoon in the Bay of Manila, embarked with its transportation and supplies from Manila, and on the first of July the Sixth Cavalry, which had been already withdrawn from its stations in the interior, sailed from San Francisco. In the meantime the foreign ministers and legations were reported to be besieged in Peking, and an expedition for their relief, under Admiral Seymour, including a small force of marines and sailors, had been attacked by imperial troops and driven back to Tien-tsin with heavy loss, and on the second of July the German minister at Peking was reported to have been murdered.

On the third of July Admiral Kempff was instructed by the Navy Department to confer with the commanding officers of other nations at Taku and to report by telegraph the proportional number of American forces considered necessary for a second expeditionary force to Peking. On the eighth he reported to the Secretary of the Navy, that a meeting had been held; that about 20,000 troops were ashore, which were necessary to hold the position from Taku to Tien-tsin, and that 60,000 troops in addition were required to march upon Peking; that our proportion of the entire allied army should be about 10,000; that reënforcements were expected within a month which, by the middle of August, would make the entire active force of other powers 40,800. . . .

The forces set in motion by the United States for the anticipated campaign in China were as follows: Infantry, 221 officers, 9,539 enlisted men; cavalry, 87 officers, 2,941 enlisted men; artillery, 23 officers, 986 enlisted men; marines, 25 officers, 756 enlisted men; and staff, medical, engineer and signal service, 79 officers, 796 enlisted men, making a total of 435 officers and 15,018 enlisted men, besides about 3,000 marines whom the Navy Department contemplated furnishing, as appears by its requirement of the Subsistence Department. Of these between 5,000 and 6,000 arrived in China before the capture of Peking.

While the climate of the province of Chili is extremely hot in summer, it is extremely cold in winter, and the river Pei-Ho and that part of the Gulf of Chili upon which Taku is situated are closed to navigation about the first of December, and remain closed until late in the succeeding spring, so that it was necessary to provide not only for the landing of the troops with their horses, transportation, ordnance, and current supplies, but for the delivery in China, not later than the middle of November, of six months' supply of food, ammunition, heavy winter clothing, fuel, stoves, lumber for quarters, medical stores and supplies of all kinds. Adequate provisions were made to meet this requirement.

The supply problem was somewhat complicated by the fact that it was impossible to discontinue the regular supply service for the army in the Philippines, in which our fleet of transports was engaged; it was impossible to withdraw from that service a sufficient number of vessels for a separate service to China, and there was not time to secure new transports. The problem was solved, however, through the courtesy of the Japanese Government, which, upon our application through the State Department, in the most friendly spirit, permitted us to use the port of Nagasaki, where the lines from the United States to Manila on the south and to Taku on the north diverged, for the transshipment of supplies and material without passing through their custom-house, and for the transfer of men (not carrying arms).

This enabled us to establish a subsidiary service, which, in connection with the main service to and from this country, distributed both men and materials between Nagasaki and Manila and between Nagasaki and Taku, practically using both our Pacific ports and Manila as main bases and Nagasaki as a secondary base of supply. This arrangement was also very convenient and, as it ultimately proved, very valuable, in enabling us to direct each organization as it left this country to look for orders at Nagasaki, so that if at any time it should become apparent, as of course we always regarded it possible, that their services were not needed in China they could be diverted from Nagasaki to the Philippines, to take the place of an equal number of volunteers. . . .

The Subsistence Department shipped from the United States and Manila 19,984,620 pounds of subsistence stores, consisting of 8,272,800 pounds of regular army rations and 5,515,200 pounds of sales stores. The Medical Department, in addition to the equipment of the hospital ship *Relief* and the regular medical attendance of the organizations, sent full equipment for a field hospital of 1,000 beds, with full medical supplies, and took the necessary steps for the establishment of an additional base hospital at Nagasaki. The Signal Corps provided all the material and personnel for the construction and operation of 235 miles of telegraph line, together with the signal flags, heliographs, lanterns, telescopes, etc., for visual signaling service. The engineer implements and materials were shipped from Manila. The necessary reserve of equipment and arms, with an adequate equipment of rapid-fire guns, with ammunition, and with over 4,000,000 rounds of small-arms ammunition, were promptly provided for by the Ordnance Department.

The gulf at Taku is too shallow for large vessels to approach within ten miles of the shore, and all of the men, animals, ordnance, and supplies had to be transported for that distance by lighters or small boats. They were much delayed at times by stormy weather, which particularly interfered with the landing of horses and mules. Besides the small vessels used in this service thirty-two large steamships were employed in the ocean transportation required.

On the twenty-sixth of June Major-General Adna R. Chaffee, U. S. V., was appointed to the command of the American forces in China. He embarked from San Francisco on the first of July, reached Nagasaki on the twenty-fourth, and Taku, China, on the twenty-eighth. . . .

In the meantime the Ninth Infantry, from Manila, reached Taku on the sixth of July. Two battalions of that regiment, under Colonel Liscum, pressed forward to Tien-tsin, reaching that point on the eleventh, and on the thirteenth took part with the British, French, and Japanese forces in an attack upon the southwest part of the walled city of Tien-tsin, which had been rendered necessary by the persistent shelling of the foreign quarters, outside of the walls, on the part of the Chinese troops occupying the city. Colonel Liscum's command formed part of a brigade under General Dorward, of the British army, and was assigned to the duty of protecting the flank of the allied forces.

In the performance of that duty it maintained a position under heavy fire for fifteen hours, with a loss of eighteen killed and seventy-seven wounded. Among the killed was the gallant Colonel Liscum, who thus ended an honorable service of nearly forty years, commencing in the ranks of the First Vermont Infantry at the outbreak of the Civil War, and distinguished by unvarying courage, fidelity, and high character. The regiment was withdrawn from its position on the night of the thirteenth, and on the morning of the fourteenth the native city was captured, and the southeast quarter was assigned to the American forces for police and protection. This duty was performed effectively until the recent withdrawal of our troops. General Dorward, writing to the then ranking officer of the American forces, on the fifteenth of July, says of the conduct of our troops:

> I desire to express the high appreciation of the British troops of the honor done them in serving alongside their comrades of the American army during the long and hard fighting of the thirteenth instant and the subsequent capture of Tien-tsin city, and of my own appreciation of the high honor accorded to me by having them under my command.
>
> The American troops formed part of the front line of the British attack and so had more than their share of the fighting that took place. The ready and willing spirit of the officers and men will always make their command easy and pleasant, and when one adds to that the steady gallantry and power of holding on to exposed positions which they displayed on the thirteenth instant the result is soldiers of the highest class.

On the seventeenth of July, upon representations made by the friendly southern viceroys of Nanking and Wuchang, the following dispatch was sent and the following answer was received:

> Commanding Officer Ninth Infantry,
> Care American Consul, Chefoo:
>
> Chinese minister has delivered following message from viceroys Nanking and Wuchang, which is transmitted for your information:
>
> "If Tien-tsin city should be destroyed it would be difficult to restore same in a hundred years. Request the powers to preserve it, as consequences would affect Chinese and foreign commerce."
>
> The President directs me to say nothing but military necessity would justify the destruction of the city, and he hopes that no such necessity may arise.
>
> Corbin.

CHEFOO.

CORBIN, Washington:

Tien-tsin, 21. Message regarding destruction Tien-tsin received. Tien-tsin captured July 14. Considerably destroyed by fire and bombardment. Meade, senior officer, will present President's instructions.

COOLIDGE.

On the twenty-first of July, owing to indiscriminate reports of pillaging in Tien-tsin, the following dispatches were sent and received:

FOWLER, Chefoo:

Send following cablegram to Coolidge, commanding United States forces, Tien-tsin:

"Reported here extensive looting in Tien-tsin. Report immediately whether American troops took part. If so, punish severely; repress sternly. Absolute regard for life and property of non-combatants enjoined."

By order of Secretary of War: CORBIN.

CHEFOO, July 29, 1900.

CORBIN, Washington:

Tien-tsin, July 25. Looting by American troops walled city Tien-tsin unfounded and denied. Silver taken from burned mint under direction Meade, commanding, who was invalided today. No property destroyed except under military exigency. American troops have orders to protect life and property non-combatants in American southeast quarter city assigned them. Will forward reports commanders of American guards in city.

COOLIDGE.

At the time of the capture of Tien-tsin the most positive and circumstantial accounts of the massacre of all the ministers and members of the legations in Peking, coming apparently from Chinese sources, had been published, and were almost universally believed. The general view taken by the civilized world of the duty to be performed in China was not that the living representatives of the Western powers in Peking were to be rescued, but that their murder was to be avenged and their murderers punished. In the performance of that duty time and rapidity of movement were not especially important.

The resolution of the commanders of the allied forces, communicated by Admiral Kempff on the eighth of July, to the effect that 80,000 men would be required — 20,000 to hold the position from Taku to Tien-tsin and 60,000 to march to Peking, while not more than 40,800 troops were expected to have arrived by the middle of August — practically abandoned all expectation of rescuing the ministers and members of the legations alive, for it proposed that after the middle of August any forward movement should be still deferred until 40,000 more troops had arrived.

On the eleventh of July, however, the American Secretary of State secured, through the Chinese minister at Washington, the forwarding of a dispatch in the State Department cipher to the American minister at Peking, and on the twentieth of July, pursuant to the same arrangement, an answer in cipher was received from Minister Conger, as follows:

> For one month we have been besieged in British legation under continued shot and shell from Chinese troops. Quick relief only can prevent general massacre.

This dispatch from Mr. Conger was the first communication received by any Western power from any representative in Peking for about a month, and although it was at first received in Europe with some incredulity, it presented a situation which plainly called for the urgency of a relief expedition rather than for perfection of preparation. It was made the basis of urgent pressure for an immediate movement upon Peking, without waiting for the accumulation of the large force previously proposed. On the thirty-first of July General Chaffee telegraphed as follows:

> CHEFOO.
>
> ADJUTANT-GENERAL, Washington:
>
> Tien-tsin, 31 July. Do not believe ministers can be relieved without overthrow of Chinese troops intrenched between here and Peking. An aggressive step probable August 3. Objective Yangtsun or crossing of railway to right bank river twenty-five miles from here. As now seems likely, English, Japanese, American troops march on right bank and hope for movement on opposite side by troops of other powers. Total available force for right bank not more 10,000; about 1,600 American.

Considerable guard necessary Tien-tsin. Assumed that defeat Chinese troops between here, Yangtsun, will stimulate favorable action Peking, as it has been assumed the fall of Tien-tsin effected cease fire on ministers. Reconnoissance by Japanese yesterday and today. Result not disclosed. Conference probable before forward movement, but not called yet. Not to exceed 20,000 troops in this vicinity. Deduct guard for Tien-tsin. Available for battle about 14,000, if all participate. Bay so rough yesterday and today little accomplished unloading. Battery and cavalry still on ship. Quartermaster started everything available working night and day. . . . CHAFFEE.

On the third of August General Chaffee telegraphed:

CHEFOO.

ADJUTANT-GENERAL, Washington:

Tien-tsin, 3d. Conference today decide battle Sunday. Chinese intrenched east and west through Pei-tsang. Left of Chinese protected by flooded ground, practically unassailable. Japanese, English, American forces about 10,000 strong. Attack Chinese right west of river in flank. Other forces, Russian, French, about 4,000 strong opposite side between river and railroad. Chinese position apparently strong. Army reported 30,000 between Pei-tsang and Yangtsun or crossing of road over Pei-ho. Yangtsun objective. Our forces 2,000 and battery. *Conemaugh* arrived. Sixth Cavalry left in Tien-tsin for guard of city and awaiting mounts. Minister safe on twenty-eighth (July). CHAFFEE.

The advance from Tien-tsin was commenced on the night of August fourth by a force composed of Japanese, Russian, British, American, and French troops, the respective numbers of which had been reported in conference of the commanding officers as follows: Japanese, 8,000; Russians, 4,800; British, 3,000; Americans, 2,100; French, 800; amounting in the aggregate to 18,700.

The American troops had, in fact, by the time of starting, been augmented to 2,500. To this was subsequently added, on the ninth of August, one troop of the Sixth Cavalry, which had succeeded in getting its horses off the transport, where they had been detained by stormy weather in the gulf. The remainder of the Sixth Cavalry and portions of other organizations were left to perform necessary duty at Tien-tsin and elsewhere on the line of communication. . . .

On the fifth of August Pei-tsang, about seven miles up the river from Tien-tsin, was captured by the Japanese troops supported by the English and Americans. On the sixth of August Yangtsun was captured, with an American loss of seven killed and sixty-five wounded. On the twelfth Tung-chow was occupied. On the fourteenth Peking was reached. At eleven o'clock in the morning of that day two companies of the Fourteenth Infantry, under the immediate command of Colonel Daggett, had scaled the wall of the Chinese city, and the flag of that regiment was the first of the foreign colors to be unfurled upon the walls of Peking. After steady fighting until about the middle of the afternoon, the Tartar city was entered, and the legations were relieved. Our casualties during the day were one officer and eleven enlisted men wounded. General Chaffee reports that he found the following conditions:

> Upon entering the legations, the appearance of the people and their surroundings, buildings, walls, streets, alleys, entrances, etc., showed every evidence of a confining siege. Barricades were built everywhere and of every sort of material, native brick being largely used for their construction, topped with sand bags made from every conceivable sort of cloth — from sheets and pillow-cases to dress materials and brocaded curtains. Many of the legations were in ruins, and the English, Russian, and American, though standing and occupied, were filled with bullet holes from small arms, often having larger apertures made by shell. The children presented a pitiable sight, white and wan for lack of proper food, but the adults, as a rule, seemed cheerful and little the worse for their trying experience, except from anxiety and constant care. They were living on short rations, a portion of which consisted of a very small piece of horse or mule meat daily. The Christian Chinese were being fed upon whatever could be secured, and were often reduced to killing dogs for meat. All the surroundings indicated that the people had been closely besieged, confined to a small area without any comforts, or conveniences, and barely existing from day to day in hope of succor.

The legations were immediately adjacent to the interior imperial city, from the walls of which the Chinese fire had been directed upon them. As these walls were still held by

Chinese troops, on the morning of the fifteenth General Chaffee proceeded to clear them of their defenders, successively forcing three gates of the imperial city, with a loss of one officer and three enlisted men killed and fifteen enlisted men wounded. The loss of the officer, Captain Henry J. Reilly, of the Fifth Artillery, is much to be deplored. He had enlisted as a private at the age of nineteen, had risen from the ranks, and had become a most efficient officer, with an enviable record of faithful attention to duty throughout his career, and of gallant and effective service in Cuba and the Philippines.

On the sixteenth the imperial city was occupied, and the entire city was divided, by agreement, among the various forces for the maintenance of order, the west half of the Chinese city and the adjacent parts of the Tartar city being placed in charge of our troops. On the twenty-eighth a formal march was made through the forbidden precincts of the imperial palace, in which the troops of all the powers participated. In the meantime Colonel Wint, with the Sixth Cavalry, had encountered and defeated a large hostile force in the neighborhood of Tien-tsin, with the loss of five wounded, and numerous detachments of our troops had been engaged with proportionate detachments from other forces in guarding the long line of communication between Peking and Tien-tsin. . . .

The Signal Corps detachment was untiring in its exertions, and rendered especially effective service. It constructed a telegraph line from Tien-tsin to Peking, practically keeping pace with the march of the relief column, and, having the first line into Peking, was able to render valuable service, not only to our own force, but to the forces of other nations and to the press. The total of American casualties during the expedition was two officers and thirty enlisted men killed and seven officers and one hundred and seventy enlisted men wounded. . . .

General Chaffee's telegraphic report of the fall of Peking was received here on the twenty-second of August, and the object of the relief expedition having been accomplished, he was instructed, on the twenty-third of August, to take no further aggressive action unless that should be necessary for defensive purposes; and orders were cabled to Nagasaki, diverting the remaining troops en route for that point to Manila, with the exception of one battery of artillery which had not left San Francisco, and which was returned to its former station at Fort Riley.

On the twenty-fifth of August General Chaffee was directed to hold his forces in readiness for instructions to withdraw, and on the twenty-fifth of September he was instructed to send to Manila all the American troops in China with the exception of a legation guard, to consist of a regiment of infantry, a squadron of cavalry, and one light battery. . . .

It is gratifying to know that the Chinese have returned in great numbers, and there has been a general resumption of business, under the protection of our forces, in that portion of Peking which was assigned to our care, and which is still under the charge of the legation guard.

THE REORGANIZATION OF THE UNITED STATES ARMY

THE INCREASE OF THE ARMY AND THE ABOLITION OF THE PERMANENT ADMINISTRATIVE STAFF DEPARTMENTS

Repeated attention had been called to the necessity for a reorganization of the American military system, particularly in its directing heads, by a series of events during the Spanish-American War. These were the absence of coördination and coöperation between the several bureaus of the War Department, such as those having charge of transportation, the equipment, the commissary supplies, the clothing, etc., of an army in motion. As stated by Mr. Root in a committee hearing, "Everybody knows that when an exigency has come, confusion has come. The confusion comes from the fact that our organization is weak at the top. It does not make adequate provision for a directing and coördinating control. It does not make provision for an adequate force to see that these branches of the administrative and the different branches of the line pull together, so that the work of each one will fit in with the work of every other, and bring out the result which always has to be the result of the conspiring of a great number of people doing a great number of duties."

The following extracts from the Annual Reports of the Secretary of War indicate the reforms in the military system which were worked out by Mr. Root during his service as Secretary and put into effect or urged upon Congress. The principal measures were:

1. The increase of the army and the abolition of the permanent administrative staff departments.
2. The establishment of a system of military education, with the Army War College at the top.
3. The creation of a General Staff.
4. The bringing of the militia system of the country under the same organization, discipline, armament, supply and accounting methods, and instruction as the regular army.

These papers show also that Mr. Root advocated the consolidation of the supply and transportation departments of the regular army which has recently been accomplished, the establishment of a reserve which is still under discussion, and the extension of the method of promotion by selection, as to which nothing has been done.

Army Reorganization

Extract from the Report of the Secretary of War for 1899[1]

BEFORE July 1, 1901, when, under existing law, the present volunteer force must be disbanded and the present regular force restored to its peace basis of 26,610, we shall be compelled to face the practical necessity of providing for some increase of the regular army. It is manifest that however speedily the insurrection in the Philippines may be quelled, we shall be required to maintain for a long time in those islands a considerable force to furnish the protection which the inhabitants are entitled to receive from us, and to maintain order among the savage and semi-civilized tribes which still exist in nearly every island. There is no occasion to doubt that the expense of this portion of the military establishment can readily and properly be defrayed from the insular revenues.

It is not conceivable that a practical people should expend the great sums we are devoting to our seacoast fortifications, and the delicate and complicated machinery of modern ordnance with which we are equipping them, and not provide an adequate force of men to care for, preserve, and become familiar with the use of the guns and machinery. An increase in our artillery force will be absolutely necessary for this purpose. The present heavy-artillery force is about one-fifth of the requisite number.

I beg to suggest that the manifold services which have been rendered by officers of the army of the United States during the past year in almost every branch of civil government, and the effective zeal and devotion which they have exhibited in succoring the distressed, teaching the ignorant, establishing and maintaining civil law, fighting against pestilence, introducing sanitary reforms, and promoting and aiding peaceful

[1] Page 44.

industry should be regarded as proof, if any were needed, that American soldiers do not cease to be American citizens, and that no danger is to be apprehended from a reasonable enlargement of the army which affords such evidence of its character and spirit.

It is greatly to be desired that at the same time, while the lessons drawn from the experience of recent war are fresh in our minds, some improvements should be made in the organization of the army.

For many years various criticisms upon our present organization have been made and discussed, and a number of measures for improvement have been recommended by my predecessors or embodied in bills introduced in Congress. Some marked improvements have been made, notably the three-battalion form of regimental organization, which, after being urged by several successive Secretaries of War and advocated by all the high military authorities in the country for a generation, was finally authorized by the act of April 26, 1898.

As to most of the proposed changes, however, there has not been a sufficient public interest in the subject or a sufficiently strong conviction of the importance of good organization to overcome the diversity of opinions and personal interests desirous of being left undisturbed.

The method of proposing and considering, one by one, specific remedies for specific defects does not seem to be an adequate treatment of the subject. It seems to me that the best course would be to settle upon the true principle which should govern the use to be made of the army and then inquire in what respect our present arrangement fails to conform to that principle, and make it conform.

Two propositions seem to me fundamental in the consideration of the subject:

First. That the real object of having an army is to provide for war.

Second. That the regular establishment in the United States will probably never be by itself the whole machine with which any war will be fought.

The first of these statements seems like a truism, and it will probably be received everywhere without conscious denial. Yet the precise contrary is really the theory upon which the entire treatment of our army proceeded for the thirty-three years between the Civil War and the war with Spain. Present utility was really the controlling consideration, and the possibility of war seemed at all times so vague and unreal that it had no formative power in shaping legislation regarding the army. The result was an elaborate system admirably adapted to secure pecuniary accountability and economy of expenditure in time of peace; a large number of small and separate commands, well officered and well disciplined, very efficient for police duty against Indians, and as separate commands unsurpassed anywhere in fighting qualities; and a class of officers most of whom were of a high order of individual excellence, who rendered valuable service in the construction of public works, as instructors in colleges, and in a great variety of professional duties at separate posts and with their commands, but who, with the exception of the general officers, were arranged in rank without any reference whatever to their respective abilities to command or to render effective service. The result did not include the effective organization and training of the army as a whole for the purposes of war. This was not because the army did not wish such organization and training, but because it was not permitted to organize and train for that object. The army has many able, educated, and competent officers who have thought much upon the subject and deeply regretted this condition, but who have been unable to secure a change.

I believe that without any revolutionary interference with the general scheme of organization or with individual rights, and without excessive expense, a great improvement can be made in the way of conforming the organization and training of the army to its true purpose. It is not reorganization which is needed, but the grant of opportunities for development along lines which are well understood and appreciated by the army itself.

The preparation of an army for war involves at least these four things:

First. Systematic study by responsible officers of plans for action under all contingencies of possible conflict, and with this, study of the larger problems of military science and the most complete information regarding it, study of the constant improvements in implements and methods of warfare, and of the adaptability of improvements and inventions for the purpose of carrying out the plans devised, and study of the arrangement of territorial and tactical organizations, and the establishment of depots, camps, fortifications, and lines of communication with reference to these plans, so that all expenditures for each separate step of development may contribute toward the practical realization of a comprehensive and consistent scheme. This requirement is not to be met by the separate study and reflection of single officers not charged with the duty or able to give effect to their conclusions. The responsibility of declared duty, the comparison of different views, the contribution of different minds, the correction and evolution by discussion, the long-continued, laborious, and systematic application of a considerable number of minds of a high order, and with a recognized status giving authority to their conclusions, are needed to produce the desired result.

To illustrate: The War Department has recently received numerous applications from different parts of the country for the acquisition of tracts of land and the establishment of permanent camping places for the encampment and training of soldiers in large bodies, which the people of the country evidently realize ought to be provided for. There are different ways in which these applications may be treated. They may be rejected or favored with reference to the advantages which they will afford to the people of the towns in the neighborhood of the proposed camps through the business which would result from the maintenance of troops there, or they may be rejected or favored according to the healthfulness of the locations and the conveniences which they will afford and the ease of access from the points whence troops would naturally be drawn. Neither of these methods is at all satisfactory. If such camps are to be established, their locations should be selected with reference to carefully devised and comprehensive plans, one feature of which consists in determining the points at which troops can most usefully be mobilized for immediate use in case of war, so that by sending troops to them in time of peace we should be doing the very same thing which we have to do in time of urgent necessity, and so that every railroad that is built, every side track that is laid, and every building that is erected will leave so much less to do when war threatens. Such plans cannot be improvised; they cannot be produced by any other process than that above indicated.

Second. The preparation of material of war, keeping pace with the progress of military science and adapted to the conditions to be anticipated when war shall arise.

Gratifying progress has been made recently in this respect, but with the restoration of peace we may apprehend that there will be to some extent a return to the same indifference which left us without smokeless powder or small-bore magazine rifles in the spring of 1898. Under such conditions it is necessary that questions as to the character and form of material should be settled by authority beyond reasonable question, and that the things which ought to be done should be indicated clearly and positively. In no other way is it possible that such things can be done. At present the opinions of the artillery or infantry using a weapon, of the ordnance officers making it, of the department commander, and of the major-general commanding the army, may all differ on such questions, and there is no way of settling them after an appropriation, except by the decision of the Secretary of War, who cannot possibly study the subject thoroughly, or before the appropriation, by a committee of Congress with whom the differing opinions naturally tend to destroy each other and to prevent any action whatever. Some body of competent men whose business it is to be familiar with the whole field of invention, to consider it, to discuss it, and to reach conclusions upon it, alone can furnish those authoritative determinations which are necessary to effective demands for adequate material.

Third. An adequate process of selection according to merit and effectiveness among the officers of the army, so that the men of superior ability and power may be known and placed in positions involving responsibility and authority.

Without some such process in time of peace the selection has to be made after war has commenced, at the expense always of treasure and of life, and sometimes of temporary failure and humiliation. Such a process of selection will necessarily at the same time afford an incentive to exertion and a reward for professional attainments and effective service, while stimulating the development of the capable officer and bringing to the front the men best able to bear responsibility and perform the difficult duties to be confronted in actual hostilities.

Fourth. The exercise and training of the officers and men of the army in the movements of large bodies of troops by brigade, division, and corps under conditions approaching as nearly as possible those to be anticipated in executing the plans devised for their action in war.

Officers who have never seen a corps, division, or brigade organized and on the march cannot be expected to perform perfectly the duties required of them when war comes. The collection of large bodies of men presents, not the same difficulties presented by a small body, multiplied or increased in degree, but entirely new difficulties which only experience can qualify men to meet. The sanitation, the care, the discipline, and many of the duties are new to the man who has dealt only with a company or a regiment. The highest efficiency under these conditions can be attained only by giving experience approximating as nearly as possible to that which will be encountered when the war machinery is required to do its proper work.

I think the following steps may be taken to advantage:

(1) An army war college should be established, which shall be composed of the heads of the staff departments, properly so called, and a number of the ablest and most competent officers of high rank in the army (including, of course, the major-general commanding), these officers to be detailed for service in the college for limited periods, so that while the college shall be continuous in records, character, and performance, it shall continually and gradually change in its personal elements. It should be the duty of this body of officers to direct the instruction and intellectual exercise of the army, to acquire the information, devise the plans, and study the subjects above indicated, and to advise the Commander-in-Chief upon all questions of plans, armament, transportation, mobilization, and military preparation and movement.

This college should have combined with it, reënforced and enlarged in its scope and effectiveness, the present division of military information of the Adjutant-General's Office, where its records and its conclusions should be preserved. It should not supersede, but should incorporate, continue, and bring under the same general management the present service schools, supplementing where it is necessary their courses, which now, so far as instruction is concerned, largely cover the ground. Its instruction would, at the outset and perhaps permanently, be given through these schools, but it should give unity, influence, authority, and effectiveness in military affairs to the work and the thought developed in them, aside from mere instruction, and a weight and utility to their records of the efficiency and merit of their pupils not hitherto accorded to them in proportion to the high character of the work they have done.

(2) Every officer of the army below the rank of a field officer, and not already a graduate of one of the service schools, should be detailed for some fixed period during his service to receive instruction at this college in the science of war, including the duties of the staff, and in all matters pertaining to the application of military science to national defense; provision should be made for the continuance of such instruction by correspondence after the expiration of the period of each officer's detail, and all officers should be invited and entitled to present, as a part of the regular course and for credit on their efficiency records, written papers and reports upon the results of their investigations, explorations, reflections, and professional and scientific work, and upon such special subjects as may be prescribed by the college.

(3) All staff appointments other than medical should hereafter be made from the line of the army for a fixed period of, say, four or five years, the holder to return to the line at the end of the period, and not to be eligible to reappointment until after at least one year's service in the line, and after the expiration of a reasonable period the selection of staff

appointments should be made on the basis of proficiency and fitness, as shown in the war college (or heretofore in the service schools), including as elements for consideration both the work done during the period of detail, and the post-graduate work. Excepting, however, that such appointments should also be permitted for gallant and meritorious conduct in the field, shown by recommendations of commanding officers for brevet promotion made during the progress of a war, and excepting that for the technical and scientific branches of Engineering, Ordnance, and Signal Service, examinations should be continued; all promotions in the staff itself should be upon the basis prescribed for original appointment, combined with efficiency of service in the staff.

(4) The present system of promotion by seniority should be modified as to all officers now or hereafter below field rank, by making a specific proportion of the promotions to each grade for seniority, and a specific proportion on the basis either of efficiency records in the war college, or heretofore in the service schools, including both elements of work done during actual attendance and subsequent thereto, or for gallantry in the field during war, or both, accompanied in each case by evidence of faithful performance of the ordinary duties of the line.

(5) All selections of candidates for staff appointments and for staff promotions and for line promotions, other than those made for seniority, should be made by boards of officers appointed for that purpose, upon an examination and estimate of the efficiency records exhibiting the grounds for appointment or promotion above stated. Nothing can be more important than that the officers of the army shall feel that their rise in rank depends upon what they do; that ability, intellectual activity, faithful performance of duty, and gallant conduct are more certain claims to preferment than social or political influence. A system of promotions

which is divorced from the efficiency record is not merely unjust, but it destroys ambition and checks the effort of the army. The way to prevent the separation is by a systematic provision to enable every officer to show what there is in him, and to preserve a full record of what he does, by providing a competent and disinterested body to pass judgment on the record, and by a law making the judgment reached on this basis the imperative and sole ground of selection for promotion.

These provisions will go far toward accomplishing results which are provided for in the organization of every considerable army in the world, and which under our organization are not the business of anybody in particular, and for the most part cannot be accomplished by any one whomsoever; and if Congress will then make the appropriations necessary for periodical mobilization and maneuvers, the four requisites of preparation for war above stated can be substantially attained. The only element in these recommendations which does not result necessarily from a statement of the requirements is the limitation on the period of staff duty and the periodical return to the line. I think this will be beneficial to the staff, and will do away with the feeling quite prevalent in the line that the staff is a privileged class, divorced from its old associates, and a tendency toward unfriendly criticism which seems to me to be prejudicial to good discipline and effective service.

Another function which is now performed to a very slight degree, and which is of very great importance, should be performed by the proposed war college acting in coöperation with the existing naval war college, that is, the union of the army and the navy in the collection and utilization of information, studying and formulating plans for defense and attack, and the testing and selection of material of war. Communication, conference, and interchange of instructors between the two institutions could not fail to be of great value to both services, and to make easier and more certain that perfect coöperation which is so essential both in forming and executing the plans which involve the operations of both forces.

There are two special changes which, I am clear, the same principles require. One is that the artillery branch of the service should have a head. At present the guns, carriages, projectiles, explosives, and all the complicated and delicate machinery which belong with them are made and delivered over to the artillery branch, and there is no one to represent or speak for the men who are to work with the tools thus furnished. There are seven colonels of artillery, and it is not the business of any one of them more than another to speak for his branch of the service. The valuable results of experience in the use of the ordnance machinery are not utilized because it is not the business of any one in particular to insist upon it. Little complaints against the ordnance or engineers which could easily be set right if it were somebody's business to attend to them, remain as causes of irritation. The use of modern ordnance is a highly specialized and scientific business, and there ought to be an expert charged with the duty and the responsibility of seeing that the officers and men of the corps understand their business and are properly trained in it. This officer should be a member of the war college, and might well be on the staff of the major-general commanding. He should not be the head of an additional bureau.

The other change referred to is the increase in the number of inspectors-general, so that the entire work of the army may be adequately inspected. Among these should be a sufficient number of inspectors-general for the sanitary, artillery, ordnance, and engineering inspection, selected for their special qualifications in those several branches and specifically assigned to those duties. Thorough inspection is essential to thorough work, but no inspector can be expected to know everything, and inspection in these matters which require special training made by a man who has not received the training is necessarily perfunctory and of little value.

The second proposition which I stated as underlying the consideration of this subject — that the regular establishment is not the whole machine with which a war will ever be fought — has been too signally illustrated both in the Civil War and in the war with Spain and the Philippine war to require further demonstration. Our method is, and always will be, immediately upon the outbreak of a war, to create an army of which the regular army on its peace footing forms but a part, and usually but a small part, and the great body of which is composed of volunteers.

That the relations between the regulars and volunteers in this new force shall be such that they shall constitute a homogeneous body, using the same arms, familiar with the same drill, answering to the same ideas of discipline, inspired by the same spirit, and capable of equal and even performance, and that the preparation of the regular army in time of peace for the event of war shall to the greatest possible extent conduce to the benefit of the whole army, both regular and volunteer, and make it easy to put that body in a state of preparation, is an end toward which the best military thought of the country may well be addressed.

It should be a special subject of consideration by the war college, and upon it that body should invite the conference and coöperation of the military authorities of the several states. As one step toward attaining the end, courses of instruction in the college should be open to officers of the National Guard of the states, and the efficiency records of such officers in the college, and written papers and reports contributed by them after their terms of instruction have ended, should be made a part of the records of the War

Department as the authorized and accepted basis of appointments to office in any volunteer force which may be raised.

The provisions of the act of March 2, 1899, under which the army now serving in the Philippines was created, partly out of the old regular force, partly by new recruits in the regular establishment, and partly by additional volunteer regiments, made a long step in advance toward attaining the homogeneity which I have endeavored to describe. The facts that the officers of the entire army receive their commissions from the same source, and look for their promotions and rewards to the same authority, while in every volunteer regiment regular officers have been joined with volunteer officers in forming, training, and commanding the regiment, produce this result to a degree not previously attained.

Following these lines and working through the methods which I have described, a permanent plan ought to be wrought out with the concurrence of the military authorities of the several states, and enacted by Congress, for the creation of a war army composed of both regulars and volunteers whenever such an army is required. The part to be taken by the regular army in the new organization and the part to be taken by the volunteers should be prescribed, and the parts should be so assigned that the new organization shall have the fullest possible benefit of the preparation of the regular army.

The form and the machinery for the organization of the new army and the part to be taken in the raising of the army by the military authorities and organizations of the several states should be indicated, so that whenever war threatens, and long before it is declared, the multitude of men who are to do the work of organization may know, without waiting for an act of Congress, what will be required of them when the hour strikes, and may be engaged in the quiet and deliberate preparation so necessary in advance of action to prevent confusion and mistake.

The value and importance of securing during the time of peace information as to the capacity and fitness of civilians instructed in military affairs, and available for volunteer commissions, cannot be overestimated. It was well illustrated by the great advantage which we had in appointing the officers of the present volunteer force by reason of having in the War Department the efficiency records of their service during the war with Spain. Without some such information all names are alike. When war has come, or is imminent, there is no time for examination or investigation. There are too many officers to be appointed in too short a time. Efficiency records can be established not only in war but in peace also. Courage may fairly be assumed among Americans, and intellectual and moral qualities can be ascertained and recorded in the way I have indicated.

The foregoing considerations naturally bring to mind the Military Academy at West Point. I believe that the great service which it has rendered the country was never more conspicuous than it has been during the past two years. The faithful and efficient services of its graduates since the declaration of war with Spain have more than repaid the cost of the institution since its foundation. But these graduates have been too few in number and most heavily burdened.

The capacity of the Academy is not sufficient for the present needs of the army on a peace footing. It will be far more deficient for the army with the absolutely necessary increase. Preparation for the greater army which we should be ready to create in case of future war should be made. Our experience during the past two years has shown that we had not too many trained officers, but too few, both in the staff and in the line, and in both the number ought to be increased.

I urgently recommend that the capacity of the Academy be enlarged and the number of its students increased. . . .

These suggestions for the improvement of our army organization should not be taken as involving a condemnation or disparagement of the system generally. Such a conclusion could be reached only by a narrow and prejudiced view looking for the defects and refusing to see the merits.

No organization which was not in the main sound and efficient could have produced the results exhibited by the army during the past two years. With its handful of regular officers and its small body of trained troops, merged with nearly double their number of raw recruits, and combined with large forces of new, untrained volunteers, it has in surprisingly short periods of time produced a great body of men, uniformly well disciplined, of good conduct and morale, patient in endurance of hardships, steady, indomitable, and heroic in action, who against the debilitating influences of tropical climates, against physical obstacles which seemed insurmountable, and against enemies of superior numbers and approved courage, and armed with weapons of modern warfare, have won a long series of victories unbroken by a single defeat.

The officers of the volunteer force are entitled to their full share of the credit of this achievement. Without the splendid virility and courage of the enlisted men it could not have been accomplished; but it is fair to all to say that the chief formative power — the dominating influence which made the achievement possible — was the organization, the training, the discipline, and the example of the officers and men of the regular army. The officers of that army have maintained the honor, advanced the interests, and exalted the reputation of our country in the discipline and command of our troops on the battlefield, and in successful civil and military administration under most difficult circumstances, where failure would have been a national humiliation. . . .

The Military Needs of the Nation

Extract from the Report of the Secretary of War for 1900 [1]

Under the existing provisions of the act of March 2, 1899, on the thirtieth of June next the present volunteer force will be discharged and the regular army will be reduced to 2,447 officers and 29,025 enlisted men.

This force is about one-third as great in proportion to the population of the country as it was thirty years ago. As our country has grown in wealth and variety of interests, and as more intimate contact with the other nations of the earth has resulted from the natural extension of our trade, there has been an increase in the duties required from the regular establishment fully equal to our increase in population. . . .

The function of the regular army in our country is to man the seacoast fortifications, which protect our harbors and great cities against hostile attack; to garrison the military posts along our frontiers and at such strategic points as Congress determines to be suitable, to be always ready to fight for the country in any sudden emergency which may come upon us before there is time to raise a volunteer force and during the time while such a force is being raised; constantly to study, experiment upon, and exercise in all the improvements in military science, both in arms, ammunition, equipment, supplies, sanitation, transportation, drill, and tactics; to furnish a nucleus of officers and men thoroughly familiar with the business for the strengthening and more ready instruction of a volunteer army whenever that shall become necessary.

In all these respects the increase of requirements from the regular army, keeping pace with the growth of the country, has been as inevitable as the requirement of a larger police force for a larger city, or of more hands to care for a greater factory and operate more complicated machinery.

[1] Page 50.

In 1888, under the impulse given by the well-timed letter of Samuel J. Tilden, a board of officers, convened during President Cleveland's first administration, under the direction of Secretary Endicott, adopted a comprehensive scheme of coast-defense fortification, which involved the expenditure of something over $100,000,000. That plan received the approval of Congress, and under that and all succeeding administrations regular appropriations have been made, and the work of fortification has steadily progressed.

We have now invested nearly $60,000,000 in a great number of forts and guns, with all the complicated and scientific engineering and electrical machinery necessary for their use. No one can use this defensive machinery or take proper care of it and keep it in order without being instructed and trained in its uses. For this purpose it is necessary to have an adequate force of artillery officers and men who make the handling of such machinery their business. This is practically a new requirement for the army. It did not exist to any considerable extent prior to the building of the new fortifications. The number of men necessary to perform this duty is capable of exact computation, and the number required according to the men most familiar with the business is, at a minimum allowance, 18,420. . . .

More than $22,000,000 have been expended in the building and equipment of military posts other than the coast-defense fortifications, and the regular army is required to garrison and care for them. The posts now in existence or required to be built provide accommodations for, and if fully garrisoned require, over 26,000 troops.

A large proportion of these posts are situated along our frontier or at strategic points, the occupation of which is desirable. The increase in their number, however, has not been the result of any administrative policy or of any suggestion from the War Department or from the army. It has been brought about by popular demands finding effect in the action of Congress.

Notwithstanding the gratifying progress which the people of Cuba are making toward the establishment of a stable government, it is not reasonable to expect that the convention now in session will conclude its labors, that the relations between that country and the United States will be agreed upon, and that the government to be provided for by the new constitution will have been elected and installed and firmly established for a considerable period. In the meantime our troops in that island cannot be withdrawn without interfering with that sense of security which is so necessary to the industry and prosperity of the island. So long as our troops are to remain, it does not seem practicable to reduce materially the present number of about six thousand.

The number of troops in Porto Rico to man the fortifications and constitute a reserve, furnishing moral support and confidence while the people of the island are learning to do their own police work and establishing their own militia, has been practically reduced to a minimum at its present figure of 1,636, which includes the 879 native troops.

In the Philippine Islands the restoration of order will necessarily be a work of time. The mountains of those islands have always been infested by bandits, who have committed depredations and levied blackmail upon the peaceful inhabitants, and for the repression of whom the Spaniards do not appear to have ever taken any very active measures.

The practical inclusion of these bands among the insurgent forces, enabling them to rob and murder under color of patriotism, has greatly increased their numbers, as the disturbed conditions of the past two years and a half have increased their opportunities. However completely the leaders and the rank and file of the real insurgents may come in and acknowledge the sovereignty of the United States, it is certain that great numbers of men who prefer to live by robbery rather than by labor will continue to call themselves guerrillas, and will require a considerable army for their suppression, and for the protection of the peaceful inhabitants in the meantime.

Much thought has been given, both by the War Department and by the commanding officers in the Philippines, to the question of organizing native troops for the performance of this duty. I have no doubt that this is practicable. The experiments which we have already made demonstrate its practicability. We have already organized several different bodies of native scouts under American officers — one under Lieutenant Batson, composed of Macabebes; one under Lieutenant Castner, composed of Tagalogs, and others of Visayans in Samar and Negros. We now have a squadron of Philippine cavalry under the command of Lieutenant Batson as major of volunteers. All of these have proved faithful, courageous, and responsive to discipline when under the immediate control of American officers. The main trouble has been to restrain them to the usages of civilized warfare.

There would be no difficulty in securing from among the natives the entire number of troops necessary for the Philippines if we wished to do so. Neither the needs of the native troops nor the customary wages in the islands would justify giving to them the same pay, allowances, and subsistence which we give to our American soldiers. One-half the cost of the American soldier in all these respects would be ample and satisfactory. The creation of such a force would require authority from Congress, and must necessarily be gradual. It can properly proceed only so rapidly as the officers available for the purpose are able not only to organize and train the new soldiers, but to cultivate in them the habit of subordination, respect for authority, self-control, and regard for the usages of civilized warfare.

The military requirements of the Philippines may accordingly be summed up as follows: We need there for the immediate future about 60,000 men. We may expect this number to be progressively decreased; first, by the gradual disappearance of real insurrection, suppression of robber bands, and restoration of order; and, second, by the substitution of native troops for the greater part of our forces, costing not more than one-half as much as American troops for their support, and not involving such an enormous transport service as we now maintain. The great wealth and rapidly increasing revenues of the islands make it evident that at no distant day the islands themselves will be able to pay whatever they justly should for the support of their own police protection.

The facts which I have now stated indicate that we require permanently an army of about 60,000 American troops, and that during the present conditions in Cuba and the Philippines about the present number of 100,000 are required. Provision should be made for a minimum force of 60,000, with an authorized maximum of 100,000, and with authority to substitute for American troops serving in the islands ceded by Spain, as that shall become practicable, native troops under the command of American officers.

In the organization of such an army as Congress may authorize, it is plainly desirable to keep in mind the relation which the different branches of the regular army will bear in case of war, to the entire body of troops, which will be composed chiefly of volunteers. Much as we desire peace, and strenuously as we shall always endeavor to preserve it, we cannot, of course, expect to be free from war in the future any more than we have been in the past. The armaments of other powers are so great that almost any conflict in which we may be so unfortunate as to become involved will require a very much larger force than any standing army which we are willing to maintain.

For such a conflict the country relies, and justly relies, for its main strength upon the volunteers who will always be available for its defense. We should arrange our regular army so that it shall be the strongest where volunteer forces are the weakest, so that the combined army of regulars and volunteers may be symmetrical, well-balanced, and properly distributed among the different branches of the service and properly trained and disciplined for every kind of military operation.

Wars, of course, always come unexpectedly, and modern wars proceed with great rapidity from the very outset.

Those elements of war, therefore, which require the longest time for preparation should receive special attention in the formation of a regular army, and those which can most speedily be made ready should be supplied by the volunteer. These considerations lead to the conclusion that the regular army should be made particularly strong in its engineering force and material; in its artillery, which cannot possibly be improvised and which cannot be handled by untrained men, and in its cavalry, which requires far greater time for selection, equipment, and training than does infantry.

I do not lose sight of the fact that there are some admirable bodies, both of artillery and cavalry, among the National Guard organizations, but their numbers are so comparatively small as not to affect the conclusions stated, and the expenditure of time and money necessary to acquire and maintain proficiency in artillery and cavalry service is so great that the numbers in those branches of the National Guard must necessarily continue small.

The same considerations also lead to the conclusion that a full supply of officers, both of the line and of the staff, should be provided for the regular army.

The problems of subsistence, clothing, equipment, transportation, sanitation, the vast and complicated business of supplying and transporting an army, of caring for the health and strength of the men, as well as the actual command of troops in battle, require long and active and devoted thought, study, and training. To send volunteers into camp or field under inexperienced officers is simply to educate the officers at the expense of the lives and the efficiency of their men.

The regular army, as now constituted, and the National Guard, both put together, can furnish only a small portion of the trained officers necessary for the performance of the duties which I have indicated, and in any volunteer force a large proportion of the officers must necessarily come from civil life and have but a small degree of the knowledge, experience, and training necessary to prevent great and needless loss of life and efficiency at the outset of any campaign. The regular establishment should include a sufficient number of officers — particularly of officers trained in the duties of the staff and supply departments — to permit of their being detailed to service in every part and organization of the combined army of regulars and volunteers, so that their training and experience may give instruction, method, and efficiency to the whole organization.

The present force has far too few officers. Notwithstanding the most painstaking effort to cut off all unnecessary details, we have now 469 officers absent from the line of the regular army — 233 as officers in the present volunteer force and 236 upon necessary detached service — leaving the regular regiments without the number of officers which they ought to have for the maintenance of discipline and effectiveness.

Having in view especially the duties to be performed by regular officers in connection with the volunteer force, I urgently renew the recommendation of my last annual report for the substitution of a system of details from the line in place of the present permanent staff and supply departments, and for the training of as many officers as possible in the variety of experience which will fit them for the duties of the staff and of general command in the combined force of regulars and volunteers.

A bill to provide for a reorganization of the army in accordance with these views has been prepared and submitted to the military committees of Congress.

It is to be hoped that the people and their representatives will realize that the surest safeguard against war is reasonable preparation for the use of the great powers of which this nation is possessed, and that while the maintenance of any army is expensive, the support of such an establishment as I have described will involve but a moderate payment for insurance against the loss which we are sure to suffer if we leave ourselves impotent for defense.

Retired Officers

The retired list of the army is now constituted as follows:

Number retired upon age limit, 64 years	180
Number retired, 62 years	11
Length of service	133
Number retired under special acts	7
Disability on account of wounds	22
Disability on account of disease	413
Total	766

I recommend that as to this last class there be further legislation to cure the evil which now exists because of the fact that retirement under the provisions of the present law is irrevocable. It not infrequently happens that officers are retired for disability arising from diseases and subsequently entirely recover, and in some cases they continue for many years in the possession of full health, engaging in ordinary vocations of life, in business and the professions, receiving at the same time a handsome income from the Government without rendering any return for it.

I recommend that in the case of officers retired for disability arising from disease alone, authority be given for a reëxamination at such time as the Secretary of War may direct, and that in case upon such reëxamination the retired officer be found fit for duty, the President be authorized, in his discretion, either to restore him to duty with the rank which he held at the time of retirement or to retire him wholly from service.

The uncertainty as to what conclusion Congress will reach as to the proper size of the army during the next fiscal year has occasioned some question as to the basis upon which the estimates for that year should be prepared. In the absence of any guide, justifying me in any assumption as to what Congress will do, I have directed that the estimates be prepared with reference to the now-existing condition for an authorized force of one hundred thousand men. In case Congress determines upon an army of a smaller number than we now have, the sums allowed for those expenditures which depend directly upon the number of troops, such as pay of the army, cost of transportation, clothing, and equipment, can readily be reduced correspondingly.

Progress of Reorganization

Extract from the Report of the Secretary of War for 1901 [1]

The act of February 2, 1901, entitled "An act to increase the efficiency of the permanent military establishment of the United States", provided for an increase of line organizations from twenty-five regiments of infantry to thirty, from ten regiments of cavalry to fifteen, from seven regiments of artillery, including sixteen field batteries, to a corps of artillery, practically equivalent to thirteen regiments under the old organization, and including thirty field batteries, and from

[1] Page 7.

one battalion of engineers to three. Minimum and maximum numbers of enlisted men for the different organizations were established by the same statute, so that the total number of enlisted men might be varied by the President, according to the exigencies of the time, from a minimum of 59,131 to a maximum of 100,000, without any change of commissioned officers or in the number of organizations.

The improvement of conditions in the Philippines during the spring and summer of this year made it unnecessary to provide the maximum number allowed by the law, and on the eighth of May an order was made fixing the enlisted strength of the several organizations in such a manner as to establish the aggregate enlisted strength of the army, including staff departments, but exclusive of hospital corps men, at 77,287. . . .

The new organizations authorized were recruited upon the basis thus prescribed, leaving the organizations in the Philippines and Cuba, which had been temporarily increased to greater numbers, to be reduced to that basis by the ordinary expiration of enlistments and by casualties. The new organizations have been completed.

The regular establishment now consists, according to the latest reports which have been received, of 3,253 officers and 76,084 enlisted men. There are also 4,336 men of the Hospital Corps, 172 volunteer surgeons in the Philippines, appointed under section 18 of the act of February 2, 1901, 4,973 native scouts under the command of 98 officers in the Philippines, and 25 officers and 815 men of the Porto Rico Provisional Regiment.

The distribution of the force is shown in the table on the opposite page.

The recruitment of the new organizations and the maintenance of the old have been accomplished without difficulty, and the material obtained appears by the reports to be of the

DISTRIBUTION OF THE ARMY, SEPTEMBER 25, 1901

Country	Officers	Enlisted Men	Total
United States	1,922	31,952	33,874
Philippine Islands	1,111	42,128	43,239
Cuba	166	4,748	4,914
Porto Rico	51	1,490	1,541
Hawaiian Islands	6	250	256
China	5	157	162
Alaska	17	510	527
Total	3,278	81,235	84,513

(In this table are included the 4,336 men of the Hospital Corps and the 25 officers and 815 men of the Porto Rico Provisional Regiment, leaving the strength of the regular army, 3,253 officers and 76,084 enlisted men.

In addition there are also in the Philippines 172 volunteer surgeons, appointed under section 18 of the act of February 2, 1901, and 98 officers and 4,973 native scouts.)

best quality. About three-fourths of the total number of applicants were rejected and about one-fourth accepted. Of those accepted about ninety per cent were native born and about ten per cent naturalized citizens. The requirements that the applicant should be in perfect health, of good character, and able to read and write have been rigidly enforced.

The reorganization provided for by the act required the selection and appointment of two hundred and ninety-eight officers of staff corps and departments, and of eight hundred and thirty-seven first and second lieutenants of the line. The staff positions have been filled, in most cases by the appointment of deserving officers who had held staff positions in the volunteer force, and as to the remaining positions, by the appointment of officers who had rendered specially meritorious service in the field.

The surgeons and chaplains constitute an exception to this statement, having been selected partly from civil life.

Vacancies in the offices of first and second lieutenants of the line existing after promotions had been made, and after the graduating class at the Military Academy had been provided for, as required by the statute, have been filled under the following provisions of section 28 of the act:

> Persons not over forty years of age who shall have at any time served as volunteers subsequent to April 21, 1898, may be ordered before boards of officers for such examination as may be prescribed by the Secretary of War, and those who establish their fitness before these examining boards may be appointed to the grades of first or second lieutenant in the regular army. . . .
>
> Enlisted men of the regular army and volunteers may be appointed second lieutenants in the regular army to vacancies created by this act, provided that they shall have served one year under the same conditions now authorized by law for enlisted men of the regular army.

In executing these provisions it seemed necessary to prescribe a uniform standard of examination, and that which has long been followed in testing the fitness of candidates for appointment from the ranks was prescribed. At the same time it was not deemed just to either officers or men who were actually in the field, or who had but recently terminated their active volunteer service, to treat them precisely the same as applicants are treated who have had abundant time and opportunity to prepare for examination, and accordingly the following order was made:

> War Department,
> Washington, April 16, 1901.
>
> In view of the long period during which volunteer officers recently serving in the Philippines have been without access to books with which they could prepare for examination, and the fact that a special test of fitness is furnished by each officer's military record, the Secretary of War directs that as to all such officers who are ordered to be examined for appointment to the regular army, and are physically qualified, the examining boards, instead of recommending appointment or rejection upon the mental examination alone, shall transmit the examination papers in each case to the War Department, with their marks or ratings, both specific and general, and with an expression of the board's estimate of the candidate's general intelligence and capacity. The question whether, upon such report and the military record taken together, the candidate's fitness has been established will then be determined by the appointing power.

In view of the fact that enlisted men who have been serving in the Philippines have also been without opportunities to prepare for examination, the Secretary of War directs that as to any of them who fail to pass the mental examination for promotion, if the examining board is of the opinion that the candidate has sufficient intelligence and capacity to fit himself readily for such an examination, and that he has failed through lack of opportunity for preparation, the board shall transmit the papers to the Department with their certificate to that effect; and thereupon, if the case seems to warrant such action, the candidate may have a further examination after reasonable opportunity to prepare therefor.

ELIHU ROOT, *Secretary of War.*

To pass upon the papers reported under the foregoing order, and the military records of the applicants in connection therewith, a board of review was organized in Washington with Brigadier-General James M. Bell, U. S. V. (now brigadier-general, U. S. A., retired), as president. To this board of review were referred the papers of all applicants, both officers and enlisted men, who failed to reach the required standard before the local examining boards, and the board of review reported as to the volunteer officers whether upon their military records, taken together with their examinations, their fitness was or was not established, and as to enlisted men whether they were or were not entitled to further examination. In all cases soldierly qualities and capacity to command as exhibited in service have been treated as the most important considerations.

I am satisfied that these duties have been performed with impartiality, fairness, and without fear or favor. Five hundred and five enlisted men have been examined, and two hundred and fourteen have been passed, declared qualified, and commissioned as second lieutenants. Eight hundred and thirty-nine volunteer officers have been ordered for examination, of whom one hundred and four declined, ninety-seven have been found not qualified, one hundred and fifty-seven remain with their cases undetermined, and four hundred and eighty-one have been accepted and commissioned.

There remain one hundred and forty-two original vacancies to be filled under the statute, and there are on file 10,362 applications.

In selecting the officers to be ordered for examination, every practicable precaution to secure good men has been taken, although, as the applications have been so numerous and the labor of examining the enormous mass of papers relating to them has been so great, many deserving applicants have doubtless been passed over. The commanding officers of all the twenty-five volunteer regiments which served in the Philippines under the act of March 2, 1899, were called upon to furnish lists of the officers of their command, whom they considered qualified for commissions in the regular army, and all of the officers whom they recommended were ordered for examination, with the exception of possibly half a dozen, against whom specific objections existed not known to the commanding officer. As to all the volunteer forces coming within the scope of the act of February 2, the rule has been rigidly followed to order no one for examination except upon military evidence of his fitness from the officers under whom he had served. Some mistakes, of course, have been made, but it is believed that in the main we have secured a very excellent body of officers, who will do credit to the service. It is especially gratifying to find so great a number of enlisted men who are able to demonstrate their fitness to receive commissions.

The selection and appointment of the new officers has very nearly kept pace with the vacancies, for the act prohibited the increase of officers of the artillery any more rapidly than the number of enlisted men of that branch was increased. In order to comply with this provision of the statute, as the increase of the artillery was practically equivalent to six additional regiments, with six full sets of officers, directions were given that the business of increasing the artillery should be treated in six separate stages, and that as each successive one-sixth part of the additional enlisted men was obtained, one-sixth part of the additional officers should be appointed by promotion or upon examination.

The last increment of enlisted men was completed on September twenty-third, and the last vacancies of first and second lieutenants in the artillery were not open for appointment until that date. The postponement in the promotion of officers of the artillery, required by this provision of the statute, has resulted in giving the greater part of the officers of artillery, commissions bearing later dates than those of the officers of cavalry and infantry, who were promoted to the extent provided for by the law immediately upon the passage of the act. Accordingly, the officers promoted from the cavalry and infantry all bear commissions dated February 2, 1901, while the officers promoted in the artillery bear commissions dated, respectively, February 2, 1901; May 8, 1901; July 1, 1901; August 1, 1901; August 22, 1901, and September 23, 1901.

I recommend action by Congress to remedy this inequality by making all the commissions bear the same date.

The Chief of Artillery

The chief of artillery, provided for by the act, has been appointed. The sixth section of the act required the Secretary of War to prescribe the duties of the new officer. In execution of that statute, the following regulation was made by the Secretary:

War Department,
Washington, April 9, 1901.

Pursuant to section 6 of the act of February 2, 1901, entitled "An act to increase the efficiency of the permanent military establishment of the United States," the duties of the chief of artillery are hereby prescribed:

1. He shall keep the Commanding General of the Army, and through

him the Secretary of War, advised at all times of the efficiency of the personnel and material of the artillery, and make such recommendations in reference thereto as shall in his judgment tend to promote efficiency.

2. He shall annually and as frequently as circumstances shall require inspect the coast and field artillery, and he shall from time to time and as frequently as once in each year report to the Commanding General, and through him to the Secretary of War, as to each coast-defense fortification, whether the same is in all respects ready for use in case of attack, and if not, in what respects the preparations are defective.

3. He shall from time to time, and as frequently as conditions require, confer directly with the Chief of Ordnance, and advise him of all matters relating to the character and preparation of artillery material which the experience and observation of the artillery arm of the service show to be of practical importance.

4. He shall have general supervision of the instruction of artillery officers and men and of examinations for promotion and for appointments and transfers of officers to the artillery arm, and shall recommend such examinations and such courses and methods of instruction in the artillery schools and otherwise as he shall deem requisite to secure a thoroughly trained and educated force.

5. He shall recommend officers for duty in coast or field artillery according to special aptitude and fitness, and is charged generally with the recommendation of officers of artillery for special duty.

6. Before any money is expended or any land is acquired for any seacoast fortification hereafter he shall advise the Secretary of War through the Commanding General whether the project under which the expenditure is to be made includes adequate provision for all the different elements of a complete coast-defense establishment, including fortification, armament, and accommodations for the use of troops; whether the land which it is proposed to acquire will be sufficient for all the purposes mentioned, and how far the appropriations available provide for the entire work. For that purpose all projects and plans for coast-defense fortifications shall upon coming into the office of the Secretary of War be referred, as of course in the first instance, to the Chief of Artillery for his report thereon.

7. He shall be a member of the Board of Ordnance and Fortification.

8. The records pertaining to the performance of the duties of the Chief of Artillery will be kept in the office of the Adjutant-General of the Army, through whom all communications relating to personnel, discipline, efficiency, transfers, and assignments should be made in accordance with existing regulations.

9. Nothing in these regulations shall be deemed to relieve the commanders of the several military departments of the duties of inspection

and command, or of responsibility for the condition and efficiency of the material and personnel of the artillery in their several departments as now provided by regulations. ELIHU ROOT, *Secretary of War.*

In pursuance of the provision of the act of February 2, 1901, which charges the coast artillery with the care and use of the fixed and movable elements of land and coast fortifications, including the submarine mine and torpedo defense, the Torpedo School at Willets Point has been transferred from the care of the engineers to the artillery, by whom it will be conducted hereafter, and the Engineer School has been removed to Washington Barracks.

Following the same design to secure enlarged activity and usefulness for the artillery arm, two additional artillery members have been appointed to the Board of Ordnance and Fortification under authority of the army appropriation act of March 2, 1901, and that important board now consists of three artillery officers, with the Lieutenant-General Commanding, the Chief of Engineers, the Chief of Ordnance, and one civilian. On the initiative of the Chief of Engineers an artillery officer has been added to the Board of Engineers, which is charged with consideration of plans of coast defense.

The two volunteer battalions in Porto Rico have been continued and reorganized as two battalions of the Porto Rico Provisional Regiment authorized by the act. It has not been deemed necessary to increase the number by the addition of a third battalion.

Twenty-seven of the thirty dental surgeons authorized by the act have been selected, after a very careful examination under the direction of the Surgeon-General. There still remain three vacancies. . . .

A board consisting of all the general officers of the line of the army now in the United States and the Chief of Artillery has been convened at Washington, and is now in session, to formulate and submit a project for the location, examinations, and surveys to be made for the permanent grounds provided for by section 35 of the act of February 2, 1901. This board is also charged with the duty of considering and reporting upon the location and distribution of military posts required for the proper accommodation, instruction, and training of the army as organized under the act of February second, not including coast fortifications, and is directed to make "recommendations in detail as to which of the existing posts should be retained or abandoned, and of those retained which, if any, should be enlarged and to what extent, and the location, size, and character of such new posts as may be necessary, having due regard in all its recommendations to the proper distribution of the different arms of the service, based upon strategic, sanitary, and economical considerations."

The provisions of section 38 of the act of February 2, 1901, prohibiting the sale of or dealing in beer, wine, or any intoxicating liquors by any person in any post exchange, or canteen, or army transport, or upon any premises used for military purposes by the United States, have been carried into full force and effect, pursuant to the directions of the statute.

When the orders were issued for the enforcement of this section of the law, the commanding officers of the various posts and military organizations were directed to report upon its effects. A great body of reports have been received, which indicate that the effect of the law is unfortunate. I think, however, that a sufficient time has not elapsed to give the law a fair trial, and the observation and report of its working will be continued during the ensuing year.

THE DISPOSITION TO BE MADE OF THE ARMY IN PEACE

Extract from the Report of the Secretary of War for 1902 [1]

THE restoration of the normal conditions of peace, and the return of the greater part of the army to the United States, have made it possible to resume with increased activity the work of preparing for future wars.

The increase of the army from 25,000 to a minimum of 60,000 has, of course, made necessary a great increase in barracks, quarters, hospitals, and all the constructions which go to make up an army post. The accommodations which had been provided before the war with Spain are now quite inadequate, and require to be more than doubled. The work of construction has been pressed vigorously by the Quartermaster's Department to the extent allowed by the appropriations made by Congress for this purpose.

The policy followed has been rather to increase the size of the posts in which the army is to be quartered than to increase the number. Two considerations have determined that policy: First, economy of administration, and second, and most important, efficiency of officers and men. The tendency of life in small one or two company posts is narrowing and dwarfing, and such posts can be justified only by necessity. On the other hand, the comparison and emulation between officers and organizations grouped in a large post, the advantages of systematic study and practice in the schools which can be maintained at such posts, the advantage of being under the immediate direction and influence of officers

[1] Page 20.

of high rank who cannot be scattered among the small posts, but can be collected in the large ones; the practical benefit derived from handling considerable bodies of troops so that company officers may be learning to handle regiments, and regimental officers to handle brigades, and so on — all these considerations, point to the large post as furnishing the conditions for increasing efficiency on the part of both officers and men.

The only argument which has been made against this view is that the scattering of the army in a great number of small posts would popularize it, and that there ought to be an equitable distribution of the troops among all the different states. I think these propositions may be dismissed with the confident assertion that the army will be popular and satisfactory to all the states in proportion as it is efficient and economical.

Another line of policy followed by the Department is, so far as practicable, to get the army posts out of the cities and large towns, and establish them upon larger tracts of cheaper land in the neighborhood of the same cities and towns, so that the men may have the benefit of country air instead of city air, and more room for training and exercise; the neighborhood of the barracks may be under military control; the rum shops and brothels may be pushed farther away from the men; and at the same time the advantages of convenient inspection, transportation and supply, and a reasonable degree of educational and social privileges, may be retained.

In order to secure a definite plan for the distribution of troops and the construction work necessary to provide for their maintenance, a board was convened in Washington in November last, composed of all the general officers of the army in the United States, under the following directions:

By direction of the Secretary of War, a board of officers is hereby appointed to meet in Washington, D. C., on the 25th day of November,

1901, to consider and report upon the location and distribution of the military posts required for the proper accommodation, instruction, and training of the army as organized under the act of February 2, 1901, not including coast fortifications. The board will make recommendations in detail as to which of the existing posts should be retained or abandoned, and of those retained which, if any, should be enlarged and to what extent, and the location, size, and character of such new posts as may be necessary, having due regard in all its recommendations to the proper distribution of the different arms of the service based upon strategic, sanitary and economical considerations.

The board will also formulate and submit a project for the location, examinations and surveys to be made for the permanent camp grounds provided for by section 35 of the act of February 2, 1901.

MILITARY EDUCATION

WEST POINT AND THE ARMY WAR COLLEGE

In his annual report to the President, November 29, 1899, Mr. Root made the first official reference to an Army War College in the United States that can be found in any War Department document. In consonance with this recommendation and with the approval of the President, the Secretary of War appointed on February 19, 1900, a board of officers to consider regulations with a view to the establishment of a War College. The board met at the War Department February 26, 1900, to consider and adopt regulations for the establishment of the college, and upon the recommendation of the Secretary of War and under his orders, Brigadier-General William Ludlow, then a member of the board, was directed to proceed to Europe for personal investigation in foreign countries regarding the organization and purposes of their war colleges, and the first appropriation for the establishment of such a college in this country was made in the Army bill, approved May 26, 1900, as follows:

> For hire of clerks, purchase of stationery, furniture, and for contingent expenses incident to the establishment of the Army War College, having for its object the direction and coördination of the instruction in the various service schools, extension of the opportunities for investigation and study in the Army and Militia of the United States, and the collection and dissemination of military information, twenty thousand dollars.

Other appropriations for the War College were made in the Army Appropriation bill for the year ending June 30, 1902, and the War College was formally established. Plans for the construction of the building for the college were approved by the Secretary of War in July of that year, and the following item inserted in the Army Appropriation Act for the year ending June 30, 1903, upon the recommendation of Secretary Root, made the first appropriation for the construction of the War College building as follows:

> For the continuance of the Army War College, having for its object the direction and coördination of the instruction in the various service schools, extension of the opportunities for investigation and study in the Army and Militia of the United States, fifteen thousand dollars.
>
> *Provided,* That the Secretary of War is hereby authorized to expend the sum of four hundred thousand dollars, or so much thereof as may be necessary, from the unexpended balance of the emergency fund appropriated in the act, approved March third, eighteen hundred and ninety-nine, for the erection of the necessary buildings for the Army War College, established at Washington Barracks, District of Columbia, for the instruction of officers of the Army and Militia of the United States.

In recognition of Mr. Root's successful advocacy of the establishment of the Army War College, a granite tablet, which carries the following inscription, has been placed near the entrance of the splendid building constructed for the college.

BECAUSE OF THE SPECIAL
INTEREST AND EFFORT OF

ELIHU ROOT
SECRETARY OF WAR
CREATOR OF THE GENERAL
STAFF OF THE ARMY

THIS BUILDING FOR THE ARMY
WAR COLLEGE WAS AUTHORIZED
BY ACTS OF CONGRESS APPROVED
JUNE 30, 1902, AND APRIL 23, 1904

ARCHITECTS
McKIM, MEAD, AND WHITE

CONSTRUCTING ENGINEER
JOHN STEPHEN SEWELL
CAPTAIN CORPS OF ENGINEERS
UNITED STATES ARMY

CORNER STONE LAID FEBRUARY 21, 1903
BUILDING OCCUPIED JUNE 30, 1907

Extract from the Report of the Secretary of War for 1901 [1]

EXISTING conditions make this subject one of primary importance at the present time. The imperative demand for the service of all our officers since the spring of 1898 has caused a practical cessation of all systematic education of commissioned officers for nearly four years. In the meantime, the ordinary additions to the number of second lieutenants have been, roughly speaking, about one-third from West Point and about two-thirds from the ranks and civil life. In the reorganization of the enlarged army about one thousand new officers have been added from the volunteer force, so that more than one-third of all the officers of the army have been without any opportunity whatever for sys-

[1] Page 20.

tematic study of the science of war. On the other hand, the rapid advance of military science; changes of tactics required by the changes in weapons; our own experience in the difficulty of working out problems of transportation, supply, and hygiene; the wide range of responsibilities which we have seen devolving upon officers charged with the civil government of occupied territory; the delicate relations which constantly arise between military and civil authority; the manifest necessity that the soldier, above all others, should be familiar with the history and imbued with the spirit of our institutions — all indicate the great importance of thorough and broad education for military officers.

I have said before that practical qualities in a soldier are more important than a knowledge of theory. But this truth has often been made the excuse for indolence and indifference, which, except in rare and gifted individuals, destroy practical efficiency. It is also true that, other things being equal, the officer who keeps his mind alert by intellectual exercise, and who systematically studies the reasons of action and the materials and conditions and difficulties with which he may have to deal, will be the stronger practical man and the better soldier.

I cannot speak too highly of the work done in our service schools for a number of years before the war with Spain. It was intelligent, devoted, and effective, and produced a high standard of individual excellence, which has been demonstrated by many officers in the active service of the past four years. There was, however, no general system of education. The number of officers who could avail themselves of the very limited accommodations afforded was comparatively small. The great body of officers were confined to the advantages offered by the post schools called "lyceums," which were, in general, unsatisfactory and futile. There was no effective method by which the individual excellence demonstrated could be effectively recognized, or the results attained be utilized.

After careful consideration and study of the subject a general scheme of instruction has been matured and embodied in an order, the general provisions of which are as follows:

Instruction of Officers

With a view to maintaining the high standard of instruction and general training of the officers of the army, and for the establishment of a coherent plan by which the work may be made progressive, the Secretary of War directs that the following general scheme be announced for the information and guidance of all concerned:

The System of Instruction

There shall be, besides the Military Academy at West Point, the following schools for the instruction of officers in the army:

1. At each military post an officers' school for elementary instruction in theory and practice.
2. Special service schools:
   - (*a*) The Artillery School at Fort Monroe, Va.
   - (*b*) The Engineer School of Application, Washington Barracks, D.C.
   - (*c*) The School of Submarine Defense, Fort Totten, N. Y.
   - (*d*) The School of Application for Cavalry and Field Artillery, at Fort Riley, Kans.
   - (*e*) The Army Medical School, Washington, D. C.
3. A General Service and Staff College, at Fort Leavenworth, Kans.
4. A War College, for the most advanced instruction, at Washington Barracks, D. C.

The War College shall be under the immediate direction of a board of five officers detailed from the army at large and the following *ex officio* members: The Chief of Engineers, the Chief of Artillery, the Superintendent of the Military Academy, the commanding officer of the General Service and Staff College.

The War College Board shall exercise general supervision and inspection of all the different schools above enumerated, and shall be charged with the duty of maintaining through them a complete system of military education, in which each separate school shall perform its proper part. Such officers as shall be requisite to assist the board in performing its duties will be detailed from time to time for that purpose. It should be kept constantly in mind that the object and ultimate aim of all this preparatory work is to train officers to command men in war. Theory must not, therefore, be allowed to displace practical application.

The officers' schools at military posts and the General Service and Staff College will be open for instruction to officers of the National Guard of the several States, to former officers of volunteers, and to graduates of military schools and colleges which have had officers of the army as instructors.

The special-service schools will be open to officers of the National Guard and former officers of volunteers who shall furnish evidence to the War Department of such preliminary education as to enable them to benefit by the courses of instruction.

The college staff at the General Service and Staff College, Fort Leavenworth, will make report to the Secretary of War of qualifications of officers of the National Guard, ex-volunteers, and graduates of military schools and colleges, who shall have attended the college or shall apply for examination, and shall further certify whether or not they are qualified for service as officers of volunteers, specifying character of the service, whether line or staff, for which they are specially qualified.

A special register of the names of persons so reported as qualified will be kept in the War Department.

A register shall also be kept in the War Department in which shall be entered the names of officers of the regular army below the grade of colonel, as follows:

First. Officers who have heretofore exhibited superior capacity, application, and devotion to duty, the names to be selected by a board of officers convened for that purpose.

Second. Officers who shall be reported as doing especially meritorious work in the above-mentioned schools, other than the officers' schools at posts.

Third. Officers who at any time specially distinguish themselves by exceptionally meritorious service.

It will be the aim of the Department to make this register the basis of selection for details as staff officers, military attachés, and for special service requiring a high degree of professional capacity.

The Army War College

A college is hereby established for an advanced course of professional study for army officers, to be known as the Army War College. Such buildings and grounds as may be available and necessary will be assigned to its use on the reservation at Washington Barracks, D. C.

The executive head of the college will be an officer of the Army, not below the grade of field officer, who will be known as the president of the Army War College, and who will preside over the War College board. A course of instruction embracing the higher branches of professional study will be arranged by the board, and this board will also prepare and submit for the approval of the Secretary of War such regulations for the government of the college as it shall deem necessary.

The officers to be detailed to pursue the course at the War College will be of two classes:

1. Those who have been recommended as distinguished graduates of the General Service and Staff College.

2. Such field officers and captains as may be specially designated by the War Department for instruction.

It is intended that the officers who have uniformly shown the greatest interest and most proficiency in the theoretical and practical courses prescribed for the officers' schools at posts, the General Service and Staff College, and the War College shall have high consideration of the War Department, with a view to the utilization of their abilities as military attachés or on special missions abroad and for the higher duties of general staff work.

This order, if loyally and persistently followed, will result in the building up of what is practically a university system of military education. The principal advantages which it is designed to secure are:

(1) The bringing of all the different branches of military education into one system under direct supervision and inspection by a body of officers whose special business it shall be to make every part of the system effective.

(2) The establishment of definite required courses of instruction in the officers' schools, which shall be the foundation of the whole system, in place of the very loosely regulated lyceums, which in most cases were not schools at all.

(3) The establishment of the General Service and Staff College, upon the foundation of the Infantry and Cavalry School at Fort Leavenworth, so that every officer who displays superior qualities in the lower schools may be instructed there in every branch of military service.

(4) The completion of the series of instruction by the War College, which shall ultimately be in effect a post-graduate course for the study of the greater problems of military science and national defense.

(5) The establishment of a record in the War Department, on which shall appear the names of officers who have exhibited special capacity, in order that they may be known by the Commander-in-Chief, and by the country whenever special service is required, and in order that, although under the law meritorious service cannot be rewarded by increase of rank or pay below the grade of general, it may receive the reward of recognition and honor and opportunity, to which it is entitled. This record shall be made by a board of officers instructed and bound to select the names of those who are worthy, without reference to any consideration but their military records.

(6) The throwing open of the schools to the officers of the National Guard, of the former volunteers, and the graduates of military colleges and schools for instruction by and with the officers of the regular army.

The courses, both of the officers' schools at the posts and the General Service and Staff College, will be arranged so that the young men wishing to fit themselves for volunteer commissions may spend their vacations in military study. It is particularly desirable that a large number of young men should be made competent to perform the duties of volunteer officers in the staff and supply departments. Without such a class at the outbreak of a war, with a large volunteer force called into being, there will always be confusion, waste, delay, and suffering, because untrained quartermasters and commissaries of subsistence cannot properly perform their duties. If the war lasts long enough they will learn in time, but at a frightful cost. There are thousands of young men in the country engaged in various kinds of civil business which make them thoroughly familiar with the subject-matter of quartermasters' and commissaries' duties, and who, with a little timely instruction and practice, could learn to apply their business knowledge in military affairs so as to be useful quartermasters and commissaries whenever called into the volunteer service.

It is hoped that, if the gentlemen to whom instruction is thus offered avail themselves of the opportunity in considerable numbers, laws may be enacted under which their proved fitness for volunteer commissions will carry a right to receive commissions whenever a volunteer force is called out, and that a selection upon the ground of ascertained competency may thus take the place of the necessarily indiscriminate appointment of volunteer officers concerning whose fitness the appointing power cannot possibly be informed.

Extract from the Report of the Secretary of War for 1902 [1]

An examination of the sources from which are drawn the officers of the army, as now constituted under the act of February 2, 1901, shows how important it is to go on with the military education of officers in some such general and systematic way as was outlined in my last report. Of the 2,900 officers of the line of the army, 1818 have been appointed since the beginning of the war with Spain. Of these 1818 but 276 were supplied by the West Point Academy; the remaining 1,542 have come — 414 from the ranks, 512 from civil life, and 616 from the volunteers of the war with Spain and in the Philippines.

The volunteers and the enlisted men have of course acquired useful experience, and they were all selected on the ground of their military conduct and intelligence. Yet it is generally true of the whole 1,542, constituting more than one half of all the officers of the line, that they have had no systematic military education. They constitute nearly the entire body of first and second lieutenants. After some years, when their seniors have passed off the stage, they will have to supply our generals and colonels and chief staff officers

[1] Page 29.

charged with the instruction, discipline, and command of our forces. Unless the theory of military education under which we have maintained the Academy at West Point for a century is all a mistake, it is very important to give to this class of young officers, now that they are in the army, some degree of the educational advantages which the West Point men get before they are commissioned. The same will be true of future accessions to the force of officers, for the West Point Academy, even with the recent enlargements, cannot be expected to fill more than about two-thirds of the annual vacancies which will occur in the ordinary course of life.

The development of the general scheme of systematic instruction, provided for by the order of November 27, 1901, annexed to my last report, has made satisfactory progress during the year. . . .

The War College Board has addressed itself especially to reinstating and regulating military instruction in the military schools and colleges of the country, which may serve as a source for future appointments of second lieutenants from civil life; to the establishment of systematic instruction of officers in the army posts, and to organizing the General Service and Staff College at Fort Leavenworth on the foundation of the Infantry and Cavalry School which existed there before the war with Spain. Seventy-seven officers have been detailed as instructors at the military schools and colleges. Ninety-seven officers have been detailed as students at the General Service and Staff College, and are now in attendance at that institution. Thirty officers are in attendance as students at the Artillery School at Fortress Monroe, ten at the School of Submarine Defense at Fort Totten, and eleven at the Engineers' School at Washington Barracks. . . .

Undoubtedly the military schools and colleges to which details of officers as instructors are made will be found to differ widely in their thoroughness and efficiency, and the maintenance of thorough inspection and supervision by the War College Board will be essential. It is the purpose of the Department to discontinue details to institutions which, upon such inspection, are found not to come up to the requisite standard, and to give to the graduates of the thorough and efficient institutions a preference in recommendations for appointment as second lieutenants in the regular army. The same observation will doubtless apply to the post schools, which will vary according to the capacity and zeal of the commanding officer. The same systematic inspection by the War College Board is designed to hold commanding officers to the same degree of responsibility for an efficient school as for a well-disciplined force. . . .

The excellent work done by the Medical Department in the Army Medical School in this city should not pass unnoticed. The school takes the young surgeon, who has already graduated from some regular medical college, and has passed his examination and received a commission in the Medical Corps, and instructs him to adapt his knowledge to the special requirements of military service in surgery, medicine, and hygiene. The general hospital on the Washington Barracks reservation which this school has been using for purposes of special instruction will no longer be available after the construction of the Engineers' School at that place. It is very desirable that new and adequate accommodations be provided for the continuance of the hospital at some other point in or near the city, and for the continuance and enlargement of this most important branch of instruction.

West Point

The Military Academy at West Point on June 11, 1902, celebrated with appropriate ceremonies the completion of a hundred years of honorable and useful service. The advance of the world in military science, the increasing complexity of the machinery and material used in warfare, and the difficulty of the problems involved in transporting, supplying, and handling the great armies of modern times, make such an institution even more necessary to the country now than when it was founded by the fathers of the Republic a hundred years ago. The efficiency of the institution and the high standard of honor and devotion to duty which have characterized its graduates justify the continuance of public confidence. The wise liberality of Congress has enabled the institution to begin its second century with the well-founded hope of larger and long-continued usefulness. The present academic year has opened with 471 cadets on the rolls of the Academy, the largest number ever belonging to it at one time. Under the new regulations relating to admissions, examinations of candidates were held on the first of May in this year, at sixteen army posts throughout the country, selected with a view to reducing to a minimum the expenses of candidates in attending. Under the authority of the act of March 2, 1901, the examinations were made to conform to the courses of study ordinarily covered in the high schools and academies of the country by boys of the average age of appointees to the Academy. Sixty-two cadets were admitted upon certificates from educational institutions in which they had prepared, following the course which has been generally adopted by the colleges and universities of this country.

The curriculum has been modified somewhat, reducing the time expended in pure mathematics and increasing the attention to Spanish, English, and military hygiene; decreasing the theoretical course in philosophy and increasing the time given to chemistry and electricity. The increase of practical instruction has been continued, and a new practice, which I hope will be long continued, has been inaugurated by taking the first class to the battlefield of Gettysburg, where for several days in April they studied the lessons of that great conflict upon the field. . . .

The provision of the Military Academy act of June 28, 1902, authorizing the enlargement and improvement of the plant at West Point upon a plan involving a total expenditure of $5,500,000, has caused much solicitude to the Department and to the officers of the Academy, lest in rearranging and rebuilding a result might be reached out of harmony with the historic traditions of the institution and the beauties of the site, with its mountains and plain and river. After much consideration the following method of working out the plan has been adopted: A board composed of officers of the Academy was convened to prepare in detail a statement of the practical requirements of the institution which were to be met by the enlargement and rearrangement.

Upon the coming in of that report, ten of the leading architects of the country were invited to submit in competition general preliminary plans showing the proposed arrangement of buildings and treatment of the ground to meet the various requirements of the Academy, based upon the data thus furnished, together with an indication of the architectural treatment of the separate buildings. From the plans thus submitted one will be selected, and the author of that plan will be expected to develop it into the complete plan authorized by the statute. Thereafter, as the statute requires, the work will proceed with the assistance of a consulting architect, who will naturally be either the successful competitor or some one connected with his establishment.

General Military Education

Extract from the Report of the Secretary of War for 1903 [1]

The organization of the General Staff relieves the War College Board of a wide range of General Staff duties orig-

[1] Page 10.

inally assigned to the Board in the absence of any more complete organization, and this has made possible a simpler organization, adapted to the performance of War College duties proper, and constituting an adjunct of the General Staff.

The following new regulations explain the organization and assignment of duties:

I. The Army War College shall be located in the city of Washington, D. C.

II. The college shall be under the direct control of the Chief of Staff.

III. Under the direction of the Chief of Staff the management of the college shall be vested in a president and two directors, who shall be assisted by a secretary.

IV. The special duty of the college shall be to assist the Chief of Staff and the General Staff in the preparation of plans for the national defense. For this purpose such number of suitable officers as may from time to time be found to be necessary by the Chief of Staff shall be detailed from the General Staff or from officers of the line, or other staff corps and departments of the army, and these officers shall work with and under the direction of the personnel provided in Paragraph III.

V. The War College will receive from time to time instructions from the Chief of Staff as to the problems which it shall take up and the general line of investigation which it shall pursue.

After the most complete study practicable, a report will be rendered to the Chief of Staff setting forth the recommendations of the college. This report will be reviewed and criticised by the Chief of Staff and such section of the General Staff as may be directed to do so by him, and if necessary will be returned to the college with these criticisms for further study and revision.

Whenever the nature of the problem is such as to require harmony of action between the two services the report will be submitted to the joint board of army and navy officers appointed by General Order No. 107, Adjutant-General's Office, 1903, and the conclusions will be further studied in the light of criticisms made by said board.

Upon the final acceptance of the report of the college by the Chief of Staff, the report will be filed in his office.

VI. From time to time, as may be determined by the Chief of Staff, a selected number of officers, to be taken from the army at large, will be assembled at the War College for the minute and detailed study, under the direction of the Chief of Staff, of the projects thus formulated.

VII. The work of the college in the preparation of its reports and in the subsequent instruction based thereon shall be confidential. . . .

Good work has been done during the year in the General Service and Staff College at Leavenworth, and in all the special service schools. Some of the student officers detailed to the Leavenworth college did not appear to understand that they were under obligation to apply themselves to their studies, and I felt bound to enforce respect for that obligation by ordering them before a court-martial for neglect of duty. Two of them were convicted, and punished by fines and reduction in lineal rank. I think the duty will be more clearly understood hereafter.

The continued establishment and perfection of officers' schools at posts is producing good results, and it is evident that when the army has become settled in the enlarged posts now in the course of construction and extension, and this system of schools has become thoroughly established, we shall be able to drop from the Leavenworth course much of the comparatively elementary instruction which we are now forced to give there and confine that institution to the more advanced instruction for which it is intended.

LETTER TO THE CHAIRMAN OF THE SENATE COMMITTEE ON MILITARY AFFAIRS

THE BILL TO INCREASE THE EFFICIENCY OF THE ARMY

War Department,
Washington, March 3, 1902.

SIR: I return you herewith the bill (S. 3917) to increase the efficiency of the army, with a corrected copy of the same. The main features of the proposed bill, which deserve most careful consideration, are the proposed consolidation of the Quartermaster's, Commissary, and Pay Departments into a new Department of Supply, making the conduct of transportation a separate division of the new department; and the provision creating a general staff.

The great work performed by the staff departments during the Civil War and the war with Spain is fully recognized, and their proposed consolidation under a single chief is in no sense a condemnation of any particular bureau. The present transportation service is part and parcel of the Quartermaster's Department, and, whether justly or not, other bureaus complain that when transportation is insufficient for all, their bureaus are prejudiced by reason of the transportation being under the direct orders of another supply bureau. With all these bureaus under one chief it will not be possible for one to interfere with another in the matter of supplies, and the army as a whole will reap the benefits arising from this change; and at the same time none of the individual bureaus loses anything of its importance. Under the present system it is entirely possible for a bureau chief to work along his own lines in ignorance of what the other bureaus are doing. Economical and business principles seem to justify the bringing together of these bureaus under a single chief, who will have general direction of all, and who will be able to decide promptly and on business principles what shall be done by each particular bureau in the mobilization and concentration of troops.

This chief will also be able to perform a great deal of the work now falling directly on the Secretary of War, who is compelled to study the minor details of each question before giving his opinion. This will be a much greater relief to the Secretary of War than would ordinarily be imagined. It is expected under this new system that much of the auditing of accounts and financial work generally of the different bureaus may be consolidated in one financial system, similar to that in vogue in great corporations, and ultimately the new system will prove vastly more economical than the present one.

In this consolidation it has not been deemed wise to ask at once a reduction in the number of officers, but it is calculated that in a very few years, when the system has become fully developed, a material reduction can be made without serious detriment to the service. At the present, however, an increase of two officers is asked — one chief of the supply department and one chief of the transportation division, to be detailed from the army for a period of four years. This legislation is involved in sections 1, 2, and 3.

The next subject, which is embodied in sections 4 to 10, inclusive, involves the introduction into the army of a general staff system. No increase of officers is asked for in the establishment of this corps, as all are to be detailed from the line of the army. There are two considerations involved in this legislation. It has long been apparent to all students of the situation that the time has arrived when it has become necessary to have for both the army and navy a body of officers trained to consider the military policy of the country and to prepare comprehensive plans for defense, and to be charged specially with those duties. The mobilization of armies and similar operations require time and consideration which can not be given to the subjects by officers who are burdened with current and official work in the army and navy departments. This work must be done before the moment of war arrives, because modern wars are so short and decisive that it would be criminal to delay the preparations until the moment of rupture.

The general staff scheme is not a new proposition, because officers of the army have always been utilized to a certain extent in this business; and in looking over the records for some years past it is observed that a number of officers have always been detailed from the army to perform such work at the War Department, but they have had no legal status. Neither law nor custom places the preparation of plans for national defense in the hands of any particular officer or body of officers, and what is everybody's business is nobody's business. It has usually been after troops were gotten together in a haphazard fashion that brigades, divisions, and corps have been organized by general and staff officers, who have been designated under the dictates of expediency rather than previous and careful selection. It has usually been because American character rises superior to system, or rather absence of system, that disaster has been avoided.

The result naturally produces much haphazard work and in the end is extremely expensive by reason of frequent changes of orders for mobilization and concentration of troops, as was evidenced in the war with Spain. It is realized, however, that no general staff or other system can be made to work properly, so long as the present unbusinesslike method prevails of having a Secretary of War and a Commanding General of the Army to control matters at the War Department. In this country, as in the British Empire, the effort to conduct the army with two heads has always failed. Many complications arise from the fact that the finances of the army must according to law be administered by the Secretary of War and are wholly within his jurisdiction and that of the various supply and financial departments, all of which are excepted from the control of the Commanding General, whose duties are generally confined to those of army administration and discipline.

There must always be great difficulty in fixing the responsibility when so many bureau chiefs and the lieutenant-general commanding are concerned in the business affairs of the army; and the army itself has continually turned toward the general staff scheme as furnishing the most probable solution of the intricate situation. A general staff added to the army as a separate corps would be powerless for good unless the abolition of the present functions of the General of the Army is pronounced coincident with the establishment of the new corps. A general staff possessing the authority of law for its existence could arrange the mass of details for the commanding generals of the various armies and order to depots the proper quantity and character of supplies essential to the success of proposed campaigns, so that independent bureaus would not provide transportation for a surplus of one class of stores while a deficiency of another equally necessary existed.

If the expense of the Civil War and the war with Spain, as carried on, could be carefully contrasted with the expense as it should have been had the military affairs of the nation been in the hands of a trained general staff corps, no further argument would be required to carry conviction that the proposed change is a real reform. The work of such a staff will not be merely that of the comparatively small regular army, but will include all of the great military questions which may concern the United States in the disposition of the greater force to be raised whenever war comes upon us. It will be an agency through which the military operations and civil policies of the country may be harmonized as becomes a republican form of government. Upon every business principle and from every military point of view, it commends itself as worthy of the most serious consideration.

It is proposed that the present lieutenant-general of the army shall be detailed as the first chief of general staff, and that upon his separation from active service the President shall detail the chief of general staff from the general officers of the army, and thereafter there shall be no more permanent appointments to the grade of lieutenant-general. The senior general officer of the army, if not chosen as chief of general staff, will be assigned to active command of troops, or such other duty as the President may direct. The officer detailed as chief of general staff will be detailed for four years, unless sooner relieved. He will have charge, under the President and Secretary of War, of executing the general military policy of the nation, and with the assistance of carefully selected officers who will not be embarrassed with handling current papers in the War Department, he will consider all questions of importance, recommend all concentration and movement of troops, assignments to command, and other important matters concerning which the President and Secretary of War require technical and professional advice.

Officers of this corps will be detailed to make all military inspections of the army and the country, and the Inspector-General's Department, as now constituted, will gradually be eliminated without interference with the equitable rights of those now holding permanent commission in that department. The memoranda for all important orders covering the affairs under the jurisdiction of the general staff corps will be sent to the adjutant-generals at the War Department or at the various geographical and army headquarters for publication. The adjutant-generals will be relieved from the consideration of important questions, which, in the absence of a general staff corps they have heretofore had to decide, and will simply issue the orders as prepared by the general staff corps, and have charge of the preparation and preservation of the records.

The inspection of money accounts is transferred to the Treasury Department. This commends itself as a business proposition, as the Auditor for the War Department and the Comptroller of the Treasury are the officials who render practically all the decisions governing the financial operations of the army. The inspection and condemnation of worn-out public property is regarded as too insignificant a duty to monopolize the time of the officers of the general staff corps, and this matter can be provided for under regulations of a very simple character.

In order to furnish a wider field of selection and some incentive to lieutenants who have shown special aptitude in their profession, it is asked that the few officers of that grade who may be selected for general staff duty may be given the rank of captain while performing such duty. The expense of this will be very slight.

The next subject covered by the bill is the modification of the present laws regulating promotions from the ranks to the grade of commissioned officer. From time immemorial it has been the custom in the army to promote from the ranks those noncommissioned officers who had distinguished themselves in action, or who had by their conduct shown a marked aptitude and ability for control of men. A few years prior to the outbreak of the war with Spain, this law was changed so as to make the promotion to vacancies in the grade of second lieutenant open to all enlisted men, including privates and musicians.

This system has produced a number of excellent young officers, but on the other hand, a number of men have been able, by virtue of mental aptitude and the ability to cram, to pass these examinations and be promoted to the grade of second lieutenant, when they did not possess the qualities sufficient to justify their promotion to the grade of corporal in their own organizations. While it is necessary to have a system of examination in order that the utterly unworthy shall not be commissioned, it is considered not in the interests of the country to continue a system of promoting men who have no aptitude for command and control of men.

In connection with the preliminary examination to establish their general character and qualifications, it is proposed to send the noncommissioned officers to the General Service and Staff College at Fort Leavenworth, Kansas, for a special course of instruction with troops, covering a period of six months. There they will have an opportunity to exercise command and show their proficiency as all-round soldiers. By this system the best men will be obtained and the unfit ones will be prevented from promotion to the commissioned list. It should be understood that after a commission is once secured under our system of seniority promotion, it is quite possible for a very unfit man to hold commission and rise through the grades without possessing any great soldierly aptitude.

Section 13 of the bill is intended to provide for those chiefs of staff who are detailed for duty in various corps or departments, and whose positions in the regular establishment were filled upon their detail to the head of a corps.

Section 14 modifies the law so as to enable disbursing officers of subsistence funds to retain small amounts in their possession for payment of public creditors.

Section 15 relates to the disposition of certain stores to avoid loss.

Section 16 provides for an increase in the number of electrician sergeants. This is rendered necessary because some of the artillery posts have more electrical appliances than can properly be supervised by one sergeant, which is all the present law allows.

Section 18, which should be transferred so as to be section 17, and follow the section concerning electrician sergeants, is provided to meet the emergency in the Philippines by authorizing more first-class sergeants in the Signal Corps.

Section 17, which becomes new section 18, is intended to extend the period during which certain volunteer surgeons may be continued in service for duty in the Philippine Islands.

Sections 19 and 20 relate to certain changes of law in regard to army transports.

Section 21 relates to the modification of the act of February 2, 1901, which provided that officers of artillery should not be promoted except as the enlisted men for that arm were obtained. When this act was under discussion, it was contemplated that the increase in the artillery might cover a period of five years, but the Department decided, after thoroughly considering the subject, to make the increase in a shorter period. This caused the promotion of the officers to be scattered over a period of about six months, giving them dates different from the officers of cavalry and infantry, varying from thirty days to six months. It would be just if the commissions of officers promoted to fill original vacancies bore the date upon which the vacancies occurred.

Section 22 provides that all patentable inventions hereafter made by army officers in active service shall be the property of the United States.

The last section, No. 23, is intended to restore to the President the power to appoint ten cadets a year, forty in all, from the country at large, to the United States Military Academy. This was the number fixed from 1846 to a few years ago, when, upon the reduction of the army, it was changed to a total of ten, instead of ten per annum. Subsequently, the number allowed the President was increased to thirty. The number of instructors and the accommodations at the Military Academy will admit of the restoration of the old number of ten per annum, or forty in all, and the necessities of the service require more officers with technical training than has ever been the case in the history of the regular army. It is earnestly recommended that the old number be restored.

In general, the provisions of this bill contemplate modifications in the business establishment of the army of far-reaching consequences to the service and the country. The fact that new officers are not created and that the business is to be placed upon a more economical and satisfactory basis should procure for this bill the serious consideration which it deserves.

With reference to the provisions of the bill relating to a general staff, and to a consolidation of supply departments, I beg to call attention to the report of the commission to investigate the conduct of the war with Spain, of which General Granville M. Dodge was president, embodied in Senate Document No. 221, Fifty-sixth Congress, first session, and particularly to the paragraphs headed "Authority and responsibility," beginning at page 115 of that document, and to the paragraphs containing the conclusions of the report relating to the Quartermaster's Department, beginning at page 147 of the same document.

This commission made a most thorough and exhaustive study of the lessons to be derived from the experience of the war with Spain. It contained a number of very distinguished officers both of the volunteer forces of the Civil War and of the regular army, and its clear and emphatic conclusion that in both respects mentioned the organization of our army requires improvement, is entitled to the highest consideration.

Very respectfully,

ELIHU ROOT,
Secretary of War.

THE CHAIRMAN COMMITTEE ON MILITARY AFFAIRS,
UNITED STATES SENATE.

THE EFFECTIVE ORGANIZATION OF THE ARMY

STATEMENT BEFORE THE SENATE COMMITTEE ON MILITARY AFFAIRS, WASHINGTON, MARCH 12, 1902

Mr. Root's statement regarding the plan and purpose of the reorganization of the army, made in a letter to the chairman of the Senate Committee on Military Affairs, March 3, 1902, followed several previous hearings before the House and Senate Committees on Military Affairs, which are omitted, the substance of his remarks appearing more fully in later hearings. On March 12, the Secretary of War appeared before the Senate Committee to describe more fully the need for and the working of his plan. On December 13, 1902, he appeared before the House Committee on Military Affairs; and on December 17, he appeared again before the Senate Committee. His several statements at these hearings are presented. Frequent interruptions and questions by members of the committees are omitted, except as they throw light on the development of his argument. These omissions are indicated by . . .

MR. CHAIRMAN, this bill contains two series of provisions of primary importance, together with a number of minor provisions on separate subjects. The provisions of primary importance are, first, a series of provisions for the consolidation of the supply departments. The second series of provisions is for the creation of a general staff. Both of these provisions seem to be of very great importance — to be necessary to an effective organization of the army. Neither of them will require any appreciable increase in the number of officers. They are simply a rearrangement of the present official force in such a way as to make that force more effective; and they are merely putting on paper the lessons which I believe have been generally deduced from observation of the working of the present system in the war with Spain.

As to the consolidation of the supply department, we have now a quartermaster, commissary, and pay department, each one running by itself.

The CHAIRMAN. You provided for a transportation division?

Secretary ROOT. Yes, General; there is a Quartermaster's Department, and the Quartermaster-General has charge of transportation. He also has charge of the purchase and manufacture of clothing. The work of his division is in two classes of duty, and no more. He transports his own clothing and the feed for the horses and a considerable variety of stores which he provides, and he also transports the subsistence which the Commissary-General provides, and the material which the Surgeon-General provides, and the ammunition and material from the Ordnance Department. The Paymaster-General pays the troops.

The Commissary-General pays for the food and the supplies which he has. Each one has his own machinery, and each one has his own business; and when it comes down to the accomplishment of any single purpose there is no one to bring them together and see that they move step by step, and that each one is doing his share in the accomplishment of that purpose, except a civilian Secretary of War, who knows nothing about it, and does not learn anything about it until it is time for him to go out of office, if he does then.

In the successful business world work is not done in that way. What would happen if a railroad company, or a steel corporation, or any great business concern, should divide its business up in that way? What would become of that business?

The Paymaster-General several years ago had a paper carefully prepared in which he proposed that he should take the payment of the bills of the quartermaster and commissary. There is no reason why he should not. That means just one step toward the consolidation. Every few weeks when operations are active, there comes in complaint that something has not yet arrived. Whose fault is it? The

Quartermaster-General blames the Commissary-General and the Commissary-General blames the Quartermaster-General. The Commissary-General wants leave to make his own shipments and take his own bills of lading and have the responsibility and authority to see that the supplies he is furnishing go to their destination, without putting them through the hands of the Quartermaster-General. Each department is trying to get from the other details which it thinks necessary to complete its own work; and when we consider each one's view of the situation and the changes that ought to be made, it is impossible not to think that they ought all to be under one head, and that head a military man.

Some time ago, I asked the different departments if they could not agree on this subject, and they all have agreed upon the general proposition. They differ as to details.

In drafting this bill I have necessarily put the details down — have arranged the method of accomplishing this result to which they all agree — as it seemed to me was best; but I suppose the committee will settle the details, if it considers favorably any method. The principle of having these great supply departments under one head is that there will be some officer whose business it is to coördinate their action, instead of leaving it all for the Secretary of War to do; and the question of method which is determined in the draft of the bill may or may not be satisfactory. The method that was adopted in the draft of the bill was to have one supply department called the Department of Supply. . . .

The Commissary-General thinks that there ought to be an absolutely hard and fast line between the members of the different divisions of the new department, just as there is now between the different departments. The Quartermaster's Department does not think that. They differ on that point. I agree with the view of the Quartermaster's Department that it should be possible to impose upon one man the duties of all three, although I think it is quite right that they should be assigned to the separate divisions; that is, that one man should be assigned to the subsistence division, another to the finance division, and so on. But I think that the War Department should be at liberty to impose upon one man the various duties of all three; that is, to require the man, even though he is assigned to the subsistence division, to do quartermaster's duty, or finance duty, wherever it is possible for one man to do all the work; that is, there ought to be some elasticity. . . .

Before leaving the subject of the consolidation of the supply departments, let me say that in my judgment it will greatly reduce the paper work necessary; it will reduce what is sometimes spoken of as red tape. It will put it within the power of the man at the head to accomplish results without carrying on a diplomatic correspondence between two departments that ought to be attending to business instead of standing off and referring matters to each other.

Now, the proposition of the bill is to make a department called the Department of Supplies, with a major-general at the head, and under it four divisions, the subsistence division, the supply and construction division, which takes one-half of the present quartermaster's duties, the transportation division, which takes the other half of the quartermaster's duties, and the finance division, which serves as a cashier for the whole business. I am confident that that would prove to be a much more practical and efficient business system than that which we have today. . . .

I started last year an improvement of Governor's Island with the idea that that should be made a great depot for the receipt and distribution of supplies, and a base for the government's use in fitting out any expedition which might be necessary along our Atlantic coast or for the West Indies. I got from the state of New York a grant of about seventy or eighty acres of land, under shallow water which lay south of Governor's Island. You made us an appropriation of $260,000, for a starter and we are at work dredging to make wharfage on the north side of the Island.

We double the area of the Island by the additional land we are filling in, and abandoning the separate ordnance depot there, the arsenal, and we are proposing to put up a series of storehouses in which can be stored all the imperishable supplies necessary for a large expedition. There will be room on the Island for troops in case we want to send out such an expedition. We can put troops on the Island and transfer them to transports of the deepest draft, which can come up to the wharf on the north side. That is utilizing our property.

Now, I want to know what is necessary for the fitting out of such an expedition. To whom do I go? I cannot tell. Military authorities have got to work it out, and it has got to be worked out in detail. That is necessary in order to determine how the money that Congress has voted, and has put in my discretion to expend in the construction there, shall be expended.

There is no single officer who could answer these questions. Indeed, I hardly know how to put the questions in detail. They should go to some military man who will say to this one, work out this part of the problem, and to another, work out that, and to another, work out that. First consider what are the ranges of possibility as to what an expedition being fitted out there would have to do, how long a time it would have to be absent, what kinds of supplies it would want, and then have the amounts of the different kinds of supplies worked out and the amount of storage room necessary for them. We must also be able to have worked out the other things for our ordinary uses that it will be necessary to do at that point. There is not anybody whose business it is to do that sort of thing except the Secretary.

THE GENERAL STAFF

STATEMENT BEFORE THE HOUSE COMMITTEE ON MILITARY AFFAIRS, WASHINGTON, DECEMBER 13, 1902

MR. CHAIRMAN and gentlemen, this bill covers but a single subject, and has but a single purpose. It is the establishment of a general staff corps, to be composed of officers detailed from the army at large, under such rules as may be prescribed by the President.

The duties of the proposed general staff corps are described in the bill as follows:

> To prepare plans for the national defense and for the mobilization of the military forces in time of war; to investigate and report upon all questions affecting the efficiency of the army and its state of preparation for military operations; to render professional aid and assistance to the Secretary of War and to general officers and other superior commanders, and to act as their agents in informing and coördinating the acts of all the different officers engaged in carrying out their orders, and to perform such other duties as may be from time to time prescribed by the President.

The bill provides that the general staff corps shall consist of one chief of staff of the army, with the rank, pay, and allowances of a lieutenant-general, one major-general, one brigadier-general, who, while so serving, shall have the rank, pay, and allowances of the grade to which detailed, all of these three to be detailed by the President from the officers of the army at large.

Mr. HAY. Would it interfere with you, Mr. Secretary, if I should ask some questions as you go along?

Mr. ROOT. Certainly not.

Mr. HAY. I want to ask if that clause would not create two lieutenant-generals of the army?

Mr. ROOT. There would be two lieutenant-generals provided at any time the officer detailed by the President to be chief of the general staff were another officer than the permanent Lieutenant-General. There would then be the same situation which existed in the latter part of the Civil War, when General Grant was in command of the army in the field and General Halleck was chief of staff conducting the administration at Washington. If, however, the President did, as he undoubtedly would do under this bill at the outset, detail the Lieutenant-General of the Army to be the chief of staff, then there would be only one lieutenant-general. That is to say, the provision affords an opportunity for adjustment to meet the exigencies of the times. . . .

The bill provides further that there shall be in the general staff four colonels, six lieutenant-colonels, twelve majors, and twenty captains, these to be detailed from the officers of the army at large, the captains to be detailed from officers of the grades of captain or first lieutenant, the details all to be for a period of four years, unless sooner relieved; and it provides that while serving in the general staff, corps officers may be temporarily assigned to duty with any branch of the army. That is the outline of the general staff corps.

Other provisions of the bill are designed to adjust the working of that corps to the working of the present organization. A portion of the members of the corps would be stationed in Washington to conduct the general business falling under the heads enumerated in the description of duties, which I have already read, and a portion of them, the larger portion of them, would be assigned to the different departments to serve under the direction of the different commanders, but maintaining their relations to the general staff corps, and reporting to the chief of staff now in Washington, very much as the assistant inspectors-general now report to the inspector-general, with the difference that the chief of staff and his assistants in Washington would be charged with advising the President or the Secretary of War of the matters in regard to which the reports showed action ought to be taken, and, under the direction of the President or the Secretary of War, seeing to it that those matters received attention.

Let me call your attention for a moment to the reason for asking you to authorize the formation of such a body of officers. We have an army excellent in its personnel, not surpassed, I believe, anywhere, in the intelligence, capacity, and devotion to duty of its enlisted men and its officers. We have the various departments of administration organized each within itself, and well enough organized for the performance of its specific duties, and we have at the head of those departments men of capacity and fidelity. The Quartermaster's Department is engaged faithfully and efficiently in conducting the transportation of the army, in supplying clothing and forage and doing construction work and a great variety of other duties. The Subsistence Department is engaged, with ability and fidelity, in furnishing the food of the army. The Signal Corps is in like manner and with conspicuous ability performing the duties of maintaining communications, building telegraph lines and operating them, and training men to do signal work.

I can go through the different branches of administration and make the same statements regarding each particular corps, department, and bureau organization. We have a nation with great wealth, willing to spend its money freely for the procurement of arms and munitions of war and supplies of all kinds. Nevertheless, no one can fail to see that there has been in the past, in the administration of the army, something which was out of joint. It is not necessary for me to go into the specification of details; for every one of us knows that whenever an exigency has come, confusion has come; and that confusion, while it is not so prominent, while it does not attract public attention to such a degree as in the days when the newspapers were full of scare headlines about the condition of affairs at Tampa, nevertheless exists in the yearly and daily transactions of the business of the War Department. The confusion comes from the fact that our organization is weak at the top. It does not make adequate provision for a directing and coördinating control. It does not make provision for an adequate force to see that these branches of the administrative staff and the different branches of the line pull together, so that the work of each one will fit in with the work of every other one, and bring out the result which always has to be the result of the conspiring of a great number of people doing a great number of duties.

While I say that the organization is weak at the top, I am not criticising any one at the top. It is weak at the top because the system is defective; because there is a distribution of powers and no coördination of the exercise of powers provided for in the system. That coördination cannot be done by any one man. It is a vast and difficult work, which can be done only by a body of men organized for that purpose and having no other duties to perform; and in all the armies of the civilized world that duty is, and during our lifetime has been, performed by a body of men who have come to be called a General Staff, — to be called a General Staff because their duties are staff duties and because their duties are general, pertaining to the general conduct of affairs, and not merely to the work of the Quartermaster's Department, as General Ludington's duties are; not merely to the work of the Ordnance Department, as General Crozier's duties are, but pertaining to the entire work.

The General Staff

Extract from the Report of the Secretary of War for 1902 [1]

The most important thing to be done now for the regular army is the creation of a general staff. I beg to call attention

[1] Page 42.

to the remarks made upon this subject under the head of "Improvement of Army Organization" in the report for 1899 and under the head of "General Staff" in the report for 1901. Since the report for 1899 was made many of the important measures then recommended for the greater efficiency of the army have been accomplished or are in course of accomplishment under authority conferred by legislation. Our military system is, however, still exceedingly defective at the top. We have a personnel unsurpassed anywhere, and a population ready to respond to calls for the increase of the personnel in case of need, up to the full limit at which it is possible to transport and feed an army. We have wealth and a present willingness to expend it reasonably for the procurement of supplies and material of war as plentiful and as good as can be found in any country. We have the different branches of the military service well organized, each within itself, for the performance of its duties. Our administrative staff and supply departments, as a rule, have at their heads good and competent men, faithful to their duties, each attending assiduously to the business of his department.

But when we come to the coördination and direction of all these means and agencies of warfare, so that all parts of the machine shall work true together, we are weak. Our system makes no adequate provision for the directing brain which every army must have, to work successfully. Common experience has shown that this cannot be furnished by any single man without assistants, and that it requires a body of officers working together under the direction of a chief and entirely separate from and independent of the administrative staff of an army (such as the adjutants, quartermasters, commissaries, etc., each of whom is engrossed in the duties of his own special department). This body of officers, in distinction from the administrative staff, has come to be called a general staff. There has been much misunderstanding as to the nature and duties of a general staff. Brigadier-General Theodore Schwan, in his work on the organization of the German army, describes it as follows:

> In Prussia, at least, the term has been exclusively and distinctively applied, since about 1789, to a body of officers to whom, as assistants to the commander-in-chief and to his subordinate generals, is confided such work as is directly connected with the designing and execution of military operations. That in Germany, as elsewhere, chiefs of special arms, heads of supply departments, judge-advocates, etc., form an important branch of the higher commands, goes without saying, but they are not included in the term "general staff." Clausewitz's dictum that the general staff is intended to convert the ideas of the commanding general into orders, not only by communicating the former to the troops, but rather by working out all matters of detail, and thus relieving the general from a vast amount of unnecessary labor, is not a sufficient definition of general staff duties, according to Von Schellendorf (upon this question certainly the better authority), as it fails to notice the important obligation of the general staff officer of constantly watching over the effectiveness of the troops, which would be impaired by a lack of attention to their material welfare. Out of this obligation grows, he says, the further duty of furnishing to the heads of the supply departments and other officers attached to headquarters such explanations touching the general military situation, or the effect of a sudden change therein, as will enable them to carry out intelligently what is expected of them. The general staff thus becomes a directing and explaining body, and its chief, therefore, is in some respects the head of the whole staff. It follows that of the two terms, staff and general staff, the Germans regard the former as the more comprehensive one and as embracing the latter.
>
> It is conceded on all hands that the almost phenomenal success that has attended the German (Prussian) arms during the last thirty years is due in a large degree to the corps of highly trained general staff officers which the German army possesses.

Neither our political nor our military system makes it suitable that we should have a general staff organized like the German general staff or like the French general staff; but the common experience of mankind is that the things which those general staffs do, have to be done in every well-managed and well-directed army, and they have to be done by a body of men especially assigned to do them. We should have such a body of men selected and organized in our own way and in accordance with our own system to do those essential things. The most intelligible way to describe such a body of men, however selected and organized, is by calling it a general staff, because its duties are staff duties and are general in their character.

The duties of such a body of officers can be illustrated by taking for example an invasion of Cuba, such as we were all thinking about a few years ago. It is easy for a President, or a general acting under his direction, to order that 50,000 or 100,000 men proceed to Cuba and capture Havana. To make an order which has any reasonable chance of being executed he must do a great deal more than that. He must determine how many men shall be sent and how they shall be divided among the different arms of the service, and how they shall be armed, and equipped; and to do that he must get all the information possible about the defenses of the place to be captured and the strength and character and armament of the forces to be met. He must determine at what points and by what routes the place shall be approached, and at what points his troops shall land in Cuba; and for this purpose he must be informed about the various harbors of the island and the depth of their channels; what classes of vessels can enter them; what the facilities for landing are; how they are defended; the character of the roads leading from them to the place to be attacked; the character of the intervening country; how far it is healthful or unhealthful; what the climate is liable to be at the season of the proposed movement; the temper and sympathies of the inhabitants; the quantity and kind of supplies that can be obtained from the country; the extent to which transportation can be obtained, and a great variety of other things which will go to determine whether it is better to make the approach from one point or from another, and to determine what it will be necessary for the army to carry with it in order to succeed in moving and living and fighting.

All this information it is the business of a general staff to procure and present. It is probable that there would be in such case a number of alternative plans, each having certain advantages and disadvantages, and these should be worked out each by itself, with the reasons for and against it, and presented to the President or general for his determination. This the general staff should do. This cannot be done in an hour. It requires that the staff shall have been at work for a long time collecting the information and arranging it and getting it in form to present. Then at home, where the preparation for the expedition is to be made, the order must be based upon a knowledge of the men and material available for its execution; how many men there are who can be devoted to that purpose, from what points they are to be drawn, what bodies of troops ought to be left or sent elsewhere, and what bodies may be included in the proposed expedition; whether there are ships enough to transport them; where they are to be obtained; whether they are properly fitted up; what more should be done to them; what are the available stocks of clothing, arms and ammunition, and engineers' material, and horses and wagons, and all the innumerable supplies and munitions necessary for a large expedition; how are the things to be supplied which are not ready, but which are necessary, and how long time will be required to supply them.

All this and much more necessary information it is the business of a general staff to supply. When that has been done the order is made with all available knowledge of all the circumstances upon which the movement depends for its success. It is then the business of a general staff to see that every separate officer upon whose action the success of the movement depends understands his share in it and does not lag behind in the performance of that share; to see that troops and ships and animals and supplies of arms and ammunition and clothing and food, etc., from hundreds of sources, come together at the right times and places. It is a laborious, complicated, and difficult work, which requires a considerable number of men whose special business it is and who are charged with no other duties.

It was the lack of such a body of men doing that kind of work which led to the confusion attending the Santiago expedition in the summer of 1898. The confusion at Tampa and elsewhere was the necessary result of having a large number of men, each of them doing his own special work the best he could, but without any adequate force of officers engaged in seeing that they pulled together according to detailed plans made beforehand. Such a body of men doing general staff duty is just as necessary to prepare an army properly for war in time of peace as it is in time of war. It is not an executive body; it is not an administrative body; it acts only through the authority of others. It makes intelligent command possible by procuring and arranging information and working out plans in detail, and it makes intelligent and effective execution of commands possible by keeping all the separate agents advised of the parts they are to play in the general scheme. . . .

It does not follow, however, that the principal and most trusted general of the army cannot exercise a great and commanding influence in the control of the army, and practically manage it in all military matters. What does follow is that he can do this only by abandoning the idea of independent command and by assuming the position and performing the functions which I have described as belonging to a chief of staff. General Schofield did this with entire success and rendered great service to the country by doing so. I quote his own words in describing the course he followed:

> Recent experience has served to confirm all the results of my life-long study and large experience that the proper position for the senior officer of the army on duty at Washington is not that of commanding general, a position which is practically impossible, but that of general-in-chief, which means in fact chief of staff to the President. The title of general-in-chief was a permanent one during the entire history of the country up to the time when General Grant became Lieutenant-General.
>
> When I became the commanding general I addressed to the President a letter in which I pointed out to him what had been the result of my study and experience, saying that the only way was to abandon entirely, which I did during my seven years of service, all pretense of being the commanding general and to content myself with acting as the chief of staff of the army under the Secretary of War and the President. The result was that perfect harmony prevailed during my time, and I did exercise a legitimate influence in command of the army, this because I did not claim to exercise anything which the law did not give me.

Everybody is not as self-restrained and sensible as General Schofield, and the best way to secure from others the same kind of good service that he rendered, is to give the officer from whom it is expected a designation which indicates what he is really to do.

Organization of the General Staff

Extract from the Report of the Secretary of War for 1903 [1]

The important military event of the year affecting the regular army has been the reorganization of the system of military control under the General Staff Act approved February 14, 1903. This Act abolished the separate office of General Commanding the Army, provided for a military Chief of Staff to the President, who, acting under the directions of the President, or of the Secretary of War representing him, should have supervision not only of all troops of the line but of the special staff and supply departments which had theretofore reported directly to the Secre-

[1] Page 3.

tary of War; and it created for the assistance of the Chief of Staff a corps of forty-four officers, who were relieved from all other duties. The function of this new corps is described by the statute in the following words:

> SEC. 2. That the duties of the General Staff Corps shall be to prepare plans for the national defense and for the mobilization of the military forces in time of war; to investigate and report upon all questions affecting the efficiency of the army and its state of preparation for military operations; to render professional aid and assistance to the Secretary of War and to general officers and other superior commanders, and to act as their agents in informing and coördinating the action of all the different officers who are subject, under the terms of this Act, to the supervision of the Chief of Staff; and to perform such other military duties not otherwise assigned by law as may be from time to time prescribed by the President.

Although, by its terms, the Act was not to take effect until August 15, 1903, it was obvious that this radical change in the administration of military affairs, and the adjustment of the new machinery to the old machinery which had been in operation for many years, would require a vast number of details to be worked out experimentally and upon full consideration by all the officers whose duties were affected. A board was accordingly convened in March to recommend selections for the new corps. It consisted of Generals Young, Chaffee, John C. Bates, Carter, Bliss, and Randolph, and Major Henry A. Greene, as recorder. The board was required under oath to recommend forty-two officers for detail upon their merits as exhibited by their military records. The order which convened the board also provided that vacancies occurring in the General Staff Corps, after its organization, should be filled upon the recommendation of a permanent board consisting of the Chief of Staff and the three senior officers of the General Staff Corps on duty at the War Department, operating in a similar manner. . . .

Upon the report of this board its recommendations were approved without change, and the officers selected were ordered to Washington to report to General Young, who was to be the first Chief of Staff. They were then organized as an experimental or provisional General Staff, and directed to work out a permanent organization and distribution of duties for the General Staff Corps, a draft of new regulations, and a revision of the old regulations made necessary by the new departure. This work was done upon full consultation with the chiefs of bureaus and taking the opinions of general officers commanding departments, and was accompanied by reference to the provisional staff organization of many tasks and problems to be worked out which were appropriate for General Staff action, in order that they might become familiar with their work, and test by experiment the best methods of accomplishing it. In this way when the act took effect on the fifteenth of August the General Staff was ready to enter upon the discharge of its duties with a fully considered organization, distribution of duties and regulations, and a considerable familiarity with the new duties which its members were to perform.

The regulations which govern the operation of the new corps were adopted on the third of August. They divide the corps into the War Department General Staff and the General Staff serving with troops (that is to say, in time of peace with the generals commanding geographical departments), and they prescribe the duties and relations of each of the two classes.

The tenth article of the regulations relating to the Chief of Staff states explicitly the new theory of control inaugurated by the General Staff Act. It will be remembered that our old plan of army administration was that there should be a General Commanding the Army in peace as well as in war, responsible for the efficiency, discipline, and conduct of the troops, but having no control over finances or the departments of supply and transportation; and that there should be a Secretary of War controlling the finances and the money-spending bureaus, but not commanding the army or responsible for the conduct of purely military affairs; and it will be remembered that the result of attempting to work upon that theory of dual and separate responsibility was almost constant discord and a consequent reduction of efficiency. The new theory is stated by the regulation. (See Regulation 10, page 437.) . . .

It will be perceived that we are here providing for civilian control over the military arm, but for civilian control to be exercised through a single military expert of high rank, who is provided with an adequate corps of professional assistants to aid him in the performance of his duties, and who is bound to use all his professional skill and knowledge in giving effect to the purposes and general directions of his civilian superior, or make way for another expert who will do so.

In this way it is hoped that the problem of reconciling civilian control with military efficiency with which we have been struggling for so many years will be solved. . . .

The general plan contemplates that every subject requiring investigation and study shall be worked out first by the officers assigned to the appropriate division and section of the staff, and, when of sufficient importance, shall then be considered by a general staff council composed of the three general officers of the corps and the heads of the three divisions, and shall then be acted upon by the Chief of Staff, or laid before the Secretary of War by him with his recommendation. It is gratifying to report that the new system of control has been accompanied by most harmonious effort and cheerful good will on the part of the members of the General Staff, the chiefs of all the War Department bureaus, and the officers of the army at large. In some cases the intervention of the Chief of Staff and his assistants has resulted in an apparent diminution of the independent authority of other officers. This has been received almost universally with a cheerful readiness to subordinate personal considerations to the good of the service. The exceptions have been so few and unimportant as to justify the belief that they will soon disappear.

Much of the work upon which the General Staff has been employed is of a confidential nature, not to be exhibited in a report which is to become a public document. Most of the work involves questions which require investigation and the collection of data; or involves several supply and construction departments, and therefore could not properly be determined by any one such department; or calls for expert opinion upon military policy or needs. Of especial importance may be noted the general subject of the distribution of troops, and the location, construction, and enlargement of army posts; the plan for the attendance of militia officers upon military schools and colleges of the regular army; the detail of student officers to the General Service and Staff College; the location of military posts in Porto Rico; the reorganization of field batteries; the prevention of desertions; the organization of maneuver divisions and plans for mobilization at West Point, Kentucky, and Fort Riley; the purchase of lands for posts and coast fortifications; the revision of Army Regulations; the revision of Infantry Drill Regulations; the location of a brigade post on the Niagara River; the examination and revision of army appropriation estimates; the details of officers for duty at military academies and colleges; regulations for muster of militia into the service of the United States; reclassification and carding of the professional data on file in the military information division; organization of Alaskan militia; the rearrangement of territorial departments; the composition, duties, and limits of the principal permanent boards in the army; the study of the storage and supply depots of all kinds with reference to the prompt and effective collection and distribution of supplies in case of war; the revision of the Articles of War for submission to Congress, adapting them to meet modern conditions and requirements; the study in detail of the supplies necessary for active military operations, including the stock on hand, the productive capacity of Government manufacturers and of private manufacturers, the sources of raw material, and the length of time necessary for production in requisite quantities; and an inquiry into all the elements of cost for seacoast defenses up to this time, and the prospective cost of continuance and maintenance.

Special credit is due to Brigadier-General William H. Carter for the exceptional ability and untiring industry which he has contributed to the work of devising, bringing about, and putting into operation the General Staff law. He brought thorough and patient historical research and wide experience, both in the line and the staff, to the aid of long-continued, anxious, and concentrated thought upon the problem of improving military administration, and if the new system shall prove to be an improvement the gain to the country will have been largely due to him.

Joint Army and Navy Board

Extract from the Report of the Secretary of War for 1903 [1]

Following the same line of policy which led to the organization of the General Staff, the Secretaries of War and the Navy entered into an arrangement, with the approval of the President, which was published to the army in General Orders No. 107.

HEADQUARTERS OF THE ARMY,
ADJUTANT-GENERAL'S OFFICE,
WASHINGTON, July 20, 1903.

GENERAL ORDERS,
No. 107.

By direction of the Secretary of War, the following order is published to the army for the information and guidance of all concerned:

[1] Page 8.

"July 17, 1903.

"The Department of War and the Department of the Navy have agreed upon the formation of a joint board to be composed of four officers of the Army and four officers of the Navy, to hold stated sessions and such extraordinary sessions as shall appear advisable for the purpose of conferring upon, discussing, and reaching common conclusions regarding all matters calling for the coöperation of the two services. Any matters which seem to either Department to call for such consideration may be referred by that Department to the board thus formed. All reports of the board shall be made in duplicate, one to each Department. All reports and proceedings of the board shall be confidential. The senior member of the board present will preside at its meetings and the junior member of the board present will act as its recorder.

"On the recommendation of the provisional General Staff of the Army the following officers are detailed by the Secretary of War to serve upon the board:

"Major-General S. B. M. Young

"Major-General Henry C. Corbin

"Brigadier-General Tasker H. Bliss

"Brigadier-General Wallace F. Randolph

"On the recommendation of the General Board of the Navy the following officers are detailed by the Secretary of the Navy to serve upon the board:

"Admiral of the Navy George Dewey

"Rear-Admiral Henry C. Taylor

"Captain John E. Pillsbury

"Commander William J. Barnette

"ELIHU ROOT, *Secretary of War.*

"WILLIAM H. MOODY, *Secretary of the Navy.*

By command of Lieutenant-General Miles: W. P. HALL,
Acting Adjutant-General."

The common understanding and mutual assistance between the two services, which it is within the power of this board to bring about, may be made to cover a wide range of subjects of great public importance, including the parts to be taken by the military and naval forces, respectively, in case of military operations on the seaboards and on navigable lakes and rivers; artillery defense of naval stations and naval defensive aid to seacoast fortifications; the exchange of information obtained by one branch of the service and useful for both; the manufacture or purchase of cannon, projectiles, explosives, small arms, ammunition, and munitions of war generally available for both services; the purchase and transportation of supplies; the transportation of men upon changes of station; the study and discussion of joint military and naval problems. In all these, and in many other respects, much greater efficiency, at much less cost, can be obtained by coöperation and mutual understanding than by separate services working in entire independence of each other. If the two forces are ever to be called upon to coöperate, the time to determine what each shall do, and the time for each to learn what the other can do, is before the exigency arises. It is hoped that this joint board, which is so constituted as to command the assistance of the General Staff in both arms of the service for the working out of its problems, will contribute materially toward the end desired.

An Act to Increase the Efficiency of the Army

Chap. 553. *Be it enacted by the Senate and House of Representatives of the United States of America in Congress assembled,* That there is hereby established a General Staff Corps, to be composed of officers detailed from the Army at large, under such rules as may be prescribed by the President.

Sect. 2. That the duties of the General Staff Corps shall be to prepare plans for the national defense and for the mobilization of the military forces in time of war; to investigate and report upon all questions affecting the efficiency of the Army and its state of preparation for military operations; to render professional aid and assistance to the Secretary of War and to general officers and other superior commanders, and to act as their agents in informing and coördinating the action of all the different officers who are subject under the terms of this Act to the supervision of the Chief of Staff; and to perform such other military duties not otherwise assigned by law as may be from time to time prescribed by the President.

Sect. 3. That the General Staff Corps shall consist of one Chief of Staff and two general officers, all to be detailed by the President from officers of the Army at large not below the grade of brigadier-general; four colonels, six lieutenant-colonels, and twelve majors, to be detailed from the corresponding grades of the Army at large, under such rules for selection as the President may prescribe; twenty captains, to be detailed from officers of the Army at large of the grades of captain or first lieutenant, who while so serving shall have the rank, pay, and allowances of captain mounted. All officers detailed in the General Staff Corps shall be detailed therein for periods of four years, unless sooner relieved. While serving in the General Staff Corps, officers may be temporarily assigned to duty with any branch of the Army. Upon being relieved from duty in the General Staff Corps, officers shall return to the branch of the Army in which they hold permanent commission, and no officer shall be eligible to a further detail in the General Staff Corps until he shall have served two years with the branch of the Army in which commissioned, except in case of emergency or in time of war.

Sect. 4. That the Chief of Staff, under the direction of the President or of the Secretary of War, under the direction of the President, shall have supervision of all troops of the line and of the Adjutant-General's, Inspector-General's, Judge-Advocate's, Quartermaster's, Subsistence, Medical, Pay, and Ordnance Departments, the Corps of Engineers, and the Signal Corps, and shall perform such other military duties not otherwise assigned by law as may be assigned to him by the President. Duties now prescribed by statute for the Commanding General of the Army as a member of the Board of Ordnance and Fortification and of the Board of Commissioners of the Soldiers' Home shall be performed by the Chief of Staff or other officer designated by the President. Acts and parts of Acts authorizing aids-de-camp and military secretaries shall not apply to general officers of the General Staff Corps.

Sect. 5. That the Chief of Artillery shall hereafter serve as an additional member of the General Staff and by and with the advice and consent of the Senate shall have the rank, pay, and allowances of a brigadier-general and when the next vacancy occurs in the office of brigadier-general of the line, it shall not be filled, and thereafter the number of brigadier-generals of the line, exclusive of the Chief of Artillery, shall not exceed fourteen; and the provisions of the foregoing sections of this Act shall take effect August fifteenth, nineteen hundred and three.[1]

Approved, February 14, 1903.

Regulations of the General Staff[2]

War Department, August 3, 1903.

The President directs that the following additional Regulations for the Army, numbered from one to twenty, inclusive, be published for the government of all concerned, and that they be strictly observed:

[1] United States Statutes at Large, Fifty-seventh Congress, Vol. 32, Part 1, pages 830–831.

[2] Report of the Secretary of War for 1903, Appendix C, page 63.

General Staff Corps

COMPOSITION

1. The General Staff Corps, created in conformity to the act of Congress approved February 14, 1903, is composed of officers of the grades and number specified in said act, detailed for service in said corps for a period of four years unless sooner relieved, under rules of selection prescribed by the President. Upon being relieved from duty in the General Staff Corps officers return to the branch of the Army in which they hold permanent commissions, and, except in case of emergency or in time of war, are not eligible to further detail therein until they have served for two years with the branch of the Army in which commissioned. This ineligibility does not apply to any officer who has been relieved prior to the expiration of four years' duty with the corps; but such officer will become ineligible as soon as he shall have completed a total of four years of said duty. While serving in the General Staff Corps officers may be temporarily assigned to duty with any branch of the Army.

RELATIONS

2. The law establishes the General Staff Corps as a separate and distinct staff organization, with supervision, under superior authority, over all branches of the military service, line and staff, except such as are exempted therefrom by law or regulations, with a view to their coördination and harmonious coöperation in the execution of authorized military policies.

DUTIES

3. The General Staff Corps, under the direction of the Chief of Staff, is charged with the duty of investigating and reporting upon all questions affecting the efficiency of the Army and its state of preparation for military operations, and to this end considers and reports upon all questions relating to organization, distribution, equipment, armament, and training of the military forces (Regulars, Volunteers, and Militia), proposed legislative enactments and general and special regulations affecting the Army, transportation, communications, quarters, and supplies; prepares projects for maneuvers; revises estimates for appropriations for the support of the Army and advises as to disbursement of such appropriations; exercises supervision over inspections, military education and instruction, examinations for the appointment and promotion of officers, efficiency records, details and assignments, and all orders and instructions originating in the course of administration in any branch of the service which have relation to the efficiency of the military forces; prepares important orders and correspondence embodying the orders and instructions of the President and Secretary of War to the Army; reviews the reports of examining

and retiring boards; and acts upon such other matters as the Secretary of War may determine.

4. The General Staff Corps, under like direction, is further charged with the duty of preparing plans for the national defense and for the mobilization of the military forces (including the assignment to armies, corps, divisions, and other headquarters of the necessary quota of general staff and other staff officers), and incident thereto with the study of possible theaters of war and of strategic questions in general; with the collection of military information of foreign countries and of our own; the preparation of plans of campaign, of reports of campaigns, battles, engagements and expeditions, and of technical histories of military operations of the United States.

5. To officers of the General Staff Corps are committed the further duties of rendering professional aid and assistance to the Secretary of War and to general officers and other superior commanders and of acting as their agents in informing and coördinating the action of all the different officers who are subject under the provisions of law to the supervision of the Chief of Staff.

They perform such other military duties not otherwise assigned by law as may from time to time be prescribed by the President. Under the authority here conferred officers of the General Staff Corps are intrusted with the executive duties hereinafter indicated.

6. Officers of the General Staff Corps assigned to duty with commanders of armies, corps, divisions, separate brigades, territorial divisions, and departments are collectively denominated the General Staff serving with troops. They serve under the immediate orders of such commander; those not so assigned perform duty under the immediate direction of the Chief of Staff, and constitute the War Department General Staff.

7. The foregoing assignment of duties to the General Staff Corps does not involve in any degree the impairment of the initiative and responsibility which special staff corps and departments now have in the transaction of current business.

WAR DEPARTMENT GENERAL STAFF

Organization

8. To facilitate the performance of its duties the War Department General Staff will be arranged in divisions, each under the direction of an officer of the General Staff Corps to be designated by the Chief of Staff. Each division will be subdivided into sections as may be directed by the Chief of Staff.

Relations and Duties

9. The War Department General Staff in its several divisions and sections stands in an advisory relation to the Chief of Staff in the performance of the duties herein devolved upon him. The distribution of duties to the several divisions and sections is regulated by the Chief of Staff.

CHIEF OF STAFF

Relations and Selection

10. Under the act of February 14, 1903, the command of the Army of the United States rests with the constitutional Commander-in-Chief, the President. The President will place parts of the Army, and separate armies whenever constituted, under commanders subordinate to his general command; and, in case of exigency seeming to him to require it, he may place the whole Army under a single commander subordinate to him; but in time of peace and under ordinary conditions the administration and control of the Army are effected without any second in command.

The President's command is exercised through the Secretary of War and the Chief of Staff. The Secretary of War is charged with carrying out the policies of the President in military affairs. He directly represents the President and is bound always to act in conformity to the President's instructions. Under the law and the decisions of the Supreme Court his acts are the President's acts, and his directions and orders are the President's directions and orders.

The Chief of Staff reports to the Secretary of War, acts as his military adviser, receives from him the directions and orders given in behalf of the President, and gives effect thereto in the manner hereinafter provided.

Exceptions to this ordinary course of administration may, however, be made at any time by special direction of the President if he sees fit to call upon the Chief of Staff to give information or advice, or receive instructions, directly.

Wherever in these regulations action by the President is referred to, the action of the President through the Secretary of War is included, and wherever the action of the Secretary of War is referred to the Secretary of War is deemed to act as the representative of the President and under his directions.

The Chief of Staff is detailed by the President from officers of the Army at large not below the grade of brigadier-general. The successful performance of the duties of the position requires what the title denotes — a relation of absolute confidence and personal accord and sympathy between the Chief of Staff and the President, and necessarily also between the Chief of Staff and the Secretary of War. For this reason, without any reflection whatever upon the officer detailed, the detail will in every case cease, unless sooner terminated, on the day following the expiration of the term of office of the President by whom the detail is made; and if at any time the Chief of Staff considers that he can no longer sustain toward the President and the Secretary of War the relations above described, it will be his duty to apply to be relieved.

The provisions of paragraph 1, regarding the re-detail of an officer who has not completed a total of four years' service, apply to the Chief of Staff.

Duties

11. The Chief of Staff is charged with the duty of supervising, under the direction of the Secretary of War, all troops of the line, the Adjutant-General's, Inspector-General's, Judge-Advocate-General's, Quartermaster's, Subsistence, Medical, Pay, and Ordnance Departments, the Corps of Engineers, and the Signal Corps. He performs such other military duties not otherwise assigned by law as may be assigned to him by the President.

12. The supervisory power vested by statute in the Chief of Staff covers primarily duties pertaining to the command, discipline, training, and recruitment of the Army, military operations, distribution of troops, inspections, armament, fortifications, military education and instruction, and kindred matters, but includes also, in an advisory capacity, such duties connected with fiscal administration and supply as are committed to him by the Secretary of War.

In respect to all duties within the scope of his supervisory power, and more particularly those duties enumerated in this and the following paragraph, he makes and causes to be made inspections to determine defects which may exist in any matter affecting the efficiency of the Army and its state of preparation for war. He keeps the Secretary of War constantly informed of defects discovered, and under his direction issues the necessary instructions for their correction.

13. Supervisory power is conferred upon the Chief of Staff over all matters arising in the execution of acts of Congress and executive regulations made in pursuance thereof relating to the militia. This supervision is especially directed to matters of organization, armament, equipment, discipline, training, and inspections. Proposed legal enactments and regulations affecting the militia and estimates for appropriations for its support are considered by him, and his recommendations submitted to the Secretary of War.

14. The Chief of Staff is charged with the duty of informing the Secretary of War as to the qualifications of officers as determined by their records, with a view to proper selection for special details, assignments, and promotions, including detail to and relief from the General

Staff Corps; also of presenting recommendations for the recognition of special or distinguished services.

15. All orders and instructions emanating from the War Department and all regulations are issued by the Secretary of War through the Chief of Staff and are communicated to troops and individuals in the military service through the Adjutant-General.

16. The assignment of officers of the General Staff Corps to stations and duties is made upon the recommendation of the Chief of Staff.

17. In case of absence or disability of the Chief of Staff the senior officer of the General Staff present for duty in Washington shall act as such chief unless otherwise specially directed by the Secretary of War.

18. In the performance of the duties hereinbefore enumerated and in representation of superior authority, the Chief of Staff calls for information, makes investigations, issues instructions, and exercises all other functions necessary to proper harmony and efficiency of action upon the part of those placed under his supervision.

THE GENERAL STAFF SERVING WITH TROOPS

Composition

19. The general staff of a command consists of general staff officers of such number and grades as may be assigned to it on the recommendation of the Chief of Staff.

Duties

20. General staff officers serving with troops are employed under the direction of the commanders thereof, upon the duties hereinbefore prescribed for officers of the General Staff Corps and provided by the second section of the act of February 14, 1903, and they shall perform such other duties within the scope of general staff employment as may be directed by such commanders. They will not be assigned to other than general staff duties except by special authority of the Secretary of War.

Elihu Root,
Secretary of War.

THE BEGINNING OF THE NEW MILITIA SYSTEM

THE ACT TO PROMOTE THE EFFICIENCY OF THE MILITIA

The need for some well defined scheme for the coördination and coöperation of the regular army with the state militia and volunteers in case of war had been demonstrated both in the Civil War and in the war with Spain. Secretary Root called attention to this subject in his annual report for 1899, and urged the necessity of legislation under which in such an emergency the regulars and volunteers should constitute " a homogeneous body, using the same arms, familiar with the same drill, answering to the same ideas of discipline, inspired by the same spirit, and capable of an equal and even performance." The Act of March 2, 1899, under which the army serving in the Philippines was created, partly out of the old regular force, partly by new recruits in the regular establishment, and partly by additional volunteer regiments, was a long step toward the attainment of this homogeneity. Mr. Root returned to the subject in his annual reports for 1901 and 1903, with the result that on January 21, 1903, there was passed by Congress " an act to Promote the Efficiency of the Militia and for other purposes," which was supplemented by an appropriation of $2,000,000 in the Army Appropriation Act of March 2, 1903. In his annual report for 1903, Secretary Root outlines in detail his ideas of the plan and method of the reorganization of the state militia, which should be effected under this act. The act in question is quoted in full at the close of this section.

That later thought and observation finally strengthened the views regarding the National Guard to be found in Mr. Root's reports as Secretary of War, is shown by the following passages from a letter to Mr. Robert Bacon, which Mr. Root wrote to be read before the annual meeting of the National Security League, held in Washington, January 20, 21, 22, 1916:

> It is idle to talk of developing the National Guard itself into an adequate army for national defense, and any such attempt would inevitably result in the failure of the whole movement and the waste of all the energy and effort devoted to it. The National Guard are primarily state troops for state purposes, and they must continue to be so. The power to raise them and to train them and to appoint their officers rests with the separate states. Under the enlightened policy of the militia act of January 1, 1903, they have been fitted to render most useful service, primarily in coast defense, in coöperation with the national army in time of war. In the time of peace they are rendering a most useful service, by training in the elements of military service a great number of young Americans, to whom the President may turn when he seeks suitable men to be appointed officers in the national army.
>
> The idea, however, that these forty-eight different bodies of troops, with officers appointed by forty-eight different governors, can be made the basis for

developing an effective mobile national army, is quite absurd. An effective army must be built up on the principle of complete unity of control. This can never be attained by developing forty-eight different bodies under forty-eight different governors, and, up to the time of war, under the direction of forty-eight different commanders-in-chief. This characteristic of the National Guard cannot be changed except by amending the Constitution of the United States, which, if practicable, would require many years, and if that were done, the result would simply be, not to develop an army upon the National Guard, but to destroy the National Guard, and to develop an army on an entirely different basis.

It seems perfectly clear to me that any effort in the direction of developing a National Guard into the required national army of defense will be worse than thrown away, because it will result in the miscarriage of the whole effort.

Let me add another practical observation. The proposal to create an adequate national army of defense involves a good deal of a shock to many Americans who do not appreciate the reasons for the great enlargement of our military forces. Many of them are afraid of militarism; they are incredulous as to the necessity; they are disinclined to incur the expense. The progress of the cause in which you are enlisted requires a good deal of education, and many, I fear, alas, need to have the true spirit of American patriotism reawakened in them.

The same view is true as to the navy. Building up the military and naval establishments to the point where they ought to be will be slow work, and we ought to begin without further delay. The people of the country will deal with their representatives for all inadequacies and shortcomings in this vital matter. But in the meanwhile let us take the first steps on any sort of a programme that is directed toward the goal we ought to attain — a trained and always available national citizen soldiery under the instruction and administration and formative leadership of an adequate though small regular army.

The reader should also see Mr. Root's letter to Lieutenant-General S. B. M. Young, which concludes this volume.

Militia and Volunteers

Extract from the Report of the Secretary of War for 1901 [1]

THE present provisions of law relating to the militia, and to the raising of volunteer forces, are quite imperfect and unsatisfactory. The militia law stands today virtually as it was enacted in 1792, and is practically obsolete. It is very desirable that Congress should now exercise the power conferred upon it by the Constitution to provide for organizing, arming, and disciplining the militia. The organization and

[1] Page 25.

armament of the National Guards of the several states, which are treated as militia in the appropriations made by Congress, should be made the same as those provided by Congress for the regular and volunteer forces. The relations of the National Guard organizations to the national forces, and the obligations and duties of those organizations in time of war, should be clearly defined, so that the confusion and distress regarding their action which accompanied the outbreak of the war with Spain may not again occur.

The reliance of the country for the large forces necessary in modern warfare must necessarily be chiefly upon volunteers. The method and procedure of raising volunteer forces should be prescribed in advance, so that instead of waiting to devise plans for a volunteer army until the excitement and haste of impending war makes perfection of design difficult and satisfactory execution impossible, Congress will have but to direct the execution of a well-understood plan by officers, each one of whom has long been familiar with the part he is to play. It is desirable that any plans adopted should provide for utilizing, in the earlier volunteer organizations called out, the training of those citizens who shall have served already in the regular and volunteer forces. If the earlier volunteer organizations can be constituted of these trained men, much valuable time and expense can be saved, and many dangers may be averted during the period the ordinary volunteers are receiving the necessary training. Provision should also be made for the selection in advance of the officers of any volunteer force which may be raised. Careful selection is impossible at the outbreak of a war. It is entirely practicable in time of peace.

I recommend that the President be authorized to convene boards of officers (including the General Service and Staff College Board) for the examination of officers of the National Guard, and other citizens who may apply to be examined, as to their qualifications to hold volunteer commissions; that the persons passing such examinations shall receive certificates, stating the office for which they are found to be qualified, and upon the calling out of a volunteer force shall be entitled to receive commissions for such offices.

I recommend that the War Department be authorized to arm the National Guard with the present service small arms used by the regular army, navy, and marine corps; that the National Guard of the several states be treated as a first reserve, to be called into the service of the United States to execute the laws of the Union, suppress insurrections, and repel invasions, the term of service under any call to be limited to nine months; that the President be authorized, on the request of the governor of any state, to detail officers of the regular army for instruction, staff, and inspection duties with the National Guard of such state; that the War Department be authorized to furnish transportation, rations, and tentage to officers and men of National Guard organizations, who shall take part with the forces of the regular army in annual encampments and maneuvers at national military camps; that the Department be authorized to allow travel pay, commutation of rations and quarters, or commutation of quarters, to officers of the National Guard attending and regularly taking part in the courses of instruction at the General Service and Staff College at Fort Leavenworth. Both of these provisions should be within reasonable limits, proportional to the numbers of National Guard organizations in the several states.

I recommend that the President be now empowered to organize the volunteer forces whenever called out, in the manner provided for by the act of March 2, 1899, for the organization of the volunteer force which has recently returned from the Philippines, with such modifications as shall be necessary to give effect to the views above expressed.

The Militia System

Extract from the Report of the Secretary of War for 1902 [1]

Early in the last session a bill was prepared by the War Department, embodying the views expressed in my last report, upon the treatment of the National Guard of the several states by the Federal Government, the relation of the Guard to the militia and volunteer systems, and preparation in advance for the organization of volunteers in time of war. This bill was submitted to the chairman of the Committee on Military Affairs of the Senate, the chairman of the Committee on Militia of the House, and to a convention of officers of the National Guard organizations which met in Washington in January, 1902. The convention appointed a special committee to consider and report upon the proposed bill, and after some modifications it was reported favorably to the convention, which after thorough discussion adopted a resolution approving the measure and requesting its enactment by Congress. . . .

I earnestly urge that this measure be made a law. It is really absurd that a nation which maintains but a small regular army and depends upon unprofessional citizen soldiery for its defense should run along as we have done for one hundred and ten years under a militia law which never worked satisfactorily in the beginning, and which was perfectly obsolete before any man now fit for military duty was born. The result is that we have practically no militia system, notwithstanding the fact that the Constitution makes it the duty of the Federal Congress " to provide for organizing, arming, and disciplining the militia," and "for calling forth the militia to execute the laws of the Union, suppress insurrections, and repel invasions." The National Guard organizations of the several states have grown up in default

[1] Page 34.

of any national system and to meet local requirements. Their relations to the Federal Government have never been defined or settled. The confusion, controversy, and bad feeling arising from this uncertain status were painfully apparent at the beginning of the war with Spain; and it must always be the same until Congress shall exercise its constitutional power over the subject. Repeated efforts have been made to accomplish this result. Two years after the passage of the present law of 1792, President Washington addressed Congress on the subject in these words:

> The devising and establishing of a well-regulated militia would be a genuine source of legislative honor and a perfect title to public gratitude. I therefore entertain a hope that the present session will not pass without carrying to its full energy the power of organizing, arming, and disciplining the militia, and thus providing, in the language of the Constitution, for calling them forth to execute the laws of the Union, suppress insurrections, and repel invasions.

President Jefferson, eleven years later, in 1805, said:

> I cannot, then, but earnestly recommend to your early consideration the expediency of so modifying our militia system as, by a separation of the more active part from that which is less so, we may draw from it, when necessary, an efficient corps for real and active service, etc.

And in 1808 he said:

> For a people who are free, and who mean to remain so, a well-organized and armed militia is their best security. It is, therefore, incumbent on us at every meeting to revise the condition of the militia, and to ask ourselves if it is prepared to repel a powerful enemy at every point of our territories exposed to invasion. Some of the States have paid a laudable attention to this subject; but every degree of neglect is to be found among others. Congress alone has power to produce a uniform state of preparation in this great organ of defense. The interest which they so deeply feel in their own and their country's security will present this as among the most important objects of their deliberation.

President Madison said in 1816:

> An efficient militia is authorized and contemplated by the Constitution and required by the spirit and safety of free government. The present organization of our militia is universally regarded as less efficient than it

ought to be made, and no organization can be better calculated to give to it its due force than a classification which will assign the foremost place in the defense of the country to that portion of its citizens whose activity and animation best enable them to rally to its standard, etc.

President Monroe said in 1817:

> An improvement in the organization and discipline of the militia is one of the great objects which claims the unremitted attention of Congress.

Almost every President, from Washington down, has urged the importance of this subject upon the attention of Congress. The chief reason why nothing has been done has been that no one system could be agreed upon. Everybody was agreed upon the general principle, but a majority of all the people interested were opposed to every particular concrete method suggested to give it effect.

The bill which has now passed the House is the result of extensive and painstaking conference among representatives of all the classes of citizens especially interested in the subject and especially qualified to express opinions upon it. It does not represent fully any one's view, but it contains many important provisions upon which a general agreement has been reached; and it will, I am sure, if enacted, be a great step in advance toward effective preparation for war otherwise than by the maintenance of a standing army.

The fundamental idea of the bill is to recognize the value to the National Government of the National Guard, which is capable of being utilized, first, as an active militia when called out by the President for the specific purposes enumerated in the Constitution; second, as an already organized volunteer force when its organizations respond as such to calls for volunteers for general military purposes under authority of Congress; and, third, as the great school of the volunteer soldier, the benefits of which are received by the country when the members of the Guard respond individually to calls for volunteers. The bill undertakes to regulate and provide for these various relations of the National Guard and its members to the general system; to conform the organization, armament, and discipline of the Guard to that of the regular and volunteer armies of the United States; to establish closer relations and better coöperation between the National Guard and the regular army; to promote the efficiency and dignity of the Guard as a part of the military system of the United States.

To aid in accomplishing these objects, and in recognition of the benefits to the General Government that come from the Guard altogether outside of its service to the individual states, the bill provides that the General Government shall furnish to the Guard the same arms which it furnishes to the regular army, and shall provide for the voluntary participation by the Guard with the regular army in maneuvers and field exercises for brief periods in each year. The bill also contains provisions making the National Guard organizations which choose voluntarily to go beyond the limitations of militia service in effect a first volunteer reserve, and further provisions for the enrollment of a second volunteer reserve not exceeding 100,000, to be composed of trained men who have served in the National Guard or in the regular army or the volunteer armies of the United States. These would constitute the first volunteer regiments after the National Guard Volunteers under any call by Congress. It also provides for ascertaining by practical tests, in advance of a call for volunteers, the fitness of members of the National Guard, graduates of the military schools and colleges, and other citizens with military training, to hold volunteer commissions, thus constituting an eligible list from which in case of a call for volunteers the officers of the second reserve must be taken, and the officers of the general body of volunteers may be taken. With the system provided for by the bill carried into effect we should be able while maintaining a standing army of but 60,000 men to put a force of at least 250,000 well-trained men into the field instantly upon a declaration of war, and the cost would be less than to maintain but a few additional regiments of regular troops.

The military force of the United States would then be as follows:

First. The regular army, capable of enlargement by the President, when he sees war coming, to 100,000.

Second. Such of the organized militia (already trained as a National Guard, and just as valuable, when used in the manner hereinafter indicated, as any other troops) as the President shall see fit to call into the service of the United States for not exceeding nine months, to repel invasion.

Third. A first volunteer reserve, composed of such companies, troops, and regiments of the organized militia already trained as a National Guard as volunteer by organizations with all their officers and men.

Fourth. A second volunteer reserve, composed of men previously enrolled and having previous military training in the National Guard, the regular army or the volunteer army, and commanded by officers whose fitness has been previously ascertained by practical tests under the provisions of the militia act.

Fifth. Such further volunteers as it may be necessary to call forth from the states, according to their respective quotas, and commanded by regimental officers appointed by the governors of the states.

A conservative estimate of the number which would be included in the first four classes of troops, who have already had military service and will be available for immediate action, is from 250,000 to 300,000.

The number of the fifth class — volunteers who may or may not have had previous service — has no limit, except the possibilities of transportation and supply.

The capacity of the National Guard organizations in general to serve effectively as organizations, either militia or volunteer, in the national army in case of war depends very largely upon the aid which they receive from the National Government. The Guard is now armed with a variety of weapons of different kinds and calibers, including two different calibers of the obsolete Springfield rifle, the Lee, the Remington-Lee, the Winchester, and the Krag-Jörgensen. In several instances different National Guard organizations of the same state are armed with different weapons of different calibers. Among all the 115,000 National Guardsmen of the different states and territories only about 4,000 have the modern service rifle of the United States army. With the exception of these 4,000 rifles the arms of the Guard would be practically worthless in time of war, not merely because they are inferior but because the Guard would have to look to the United States Government for their ammunition, and the Government would have no ammunition for the kind of rifles they carry: they would have to look to the Government to replace the arms lost or broken in service, and the Government would be unable to supply the same kind. The militia and the volunteer National Guard organizations in general would, therefore, be obliged to throw away their present arms at the beginning of a war and get reëquipped with weapons the use of which they had never learned.

The Militia and Coast Defense

Extract from the Report of the Secretary of War for 1902 [1]

One of the most valuable services which can be rendered to the country by its militia, and the one which can be made the easiest and most natural for it to render, is to supplement the regular force in manning the coast defenses in time

[1] Page 38.

of war. Our present regular force is none too large to take care of the guns and the machinery of the fortifications in time of peace. It will be quite insufficient in war. The number of artillerymen for which Congress was asked to provide in the act of February 2, 1901, was intentionally made small in view of the manifest practicability of supplementing it by a well-trained militia force, available in case of threatened attack. Manning the coast fortifications is constitutional militia work, for it is always to repel invasion. It can be undertaken by citizens living in the neighborhood of the fortifications with less disturbance and sacrifice than any other military duty, because it does not take them far away from their homes and their business.

The handling of the modern high-power and rapid-fire guns and the complicated machinery by which they are worked requires, it is true, special training, but there is no trouble in securing a reasonable degree of that for heavy artillery militia organizations. For the past three years I have been following closely the work of the First Massachusetts Heavy Artillery, which has been admitted each year to one or another of the defenses on that coast for practice. The officers at all the fortifications speak in high terms of the intelligence and readiness with which these men have acquired facility in doing the work. Many of them are mechanics and take naturally to the machinery of defense. On the other hand, the members of the regiment evidently take great and sustained interest and satisfaction in the performance of their duties. The same is true of the Connecticut artillery organization which took part in the recent seacoast maneuvers, and of the Thirteenth New York Heavy Artillery, and I doubt not of other organizations with which I am less familiar.

If the militia bill above described becomes a law, an effort should be made to procure the organization of a National Guard force of heavy-artillerymen in the neighborhood of each coast-defense fortification, with the understanding that whenever the President finds occasion to call out militia to repel invasion that organization will be called into that fortification. In the meantime an immediate and special relation should be established between the militia organization and the fortification for the purpose of practice and instruction. They should be made as familiar as possible with the use of the guns and methods of defense at that particular point. In many cases it will be practicable to give them facilities for meeting and keeping their equipment on the military reservation, which would make unnecessary any outside armory for their use. Such an organization could readily perform all its duties to the state serving as infantry, but it could at the same time be distinctly known, and constantly prepared for service, as the militia reserve of the fortification with which it sustains the relations described.

Another very important function to be performed by militia, and having the same characteristic of not requiring militiamen to render any service except for the defense of their homes, is the service to be rendered by infantry in the defense of our coast fortifications against attack in reverses by land. That is a subject which ought to receive early and earnest attention on the part of the Federal Government. It is of great importance that an adequate force should be ready to perform that service, should be ready to take their places without confusion, and that there should be a perfect understanding as to where the force are to come from, where they are to be posted, and how they are to be supplied and maintained.

The National Guard contains two widely different elements. One is composed of men who wish to perform their duty to the state and as members of the militia, but do not wish, or do not feel at liberty, to leave their families or their business interests and become soldiers for all purposes, liable to be sent away for distant military operations. The other element wish to go wherever there is adventure and a chance to fight. The amount of strictly local military work of the highest importance to be done in case of war is so great that the whole National Guard force, of the seacoast states at all events, can be made just as useful as if they all became volunteers for all purposes. In order to accomplish this, however, there should be a careful prearrangement as to the distribution of duties.

Fort Riley Maneuvers and Camp Sites

Extract from the Report of the Secretary of War for 1902[1]

A good example of what can be done in the way of joint maneuvers and exercise by regulars and militia, to the great advantage of both, in preparation for general military service, has been furnished by the concentration and exercise of troops at Fort Riley in the latter part of September. Three regiments of regular infantry, two regiments of infantry of the National Guard of Kansas, a battalion of Colorado infantry, a regiment of regular cavalry, five batteries of regular field artillery, two batteries of Kansas field artillery, a battalion of regular engineers, and detachments of the regular Signal Corps and Hospital Corps were concentrated at that point and engaged for from five days to two weeks in practicing field operations, involving work from the simplest outpost and patrol duties up to and including maneuvers by brigade and division.

A large number of National Guard officers, besides those commanding troops in the maneuvers, and representing twenty different states and two territories, were present. A large number of National Guard troops of other states would have been present had there been any appropriations to pay their expenses. Both the officers of the Guard and

[1] Page 40.

of the regular army unite in the opinion that both branches of the service received great benefit; and the good understanding and friendly feeling established between the two classes of officers who were present at the maneuvers are most gratifying. Jealousy, superciliousness, or a suspicion of it, and bad feeling between regular and volunteer officers have been some of the most fruitful causes of dissension and hindrance to general military efficiency in this country. The best way to put an end to this is to bring the officers together and get them to know each other and work with each other with a common purpose.

General Bates, the commander of the Department of the Missouri, says in his report:

> The value of such concentrations and maneuverings cannot be overestimated, either to the regular forces or to the National Guard, as it gives to both an opportunity for observing the appearance and formation of a division under various conditions, and affords to officers of the several arms of the service a chance for seeing the evolutions and capabilities of the other arms, and enables them to enlarge their circle of military acquaintanceship, which can rarely be done without absorbing new ideas upon military subjects. During the exercises under discussion young officers had constantly impressed upon them the value of studying the terrain, with a view to protecting their commands by the accidents of the ground, and of seizing advantageous positions. The lessons learned in this connection at Fort Riley may be the means of saving many lives in future hostilities. The power of modern weapons was well illustrated and accentuated by each opponent maneuvering for position.

At the end of the encampment the officers representing Maryland, Texas, Nebraska, Pennsylvania, New Jersey, North Dakota, Michigan, Rhode Island, Massachusetts, Ohio, Indiana, Georgia, Illinois, California, Florida, New York, Virginia, and Oklahoma met and passed resolutions expressing their opinion as to the benefit of what had been done. . . .

It is to be hoped that before another autumn the passage of the militia bill will enable the War Department to facilitate the attendance of greater numbers of National Guard troops for a repetition of these maneuvers on a larger scale.

Section 35 of the act of February 2, 1901, directed the Secretary of War to cause preliminary examinations and surveys to be made for the purpose of selecting four sites with a view to the establishment of permanent camp grounds for instruction of troops of the regular army and National Guard. In compliance with this direction such preliminary examinations and surveys have been made at places selected by the board of general officers upon military posts and camp sites already mentioned in this report; and on May 19, 1902, the reports of the examinations and surveys were transmitted to Congress.[1] The sites selected by the board were at Fort Riley, Kansas, where the present reservation consists of about 20,000 acres; one in the vicinity of Chickamauga Park, Georgia, where a not very expensive addition to the present park grounds now owned by the Government would suffice; one in the Conewago Valley in Lebanon, Dauphin, and Lancaster counties, Pennsylvania; and one on the Nacimiento Ranch, in Monterey and San Luis Obispo counties, California.

Reports of examinations and estimates of the cost of several other sites in Indiana, Kentucky, New Mexico, Texas, and Wisconsin were also transmitted for the consideration of Congress. It is to be hoped that Congress will proceed to carry out the design of the act of February 2, 1901, by authorizing the purchase of a sufficient number of sites in different parts of the country to make it possible to give to the National Guard of all the states, and to the regular troops stationed in each section, the benefits of annual maneuvers similar to those which have been inaugurated at Fort Riley.

[1] House Document No. 618, Fifty-seventh Congress, first session.

PROGRESS OF THE MILITIA REORGANIZATION

Extract from the Report of the Secretary of War for 1903[1]

Of equal importance with the General Staff act in its relation to the general military efficiency of the country is the act to promote the efficiency of the militia, approved January 21, 1903, supplemented by an appropriation of $2,000,000 in the army appropriation act of March 2, 1903. The militia act had its origin in an agreement between the regular army, represented by the War Department, and the National Guards of the states, represented by a convention which met in Washington in January, 1902, upon the main and fundamental provisions necessary to give vitality and effectiveness to our militia system. Upon the presentation of these provisions to Congress, the Committee on Militia of the House took up the subject with great public spirit and industry, and on that basis wrought out a bill which, with but a few changes, was passed and approved in the form of the present act. The act proceeds upon the following ideas:

That whenever the United States becomes involved in war, the regular army will form but a small part of its armed force; and the country must also rely, for immediate and special exigencies, upon militia; and for service going beyond the proper limits of militia duty, upon volunteers.

That it is of vital importance to have a trained force of militia ready for instant service when called upon, and also to have a large number of citizens sufficiently instructed and exercised in the art of war, to organize, train and command volunteer forces.

That the best way for the National Government to secure both these requisites is by turning to the National Guards of the states, which have grown up as state organizations intended for state purposes, but are composed of citizens

[1] Page 13.

liable to be called upon by the National Government for military duty, and willing to devote a considerable part of their time to fitting themselves for the performance of that duty.

That, without at all interfering with the services of these organizations to their respective states in time of peace, they can be treated as a national militia to be called into the service of the United States in time of war; and that it is for the interest of the National Government to make these organizations as effective as possible, having in view their prospective national service as militia and their immediate service as the school of the national volunteer soldier.

That as the militia when called into the service of the United States and the volunteer forces commanded by the citizens trained in this school of arms, will form, together with the regular troops, but one army, subject to the same command, drawing arms, ammunition, and supplies from the same source, and subject to the same general system of accountability for property, it will be important that all parts of this greater army shall have used and shall be familiar with the same arms, ammunition, supplies, and forms and methods of transacting business, and shall have similar organization and discipline.

In this act, accordingly, Congress declared the National Guard organizations to be the organized militia, and provided for calling them into the service of the United States, whenever required, for the constitutional purposes of repelling invasion, suppressing insurrection, and executing the laws of the Union. And Congress also exercised its constitutional power "to provide for organizing, arming, and disciplining the militia" by a series of provisions designed to promote the strength, efficiency, and prosperity of these militia organizations; to make them and the regular army a homogeneous force; and to bring about a habit of coöperation and mutual respect and good understanding between the officers of the two forces.

To accomplish these purposes, the act provides that the organization, armament, and discipline of the organized militia shall be the same as that prescribed for the regular army. It authorizes the Secretary of War to issue to the militia, at the expense of the National Government, the same arms, ammunition, and supplies which are provided for the regular army. It provides for regular inspections by officers detailed by the Secretary of War and for regular returns by the adjutants in the several states to the Secretary of War. It authorizes participation by the organized militia in joint maneuvers with the regular army, and provides that in such case the organized militia so participating shall receive the same pay, subsistence, and transportation as is provided by law for the officers and men of the regular army, to be paid out of the regular appropriations for the support of the army. It provides for furnishing aid to separate state encampments of the militia by allowing, out of an annual appropriation of $1,000,000 for militia purposes, to the officers and enlisted men engaged in such encampments, the same pay, subsistence, and transportation or travel allowances as are made for similar purposes to officers and enlisted men of the regular army. It provides for detailing officers of the army to attend encampments upon the request of the governors of the states to give instruction and information, and for detailing officers to report to the governors for duty generally in connection with the militia. And it provides that for the purpose of securing a list of persons specially qualified to hold commissions in any volunteer force which may be called out hereafter, examinations shall be held, open to any one serving or who has served in the organized militia, to determine the fitness of the applicant to hold a volunteer commission. The persons passing such examination are to be certified and registered, and are to constitute an eligible class for appointment as officers of any future volunteer force; and they are authorized to attend any military school or college of the United States except the Military Academy at West Point, and to receive the same allowances and commutations during such attendance as are provided for the officers of the regular army.

This statute plainly opens a wide field of new duty for the officers of the regular army. They can no longer fill the measure of their obligation to the country by perfecting themselves and the forces under their command in the performance of their own military duties. They are charged with the further duty of applying their military skill and experience to the preparation of the militia and volunteer force which will be associated with them in the next war, for effective service. A new responsibility also rests upon the officers of the National Guard to render to the nation full and unstinted return for the enlarged means and opportunities which the liberality of Congress has afforded to them.

It is gratifying to report that the officers of both services have entered upon the execution of the new statute with an evident desire to discharge these obligations and attain the purposes of the law.

Following is a review of the principal things already done under the law:

Militia Inspection under Section 14. Section 14 of the act makes it the duty of the Secretary of War to cause to be made at least once in each year, by officers detailed for that purpose, inspections to determine whether the organized militia is sufficiently armed, uniformed, and equipped for active duty in the field, as a condition precedent to the use of its allotment under section 1661, Revised Statutes, for the payment, subsistence, and transportation of such portion of the organized militia as shall engage in actual field or camp service for instruction. Hitherto the entire expense of state encampments has been a charge which the states have had to meet. A special inspection of the entire organized militia of the country was promptly made after the passage of the law. This inspection was thoroughly and effectively conducted by 87 selected officers of the army, who in the aggregate visited 1,196 towns and cities, and inspected 196 regiments, separate battalions and squadrons, and 1,943 companies, troops, batteries, and staff organizations. The total number of the organized militia, including officers of every rank and grade, was ascertained to be 116,542, of which 7,610 were officers of the line and 1,510 officers of the staff, making a total of 9,120 commissioned officers and 107,422 enlisted men; of this number 6,695 officers and 81,007 men were present at inspection. Their distribution among the arms of service was as follows:

	Officers	Enlisted Men	Aggregate
General and Staff	1,360	....	1,360
Cavalry	350	4,740	5,090
Artillery	498	6,754	7,252
Infantry	6,782	93,314	100,096
Engineers	63	1,011	1,074
Signal Corps	52	680	732
Hospital Corps	15	923	938
Total	9,120	107,422	116,542

Among the immediate results of the special inspection were the disbandment and muster out of many companies, the recruitment of others, and the entire reorganization of the organized militia of several states and territories, as well as a material change in the organized strength of nearly every state from that last report by the adjutant-generals.

Inspection under Section 18. Another feature of this inspection, made mandatory by section 18 of the law, in order to entitle the states and territories to the benefit of the appropriation under section 1661, Revised Statutes, relates to the system of drill and inspection required by the states during the year next preceding each annual allotment of funds. The law requires that each state or territory shall have required during the preceding year every company, troop, and battalion in its organized militia, not excused by the governor, to participate in practice marches or to go into camp of instruction at least five consecutive days, and to assemble for drill and instruction at company, battalion, or regimental armories or rendezvous, or for target practice, not less than twenty-four times, and shall also have required during such year an inspection of each such company, troop, and battalion to be made by an officer of such militia or an officer of the regular army.

As the result of this inspection it was learned that 1,337 organizations have participated in practice marches or gone into camps of instruction at least five consecutive days during the year preceding June 30, 1903, and 1,740 organizations have assembled for drill and instruction at armories or rendezvous or for target practice not less than twenty-four times during that period. The number of organizations not participating in the first class of military exercise is 557, and not participating in the second class, 154. The value of the aid rendered by the Federal Government in furnishing material of war and paying certain necessary expenses of encampments is so manifest that it is to be presumed that all organizations of the Guard will in the future make every effort to comply with the conditions which must hereafter govern in the allotment of this annual appropriation for the support of the militia. . . .

Participation of Militia in Combined Maneuvers. The participation by any part of the organized militia of any state or territory, on request of the governor, in the encampment, maneuvers, and field instruction of any part of the regular army at or near any military post or camp or lake or seacoast defenses of the United States is authorized under section 15. The militia taking part in these maneuvers are to receive the same pay, subsistence, and transportation as are provided for officers and men of the regular army, to be paid out of the appropriations for the support of the army.

The militia organizations availing themselves of this privilege were the National Guard of Hawaii, with the troops at Camp McKinley, near Honolulu, June tenth to fourteenth; the entire militia of Maine, and one regiment of coast artillery from Massachusetts, in the combined maneuvers of the army and navy in the artillery district of Portland, Maine, from August twenty-second to twenty-ninth; two companies of coast artillery of Connecticut and one regiment of coast artillery of New York in operations at the eastern entrance of Long Island Sound, July tenth to twentieth; three regiments of infantry and one field battery of the Indiana National Guard, three regiments and one battalion of the Michigan National Guard, two regiments of infantry and a battalion of artillery of the Kentucky State Guard, one regiment of infantry and a field battery of the Ohio National Guard, and one regiment of infantry of the Wisconsin National Guard in the maneuvers at West Point, Kentucky, September twenty-fifth to October sixteenth; one battalion of infantry of the Colorado National Guard, one regiment of infantry of the Iowa National Guard, two regiments of infantry and two batteries of field artillery of the Kansas National Guard, one regiment of infantry of the Missouri National Guard, one regiment of infantry and one company of the signal corps of the Nebraska National Guard, and one regiment of infantry of the Texas National Guard in the maneuvers at Fort Riley, Kansas, from October fifteenth to twenty-seventh.

These organizations had present approximately 1,000 officers and 13,000 men.

These general field exercises have proved of great value to the militia, affording it opportunity to take part in military maneuvers on an extended scale, and to come into actual contact with the regular army under the conditions of simulated warfare; and they tend to infuse into the militia a spirit of discipline and respect for army standards and efficiency. They have also proved of material advantage to the regular army through the association of the two forces. The relations of mutual respect, good feeling, and common understanding established between the great numbers of officers of both services, who have been working together in these maneuvers, will prove of incalculable benefit whenever those officers are found serving in the same army engaged in actual hostilities.

Issue of Arms and Equipment. One of the cardinal purposes of the law being to secure uniformity of armament between the militia and the regular army, the Secretary of War is authorized under section 13 to issue upon the requisitions of the state authorities such number of the United States standard service magazine rifles, with necessary equipments and accouterments as are required to arm all the organized militia, without charging the cost under section 1661, Revised Statutes, or requiring payment therefor, and to make the necessary exchange of ammunition for the new arms.

Under this provision the Chief of Ordnance has issued 88,031 magazine rifles and carbines, and credited back to various states and territories $336,893.09 which had been charged to them for similar issues since December 1, 1901. All of the states and territories but three have been fully supplied, and of these three the principal one is, by preference, waiting for a change of sights upon the rifles which are ready to be delivered. The reärmament may, accordingly, be regarded as substantially accomplished.

Allotments to the Militia under Section 1661, Revised Statutes. In the distribution and use of the $1,000,000 annually appropriated under section 1661, Revised Statutes, the limitations which have heretofore governed the use of the appropriation have been removed by section 17 of the new act, so that instead of its being confined to the purchase of ordnance and quartermaster stores, as was formerly the case, it is available for the purpose of providing for the use of the organized militia any stores and supplies or publications which are supplied to the army by any department. In addition it is applicable to the pay, subsistence, and transportation of militia participating in state encampments under section 14, as already stated above. In lieu of the limitations which formerly governed this appropriation, Congress has substituted those set forth in sections 14 and 18 of the act, requiring a definite and satisfactory showing of the militia's preparedness for military duty and the genuineness of its claims for consideration as a military organization.

Further authority is conferred upon the states to purchase for cash, for the use of its militia, materials of war and military publications at the prices at which they are issued to the army, with the cost of transportation added.

Militia Allotments under Act of March 2, 1903. The allotments under section 1661, Revised Statutes, are made to the states upon the basis of representation in Congress. The act of March 2, 1903, provided for the procurement and issue of certain articles of armament and equipment to the militia, with a view to conforming its equipment in its entirety to that of the regular army, so that it became the duty of the Department to procure and furnish the equipment in kind, using this appropriation as far as it would go toward completely equipping the entire militia. That the sum appropriated was inadequate for the purpose was manifest, and it was therefore necessary to determine what portion of the supplies required by each state could be furnished.

An article of issue of prime importance was the field gun of the model about to be adopted by the army to replace the old field guns of 3.2 caliber in use by the militia. As a result of special inspection it appears that there are in the possession of the militia seventy-two field guns of 3.2 inch caliber, which number would constitute eighteen batteries of the army organization. The Secretary of War therefore directed that the sum of $700,000 should be set aside from this appropriation for the procurement by the Chief of Ordnance of field artillery. This sum is sufficient to equip about fourteen batteries of four guns each. A provisional apportionment to the states and territories of $1,000,000 of this appropriation, upon the basis of the organized strength of the militia as reported to Congress under date of February 2, 1903, was directed by the Secretary of War. The states have availed themselves of this provisional allotment by calling for articles of clothing, equipage, ordnance, medical and signal supplies. Under this appropriation blank forms of requisitions, returns, and many other papers used by the regular army have been distributed to the militia in order to bring the paper work of the two forces into conformity.

Detail of Officers with States and Territories. As an additional means of aiding the state authorities in developing the militia under the system prescribed by Congress, authority was conferred upon the Secretary of War by section 20 of the act to detail, in his discretion, upon the application of the governors, one or more officers of the army to report to them for duty in connection with their organized militia. The act of March 2, 1903, authorized a similar detail of not exceeding twenty retired officers. As the conditions of the service at this time do not permit the detail of officers on the active list for this duty, steps have been taken to detail the twenty retired officers. The governors of the states, in the order of the strength of their organized militia, have been afforded opportunity to secure such details, and six officers have already been assigned to this duty. Notifications have been sent to the governors of all the states to indicate their wishes as to the detail of retired officers, and these requests will be disposed of in the order of the organized strength of the militia, until the number of retired officers authorized by law is exhausted.

Conformity to Army Standards. The requirement of the law that the organization of the militia shall conform to that of the regular army within five years from the date of the approval of the act is one which mainly falls upon the states and territories to carry out, but the Department has endeavored to facilitate this end by submitting for the consideration of the state authorities a proposed code of militia law covering in detail features of organization. This code is comprehensive in its treatment, embodying the most approved machinery for the government of the militia, and while it is offered to the states only by way of suggestion, it is hoped that the substance of its provisions will be adopted, thereby furnishing a fairly uniform basis of administration for the National Guard.

The inherent difficulties of conforming in all particulars to army organization are thoroughly appreciated by the Department, but it is confidently believed that the earnest coöperation of the state authorities will enable the necessary changes to be gradually effected. This act provides that the President of the United States may in time of peace, by order, fix the minimum number of enlisted men in each company, troop, battalion, signal corps, engineer corps, and hospital corps. In the proposed code the suggested minimum strength of the tactical units of the several arms of the service will be found, with the exception of the engineer companies, the minimum strength of which, it is thought, should be the same as that of the infantry.

Military Education of Militia and Volunteer Officers. Very liberal means have been afforded by section 16 and 23 for the instruction of militia officers at military schools and colleges of the United States. Such student officers receive the same travelling allowance and quarters or commutation of quarters, that officers of the regular army would be entitled to while in attendance at such schools, together with an allowance for subsistence. Section 23 provides for the creation in the Department of a roster of militia officers who are especially qualified to hold commissions in any volunteer force which may hereafter be called for and organized under authority of Congress. The General Staff has prepared regulations for examining boards to determine the qualifications of such applicants. These regulations have been approved by the Department, and will shortly be issued.

While the army service schools are fully taxed by the present attendance of regular officers, the necessary steps will be taken to provide accommodations for student militia officers as soon as they become eligible to attend under the requirements of the law and the regulations of the Department.

Regulation of Use of Militia for National Defense. As the chief interest of the United States in the militia lies in its availability for national protection upon occasions of emergency, one of the underlying objects of this law is to prescribe the way to make it available as a fighting force. The constitutional purposes for which the militia can be called into the active service of the United States are embodied in section 4, the terms of service in section 5, the apportionment of the militia when called into service in section 6, while sections 7 to 11 provide for the muster into service, courts-martial, pay and allowances, and other miscellaneous subjects. Regulations to govern the muster of the militia into the service of the United States under section 7 have been framed by the General Staff and have received the Department's approval.

In considering the availability of the militia for national defense, a most pertinent inquiry is that of dependable strength. With a view to obtaining a definite idea as to what this dependable strength would be at this time, a thorough canvass of the National Guard was made, from which it appears that of the 1,943 separate bodies in the organized militia the men of 1,586 had a thorough understanding of their obligations under the statute, 250 organizations had no such idea, and 57 had a partial idea. Of the 116,542 officers and men now in the service of the organized militia, 100,345 declared themselves ready to respond to a sudden call of the President.

Promotion of Rifle Practice

Extract from the Report of the Secretary of War for 1903 [1]

The Army Appropriation act of March 2, 1903, provided —

> That for the purpose of furnishing a national trophy and medals and other prizes, to be provided and contested for annually, under such regulations as may be prescribed by the Secretary of War, said contest to be open to the army and the National Guard, or organized militia of the several states, territories, and of the District of Columbia, and for the cost of the trophy, prizes, and medals herein provided for, the sum of two thousand five hundred dollars be, and the same is hereby, annually appropriated out of any money in the Treasury not otherwise appropriated, to be expended for the purposes hereinbefore prescribed, under the direction of the Secretary of War.

The very great importance of this subject led the Secretary of War to exercise the authority vested in him by this provision to make regulations for the government of this annual contest in such form as to promote the purpose of the statute

[1] Page 25.

by securing a comprehensive and progressive treatment of the whole subject of improving the marksmanship of the army and the militia. For that purpose a board was established composed of five members from the regular establishment, including the Assistant Secretary of War, two officers of the army, an officer of the navy, and an officer of the marine corps, detailed by special authority of the Secretary of the Navy; the trustees of the National Rifle Association, eight in number; and eight citizens who had shown special interest in the subject, appointed from the country at large. Nearly all of the members of the last two classes are prominent officers of the National Guard, representing thirteen different states and territories. This board formulated rules and conditions for the first contest under the statute, which received the approval of the Secretary of War; and the contest was held on the eighth and ninth of September. The board has also had under consideration a number of important questions relating to the promotion of rifle practice, and will, I am satisfied, if properly sustained in its efforts, prove a most useful agency in the conduct of this necessary work. I know of nothing more important in the way of preparation for war than teaching the young men of the country to shoot straight. It is especially important to the efficiency of our volunteer armies in the future. It is of no use to pay, equip, subsist, and transport a soldier to the battlefield unless he can hit an enemy when he shoots at him. Two recent changes in conditions require that we should make continuous and active effort in this direction if we are to have this necessary element of efficiency. One is the greatly increased range of modern rifles which determines battles in which the combatants are at great distances from each other, and which makes practice more necessary for good marksmanship than ever before. The other is the decline in the use of firearms among the greater part of our people. Formerly when our population was scattered and game was abundant in all parts of the country every house had its rifle or its shotgun, and every boy learned to shoot them. Now it is probable that a majority of the young men in the thickly settled parts of the country have never fired a gun, and would be quite harmless to an enemy until taught to shoot. The time to give that instruction is now. We ought not to wait until we are actually engaged in hostilities. When that time comes the enemy will not wait for us to give the instruction. I recommend that an appropriation be made to pay the necessary expenses of the board for the promotion of rifle practice; that the statute be amended so as to include the navy and the marine corps, and that an additional sum be appropriated for the promotion of rifle practice by the formation of rifle clubs and contests to which citizens generally shall be admitted; to be expended upon the recommendation of the board with the approval of the Secretary of War.

The Act to Promote the Efficiency of the Militia

Be it enacted by the Senate and House of Representatives of the United States of America in Congress assembled, That the militia shall consist of every able-bodied male citizen of the respective States, Territories, and the District of Columbia, and every able-bodied male of foreign birth who has declared his intention to become a citizen, who is more than eighteen and less than forty-five years of age, and shall be divided into two classes — the organized militia, to be known as the National Guard of the State, Territory, or District of Columbia, or by such other designations as may be given them by the laws of the respective States or Territories, and the remainder to be known as the Reserve Militia.

Sec. 2. That the Vice-President of the United States, the officers, judicial and executive, of the Government of the United States, the members and officers of each House of Congress, persons in the military or naval service of the United States, all custom-house officers, with their clerks, postmasters, and persons employed by the United States in the transmission of the mail, ferrymen employed at any ferry on a post-road, artificers and workmen employed in the armories and arsenals of the United States, pilots, mariners actually employed in the sea service of any citizen or merchant within the United States, and all persons who are exempted by the laws of the respective States or Territories shall be exempted from militia duty, without regard to age: *Provided,* That nothing in this Act shall be construed to require or compel any member of any well-recognized religious sect or organization at present organized and existing whose creed forbids its members to participate in war in any form, and whose religious convictions are against war or participation therein, in accordance with the creed of said religious organization, to serve in the militia or any other armed or volunteer force under the jurisdiction and authority of the United States.

Sec. 3. That the regularly enlisted, organized, and uniformed active militia in the several States and Territories and the District of Columbia who have heretofore participated or shall hereafter participate in the apportionment of the annual appropriation provided by section sixteen hundred and sixty-one of the Revised Statutes of the United States, as amended, whether known and designated as National Guard, militia, or otherwise, shall constitute the organized militia. The organization, armament, and discipline of the organized militia in the several States and Territories and in the District of Columbia shall be the same as that which is now or may hereafter be prescribed for the Regular and Volunteer Armies of the United States, within five years from the date of the approval of this Act: *Provided,* That the President of the United States, in time of peace, may by order fix the minimum number of enlisted men in each company, troop, battery, signal corps, engineer corps, and hospital corps; *And provided further,* That any corps of artillery, cavalry, and infantry existing in any of the States at the passage of the Act of May eight, seventeen hundred and ninety-two, which, by the laws, customs, or usages of the said States have been in continuous existence since the passage of said Act under its provisions and under the provisions of section two hundred and thirty-two and sections sixteen hundred and twenty-five to sixteen hundred and sixty, both inclusive, of Title sixteen of the Revised Statutes of the United States, relating to the Militia, shall be allowed to retain their accustomed privileges, subject, nevertheless, to all other duties required by law in like manner as the other Militia.

Sec. 4. That whenever the United States is invaded, or in danger of invasion from any foreign nation, or of rebellion against the authority of the Government of the United States, or the President is unable, with the other forces at his command, to execute the laws of the Union in any part thereof, it shall be lawful for the President to call forth for a period not exceeding nine months, such numbeı of the militia of the State or of the States or Territories or of the District of Columbia as he may deem necessary to repel such invasion, suppress such rebellion, or to enable him to execute such laws, and to issue his orders for that purpose to such officers of the militia as he may think proper.

Sec. 5. That whenever the President calls forth the militia of any State or Territory or of the District of Columbia to be employed in the service of the United States, he may specify in his call the period for which such service is required, not exceeding nine months, and the militia so called shall continue to serve during the term so specified, unless sooner discharged by order of the President.

Sec. 6. That when the militia of more than one State is called into the actual service of the United States by the President he may, in his discretion, apportion them among such States or Territories or to the District of Columbia according to representative population.

Sec. 7. That every officer and enlisted man of the militia who shall be called forth in the manner hereinbefore prescribed and shall be found fit for military service shall be mustered or accepted into the United States service by a duly authorized mustering officer of the United States: *Provided, however*, That any officer or enlisted man of the militia who shall refuse or neglect to present himself to such mustering officer upon being called forth as herein prescribed shall be subject to trial by court-martial, and shall be punished as such court-martial may direct.

Sec. 8. That courts-martial for the trial of officers or men of the militia when in the service of the United States, shall be composed of militia officers only.

Sec. 9. That the militia, when called into the actual service of the United States, shall be subject to the same Rules and Articles of War as the regular troops of the United States.

Sec. 10. That the militia, when called into the actual service of the United States, shall, during their time of service, be entitled to the same pay and allowances as are or may be provided by law for the Regular Army.

Sec. 11. That when the militia is called into the actual service of the United States, or any portion of the militia is accepted under the provisions of this act, their pay shall commence from the day of their appearing at the place of company rendezvous. But this provision shall not be construed to authorize any species of expenditure previous to arriving at such places of rendezvous which is not provided by existing laws to be paid after their arrival at such places of rendezvous.

Sec. 12. That there shall be appointed in each State, Territory, and District of Columbia an adjutant-general, who shall perform such duties as may be prescribed by the laws of such State, Territory, and District, respectively, and make returns to the Secretary of War, at such times and in such form as he shall from time to time prescribe, of the strength of the organized militia, and also make such reports as may from time to time be required by the Secretary of War. That the Secretary of War shall, with his annual report of each year, transmit to Congress an abstract of the returns and reports of the adjutant-generals of the States, Territories, and the District of Columbia, with such observations thereon as he may deem necessary for the information of Congress.

Sec. 13. That the Secretary of War is hereby authorized to issue, on the requisitions of the governors of the several States and Territories, or of the commanding general of the militia of the District of Columbia, such number of the United States standard service magazine arms, with bayonets, bayonet scabbards, gun slings, belts, and such other necessary accouterments and equipments as are required for the Army of the United States, for arming all of the organized militia in said States and Territories and District of Columbia, without charging the cost or value thereof, or any which have been issued since December first, nineteen hundred and one, or any expense connected therewith, against the allotment to said State, Territory, or District of Columbia, out of the annual appropriation provided by section sixteen hundred and sixty-one of the Revised Statutes, as amended, or requiring payment therefor, and to exchange, without receiving any money credit therefor, ammunition, or parts thereof, suitable to the new arms, round for round, for corresponding ammunition suitable to the old arms theretofore issued to said State, Territory, or District by the United States: *Provided*, That said rifles and carbines and other property shall be receipted for and shall remain the property of the United States and be annually accounted for by the governors of the States and Territories as now required by law, and that each State, Territory, and District shall, on receipt of the new arms, turn in to the Ordnance Department of the United States Army, without receiving any money credit therefor, and without expense for transportation, all United States rifles and carbines now in its possession.

To provide means to carry into effect the provisions of this section, the necessary money to cover the cost of exchanging or issuing the new arms, accouterments, equipments, and ammunition to be exchanged or issued hereunder is hereby appropriated out of any moneys in the Treasury not otherwise appropriated.

Sec. 14. That whenever it shall appear by the report of inspections, which it shall be the duty of the Secretary of War to cause to be made at least once in each year by officers detailed by him for that purpose, that the organized militia of a State or Territory or of the District of Columbia is sufficiently armed, uniformed, and equipped for active duty in the field, the Secretary of War is authorized, on the requisition of the governor of such State or Territory, to pay to the quartermaster-general thereof, or to such other officer of the militia of said State as the said governor may designate and appoint for the purpose, so much of its allotment out of the said annual appropriation under section sixteen hundred and sixty-one of the Revised Statutes as amended as shall be necessary for the payment, subsistence, and transportation of such portion of said organized militia as shall engage in actual field or camp service for instruction, and the officers and enlisted men of such militia while so engaged shall be entitled to the same pay, subsistence, and transportation or travel allowances as officers and enlisted men of corresponding grades of the Regular Army are or may hereafter be entitled to by law, and the officer so designated and appointed shall be regarded as a disbursing officer of the United States, and shall render his accounts through the War Department to the proper accounting officers of the Treasury for settlement, and he shall be required to give good and sufficient bonds to the United States, in such sums as the Secretary of War may direct, faithfully to account for the safe-keeping and payment of the public moneys so intrusted to him for disbursement.

Sec. 15. That the Secretary of War is hereby authorized to provide for participation by any part of the organized militia of any State or Territory on the request of the governor thereof in the encampment, maneuvers, and field instruction of any part of the Regular Army at or near any military post or camp or lake or seacoast defenses of the United States. In such case the organized militia so participating shall receive the same pay, subsistence, and transportation as is provided by law for the officers and men of the Regular Army, to be paid out of the appropriation for the pay, subsistence, and transportation of the Army: *Provided*, That the command of such military post or camp and of the officers and troops of the United States there stationed shall remain with the regular commander of the post without regard to the rank of the commanding or other officers of the militia temporarily so encamped within its limits or in its vicinity.

Sec. 16. That whenever any officer of the organized militia shall, upon recommendation of the governor of any State, Territory, or general commanding the District of Columbia, and when authorized by the President, attend and pursue a regular course of study at any military school or college of the United States such officer shall receive from the annual appropriation for the support of the Army the same travel allowances, and quarters, or commutation of quarters, to which an officer of the Regular Army would be entitled if attending such school or college under orders from proper military authority, and shall also receive commutation of subsistence at the rate of one dollar per day while in actual attendance upon the course of instruction.

Sec. 17. That the annual appropriation made by section sixteen hundred and sixty-one, Revised Statutes, as amended, shall be available for the purpose of providing for issue to the organized militia any stores and supplies or publications which are supplied to the Army by any department. Any State, Territory, or the District of Columbia may, with the approval of the Secretary of War, purchase for cash from the War Department, for the use of its militia, stores, supplies, material of war, or military publications, such as are furnished to the Army, in addition to those issued under the provisions of this Act, at the price at which they are listed for issue to the Army, with the cost of transportation added, and funds received from such sales shall be credited to the appropriations to which they belong and shall not be covered into the Treasury, but shall be available until expended to replace therewith the supplies sold to the States and Territories and to the District of Columbia in the manner herein provided.

Sec. 18. That each State or Territory furnished with material of war under the provisions of this or former Acts of Congress shall, during the year next preceding each annual allotment of funds, in accordance with section sixteen hundred and sixty-one of the Revised Statutes as amended, have required every company, troop, and battery in its organized militia not excused by the governor of such State or Territory, to participate in practice marches or go into camp of instruction at least five consecutive days, and to assemble for drill and instruction at company, battalion, or regimental armories or rendezvous or for target practice not less than twenty-four times, and shall also have required during such year an inspection of each such company, troop, and battery to be made by an officer of such militia or an officer of the Regular Army.

Sec. 19. That upon the application of the governor of any State or Territory furnished with material of war under the provisions of this Act or former laws of Congress, the Secretary of War may detail one or more officers of the Army to attend any encampment of the organized militia, and to give such instruction and information to the officers and men assembled in such camp as may be requested by the governor. Such officer or officers shall immediately make a report of such encampment to the Secretary of War, who shall furnish a copy thereof to the governor of the State or Territory.

Sec. 20. That upon application of the governor of any State or Territory furnished with material of war under the provisions of this Act or former laws of Congress, the Secretary of War may, in his discretion, detail one or more officers of the Army to report to the governor of such State or Territory for duty in connection with the organized militia. All such assignments may be revoked at the request of the governor of such State or Territory or at the pleasure of the Secretary of War.

Sec. 21. That the troops of the militia encamped at any military post or camp of the United States may be furnished such amounts of ammunition for instruction in firing and target practice as may be prescribed by the Secretary of War, and such instruction in firing shall be carried on under the direction of an officer selected for that purpose by the proper military commander.

Sec. 22. That when any officer, noncommissioned officer, or private of the militia is disabled by reason of wounds or disabilities received or incurred in the service of the United States he shall be entitled to all the benefits of the pension laws existing at the time of his service, and in case such officer, noncommissioned officer, or private dies in the service of the United States or in returning to his place of residence after being mustered out of such service, or at any time, in consequence of wounds or disabilities received in such service, his widow and children, if any, shall be entitled to all the benefits of such pension laws.

Sec. 23. That for the purpose of securing a list of persons specially qualified to hold commissions in any volunteer force which may hereafter be called for and organized under the authority of Congress, other than a force composed of organized militia, the Secretary of War is authorized from time to time to convene boards of officers at suitable and convenient army posts in different parts of the United States, who shall examine as to their qualifications for the command of troops or for the performance of staff duties all applicants who shall have served in the Regular Army of the United States, in any of the volunteer forces of the United States, or in the organized militia of any State or Territory or the District of Columbia, or who, being a citizen of the United States, shall have attended or pursued a regular course of instruction in any military school or college of the United States Army, or shall have graduated from any educational institution to which an officer of the Army or Navy has been detailed as superintendent or professor pursuant to law after having creditably pursued the course of military instruction therein provided. Such examinations shall be under rules and regulations prescribed by the Secretary of War, and shall be especially directed to ascertain the practical capacity of the applicant. The record of previous service of the applicant shall be considered as a part of the examination. Upon the conclusion of each examination the board shall certify to the War Department its judgment as to the fitness of the applicant, stating the office, if any, which it deems him qualified to fill, and, upon approval by the President, the names of the persons certified to be qualified shall be inscribed in a register to be kept in the War Department for that purpose. The persons so certified and registered shall, subject to a physical examination at the time, constitute an eligible class for commissions pursuant to such certificates in any volunteer force hereafter called for and organized under the authority of Congress, other than a force composed of organized militia, and the President may authorize persons from this class, to attend and pursue a regular course of study at any military school or college of the United States other than the Military Academy at West Point and to receive from the annual appropriation for the support of the Army the same allowances and commutations as provided in this Act for officers of the organized militia: *Provided*, That no person shall be entitled to receive a commission as a second lieutenant after he shall have passed the age of thirty; as first lieutenant after he shall have passed the age of thirty-five; as captain after he shall have passed the age of forty; as major after he shall have passed the age of forty-five; as lieutenant-colonel after he shall have passed the age of fifty, or as colonel after he shall have passed the age of fifty-five: *And provided further,* That such appointments shall be distributed proportionately, as near as may be, among the various States contributing such volunteer force: *And provided,* That the appointments in this section provided for shall not be deemed to include appointments to any office in any company, troop, battery, battalion, or regiment of the organized militia which volunteers as a body or the officers of which are appointed by the governor of a State or Territory.

Sec. 24. That all the volunteer forces of the United States called for by authority of Congress shall, except as hereinbefore provided, be organized in the manner provided by the Act entitled "An Act to provide for temporarily increasing the military establishment of the United States in time of war, and for other purposes," approved April twenty-second, eighteen hundred and ninety-eight.

Sec. 25. That sections sixteen hundred and twenty-five to sixteen hundred and sixty, both included, of title sixteen of the Revised Statutes, and section two hundred and thirty-two thereof, relating to the militia, are hereby repealed.

Sec. 26. That this Act shall take effect upon the date of its approval.

Approved, January 21, 1903.

Extract from the Army Appropriation Act Approved March 2, 1903

Provided further, That for the purpose of furnishing the necessary articles requisite to fully arm, equip, and supply each regiment, battalion, squadron, company, troop, battery, signal, engineer, and hospital corps and medical department of the organized militia of the several States, Territories, and the District of Columbia with the same armament and equipment as are now prescribed for corresponding branches of the line or staff in the Regular Army, without cost to said States, Territories, or the District of Columbia, but to remain the property of the United States, and to be accounted for in the manner now prescribed by law, the Secretary of War is hereby authorized, under such regulations as he may prescribe, on the requisitions of the governors of the several States and Territories, or the commanding general of the militia of the District of Columbia, to issue the said armament and equipment to the organized militia; and the sum of two million dollars is hereby appropriated and made immediately available until expended for the procurement and issue of the articles constituting the same. . . .

PROMOTIONS IN THE ARMY

EXTRACTS FROM A HEARING BEFORE THE HOUSE COMMITTEE ON MILITARY AFFAIRS IN JANUARY, 1904

I WANT to say something about the subject of promotion. The only system of promotion by selection that we have is that of general officers. When a vacancy in a general office is to be filled, there are always two entirely different considerations that come up. One is a desire to reward long and faithful and meritorious service; the other is the duty of securing men for a position most competent to do the work that has to be done. Those two do not always coincide; it frequently happens that they do not coincide.

Under our system of promotion by seniority alone, for grades below the grade of general officer, there is no presumption whatever that the best man will be at the top on the list of colonels. There is no presumption whatever that a colonel is better able to perform the duties of a general than any one on the list below, because the only thing that has made him a colonel is the fact that he has been longer in the service, in his own branch of the service. When the two considerations — that is, the desire to reward long and faithful service and the necessity to get a man that can do the work to be done — coincide, it is all perfectly plain. When they do not coincide, my idea has been, and President McKinley and President Roosevelt have both agreed with it, that there should be a fair and reasonable division, and that a reasonable part of the promotion to general office should be made primarily with the idea of reward and that a reasonable part should be made primarily with reference to the performance of duty.

That has always been assented to in time of war. The idea that it should not be done in time of peace proceeds entirely upon the theory that there is nothing that it is necessary to have done in time of peace, which is a false idea. It is of the highest importance that the army should have in general office in time of peace men of ability, competent soldiers, and men who have vigor and ambition and initiative. Now, if you are going to make all your appointments to general office with the view to reward, inasmuch as all our men do not get up to the point where they are colonels, in the ordinary course of seniority, until they are nearly at the end of their service, you would have an army commanded by generals substantially all of whom are just closing their careers and are in the last year, or two or three last years of their active service.

Many of them have come to a point where they have passed the enthusiasm, and ambition, and activity of youth, and have reached the period of repose; and you cannot have a live and efficient army which is ready to meet any contingencies that arise with the greatest force and efficiency, which is generaled entirely by men who are just closing their careers. You must have a reasonable proportion of your general officers taken from men who are in the prime of life and who have activity and efficiency. For that reason, while the great majority of men who have been made general officers during the time that I have been here have been men who were approaching the end of their careers, and who have been promoted primarily with the view to reward of service, there has been a small part of the generals selected from the men who have shown that they had the greatest ability to do the work that is to be done, and who have the vigor and force of life left in them, and who can be in office long enough to do work in the making of a career, and long enough to have some continuity of policy and of effort in the working out of plans which require years to work out.

Now, the public discussion upon promotions to general office proceeds always entirely upon the idea of reward and only of reward; but the men who are responsible for the efficiency of the army are certainly bound to keep the other idea in mind and to see to it that there are among the general officers of the army some men who are discovered by what they do to be men of exceptional capacity, and who have left the vigor and energy and physical power to go into the field and do the active work that some general officer has to do if war comes.

Mr. Parker. There is a matter which I am interested in, which seems to be germane now. When a man from West Point goes into the army he is trained in the artillery, the cavalry, the infantry, and engineering to a certain extent. The young man from civil life has to learn his duties in one of those arms of the service. Would it be practical or beneficial to transfer a man for the first six years so he would have two years in each of these different arms before he finally took his place, so that when he finally became a field officer he would know how to ride, and when he became a general officer he would understand the application of the arms which came under his command?

Secretary Root. I think it very desirable that the result should be obtained. That is exactly what we are trying to accomplish now by our system of schools. The whole policy in expending the money you have voted for the increase of military posts to accommodate the enlarged army, has been to make the provision by enlarging posts rather than by increasing their number; and it contemplates having a considerable number of posts of all arms of the service; so that the young officers will be familiar with the operations of the other arms; and in the post schools, in which all of the junior officers will be trained, and so far as we have been able to establish them up to this time, all are being trained, they will be taught not merely the duties of their particular branch, but of all branches. It is the object of the general service college at Leavenworth, where we have at the full war strength representatives of all arms of the service — infantry, cavalry, engineers, artillery, and signal corps, the full outfit of a brigade — it is the object of that school to train an officer as an all-round officer, and train him in the use and the command of organizations of every branch of the service.

I think that that kind of training will be useful, however, for only a part of the officers of the army. Inevitably we will find that a considerable portion of the officers of the army are competent to be good officers of infantry, of cavalry, of artillery, to perform the duties of their own branch, but have not the capacity which will ever lead to their being called upon to command an army; while another part of the officers who have superior capacity ought to be educated with the view of being called upon to perform such higher duties. The idea of the system we are trying to work out is, that we will gradually differentiate those two classes, and that we will move along the men who show superior capacity and give them the all-round education for performing the higher duties that they are competent for, while we will leave the men of inferior capacity to the work of their own branches. . . .

Since we have gone into a discussion of military preparation, I should like to say something also about the promotion of rifle practice.

Congress last year appropriated $2,500 for a trophy or trophies, as prizes for a competition in sharp-shooting, to which the army and the National Guards should be admitted, the trophy to be contested for under regulations to be prescribed by the Secretary of War and the money to be expended under his direction. I thought that in the exercise of that authority it was desirable to make regulations which would lead to—at all events would begin — a general comprehensive treatment of the subject of instruction in rifle practice; and accordingly I made the regulations provide for a board for the promotion of rifle practice which should take charge of this trophy competition. I made the board consist of twenty-one members, put on it five members from the regular establishment, the Assistant Secretary of War at the head, two officers of the army, an officer of the navy, and an officer of the marine corps, whom the Secretary of the Navy detailed, the president and trustees of the National Rifle Association, eight in number, and then eight citizens from different parts of the country, who had shown an interest in the subject of rifle practice.

Of course the two last classes were composed almost entirely of National Guardsmen, National Guard officers, either active or retired. Those sixteen represented thirteen different states and territories. That board met and formulated the rules for the conduct of the competition for the trophy, and the match was had in September under their direction. They have also had under consideration, without any power to act, a number of matters which affected the general subject of the promotion of rifle practice in this country. I should be very glad if Congress would do two or three things about that. It is plain that the navy and the marine corps ought to be included in the classes eligible to compete. They did send teams to Sea Girt at the time of competition. These teams went into the competition, but were not permitted to have any chance for the prizes because the statutes did not name them. That ought to be changed.

I think the board will be useful enough to justify a small appropriation to pay their expenses. At present they have to pay their own expenses — their travelling expenses.

And then I wish very much that you would make a moderate appropriation which the board can use under the direction, under the approval, of the Secretary of War, for the promotion of rifle practice generally, so that rifle practice can have some stimulus given it. It is of no use to raise volunteer forces composed of men who cannot shoot. It is no use to enlist and clothe and feed and transport forces to the field, if they cannot hit an enemy when they shoot at him; and the changing conditions make it necessary that some effort should be made, if the young men of the country are going to be able to hit an enemy when they go out as a volunteer force.

The change in small arms, the greatly increased range, makes practice much more necessary than it was when you did not shoot at a man until you could see the whites of his eyes. And then our young men are less and less familiar with firearms. When I was a boy, and some of the more venerable members of the committee were boys, every house had its rifle or shotgun, and the boys learned to use them. There was game about all over the country, and the boys learned to shoot. But in the thickly settled portions of the country today a large proportion, I should say a majority, of the boys grow up without ever having fired a gun. And when war comes and they are called out into the volunteer force, there will not be time to train them, and we cannot wait for them to be trained. They will have to go into the field and go to spending ammunition.

I think it is a matter of great interest and importance for the Government of the United States to spend small sums in promoting exercises in the use of the rifle among the young men of the country. I made the organization under the regulations for this particular trophy in accordance with the spirit of the appropriation to further work in that direction; and it affords a harmonious coöperation of the regular army, and the navy, and the National Guard for that purpose, and I hope you will promote it. So that if in Des

Moines, or Newark, or in Akron, the young men choose to get together and form a rifle club, there can be some objective point to work for in the way of some simple competition. That can readily be arranged so that competitions can be put about in different parts of the country. . . .

I shall be very glad to come before the committee any time that the committee thinks my presence will be useful to them.

Mr. Capron. I could not let you go away, Mr. Secretary, without saying — and I voice the sentiment of every member of the committee, I am sure, — that it is with deep regret down in our hearts that we approach the time when you are no more to come here as our adviser, and when we are to depend on some source of information other than that on which we have depended so long and so reliably; I can only say that this regret is coupled with the hope that you will not forget that this committee and Congress and the country will look to you hereafter, as they have in the years just passed, for such advice as we believe you can give for the improvement of the military service.

Secretary Root. You are very kind, and I am deeply appreciative of what you say. I want to say that I very keenly appreciate not merely the courtesy and kindness but the public-spirited and generous consideration that I have received from this committee. The association has been most delightful, and it is peculiarly pleasant to feel that it has been without any division or distinction or prejudice upon the score of party or locality. I do not expect ever to find myself working with men more single-minded in the desire to promote the public interest than the men of your committee, Mr. Chairman, with whom I have been working for the past four years and a half; and while I shall be glad to get home and get back to my own proper work in the practice of law, I shall leave Washington with great regret in parting from you all.

THE SPIRIT OF NATIONAL SERVICE

As stating Mr. Root's views concerning the military policy which the United States should now adopt and should pursue in the future, the volume devoted to the Military and Colonial Policy of the United States may be closed appropriately with the following letter to Lieutenant-General S. B. M. Young, president of the Association for National Service:

CLINTON, N. Y., September 17, 1916.

MY DEAR GENERAL:

I am obliged to you for sending me the papers relating to the Association for National Service. We certainly need the spirit of national service in our country. It is a mistake to suppose that a people can have good government, peace, order, and progress for any long period without any effort on their part. We in the United States need to have our patriotism awakened, to throw off our indifference, and to think more of our duties as well as of our rights.

Every one who is fit to be a citizen of a free country ought to be willing to serve the country when called upon, in accordance with his ability. The young men who are physically fit for military duty should hold themselves ready to fight for their country if need be, and if they are not ready when the need comes they will not long have any country, and they will not deserve to have any. The vast change in the way of carrying on war which has occurred within a very few years has created a situation in which it is perfectly plain that no country can be ready to defend her independence against foreign aggression except by universal military training and a resulting universal readiness for military service.

The old way of waiting until war came and then calling for volunteers has become obsolete, and is no longer effective.

The National Guard system is not adequate and cannot be made adequate to meet the needs of national defense under any real assault upon our right. It is impossible to have an effective body of soldiers who serve two masters and are raised and organized to accomplish two different purposes. Universal training and readiness for service are not only demanded by plain common sense, but they are essentially democratic. They were required by law during the early years of our Republic, for every male citizen between the ages of eighteen and forty-five was required to be ready to fight for his country and was required to be trained and provided with arms in accordance with the simple needs of warfare in those days. It is only necessary now to apply the principles and requirements of the national law of May 8, 1792, adapted to present conditions.

You have my best wishes in your patriotic endeavors. With kind regards I am always faithfully yours,

ELIHU ROOT.

Lieut.-Gen. S. B. M. YOUNG,
President Association for National Service, Washington, D. C.

INDEX

INDEX